Scaling Agile with Jira Align

A practical guide to strategically scaling agile across teams, programs, and portfolios in enterprises

Dean MacNeil

Aslam Cader

Packt>

BIRMINGHAM—MUMBAI

Scaling Agile with Jira Align

Commissioning Editor: Richa Tripathi
Acquisition Editor: Alok Dhuri
Senior Editor: Rohit Singh
Content Development Editor: Kinnari Chohan
Technical Editor: Gaurav Gala
Copy Editor: Safis Editing
Project Coordinator: Deeksha Thakkar
Proofreader: Safis Editing
Indexer: Manju Arasan
Production Designer: Nilesh Mohite

First published: November 2020

Production reference: 2040121

Published by Packt Publishing Ltd.
Livery Place
35 Livery Street
Birmingham
B3 2PB, UK.

ISBN 978-1-80020-321-1

www.packt.com

For those on the journey toward business agility—may you find something here to help you achieve great outcomes.

Packt>

Contributors

About the authors

Dean MacNeil has been passionate about agile practices and tools since before they were called "agile," having pioneered a form of iterative and incremental product delivery at the world's leading music company in the mid-1990s. As an Atlassian Certified Consultant and Enterprise Agile Coach, MacNeil has helped companies of diverse sizes and verticals, including some of the world's largest and fastest-growing companies, to improve business agility and outcomes. MacNeil also writes about music and is a lifelong musician. He lives in Los Angeles, where he enjoys hiking, biking, and sailing with his son.

Aslam Cader is a software professional with over 10 years of experience working with teams at all levels to solve complex business problems while improving business productivity and agility. As an Atlassian Certified Consultant, Cader has helped companies standardize business processes around lean, agile, ALM, ITSM, DevOps, and digital transformation programs. He is particularly passionate about scaling agile, governance, and best practices to support the scaled use of Atlassian stack, cloud, and ecosystem solutions. He lives in London and enjoys traveling and time with his family.

Acknowledgments

We'd like to thank the Atlassian Jira Align Community and Enterprise Solution Architects for their knowledge and wisdom, Jira Align Support for their responsiveness, and especially Valiantys, an Atlassian Platinum Solution Partner, for leading the way and continuously raising the bar in helping enterprises find success with Jira Align.

About the reviewer

Afsana Atar is an author, speaker, and accomplished test engineer with 12 years of extensive experience in software testing. She extends her thought leadership to teams in a variety of domains, from digital advertising, education, and healthcare to the financial sector. She has worked for various organizations, including Google, IBM, Principal Financial Group, and The Children's Hospital of Philadelphia. Currently, she works for Susquehanna International Group, a financial trading firm. She is a **Certified Scrum Professional Scrum Master (CSP-SM)**, **Product Owner (CSPO)**, an agile scrum practitioner, and part of the Scrum Alliance community. She believes in sharing her experience with the testing community to help foster greater learning and innovation.

Gregory Kneller began as a developer in early 199x, developed desktop and web applications in various languages, worked as a support engineer, solution architect, and product designer. Since 2010 he has focused solely on Atlassian products and covers all topics of configuration, customization, and implementation. His customers are UNFCCC, eBay, Alstom, Tipico, Agilent, Allianz, and others. He is an Atlassian Certified Professional since 2016.

Packt is searching for authors like you

If you're interested in becoming an author for Packt, please visit `authors.packtpub.com` and apply today. We have worked with thousands of developers and tech professionals, just like you, to help them share their insight with the global tech community. You can make a general application, apply for a specific hot topic that we are recruiting an author for, or submit your own idea.

Table of Contents

3
Navigating Jira Align

Section 2:
Problem-Solving with Jira Align

4
Team Challenges

5

Program Planning Challenges

6

Program Execution Challenges

7

Enterprise and Portfolio Challenges

Section 3:
Special Use Cases and Add-Ons

8

Bimodal Development, Advanced Data Security, and Analytics

Assessments

Other Books You May Enjoy

Index

Preface

Every good agilist knows that individuals and interactions are valued over processes and tools. This first tenet of the manifesto endures two decades since its formation. Yet in today's world of digital disruption, the right practices and tools can mean the difference between surviving and thriving.

What if we told you about a tool that was built by agilists for agilists, supports all leading frameworks, enables you to scale agility from the team to the enterprise, and visualizes all key dimensions including people, work, time, and outcomes? Well, that tool is here, and it's called Jira Align.

This book serves as a foundation for those who are looking to begin their journey with Jira Align and a companion to those who already use Jira Align. Starting with an introduction to the platform and its features, you'll learn how to implement and leverage Jira Align to maximize outcomes and mitigate common team, program, and portfolio-level challenges in enterprises.

Get ready for a wealth of knowledge on this leading **enterprise agile planning (EAP)** platform. From running remote agile ceremonies, to generating live product roadmaps, to tracking **objectives and key results (OKRs)**, you'll learn all the key features of Jira Align and how they support agility at every level of scale.

Thank you for joining us and may you find much success in your journey!

Who this book is for

This book is for portfolio managers, program managers, product managers, product owners, executives, release train engineers, and scrum masters who want to empower their teams to deliver the right things at the right time and quickly respond to changes in the market.

What this book covers

Chapter 1, *Introducing Jira Align,* covers connecting with Jira Align, the ideal candidate for Jira Align, assembling the Jira Align Core Team, selecting a framework, and working with an Atlassian Solution Partner.

Chapter 2, Implementing Jira Align, covers analyzing existing programs in Jira, mapping people, work, time, and outcomes, setting up Jira Align, connecting to Jira, and extending to the portfolio.

Chapter 3, Navigating Jira Align, covers getting around Jira Align, facilitating onboarding, creating and refining backlogs, and collaborating in Jira Align.

Chapter 4, Team Challenges, covers ensuring that teams are connected, sizing stories with estimation games, loading sprints during remote planning, conducting ceremonies and meetings, and reviewing sprints and giving shoutouts.

Chapter 5, Program Planning Challenges, covers building product roadmaps, planning for value delivery as a program, organizing around value to reduce dependencies, and visualizing program velocity for planning and predictability.

Chapter 6, Program Execution Challenges, covers overseeing the program room, negotiating and visualizing dependencies, reducing waste, managing scope, and communicating progress.

Chapter 7, Enterprise and Portfolio Challenges, covers connecting strategy to execution, implementing lean portfolio management, and promoting innovation.

Chapter 8, Bimodal Development, Advanced Data Security and Analytics, covers developing products bimodally, handling time tracking, advanced data security, government reporting, and integrating with business intelligence and other solutions.

To get the most out of this book

Familiarity with agile frameworks and Jira Software is necessary; we will teach you the rest.

Download the color images

We also provide a PDF file that has color images of the screenshots/diagrams used in this book. You can download it here:

```
https://static.packt-cdn.com/downloads/9781800203211_ColorIm-
ages.pdf.
```

Conventions used

Bold: Indicates a new term, an important word, or words that you see onscreen. For example, words in menus or dialog boxes appear in the text like this. Here is an example: "To manage snapshots, click on the **Strategic Snapshots** button near the top-right corner of the strategy room or go to the navigation menu and select **Enterprise | Manage | Strategic Snapshots**."

> **Tips and tricks**
> Appear like this.

Get in touch

Feedback from our readers is always welcome.

General feedback: If you have questions about any aspect of this book, mention the book title in the subject of your message and email us at `customercare@packtpub.com`.

Errata: Although we have taken every care to ensure the accuracy of our content, mistakes do happen. If you have found a mistake in this book, we would be grateful if you would report this to us. Please visit `www.packtpub.com/support/errata`, selecting your book, clicking on the Errata Submission Form link, and entering the details.

Piracy: If you come across any illegal copies of our works in any form on the Internet, we would be grateful if you would provide us with the location address or website name. Please contact us at `copyright@packt.com` with a link to the material.

If you are interested in becoming an author: If there is a topic that you have expertise in and you are interested in either writing or contributing to a book, please visit `authors.packtpub.com`.

Reviews

Please leave a review. Once you have read and used this book, why not leave a review on the site that you purchased it from? Potential readers can then see and use your unbiased opinion to make purchase decisions, we at Packt can understand what you think about our products, and our authors can see your feedback on their book. Thank you!

For more information about Packt, please visit `packt.com`.

Section 1: Preparing for Jira Align

In this section, you will be introduced to Jira Align and will learn the characteristics of an organization that can benefit from implementing Jira Align. It then shows how to implement the solution by mapping the people, work, time and outcomes. Finally, it shows how to navigate Jira Align and facilitate onboarding and collaboration.

This section comprises of the following chapters:

- *Chapter 1, Introducing Jira Align*
- *Chapter 2, Implementing Jira Align*
- *Chapter 3, Navigating Jira Align*

1
Introducing Jira Align

This chapter provides an introduction to Jira Align. You will learn about the past and present of Jira Align and the company that brought it to the market. This chapter also covers the types of organizations that can benefit the most from implementing Jira Align and the key factors for success. Lastly, you will learn how Jira Align supports organizations in using a scaling agile framework.

We will cover the following topics:

- Connecting with Jira Align
- The ideal candidate for Jira Align
- Assembling the Jira Align Core Team
- Selecting a framework
- Working with an Atlassian Solution Partner

Connecting with Jira Align

Jira Align is a product whose time has come. Its story begins with agile frameworks created in the 1990s for development teams to deliver quality products early and often. When leaders of these frameworks met in Snowbird, Utah, to formulate the Agile Manifesto in 2001, team-level execution was still the focus. But the world has grown more complex in the two decades since, with the need for diverse sectors such as banking, automotive, and government to embrace digital transformation. As organizations struggle to create ever larger and more complex systems and even systems of systems (such as aerospace and military applications), the need to coordinate the delivery of numerous agile teams has grown more pressing.

In 2007, entrepreneur and technology executive Steve Elliott teamed up with a talented engineer to answer this challenge by creating what would become AgileCraft and later Jira Align – a way to break down the barriers between product management, project management, and engineering to coordinate and deliver complex product development efforts. As the tool was taking shape, a new type of agile framework was emerging, one that harnessed the power of successful agile team delivery and scaled it both upward to teams within teams and ultimately the enterprise, and outward to parts of the organization not traditionally associated with agile.

AgileCraft has had a close working relationship with the **Scaled Agile Framework** (**SAFe**), the leading framework for agile at scale, since SAFe was launched in 2011. After 7 years of rigorous, real-life testing during his tenure as a technology executive, Steve left his day job and launched AgileCraft in 2013 to help companies achieve *enterprise agility at start-up speed*. By 2015, AgileCraft was named a Scaled Agile Gold Partner and Gartner Cool Vendor.

In 2016, Team AgileCraft scored its first Fortune 10 client, AT&T, which adopted it as a companywide standard in 2017 after delivering its mobile TV product using the platform. In 2018, Gartner named AgileCraft a *visionary* in the Magic Quadrant for **Enterprise Agile Planning** (**EAP**) Tools. In 2019, Gartner named it a *leader* and Atlassian acquired AgileCraft. Today, known as Jira Align, it is still a leader, if not *the* leader. Moreover, the product is continuously improving, with new features and enhancements released every 2 weeks.

The ideal candidate for Jira Align

Jira Align is not for every organization. It is vast in breadth and depth, built from the ground up as an agile-first platform, unlike competitors that attempt to transform waterfall **project portfolio management (PPM)** solutions into EAP tools. Much as SAFe builds upon team-level agile delivery and scales it to the program, solution, portfolio, and enterprise levels, Jira Align too works in concert with the top team-level agile tool, Jira Software, extending it to all levels of scale. It natively supports a variety of frameworks and approaches beyond SAFe, including **Disciplined Agile Delivery (DAD)**, **Large-Scale Scrum (LeSS)**, **Scrum@Scale**, **Spotify**, **Lean Startup**, custom frameworks, and any combination of these. It is therefore geared toward larger organizations that have or seek a more formal approach to agile at scale.

The ideal candidate for a successful Jira Align implementation meets the seven qualifications listed here:

1. **500+ developers using Jira Software**: Functionally, Jira Align can support hundreds to thousands of users across all levels of an organization. The quantity of developers using Jira Software is often a good indication of whether an organization's size is well suited for Jira Align. If you have 500 or more developers using Jira Software, then Jira Align may be worth your investment. For fewer than 500 developers, Jira Software alone or in combination with Atlassian Marketplace apps may suffice.

2. **Following an agile scaling framework**: There are two rules of thumb that apply when selecting a tool to support agile at scale. The first is that you cannot scale the unscalable. The second is that any tool is only as good as the underlying data, organizational structures, and agile practices that it visualizes and supports. Therefore, having a formal practice around agile at scale is often a leading indicator of successful outcomes with Jira Align. See the *Selecting a framework* section later for more information.

3. **Has executed two or more quarterly planning events**: Quarterly planning and execution focused on the highest-ranking features in the product backlog have become standard practice among companies engaged in agile delivery. The Program Board is one of the key pieces of functionality in Jira Align used to support this practice. But it's best to have practical experience of a methodology before applying a tool to it, especially one that is so feature-rich it could be overwhelming at first. Therefore, it's sensible to have at least two quarterly planning increments under your belt before introducing Jira Align.

4. **Has an established team agile practice for at least 6 months**: Successful agile delivery at the team level is a prerequisite to scaling with frameworks and tools. Just as you would not scale buggy code, you would not want to scale suboptimal product delivery methods. A good way to gauge the effectiveness of your teams is to review the 12 principles behind the Agile Manifesto. If your teams are regularly enacting at least 7 or 8 out of 12, such as satisfying the customer through early and continuous delivery of valuable product features (Principle 1), then they've achieved a high degree of agility. Your organization can then build upon this foundation by scaling it to achieve goals such as the following:

- Delivering larger and more complex initiatives
- Expanding agile methods to more areas of the company
- Connecting execution with strategy

It all begins with your agile teams, so get them the training and experience they need. Jira Align will then allow you to connect their skilled tactical execution to corporate strategy.

5. **Each program has 5–12 teams**: Whether you call it a program, **agile release train (ART)**, tribe, or something else, the team of teams construct has proven successful for delivering higher quality products faster to market. There are two important considerations when structuring these groups of teams.

The first is that each group of teams should be able to deliver product features independently, on cadence (typically quarterly), with minimal dependencies on other groups. The second is that each group should comprise 50–125 individuals (5–12 agile teams) due to the inherent limitations on cohesion in larger groups observed by anthropologist Robin Dunbar in the 1990s.

6. **Executive sponsorship for the agile at scale transformation**: Agile at scale, and the tools to support it, needs buy-in from executives. This is not merely a matter of funding, but one of embracing and leading the change. This requires openness and commitment to shifting the internal culture. According to the 13th annual State of Agile survey, the top three impediments to successful transformations are culture-related:

- Organizational culture at odds with agile values
- General organization resistance to change
- Inadequate management support and sponsorship

These 3 remain in the top 5 of the 14th annual State of Agile survey, published in May 2020. Additionally, a new impediment reached the top 5 in that report: *Not enough leadership participation*. This speaks to the importance of leaders embracing the agile mindset, first by learning it themselves, then by *walking the talk* – advocating the principles, exhibiting the practices, and coaching others. Start small with a few showcase programs, generate short-term wins, then consolidate gains and produce more wins. John Kotter, author of *Leading Change*, has shown that this is the way to anchor new approaches in the culture. When teams experience wins, their energy shifts. They move from merely *doing* agile toward *being* agile.

7. **Center of Excellence (CoE) or governing body in place for agile practice, with funding**: The CoE is a team dedicated to implementing and supporting the agile transformation. It is a key differentiator separating companies who are agile in name only from those who are achieving the best outcomes. Functions of the CoE include training staff in the new methods, sourcing specialized roles such as **product owner (PO)** and **scrum master (SM)**, and the all-important practice of coaching.

   For three years in a row, 2017–2019, respondents surveyed for the annual State of Agile report designated Internal Agile Coaches as the top tip for success with scaling agile. This makes sense, as it reduces dependency on outside consulting firms and creates a sustainable agile capability. Even apart from agile, professional coaching is taking hold within many Fortune 1,000 companies. A recent study by the **International Coach Federation (ICF)** found that the typical company can expect a return of 7 times its initial coaching investment. It's important to note, however, that there's a wide range of expertise among those who practice coaching. The best agile coaches we've seen are ICF certified in addition to holding agile-specific certifications.

The better an organization meets these seven parameters, the better the outcomes it will achieve. These are the key success factors that have worked for AgileCraft and then Jira Align throughout the years. But once again, it's important to remember that a tool is only as good as the underlying data, organizational structures, and agile practices it supports.

It's one thing to have success at the team level, but if you are going to scale throughout the organization, you will need to standardize methods and tools for product delivery so that you can achieve the following:

- Numerous teams can seamlessly collaborate to deliver large and complex solutions.

- Various parts of the organization speak the same language and work toward common strategic objectives.

- Dispersed tactical information can connect uniformly with the highest-level corporate strategy and objectives.

So, it is important to get the house in order before implementing Jira Align. But don't worry, we will guide you through the pitfalls and challenges, providing tips and tricks learned in numerous Jira Align implementations to help ensure your success. Whether you're a hyper-growth tech start-up, an old school telecoms company, or a government agency, we'll show how Jira Align can work for you.

Assembling the Jira Align Core Team

The work of John Kotter, author of *Leading Change*, has shown the importance of a guiding coalition for any transformation effort. The first order of business is to assemble a guiding team for the Jira Align implementation, including roles such as the following:

- Implementation Lead

- Agile Practice Lead or Representative

- Product Management

- Program Management

- Jira Align Administrator

- Jira Administrator

These are individuals *with skin in the game* who are willing to embrace change and lead by example. The Jira Align implementation approach is to start small with a few showcase programs, generate short-term wins, then consolidate gains and produce more wins. As Kotter has shown, this is the way to anchor new approaches in the culture. This technique works well with teams and teams of teams, but true enterprise transformation requires an even more disciplined and holistic approach. At this level, the scaling framework you choose will help you achieve a connected knowledge environment supported by Jira Align.

Selecting a framework

In successful enterprise transformations, all levels of an organization work toward a common understanding of how people, practices, and tools are orchestrated for efficient and effective delivery. In the best cases, your practices and tools work in unison to create competencies that allow your organization to scale and stay competitive in the market. This setting combined with engaged leadership creates a knowledge environment geared toward continuous learning, business agility, and innovation.

The knowledge environment is not a state but an evolving journey. Any organization can start from where they are. The following illustration represents how an organization can align toward transformation by connecting strategy with execution:

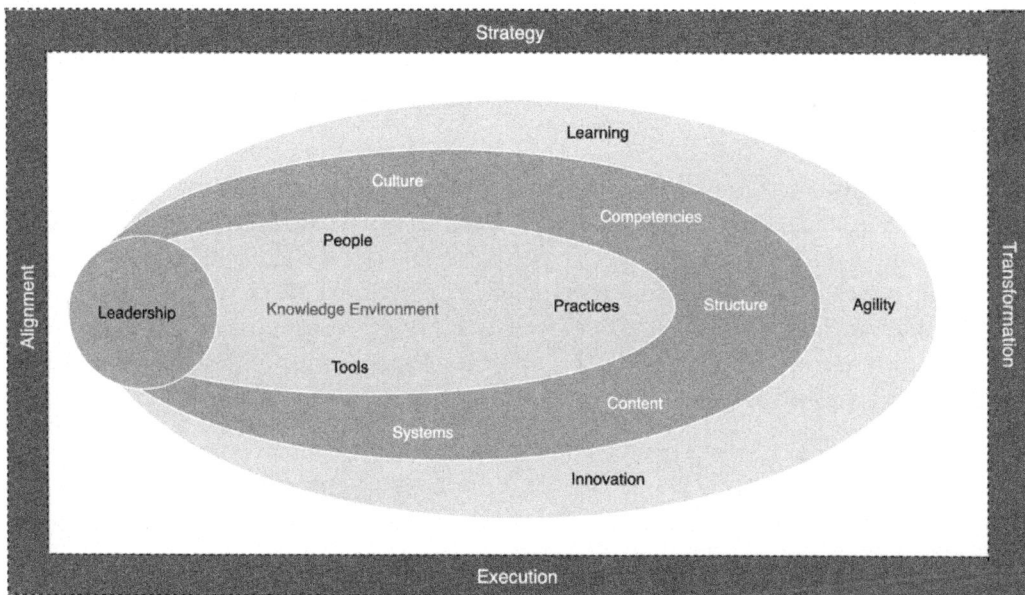

Figure 1.1 – Alignment toward transformation by connecting strategy with execution

Earlier, we spoke of the importance of leadership in any transformation effort. Here, we see that when leaders at all levels work together to align people, practices, and tools in a connected knowledge environment, they create a positive ripple effect through culture, competencies, structure, content, and systems toward continuous learning, business agility, and innovation – the fruits of transformation. The path may not be easy, but those who have blazed the trail have told of three waypoints you will encounter along the way.

Beginning with Dr. Alistair Cockburn, co-author of the *Agile Manifesto* and author of *Agile Software Development*, the practice of frameworks to acquire the agile mindset has been likened to the stages of developing expertise in the martial arts, Shu-Ha-Ri:

- In the Shu stage, you are learning the forms and becoming proficient by following the guidelines set by your teacher.

- In the Ha stage, you've gained a level of proficiency in how to use the forms and may safely bend some of them when necessary.

- Ri is the stage of the masters who break with tradition and create their own forms after practicing for years at the levels of Shu and Ha.

Another popular three-phase model for understanding where you are in your agile journey is *Crawl-Walk-Run*.

In either model, assess where you are and know that success lies in the journey itself, not the destination.

A scaling framework is an essential companion in your agile journey. You will likely select one because it is a proven method backed by numerous case studies. Therefore, resist the urge to modify the framework from the start. That would be analogous to an apprentice attempting to create their own form, skipping the Shu stage, and the results would not likely be optimal. Similarly, resist the tendency to think your organization is unique. Look for a case study analogous to your industry to see the results your peers are achieving and stick with the approach to yield your own great results.

It is common for agile teams to practice scrum, kanban, or a blend of both. According to the 14th Annual State of Agile Report, scrum is the leading agile methodology practiced by a majority of teams around the world, followed by hybrid approaches, scrumban, and kanban. Scrum is a lightweight agile framework practiced by teams of 5–9 members who collaboratively manage complex knowledge work to iteratively and incrementally deliver products of the highest possible value.

Organizations operating with hundreds of teams find that scrum alone does not suffice to deliver optimal results at scale and struggle with alignment, dependencies, risks, and collaboration across teams. In the 2000s and 2010s, scaling frameworks emerged to answer these needs. According to the 14th Annual State of Agile Report, SAFe is the most adopted and leading framework named year on year.

SAFe is a full-fledged knowledge base of proven, integrated principles, and competencies with guardrails to implement lean, agile, and DevOps practices at scale. However, there are several other frameworks worth considering. Creating a scorecard or matrix such as the following, with the most meaningful parameters to your organization, can help guide decision making:

Factor	eScrum	SAFe	LeSS	DAD	Scrum@Scale	Nexus
Simple	✓	✓	✓	✓	✓	✓
Well-Defined		✓	✓	✓	✓	✓
Web Portal		✓	✓			
Books	✓	✓	✓	✓		✓
Case Studies		✓	✓	✓	✓	✓
Training & Cert	✓	✓	✓	✓	✓	✓
Consultants		✓	✓		✓	
Tools		✓	✓	✓	✓	
Popularity		✓		✓		
International		✓	✓	✓	✓	✓
Fortune 500	✓	✓	✓	✓	✓	
Government		✓				
Lean-Kanban		✓	✓			
Affiliation	Enterprise Scrum, Inc.	Scaled Agile, Inc.	Scrum Alliance	Project Management Institute	Scrum Alliance & Scrum, Inc.	Scrum.org

Figure 1.2 – Scaling framework comparison, adapted from Rico, D. F. (2014)

If you have yet to choose your framework, the Agile CoE with co-leadership from the Jira Align core team can lead the way to recommend one that suits your industry and culture. Practicing the framework will involve the key effort of coaching and training teams to create a consistent operational understanding and aligning the language between teams across the organization. Your next step will be to engage an Atlassian Solution Partner for your Jira Align implementation. Unlike Jira Software, which can be purchased on a credit card and implemented on your own, you will not be alone with the sizeable undertaking of implementing Jira Align.

Working with an Atlassian Solution Partner

If you haven't previously worked with a solution partner, Atlassian can help you find one. Simply go to www.atlassian.com/partners. The partner will guide you through workshops to discover what is most important to your business and how Jira Align will support your goals. With this understanding, the partner can ensure that the platform is configured to support your highest-ranking business goals, helping you achieve the best outcomes. Atlassian wants you to be successful, so they require working through a partner. There are, for example, more than 769 different configuration toggles in the platform, so you will want to leverage the partner's experience and expertise to help you succeed. In the next chapter, we'll introduce the fundamentals of implementing Jira Align, beginning with a quick setup. This will provide foundational knowledge to help you work with your solution partner and jumpstart the role-based training that the partner will provide as part of the implementation.

Summary

In this chapter, we introduced Jira Align and the company that created it. We discussed what the ideal Jira Align candidate looks like, including seven success factors. We covered the importance of assembling a Jira Align Core Team and of selecting and following a framework. Lastly, we introduced the necessity of working with an Atlassian Solution Partner on your Jira Align implementation.

Now you know the purpose of Jira Align and who can benefit the most from it. You're equipped with the seven key parameters for a successful implementation, and you know the importance of the core team, scaling framework, and solution partner.

In the next chapter, we'll build upon what we've learned and get into the fundamentals of implementing Jira Align.

Questions

1. What circumstances gave rise to the agile platform now known as Jira Align?

2. Which scaling framework has a longstanding relationship with Jira Align?

3. How many agile teams can belong to a program or *team of teams*?

4. What role does leadership play in a Jira Align implementation?

5. Why is it important to have a Jira Align Core Team?

Further reading

- *Enterprise Agility* by Sunil Mundra (Packt, 2018)
- *Agile Technical Practices Distilled* by Pedro M. Santos (Packt, 2019)

2
Implementing Jira Align

In this chapter, we will go through the fundamentals of implementing Jira Align to map the key objects and attributes. You will learn what is required to analyze an existing program in Jira Software and what it takes to translate the actual work into Jira Align. This chapter further elaborates on the dimensions of people, work, time, and outcomes, which are supported within your Jira Align and Jira Software toolset. Lastly, you will learn an approach to extend from program to portfolio and bridge strategy with execution.

In this chapter, we will cover the following topics:

- Analyzing existing programs in Jira
- Mapping people, work, time, and outcomes
- Setting up Jira Align
- Connecting to Jira
- Extending to the portfolio

Analyzing existing programs in Jira

A key factor in the success of Jira Align is the quality of underlying data from Jira Software. As a part of the tool solution integration, you'll want to analyze the team-level data in Jira to determine whether it is scalable and connectable. If not, you'll want to standardize and optimize the data prior to integrating with Jira Align.

We will now perform the following steps to start the health check of your data:

1. Download the Jet by Jira Align app from the Atlassian Marketplace, as shown in the following screenshot, available for Jira Cloud, Server, and Data Center hosting options. Ask your Jira administrator to install the app on your Jira instance:

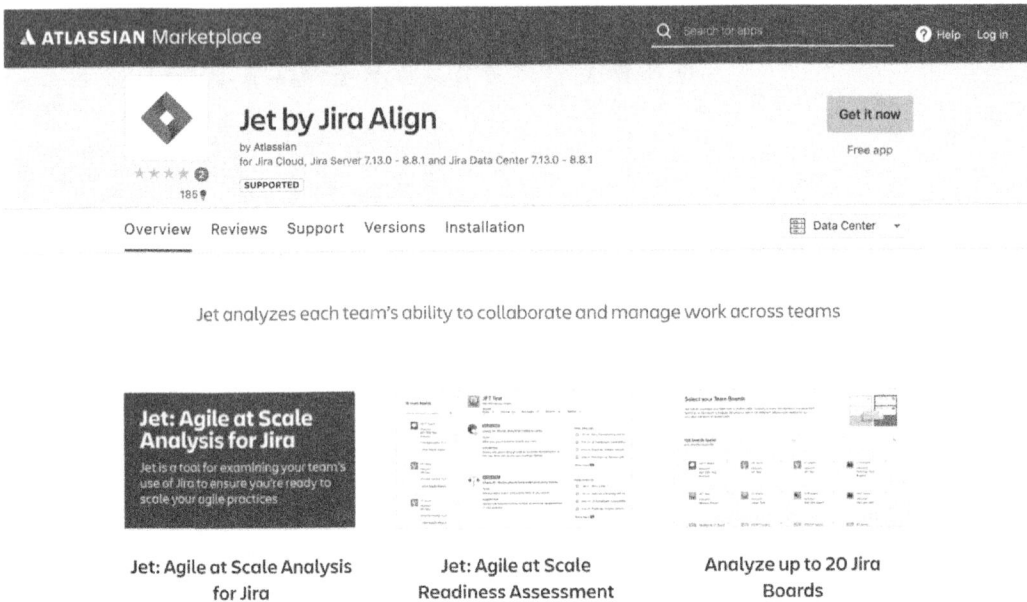

Figure 2.1 – Jet by Jira Align, Atlassian Marketplace

Jet by Jira Align is a native Jira app built for analyzing the underlying health of your team data and practices in Jira. The app runs seven prioritized health checks and provides detailed insights by highlighting the areas requiring action to fix or improve the data. The more health checks that pass, the smoother your integration with Jira Align will be.

2. Access the Jira wizard under **Jira Administration | Manage apps | Jira Align | Jet**. You will see the following start screen for the step-by-step wizard:

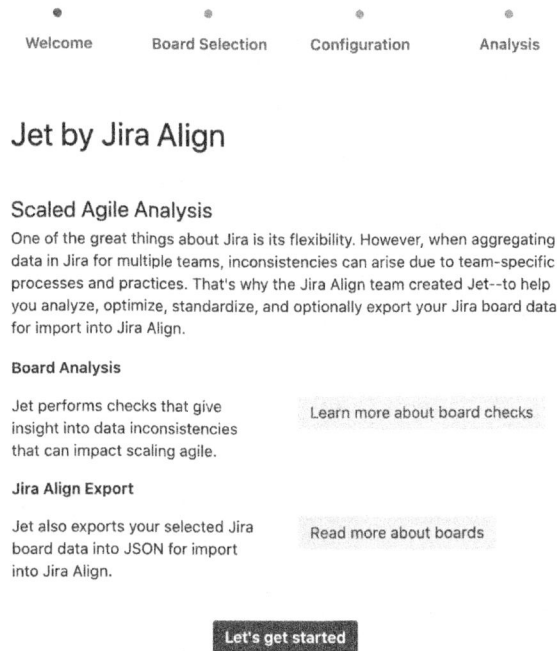

Figure 2.2 – Jet by Jira Align, step-by-step wizard

3. Once you get started, you can select up to 20 boards to analyze. A board typically represents one agile team. You may select multiple boards that belong to a single team of teams or program.

> **Tips and tricks**
>
> A Scrum team will work off of a sprint tied to a Jira board and all Jira issues planned within a sprint will belong only to a single team. It is important that only one team works off of a Jira board. This principle applies to Kanban team boards as well.
>
> When selecting multiple boards for analysis, it's best to select boards from the same project or that share the same field and issue type configurations. Selecting boards from different projects can cause field mapping discrepancies that skew results.
>
> For Jira Cloud, next-gen boards are not officially supported. This is due to the unique field structure in next-gen. You could still analyze next-gen project boards by choosing to run each board individually.

Here's how the board selection screen appears:

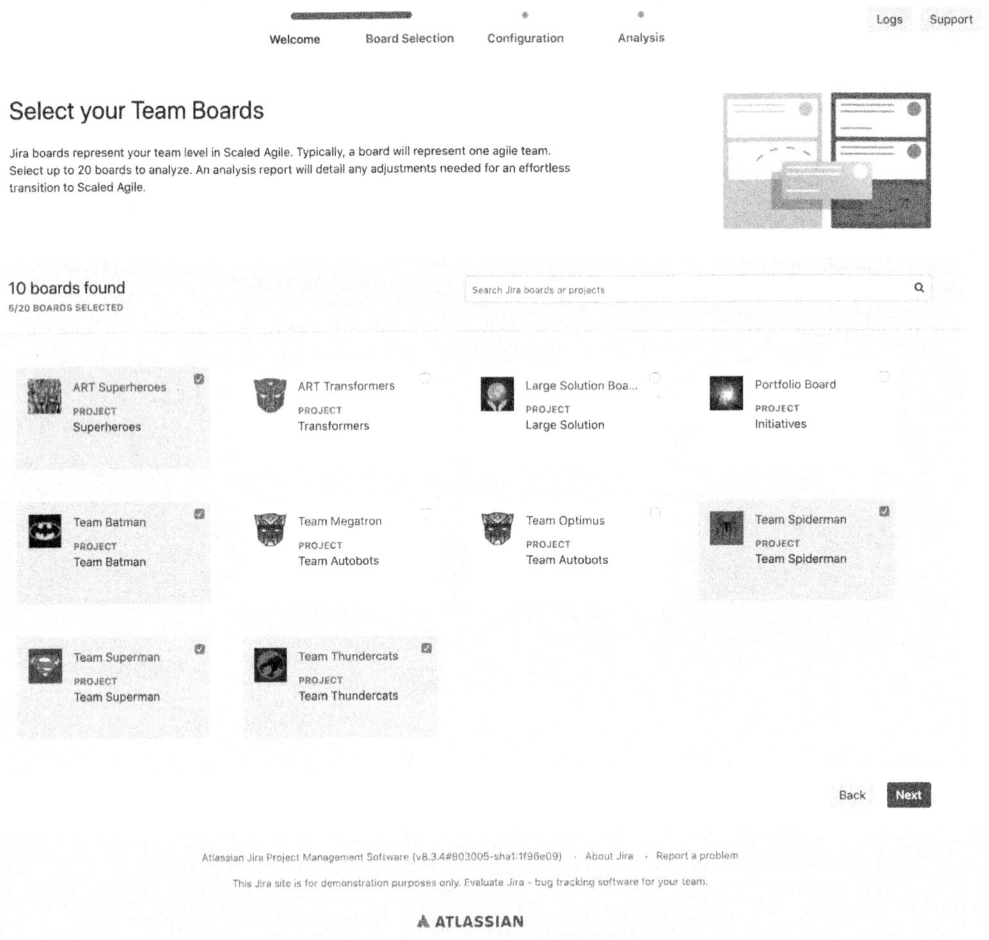

Figure 2.3 – Jet by Jira Align, step 2 – select your team boards

4. Next, you will map the Jira fields and issue types to compare the Jira data structure against the seven health checks and analyze the health of the boards:

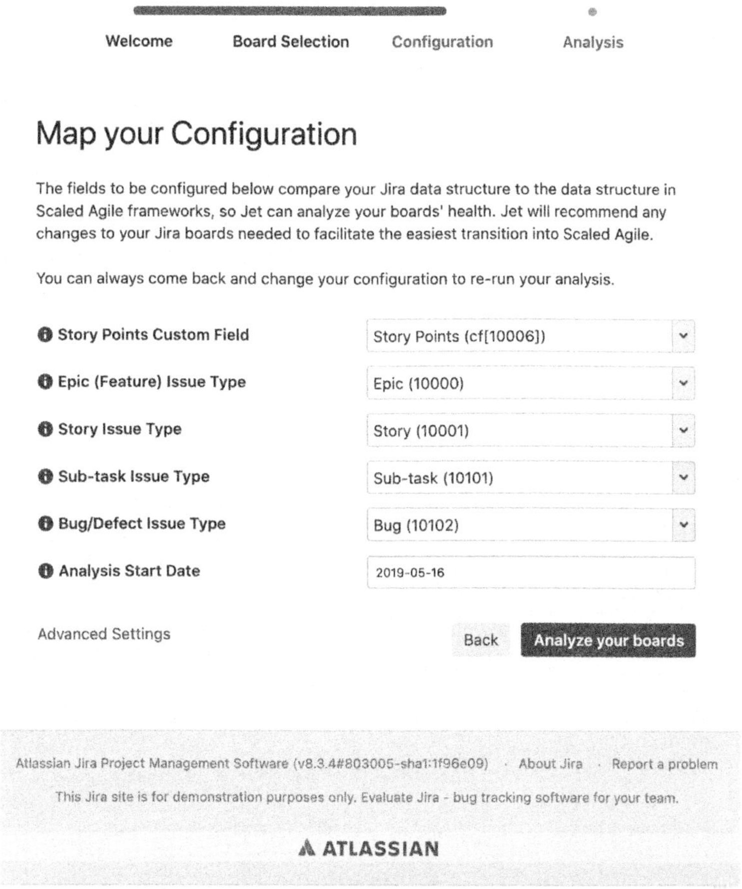

Figure 2.4 – Jet by Jira Align, step 3 – map your configuration

If you click on the **Advanced Settings** link, it will open the **Advanced Settings** screen, as follows:

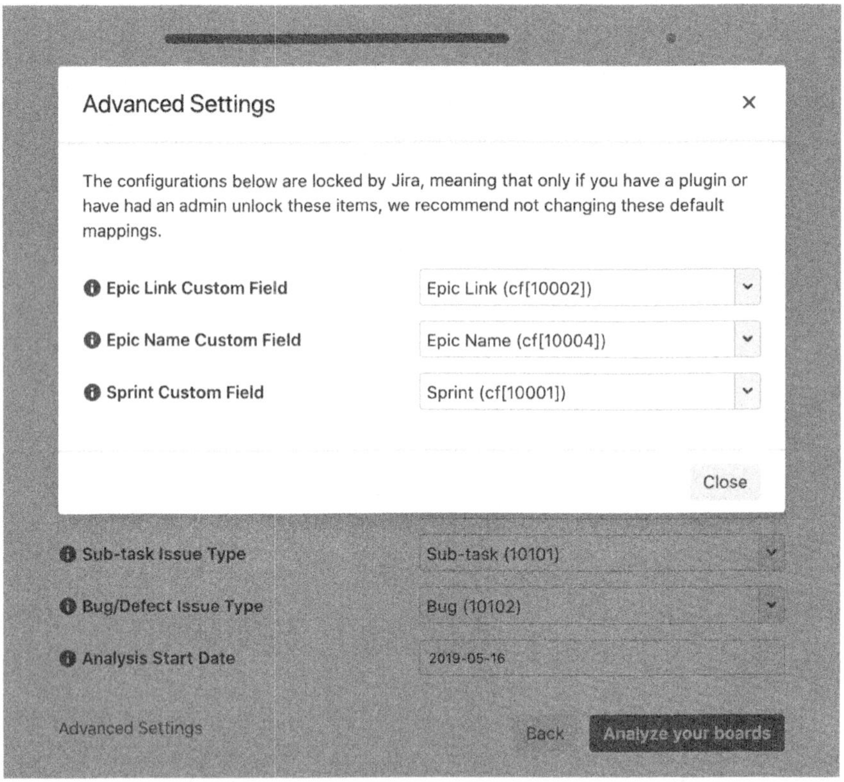

Figure 2.5 – Jet by Jira Align, step 3 – advanced settings

5. Analyze your boards and check the progress in terms of checks passed. When the board analysis is complete, you can view the **Health Report**. For the checks displaying **Needs Work**, follow the recommended action to improve the data and rerun the health check:

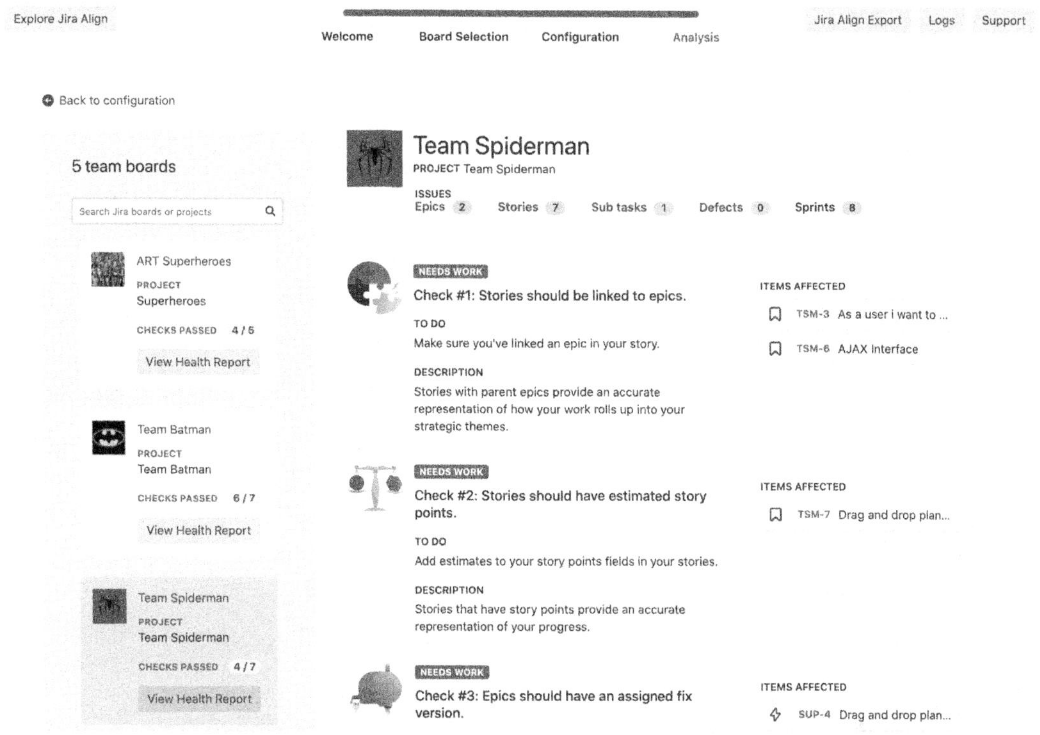

Figure 2.6 – Jet by Jira Align, step 4 – health report analysis

Let's now discuss the seven health checks, including their criticality on a scale of 1 to 5, with 5 being the most critical, and recommended actions if **Needs Work** is displayed.

Health check #1: Stories should be linked to epics.

Criticality: 3

Stories with parent Jira epics represent how team-level work connects to strategic work. All team-level work should be traceable and reportable against a measurable goal. This check ensures that tactical execution in Jira can connect to strategy in Jira Align.

You can simply treat it by linking orphan stories to parent Jira epics.

Health check #2: Stories should have estimated story points.

Criticality: 2

It is recommended that stories are estimated using story points to provide progress visibility in burndown charts and improve planning based on historical velocity (points per sprint). Ensuring that all stories are estimated will improve your delivery predictability based on actual velocity.

You can improve it by adding point estimates to your unestimated stories.

Health check #3: Epics should have an assigned fix version.

Criticality: 3

An assigned fix version for a Jira epic defines the release in which the feature will be shipped. The releases are tied to a project in Jira where the Jira epics are located. Fix versions are equivalent and map to release vehicles in Jira Align.

You can fix it by assigning a fix version to all planned Jira epics.

Health check #4: There should only be one project assigned to a Jira board.

Criticality: 5

An agile board in Jira should represent a team. Having multiple projects linked to a single board can make it difficult to measure team-level progress. For example, you may struggle with multiple team sprints with overlapping dates.

You can fix it by ensuring that only one project is linked to a board by navigating to **Board Settings**, selecting **Edit Filter Shares**, and removing all but one project. You may also fail this check if there are no projects associated with your board.

Health check #5: Mark custom fields as optional, not required.

Criticality: 5

Custom field configuration can affect your ability to integrate with Jira Align. Any Jira custom field that is set as mandatory will fail to sync between Jira and Jira Align.

You can fix this by making your Jira issue custom fields optional.

Health check #6: A single sprint should only be tied to one board.

Criticality: 5

Because a board should only represent one team, if you have a sprint on multiple boards, it can be difficult to measure team-level progress.

Similar to health check #4, follow the instructions to make sure you only have one project per board. If your team is structured such that you can't edit **Filter Shares**, instead select **Edit Filter Query** and ensure that only a single team's sprints are tied to a Jira board.

Health check #7: Sprints on a Jira board should not have overlapping dates.

Criticality: 5

Sprints represent a (usually 2-week) planning and execution time slot for a single team. Only one sprint should be active at a time.

You can improve it by making sure the start and end dates for your sprints don't overlap and that there is only one active sprint at a time.

Tips and tricks

Health checks #1, #2, and #3 are great to have when scaling; however, they won't stop you from moving ahead with your Jira Align journey.

Health checks #4, #5, #6, and #7 are very important to get right before connecting to Jira. The affected data will impact how work is visualized and synced into Jira Align.

Health checks #6 and #7 do not apply to Kanban team boards. However, the Kanban teams should have an agreement to work on a common cadence aligned to sprints and a PI.

To bring predictability and forecast insights into Jira Align, define a dataset and import only data completed within the last quarter, currently in progress, and future planned work.

We have identified which data needs improving by analyzing existing programs in Jira. Let's now set the boundaries and map people, work, time, and outcomes.

Mapping people, work, time, and outcomes

Jira Align provides a holistic view of how people engage in work over periods of time in order to achieve outcomes. These four dimensions are key to planning and alignment and play a significant role in business agility. While the teams continue their work in the best-of-breed Jira Software, Jira Align connects team-level execution with top-level strategy.

There are a number of ways in which team-level work can be organized in Jira. Keep in mind that a *project* in Jira represents a container for work items and is hence analogous to a backlog. Also note that there is not a *team* entity in Jira's database. Therefore, Jira Align will derive teams based on Jira project/board combinations. Here are the two top options for mapping projects/boards in Jira to teams in Jira Align:

- One Jira project per team of teams, one board per team, and one active sprint per board. This option requires a custom team field in Jira to drive each board. We recommend including Jira epics in the same project when using this option.

- One Jira project per team, one board per team, and one active sprint per board. For this option, you need an additional Jira project to contain Jira epics.

Which option should you choose? Either one project per team of teams or one project per team is acceptable. Let's now take a look at how to use one project per team of teams:

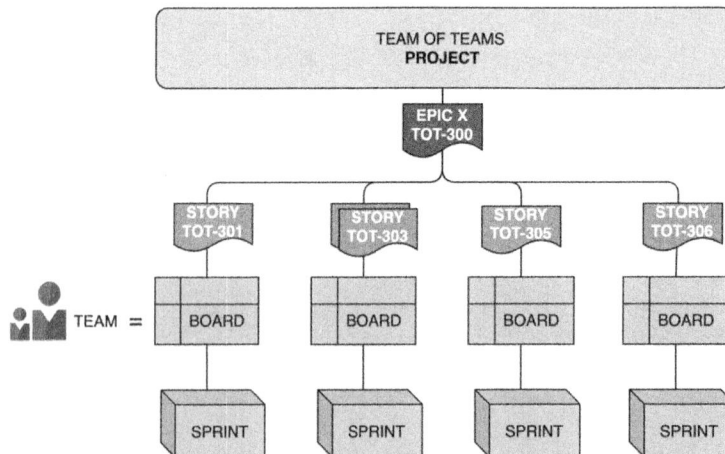

Figure 2.7 – One team of teams project structure

One project per team of teams requires the use of a custom field for teams in Jira to separate team boards. Jira issues don't store the board ID, and a single team selector field should be used to identify the team assignment for each story. The team field sets the board filter and prevents a sprint from being shared by multiple team boards in one Jira project. Teams can create additional boards and workflows for visualizations, but those won't be mapped to Jira Align. It's best to come up with a naming convention for the team boards that are connected to Jira Align. Larger organizations tend to opt for one project per team of teams to reduce the number of projects in Jira. For example, if there are 20 portfolios, each with 10 programs, each with 10 teams, that would be 2,000 Jira projects.

The smaller the company, the more it makes sense to go with the best practice of one project per team – it's simpler and doesn't require a team custom field. An organization can also use a combination of the approaches if need be. Here is the structure for one program project with many team projects:

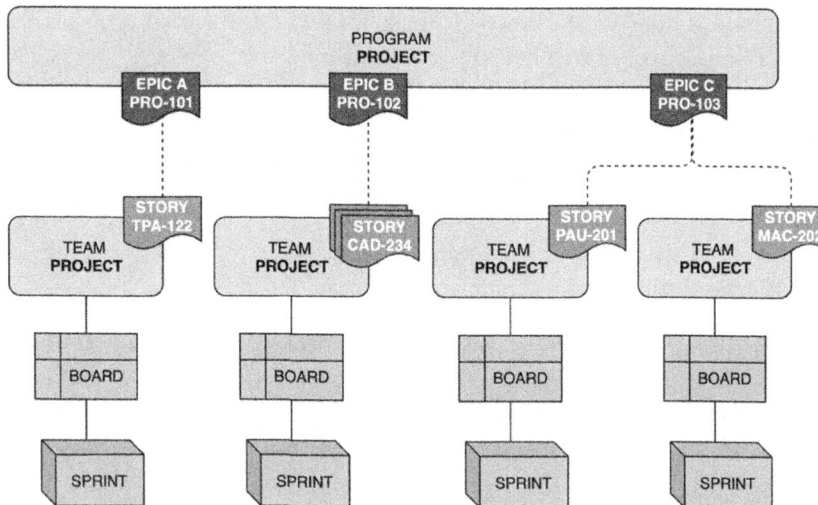

Figure 2.8 – Many team projects structure

Note that with this option, the program project should contain only Jira epics, which will get synced with Jira Align features.

Tips and tricks

Be sure to have only one active sprint per team agile board (teams can have future sprints planned without activating them).

Avoid overlapping sprint dates and maintain a common sprint cadence between teams, a best practice for agile at scale.

It's recommended for a story to be completed by one team in a single sprint. If a story needs to be shared, then clone it for each individual team.

If there are any unfinished stories at the end of a sprint, split them or move them to the backlog before completing the sprint.

For a Jira project with many team agile boards, do not share sprints across boards as this will create a conflict between boards.

Avoid creating fake sprints as an extra holding sprint or backlog within the backlog. Jira Align will assume these are real planned future sprints.

Now that we've got containers for team-level work items in Jira, we return to the concept that people perform work over time to achieve outcomes. Team-level work is executed in Jira while Jira Align sits on top of Jira to connect execution with strategy. Teams track work in Jira using the native issues and a hierarchy of Jira epics, stories, and sub-tasks. Jira epics represent a feature at the program level that teams deliver within a program increment or business quarter. Jira epics are broken down into stories, and further still into sub-tasks, to be delivered within a single sprint.

At the portfolio level, you track high-level work items called *themes* and *portfolio epics*, which are linked to your program-level work items, Jira epics or *features*. Organizations developing complex systems often require an additional work level between portfolio epics and features called *capabilities*. Introduce the additional level with caution as it adds extra levels of complexity that require added resources and measures to manage, maintain, and report at the capability level.

At each level, work items contribute to measurable outcomes, roll up to parent work items, and ultimately connect to the enterprise strategy, as depicted in the following diagram. Notably, your toolset should support these practices at each level:

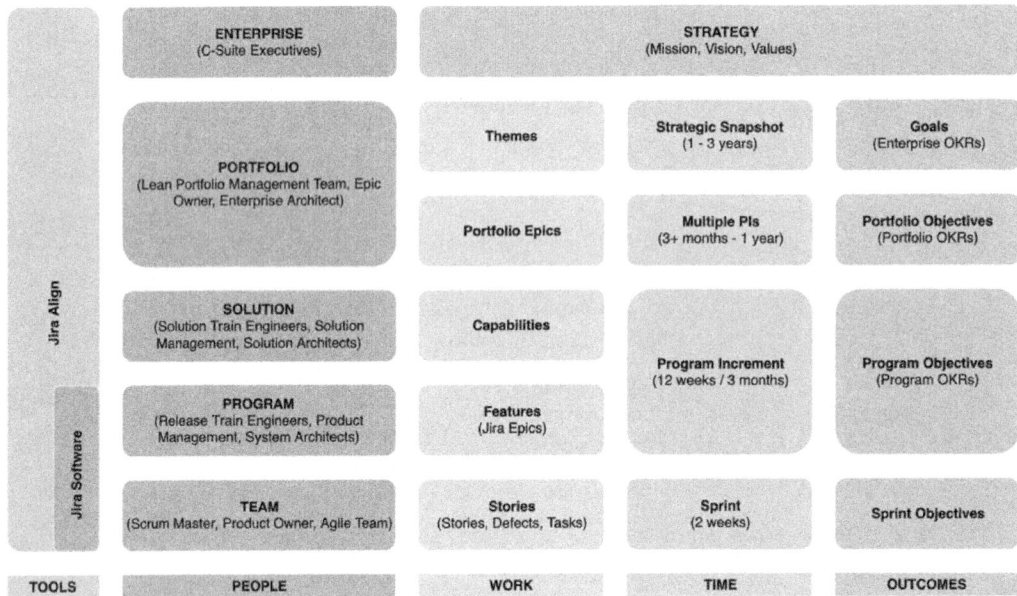

TOOLS	PEOPLE	WORK	TIME	OUTCOMES
	ENTERPRISE (C-Suite Executives)		**STRATEGY** (Mission, Vision, Values)	
	PORTFOLIO (Lean Portfolio Management Team, Epic Owner, Enterprise Architect)	**Themes**	**Strategic Snapshot** (1 - 3 years)	**Goals** (Enterprise OKRs)
Jira Align		**Portfolio Epics**	**Multiple PIs** (3+ months - 1 year)	**Portfolio Objectives** (Portfolio OKRs)
	SOLUTION (Solution Train Engineers, Solution Management, Solution Architects)	**Capabilities**	**Program Increment** (12 weeks / 3 months)	**Program Objectives** (Program OKRs)
	PROGRAM (Release Train Engineers, Product Management, System Architects)	**Features** (Jira Epics)		
Jira Software	**TEAM** (Scrum Master, Product Owner, Agile Team)	**Stories** (Stories, Defects, Tasks)	**Sprint** (2 weeks)	**Sprint Objectives**

Figure 2.9 – Tools with people, work, time, and outcomes

It is critical that the organization comes to a common agreement on how to align tools with people, work, time, and outcomes to successfully set up Jira Align. A key aspect of alignment is agreeing upon terminology. Whether your organization adopts SAFe or not, we recommend referring to the SAFe glossary as a reference when defining your dimensions: `https://www.scaledagileframework.com/glossary/`.

Note that the model shown in *Figure 2.9* also leads to *Chapter 3, Navigating Jira Align*, where you will learn to load, visualize, and report upon work at various levels of scale.

Let's get started and set up Jira Align by going through a quick fundamental setup and apply what we have discovered so far.

Setting up Jira Align

To get started with Jira Align, we will look at how to perform a quick setup using the information you discovered during the previous two phases: analyzing existing programs in Jira and mapping people, work, time, and outcomes. We will then onboard new users into Jira Align.

As part of organizational alignment for transformation, it is important that everyone speaks a common language. As illustrated in *Figure 1.1, Alignment toward transformation by connecting strategy with execution*, language helps an organization shape their culture by improving transparent communication flowing from leadership to the knowledge workers and vice versa. Experience has shown that it is important to keep the language as close to the common industry terminology or chosen framework as possible. This not only helps develop competencies internally, but also makes onboarding faster with effective communication when a new knowledge workforce joins an organization.

As the organization matures in language, they start developing a shorthand form of communication that abbreviates useful principles and practices. This often creates a sense of togetherness and identity. When everyone speaks the same language, it feels cohesive and creates stronger relationships to bridge differences. The consistency in language has a positive ripple effect both inside and outside the organization, helping to build trust, reliability, and credibility. Overall, the alignment in language helps reduce misunderstandings and increases productivity.

Jira Align is designed to adapt to your organization's transformation journey. You can rename the work objects, navigation menus, date labels, release attributes, currency, and finance terminologies in Jira Align to allow your organization to closely match your chosen practices and team tools. You can configure the platform terminology in Jira Align to match your framework, such as **Large-Scale Scrum (LeSS)**, **Scaled Agile Framework (SAFe)**, and **Disciplined Agile Delivery (DAD)**. For example, a *driver* in LeSS can be identified as a *business driver* in SAFe and a *goal* in DAD. Likewise, you may want to call your Jira epic a *feature*, your sprint an *iteration*, and so on.

You can configure platform terminology under **Administration | Settings | Platform Terminology**, and user record terminology under **Administration | Settings| User Record Terminology**. Once you update the terminologies, be sure to click on the **Update Terminology** button to save the changes and re-login to Jira Align for the updates to take effect. Here is the platform terminology setup screen:

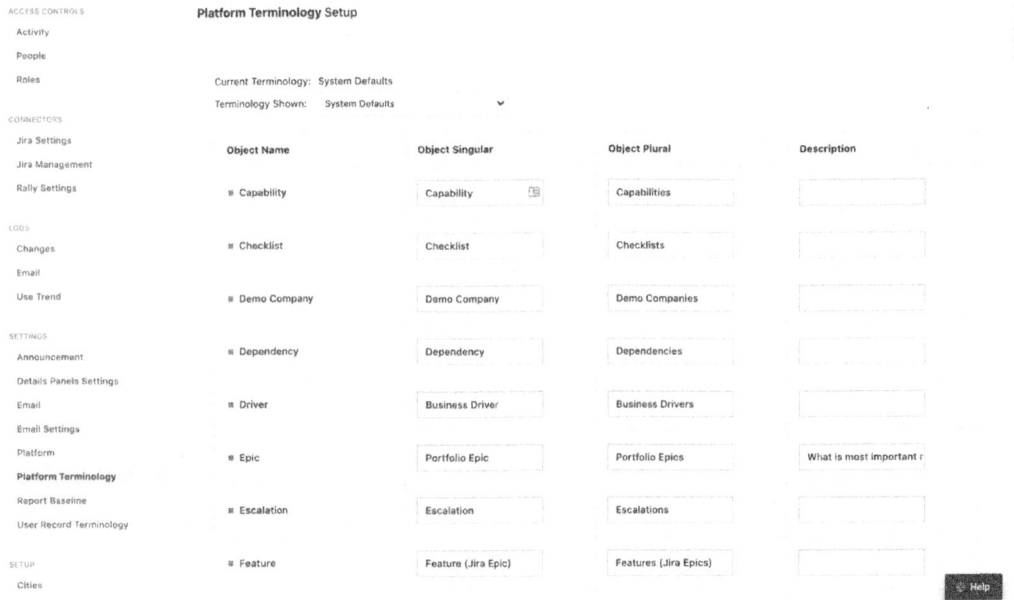

Figure 2.10 – Jira Align platform terminology setup

Once the terminologies are configured, we will start creating the entries for the physical and virtual organizational attributes in Jira Align. The physical attributes include the enterprise's organization structure and operational regions. Next, for the virtual organization, we will create a portfolio and associate multiple programs.

You will first create the organization structure under **Administration | Setup | Organization Structure** by clicking on the **Add New** button, which presents the following screen:

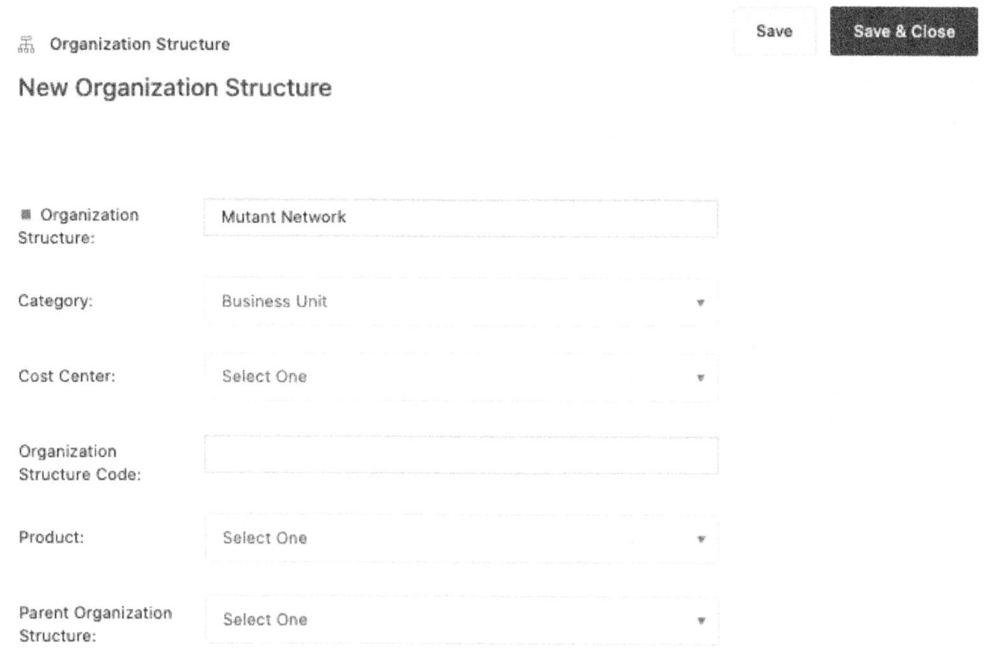

Figure 2.11 – Jira Align organization structure setup

The organization structure allows you to represent your organizational business units and how they relate to one another.

Next, we will create the physical regions in which your organization operates. This information is used when creating portfolios, programs, users, and releases for functionalities tied to time tracking in Jira Align. You can add regions under **Administration | Setup | Regions** by clicking on the **Add Regions** button to open the following screen:

Figure 2.12 – Jira Align regions setup

We will now create the virtual organization attributes, beginning with the portfolio by going to **Administration | Setup | Portfolios** and clicking on the **Add Portfolio** button. Creating a portfolio requires the following mandatory details:

- **Portfolio Name**: Name your portfolio `Mutants`.

- **Description**: Add a description to your `Mutants Portfolio` portfolio.

- **Parent Organization**: Associate the portfolio with the applicable organization structure, `Mutants Network`.

- **Team Description**: Name the portfolio leadership team to be created `Mutants Portfolio Leadership Team`.

- **Region**: Choose the applicable region from where your portfolio will be managed, in this instance, `Europe`.

These settings are shown in the following screenshot:

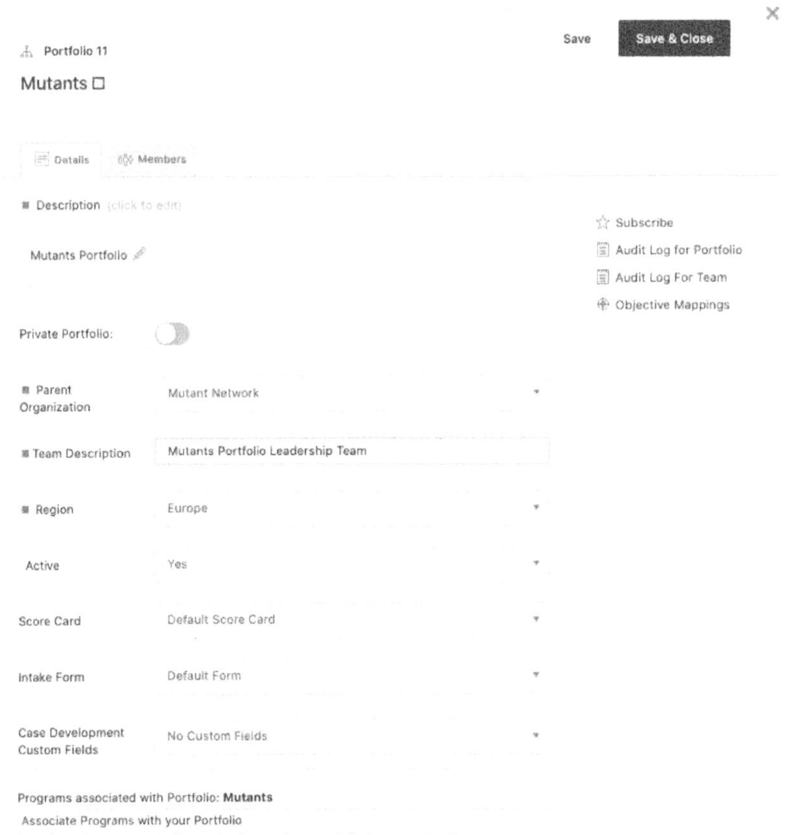

Figure 2.13 – Jira Align portfolio setup

Once you have completed the required details, click on **Save**. You can now add the individual portfolio leadership team members under the **Members** tab.

Next, we will create the programs and link them to the portfolio by going to **Administration | Setup | Programs** and clicking on the **Add Program** button. Creating a program requires the following mandatory details:

- **Program Name**: Name your program `Superheroes`.

- **Portfolio**: Associate the program with the applicable portfolio, `Mutants`.

- **Team Description**: Name the program leadership team to be created `Superheroes Program Leadership Team`.

Once you complete the required details, click on **Save**. You can now add the individual program leadership team members under the **Members** tab. When you need to run more than one program, you can repeat the steps to create and associate multiple programs with the portfolio. For example, we have created and associated the **Transformers** program and the **Superheroes** program:

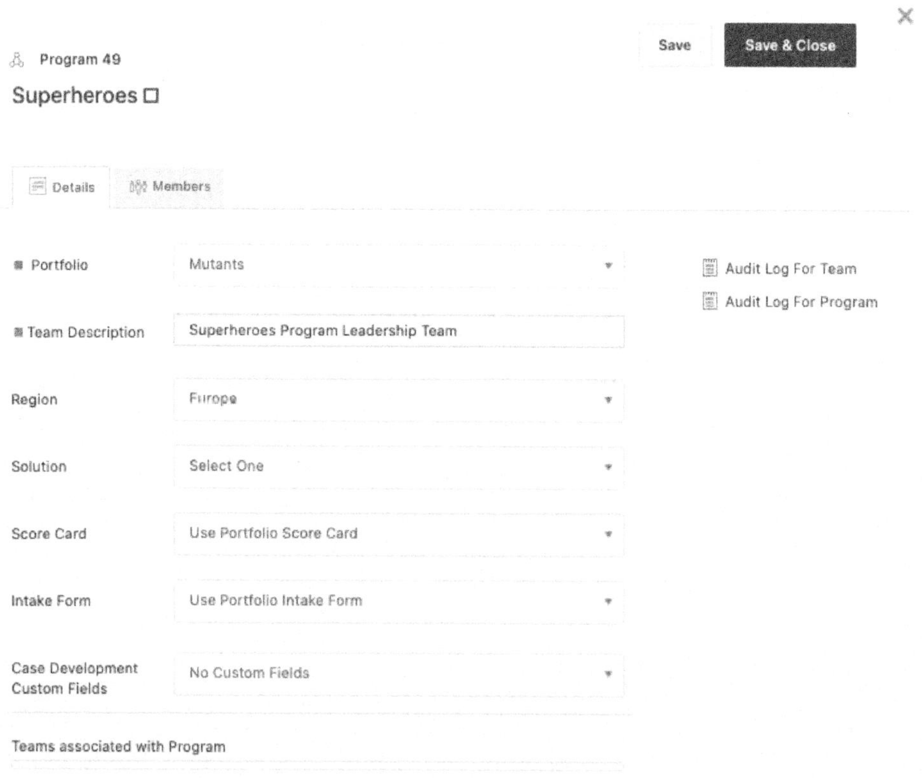

Figure 2.14 – Jira Align program setup

You may create and manage additional attributes, such as customers, cost centers, countries, cities, and custom hierarchies under the **Administration | Setup** menu to further define your views and reporting in Jira Align.

We will next create teams and associate them with the program. The teams will be created by going to **Team | Manage | Teams** and clicking on the **Add Team** button. Creating a team requires the following mandatory details:

- **Type**: Choose **Agile Team** for creating a Scrum team and **Kanban Team** for a Kanban team. Let's create an agile team for the Superheroes program.

- **Team**: Add the team name. Let's call it `Team Batman`.

- **Description**: Add a description for your team.

- **Team Short Name**: Add a five-character short name.

- **Sprint Prefix**: Add a team prefix to your team sprints.

- **Program**: Choose the program that your team belongs to.

Once you have completed the required details, click on **Save**. You can now add the team photo under the **Details** tab and individual team members under the **Members** tab:

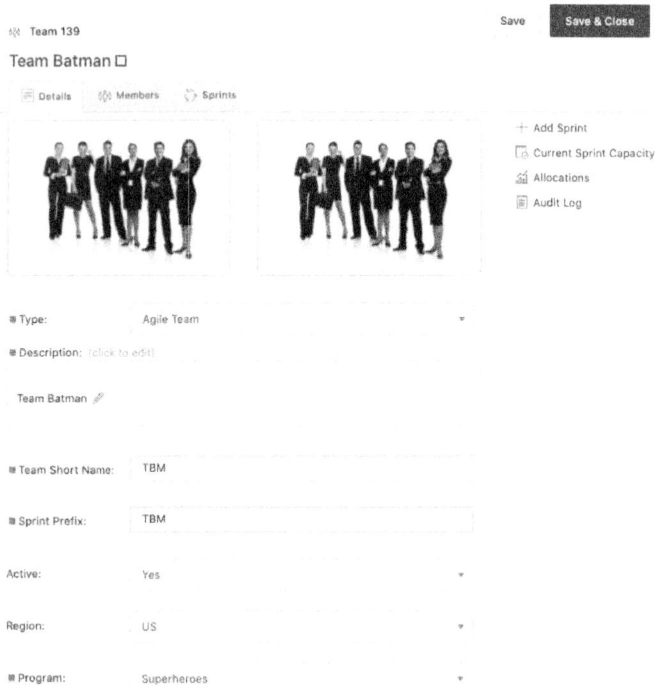

Figure 2.15 – Jira Align team setup

You will repeat these configuration steps to create your virtual structure and then use the **Configuration** bar to navigate the virtual organization:

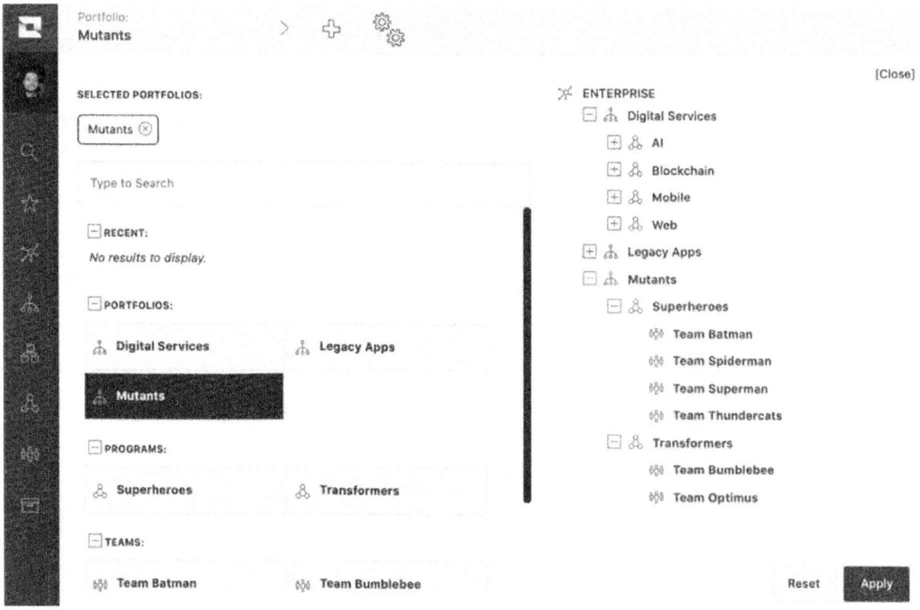

Figure 2.16 – Jira Align virtual organizational structure

Finally, we will create a program increment cadence and the related anchor sprints in Jira Align as preparations to connect to Jira. The program increment will be created by going to **Program | Manage | Program Increments** and clicking on the **Add Program Increment** button. Creating a program increment requires the following mandatory details:

- **Portfolio**: Choose the applicable Mutants portfolio.

- **Program**: Choose all the programs that will share the program increment cadence *Superheroes and Transformers.*

- **Program Increment #**: Add a program increment number, 2020 Q4.

- **Program Increment Name**: Add a program increment name, 2020 Q4.

- **Short Name**: Add a short name to the program increment, 20Q4. This will be used for reporting purposes.

- **Start Date**: Add a start date to your program increment.

- **Finish Date**: Add a finish date to your program increment.

- **Description**: Add a description to your program increment.

- **Status**: Choose a status to track your program increment. The available statuses are **Planning**, **In Progress**, **Done**, and **Archive**.

Once you complete the required details, click on **Save**:

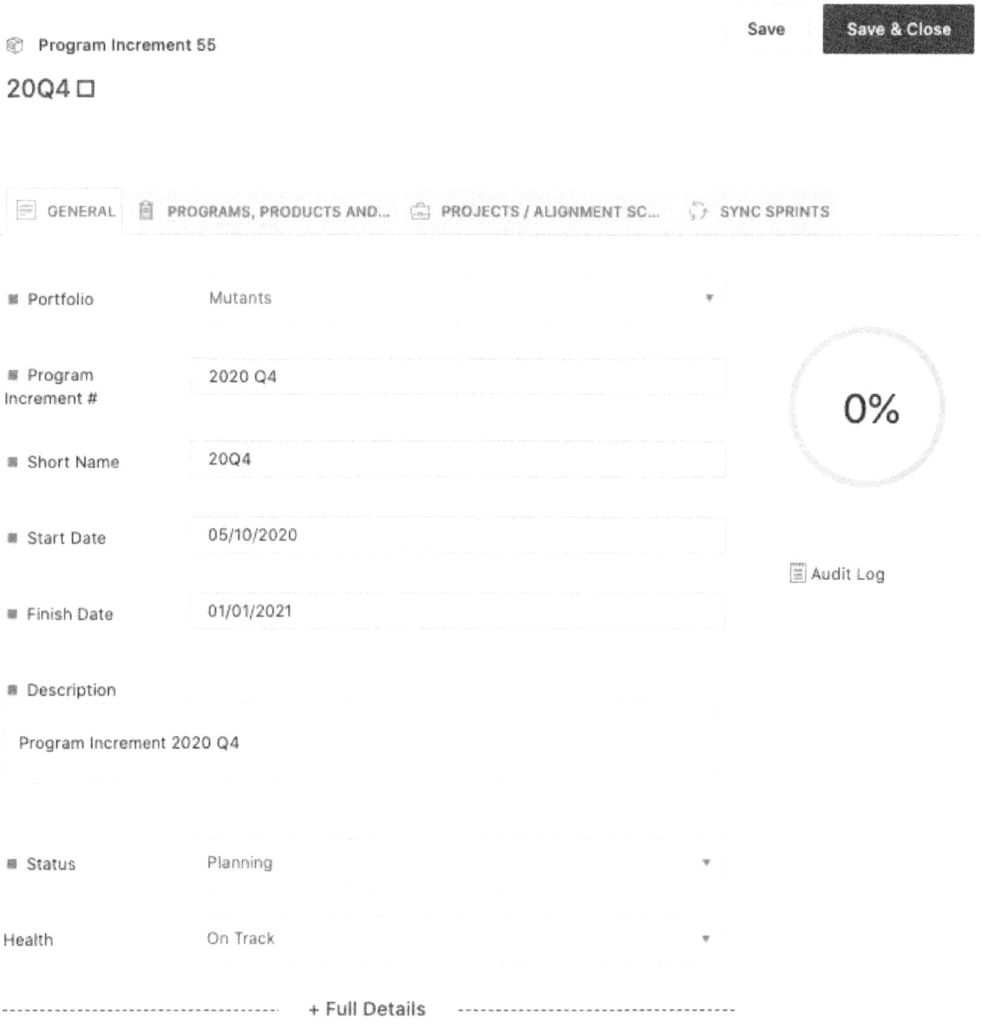

Figure 2.17 – Jira Align program increment setup

If your programs do not share a common program increment, then repeat the preceding steps and ensure that you add a prefix to your program increment number, name, and short name to uniquely identify the other program increment cadences.

We can now create anchor sprints for the program increment. For this, choose the **Sync Sprints** tab under the selected program increment. You can mass add anchor sprints that follow a common sprint cadence or you can add a single anchor sprint that can represent your **IP (innovation and planning)** sprint.

To mass add anchor sprints, select the **Mass Add** toggle and provide the following details:

- **Sprint Prefix**: Add a prefix to identify the sprints in the program increment, Q4S.

- **First Date**: Add the first sprint start date.

- **Type**: Choose the anchor sprint type Standard Sprint.

- **Duration**: Choose the duration of your sprint. Choose 10 Week Days to select a 2-week cadence.

- **Daily Max**: Choose the maximum daily work allocation in hours.

- **Daily Defect**: Choose the expected daily defect allocation in hours.

- **Total Anchors**: Choose the number of anchor sprints to generate. Choose **5** to create five anchor sprints.

Next, click on the **Create Anchors** button:

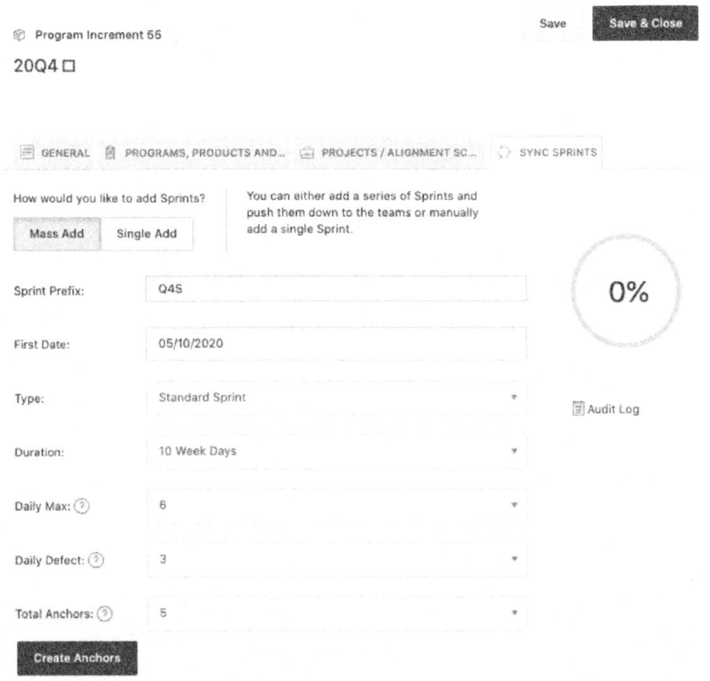

Figure 2.18 – Jira Align anchor sprint mass add

To add a single anchor sprint, select the **Single Add** toggle and provide the following details:

- **Sprint**: Add a name to identify the single sprint, Q4S6 (12/14-01/01).
- **Short Name**: Add a short name to identify the sprint, Q4S6.
- **Dates**: Add a sprint start date and finish date.
- **Type**: Choose the anchor sprint type *IP (Innovation & Planning) Sprint*.
- **Duration**: Choose the duration of your sprint if you haven't added a sprint finish date.
- **Daily Max**: Choose the maximum daily work allocation in hours.
- **Daily Defect**: Choose the expected daily defect allocation in hours.

Next, click on the **Create Sprint** button:

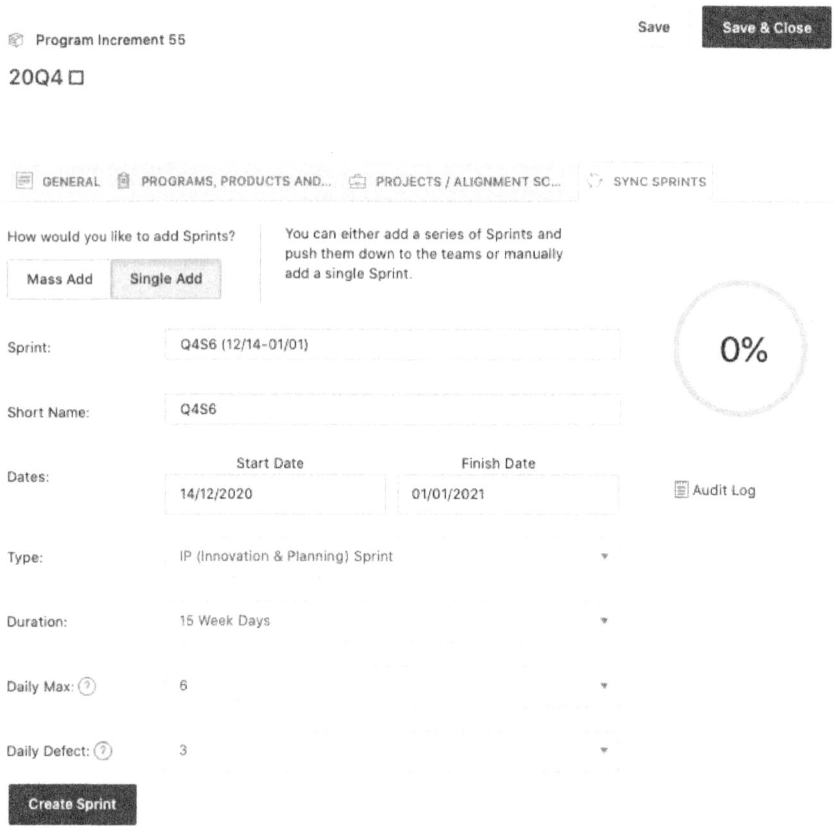

Figure 2.19 – Jira Align anchor sprint single add

Once all the anchor sprints are created, you can now generate the team sprints in bulk using the **Generate Team Sprints** button, as shown:

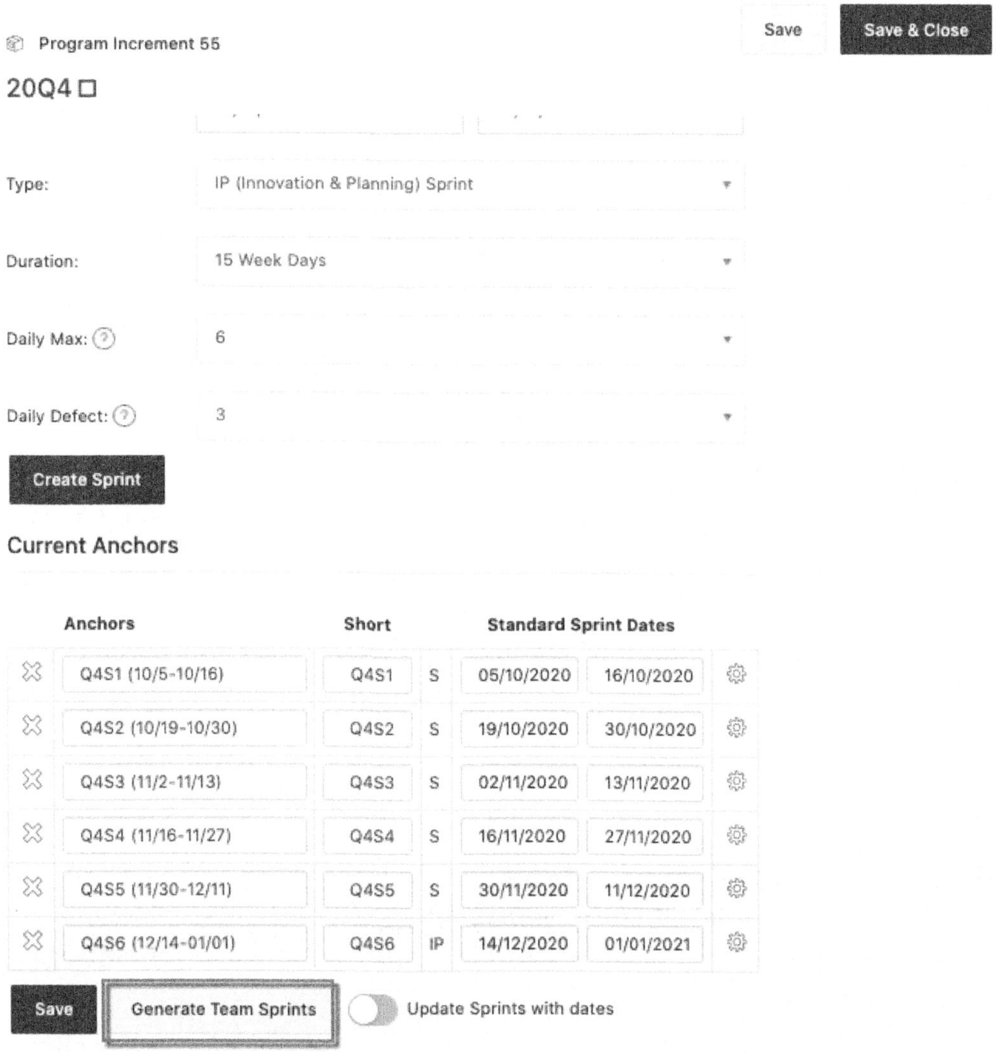

Figure 2.20 – Jira Align team sprints generation

Once you confirm, Jira Align will generate the associated sprints for all the teams in the chosen programs and program increments.

You will repeat these steps to generate as many program increments as you need for planning and executing work. The program increments will now be available to the applicable programs and will be available to choose from the **Program Increment** filter in the **Configuration** bar:

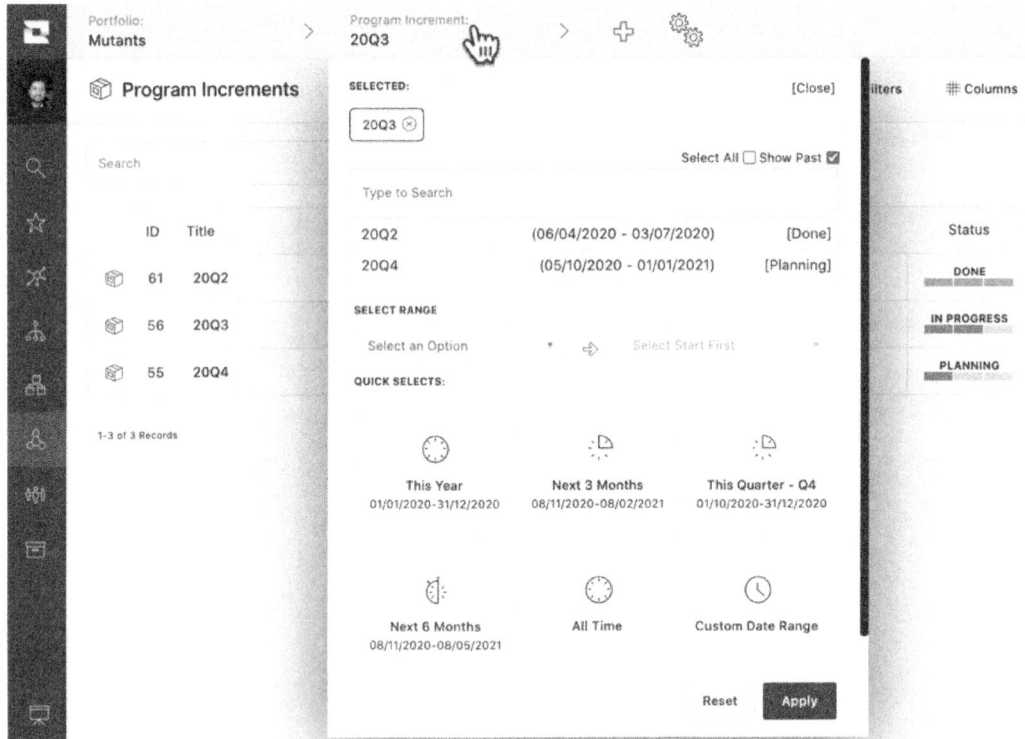

Figure 2.21 – Jira Align program increment configuration bar

Now we can onboard new users into Jira Align by going to **Administration | Access Control | People** and clicking on the **Add User** button. Adding a new user requires the following mandatory details:

- **User Type**: Choose **Internal** to create fully functional, role-based Jira Align users. For users who only require access to the ideation module, choose **External**.

- **First Name**: Add the user's first name.

- **Last Name**: Add the user's last name.

- **Email**: Add the user's email address. Jira Align will send all user correspondence to the given email.

- **Title**: Add a title for the user.

- **Role**: Choose a role from the list.
- **Enterprise Hierarchy**: Choose the organization.
- **Region**: Choose the region.
- **City**: Choose the city.
- **Cost Center**: Choose the applicable cost center.

Next, click on the **Save** button to create the new user. Jira Align will send a new user setup invitation via email to onboard the user onto the platform:

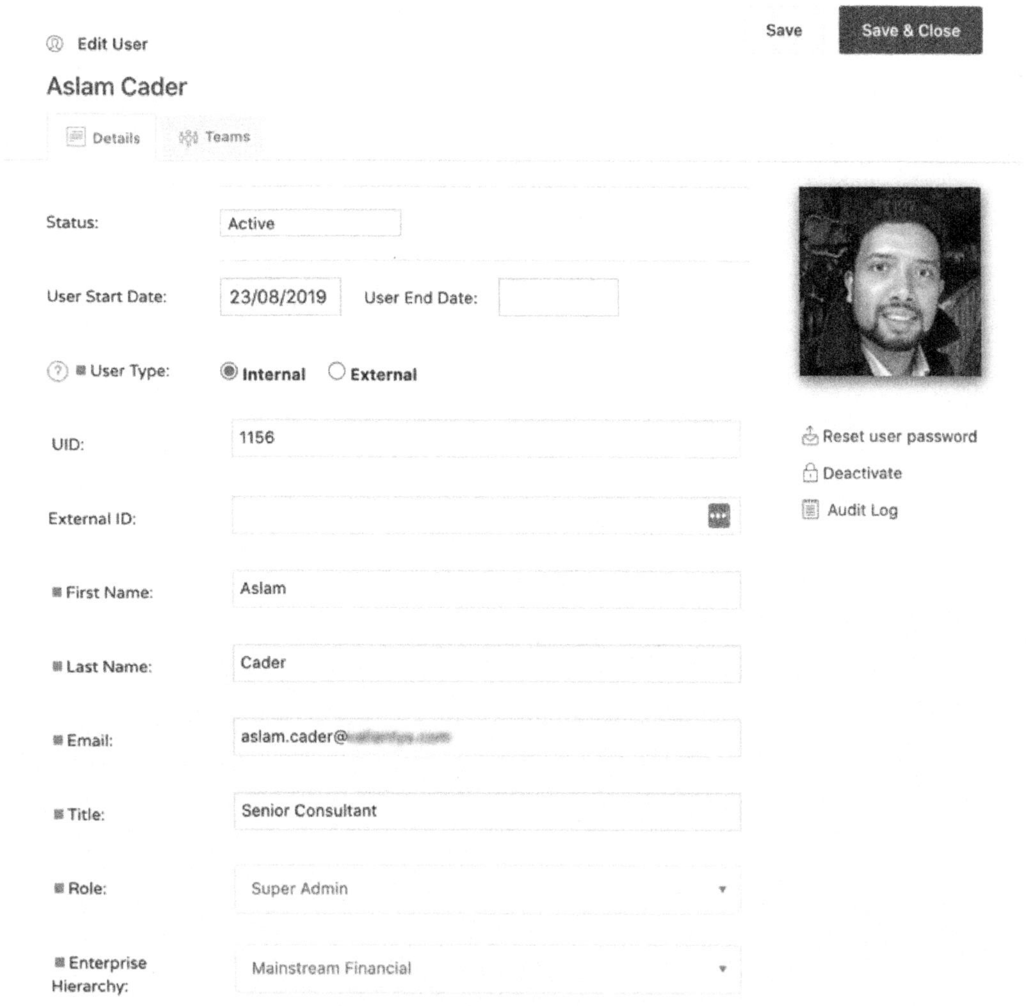

Figure 2.22 – Jira Align user account

> **Tips and tricks**
>
> User access control in Jira Align is based on roles. There are predefined sets of roles that can be used or copied to create new roles. Roles are configured using functionality toggles at different levels of the application, such as the Team, Program, Solution, and Portfolio levels.
>
> If you want to mass import users, you can go to **Administration | Access Control | People | More Actions** and click on **Import User Records**. This will provide a user import template to guide you through the bulk user import.
>
> To avoid updating user records in the **user interface (UI)**, you can export user records by going to **Administration | Access Control | People | More Actions**, clicking on **Export**, and then editing and re-importing the file into Jira Align.

Jira Align supports **single-sign-on (SSO)**, which can be configured by going to the **Administration | Settings | Platform | Security** tab and providing the following details:

- **Enable SSO**: Set the option to **Yes**. This option will display when **Disable Manual Sign In** is set to **Yes** (see next item).

- **Disable Manual Sign In**: The default value is **No**. Setting the option to **Yes** will disable manual sign in, along with the security settings, resend password option, login page, and new user setup email.

- **SAML 2.0 Identity Providers**: Click on the **Add SAML Provider** button and then copy and paste the SAML 2.0 (security assertion markup language) XML (extensible markup language) metadata. Under **NameID Lookup By**, select either the **Email** or **External ID** field for user authentication. A user's external ID can be set on the **Edit User** page and synced through the external connectors.

- **Sign In URL**: This option is only available if the manual sign in option is disabled. Set the URL that you want to direct users to when they try to access Jira Align.

- **Sign Out URL**: Set the URL that you want to redirect users to when they click **Sign Out**.

In addition to the preceding details, once you connect to Jira, there will be Jira-integrated users who will obtain access to Jira Align. Let's now connect Jira Align to Jira and start mapping the objects and fields with Jira.

Connecting to Jira

In Jira Align, you will create and manage portfolio and program backlogs while agile teams continue to work in Jira Software with zero to minimal disruption. Jira Align connects to one or many Jira instances and the connector supports all three Jira hosting platforms: Atlassian Cloud, Server, and Data Center. Jira Align is a SaaS first solution with enterprise-grade hosting. A Jira Align on-premises solution is available for organizations that require additional controls in terms of their data security and privacy. The following diagram represents how the Jira Align platform connects to one or many Jira platforms:

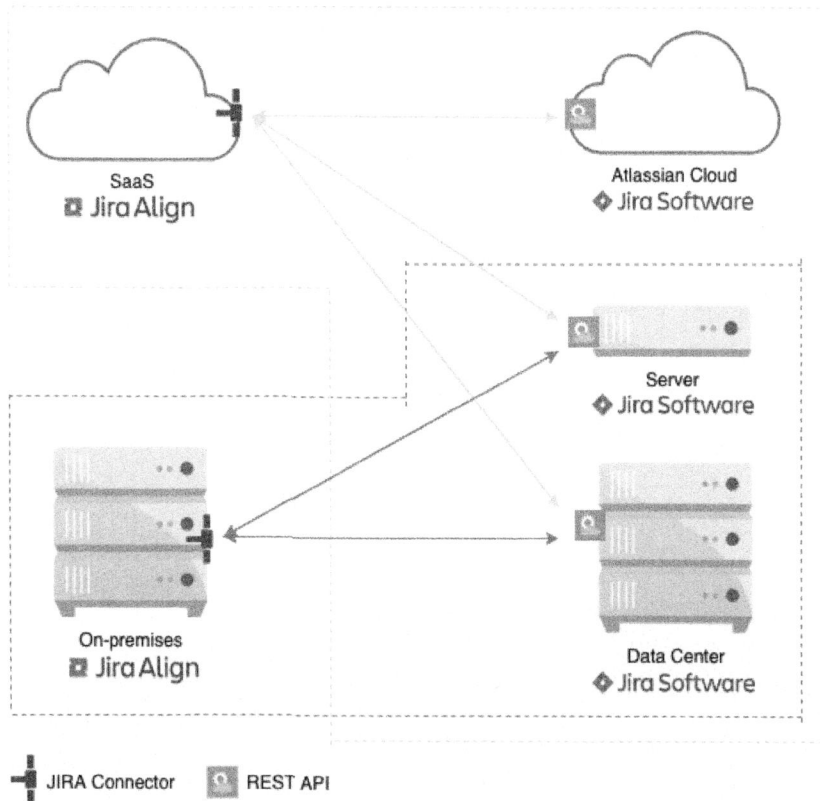

Figure 2.23 – Jira connector hosting platforms

> **Tips and tricks**
>
> Jira Align on-premises has the same code base as Jira Align SaaS and supports integration with the Atlassian Cloud Jira Software. If you chose to deploy Jira Align on-premises, you are most likely to integrate with Jira Software Data Center, as illustrated in *Figure 2.23*.

For physically connecting to Jira Software, it is required to establish a permanent application link between Jira and Jira Align via the Jira Connector. To establish the connection, you will need a Jira service account with permission to access the data in Jira.

You will first create and configure an application link in Jira Software by going to **Administration | Applications | Application Links**, adding the Jira Align URL link, and then clicking on the **Create new link** button. To create the application link, you will only need to provide the application name, Jira Align, and application type, Generic Application:

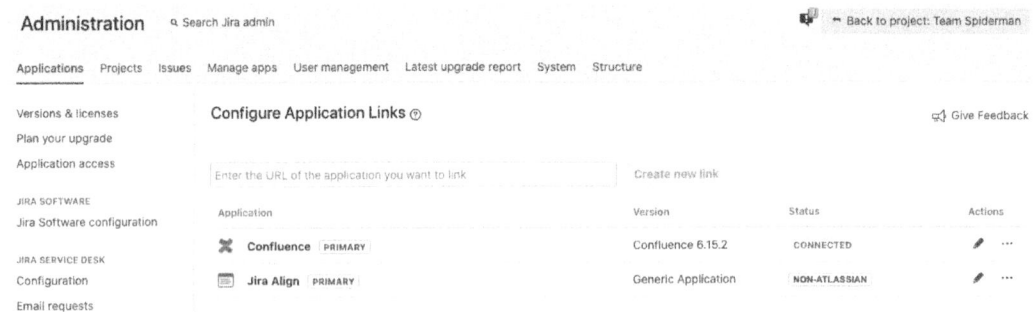

Figure 2.24 – Jira application link

Now switch to Jira Align, go to **Administration | Jira Settings**, and click on the **Jira Connectors** button. Add a connector and then complete the following details for the connection before you click on the **Active** button. This will prompt you to enter the Jira service user login details for the Jira connector to access Jira via the API:

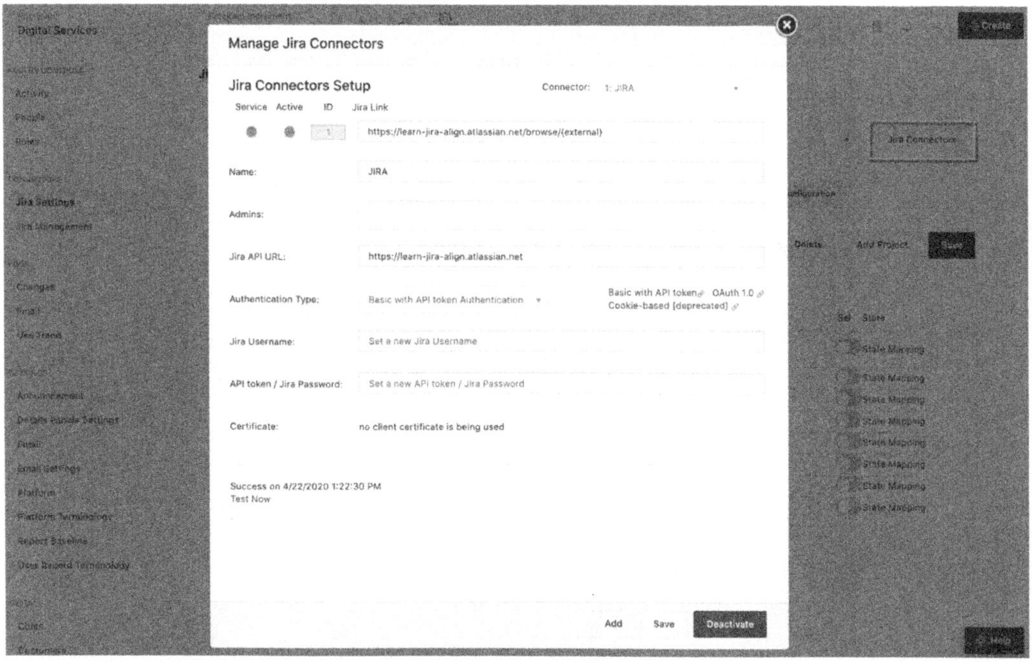

Figure 2.25 – Jira Align, manage Jira connectors

Here are the technical prerequisites for integration:

Jira instance accessibility: The Jira instance should be accessible to Jira Align via the internet or the **virtual private network** (**VPN**).

Jira instance with secure access: The Jira instance should have a publicly trusted **SSL** (**secure socket layer**) certificate for secure **HTTPS** (**hypertext transfer protocol secure**) access.

Jira user access: You will need a dedicated Jira service user provisioned with the following project permissions: Create Issues, Edit Issues, Assign Issues, Manage Sprints, Browse, and Manage Reporter.

The Jira connector requires access to the Jira API, which should be exposed outside the firewall to access from the Jira Align application. If your Jira is hosted in the Atlassian Cloud, then it is pretty straightforward connecting to the Jira API. If your Jira is hosted on-premises, then your Jira most probably sits behind a firewall, and enabling external access to the Jira API and integrating to Jira becomes a challenge to address. The following diagram represents how the Jira API should be exposed and accessible to the Jira connector in Jira Align:

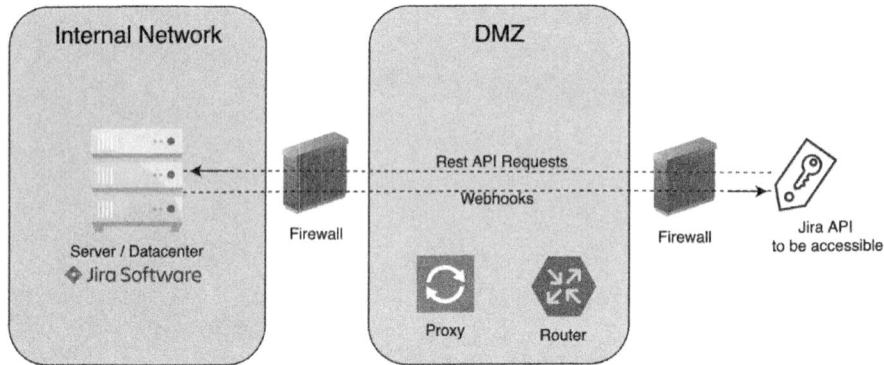

Figure 2.26 – Jira Connector API access and connectivity

You may achieve this by one or a combination of three options after Jira has been configured:

- Opening firewall ports/whitelisting
- Reverse proxy and/or API gateway
- On-premises agent

Due to an organization's network policies, complex infrastructure, and security requirements, you may need to involve various technical roles, including Edge Network Security, Sysadmin, Jira Admin, Network Admin, and IT C-suite executives, to successfully enable and allow the Jira API access to the Jira connector. These are the four API-based URLs that the Jira connector requires:

- `/rest/auth/`
- `/rest/api/2/`
- `/rest/agile/1.0/`
- `/rest/greenhopper/1.0/`

The verbs needed for each of these are as follows:

- `GET /rest/**`
- `POST /rest/**`
- `DELETE /rest/**`
- `PUT /rest/**`

Here, /rest/** should be replaced with the endpoints listed previously, for example /rest/auth.

Once the connection is established, we will start connecting the Jira artifacts. The following image based on the 10X: Jira Integration Guide document details how Jira and Jira Align artifacts are mapped and synced via the Jira API connector:

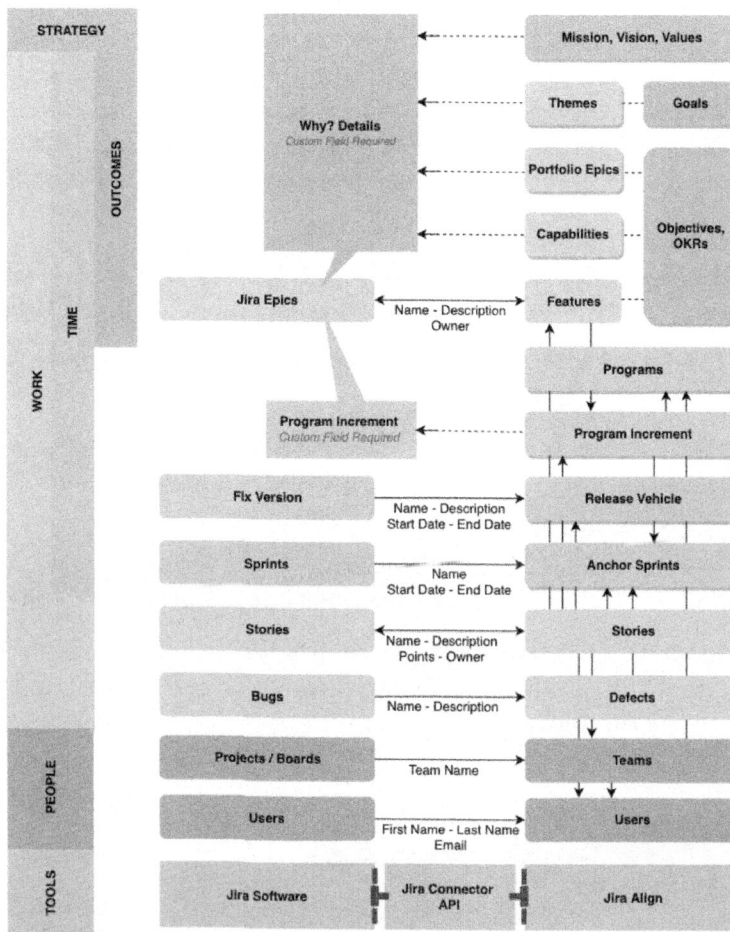

Figure 2.27 - Jira Align Jira integration mapping, adapted from 10X: Jira Integration Guide

You can access the Jira Integration Guide by going to the user menu, selecting **Help | Quick Links | Guides,** and then clicking on **10X: Jira Integration Guide**.

Tips and tricks

It is important to understand the core data mapping between Jira Align and Jira Software projects, boards, work item types, and fields.

Atlassian provides templates for Jira Integration Data Collection to facilitate data mapping during preliminary requirements gathering. You can download the templates by going to the user menu, selecting **Help | Knowledge Base | Integrations | 10X: Jira Integration Guide,** and then clicking on **10X: Jira Integration Data Collection**.

In addition to the field mappings required as discussed earlier, there are some recommended optional Jira Align field mappings between Jira epics and Jira Align features. You can configure them under the **Administration | Connectors | Jira Settings | Jira Setup** tab and look for the **Custom Fields** section. Next, you will enter your custom field ID in the following format: **customfield_100xx**, where *100xx* is the ID located in Jira Software. Keep in mind that these will require you to create custom fields in Jira Software as follows:

- **MMF (Minimum Marketable Feature**): A **Yes/No** field that syncs bi-directionally to indicate whether the feature represents the minimum marketable functionality

- **Feature Product**: A single selection drop-down field that syncs bi-directionally to display the product with which a feature is associated

- **Why? Details**: A multiline text field that syncs one way (Jira Align to Jira) to display details on why a work item is in the backlog and how it connects to strategic objectives

- **Feature Parent**: A single selection drop-down field that syncs one way (Jira Align to Jira) to display the parent work item (capability or portfolio epic) of the feature

- **Program increment**: A single selection drop-down field that syncs one way (Jira Align to Jira) to display the program increment or business quarter in which the feature will be delivered

Tips and tricks

The **Jira Align Why? definition**, a custom text (multiline) field, should be created in Jira Software and added to the applicable Jira epic issue screen. Next, the custom field should be configured as a **Wiki style renderer** in the Jira field configuration. This configuration would allow the **Why?** button data to be presented in a wiki-formatted table.

The data syncs one way, from Jira Align to Jira Software. We recommend that the Jira Align Why? definition custom field is set as read-only, or any changes made in the custom field will be overwritten upon the next sync with Jira Align.

In addition, any required custom fields in Jira Software should be set as optional in order for the custom fields to successfully sync with Jira Align.

If you use Rich Text Format in Jira fields to be integrated with Jira Align, go to the **Administration | Connections | Jira Settings | Jira Setup** tab and choose **HTML** as the option for **Rich Text Format**.

We saw how Jira issue types (epics, stories, and bugs) map to Jira Align work items (features, stories, and defects). Note, too, that Jira sub-tasks map to Jira Align tasks and that Jira tasks can be mapped to a Jira Align story of *type = task*. But what about the status of these Jira issue types? Jira workflows are comprised of the statuses and transitions that issues move through as part of the development life cycle. These workflows are connected to Jira Align via a mapping of Jira statuses to Jira Align states (forward mapping) and of Jira Align states to Jira statuses (reverse mapping). Note that ideally, all workflows connected to Jira Align are consistent to make administration easier, but whatever workflows are agreed upon must not be altered without coordination with the Jira Align administrator.

Let's now configure the forward state mapping between Jira and Jira Align. You can configure the state mapping under the **Administration | Connectors | Jira Settings | State Mapping** tab. The forward state mapping is a global setting and can be configured for the following work items: features (Jira epics), stories, tasks (Jira sub-tasks), and defects (Jira bugs). You will need to set the Jira Canceled State ID to allow any issues canceled in Jira to move to the canceled recycle bin in Jira Align. Any canceled work item in Jira Align will set the issues in Jira to the canceled state. The following screen shows how to configure the forward state mapping in Jira Align:

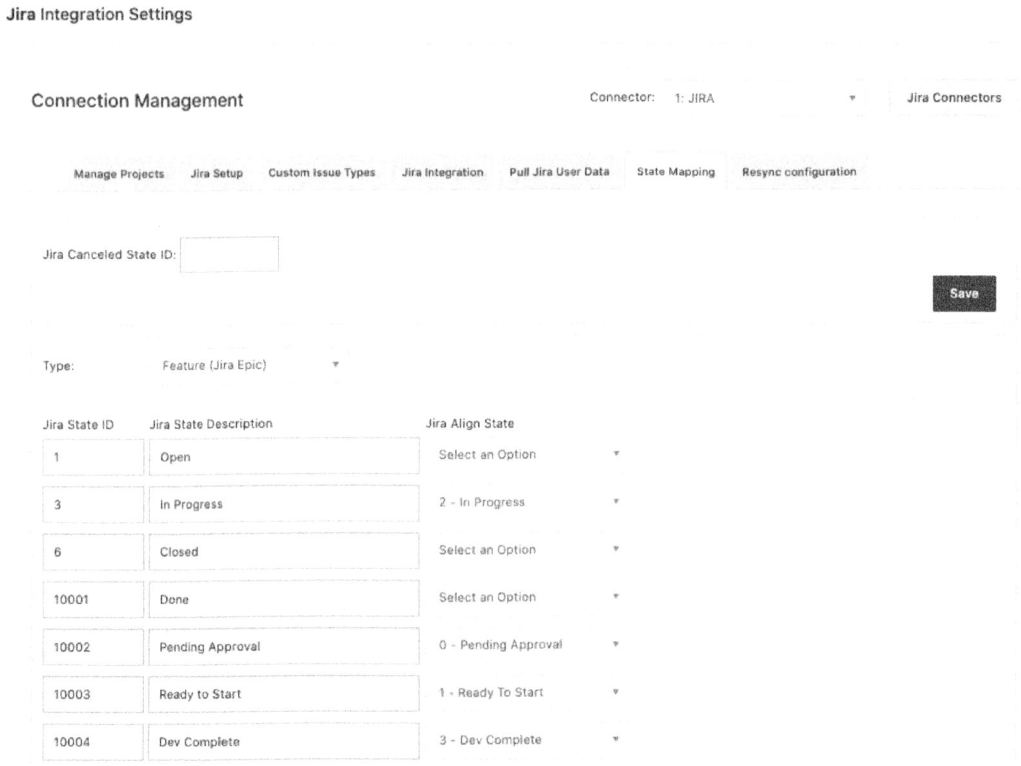

Jira Integration Settings

Connection Management
Connector: 1: JIRA   ▼   Jira Connectors

Manage Projects   Jira Setup   Custom Issue Types   Jira Integration   Pull Jira User Data   State Mapping   Resync configuration

Jira Canceled State ID: [   ]

[Save]

Type: Feature (Jira Epic)   ▼

Jira State ID	Jira State Description	Jira Align State
1	Open	Select an Option ▼
3	In Progress	2 - In Progress ▼
6	Closed	Select an Option ▼
10001	Done	Select an Option ▼
10002	Pending Approval	0 - Pending Approval ▼
10003	Ready to Start	1 - Ready To Start ▼
10004	Dev Complete	3 - Dev Complete ▼

Figure 2.28 – Jira Align forward state mapping

Next, we will set the reverse state mapping between Jira Align and Jira. For this you will first need to manage Jira projects under **Administration | Connectors | Jira Settings | Manage Projects**. To add a new Jira project, click on the **Add Project** button and provide the project key, project name, choose the associated program, and then click on **Save**:

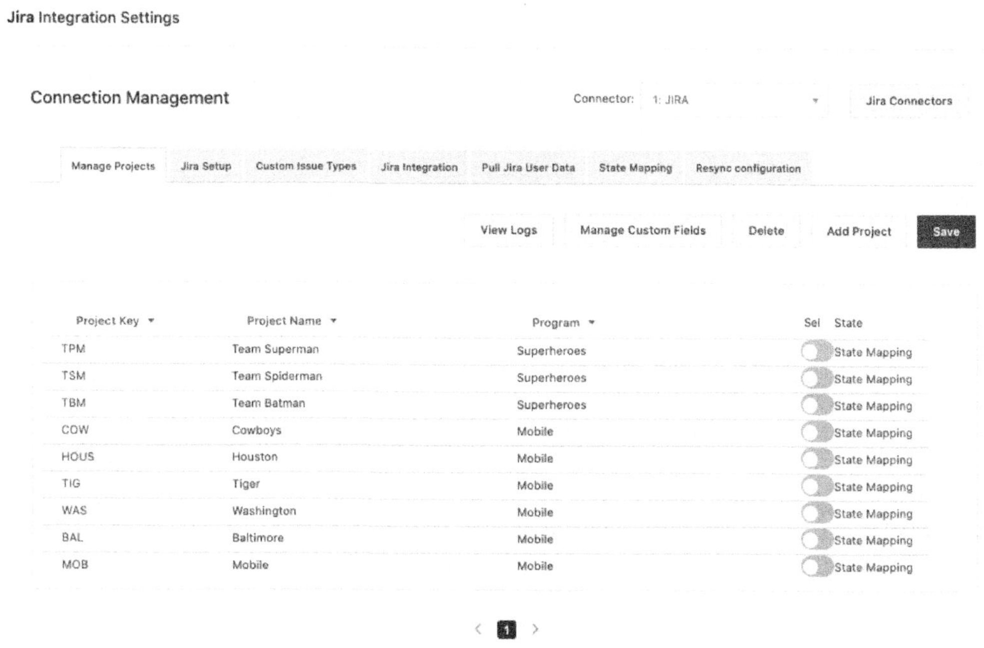

Jira Integration Settings

Connection Management   Connector: 1: JIRA   ▼   Jira Connectors

Manage Projects   Jira Setup   Custom Issue Types   Jira Integration   Pull Jira User Data   State Mapping   Resync configuration

View Logs   Manage Custom Fields   Delete   Add Project   Save

Project Key ▼	Project Name ▼	Program ▼	Sel	State
TPM	Team Superman	Superheroes		State Mapping
TSM	Team Spiderman	Superheroes		State Mapping
TBM	Team Batman	Superheroes		State Mapping
COW	Cowboys	Mobile		State Mapping
HOUS	Houston	Mobile		State Mapping
TIG	Tiger	Mobile		State Mapping
WAS	Washington	Mobile		State Mapping
BAL	Baltimore	Mobile		State Mapping
MOB	Mobile	Mobile		State Mapping

< **1** >

Figure 2.29 – Jira Align manage projects

The reverse state mapping is available for each Jira project for the following work items: features (Jira epics), stories, and defects (Jira bugs). You will need to click on the **State Mapping** link for each Jira project to configure the reverse state mapping. The following screen shows how to configure the reverse state mapping for a chosen Jira project in Jira Align:

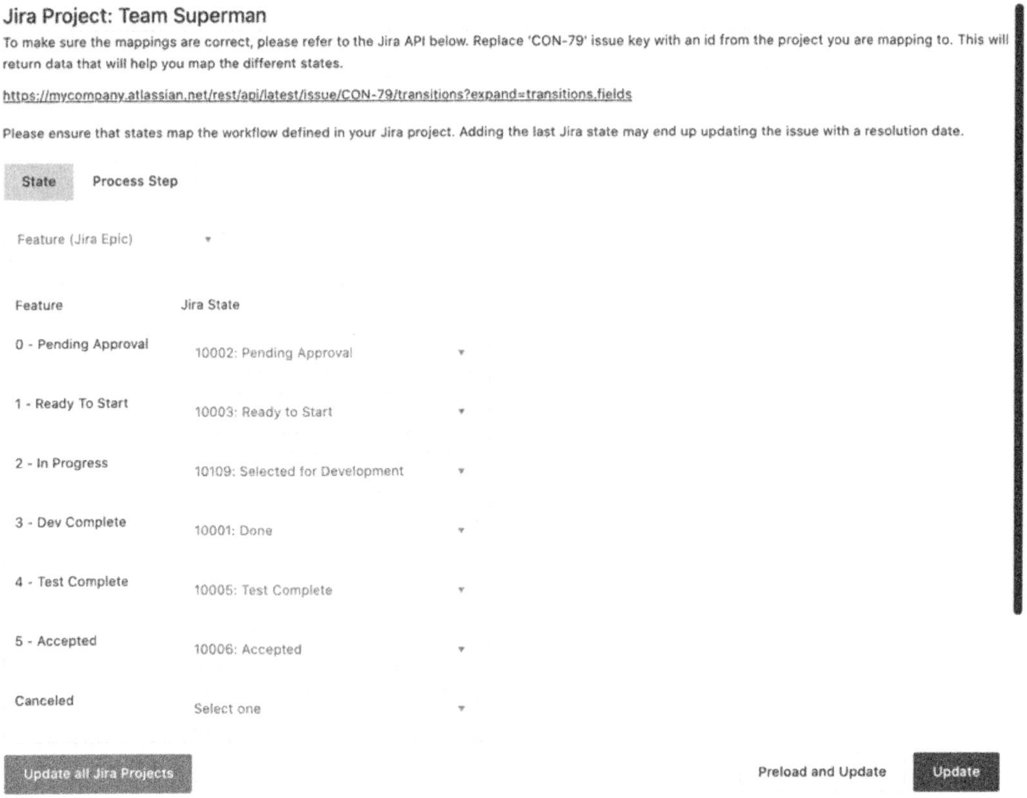

Figure 2.30 – Jira Align reverse state mapping

Once the mapping is configured, you can click on **Update** to save it to the project or click on the **Update all Jira Projects** button to apply the reverse state mapping to all available Jira projects in Jira Align.

Next, you will configure the field mappings for each Jira project by going to the **Manage Projects** tab and clicking on the **Manage Custom Fields** button. Here you will configure the Jira custom field mappings: Jira Team and Team values, Jira Link Actions, Jira Product, Jira MMF, and Jira Priority field values, as shown:

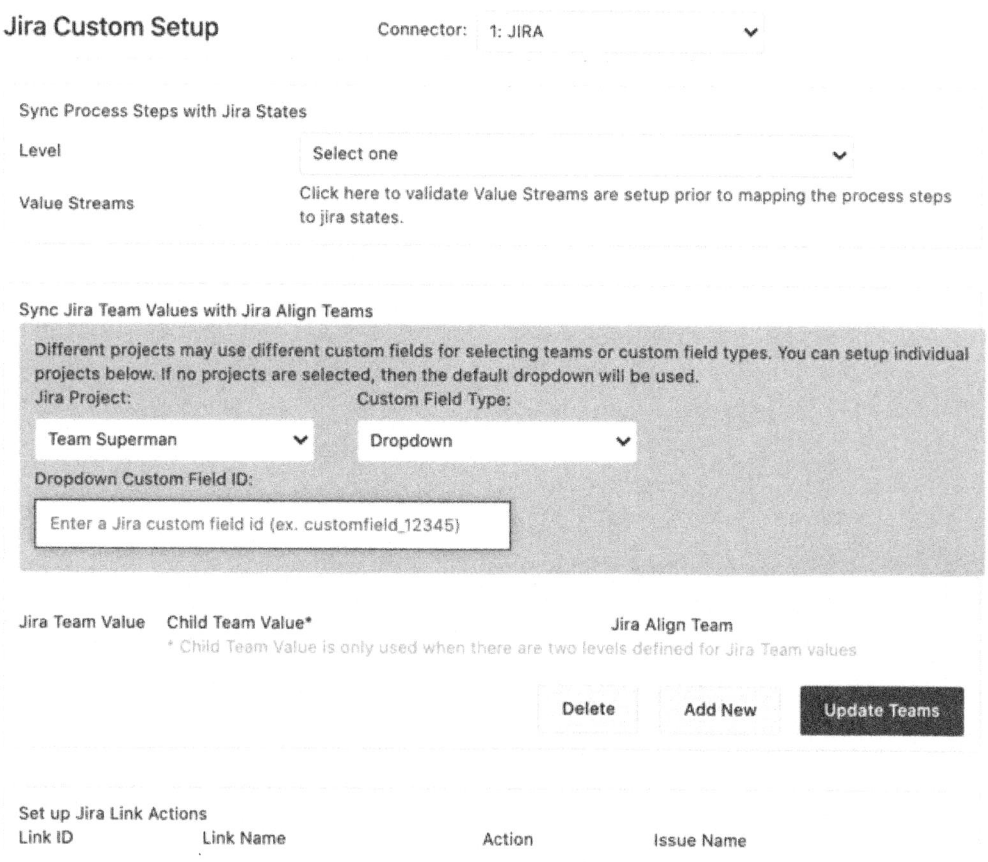

Jira Custom Setup

Connector: 1: JIRA

Sync Process Steps with Jira States

Level   Select one

Value Streams   Click here to validate Value Streams are setup prior to mapping the process steps
                              to jira states.

Sync Jira Team Values with Jira Align Teams

Different projects may use different custom fields for selecting teams or custom field types. You can setup individual
projects below. If no projects are selected, then the default dropdown will be used.

Jira Project: Custom Field Type:

Team Superman   Dropdown

Dropdown Custom Field ID:

Enter a Jira custom field id (ex. customfield_12345)

Jira Team Value   Child Team Value*   Jira Align Team
                   * Child Team Value is only used when there are two levels defined for Jira Team values

                                          Delete   Add New   Update Teams

Set up Jira Link Actions
Link ID   Link Name   Action   Issue Name

Figure 2.31 – Jira Align reverse custom field mapping

Now that fields and states are mapped, let's see how to audit changes and orphan records. You can report on Jira issues that Jira Align no longer has access to via the API. These issues are known as orphans and you can report on them under the **Administration | Connectors | Jira Management | Jira Deleted Issue** tab. The resulting orphan Jira issues report lists two types of missing issues:

- Any Jira Align-linked Jira issues that were permanently deleted by a user in Jira. The issues are displayed with a red warning icon.

- Any Jira issues that had their parent project permission changed such that the Jira service account no longer has access to the issue.

> **Tips and tricks**
> Note that the report also displays API parsing errors via a yellow icon, which can be ignored or filtered out using the error types, as the issues still exist in Jira.

It is recommended to run this report once a week and schedule the run during non-working hours to prevent any interruptions to the regular syncing of data.

Next, let's see how to view an audit log. Simply go to the **Manage Projects** tab and click on the **View Logs** button to view audit logs on the Jira synchronization process. The log captures changes to the data regarding managing projects, Jira setup, custom issue types, Jira integration, pulling Jira user data, and state mappings. You can filter the Jira log report according to the following items: Configuration, Jira API, Issues, Sprints, and Release Vehicles. You can filter the configuration data further by date, and it serves as a change log if you need to track who changed what and when on the Jira Connector configurations.

Now that you have connected to Jira, let's explore how to connect tactical execution in Jira to strategy in Jira Align by extending to the portfolio.

Extending to the portfolio

A portfolio is more than a collection of programs. It is the unit responsible for linking strategy to execution. The portfolio team translates mission and vision into strategic themes and lightweight business cases for epics through which the themes are realized. But extending Jira Align to the portfolio level traditionally comes later in an enterprise implementation after several successful programs are up and running.

For years, the Jira Align implementation roadmap has closely followed that of the leading framework it supports, SAFe, beginning with the establishment of the core leadership team who are not only bought in, but drive the transformation day to day. From there, programs (teams of teams) are identified, trained, and onboarded in Jira Align where they refine their backlogs and prepare for quarterly planning (PI planning if following SAFe). They leverage Jira Align's powerful Product Roadmaps, Program Room, Program Board, Dependency Maps, Risk ROAM report, and so on, to execute their quarterly increment. Then, building on the success of the first launched program, the guiding group engages in a *rinse and repeat* for the next program, and so on. One of our successful clients launched seven programs this way in the course of a year, realizing 33% faster time-to-market in year 1, 37% in year 2, and 45% in year 3.

Program-level success, where teams of teams deliver features to market faster, with higher quality and higher value has traditionally been the sweet spot of both scaling frameworks and tools that support them. For this reason, extending program-level success to the portfolio has come later, after launching several programs. However, there is a more recent trend to establish the portfolio level in Jira Align early on and connect it with program-level execution concurrent with launching the first few programs.

Using this approach, portfolio leadership may be onboarded in Jira Align prior to the first programs and begin creating high-level work items: themes that may span years and portfolio epics that span business quarters. They may also create high-level goals, such as annual OKRs that will be realized through the work of programs as they are onboarded. A portfolio-level funnel can be created in Jira Align using process steps visualized on a Kanban for leadership to track the state of epics from concept through to delivery. This is done as shown in the following screenshot:

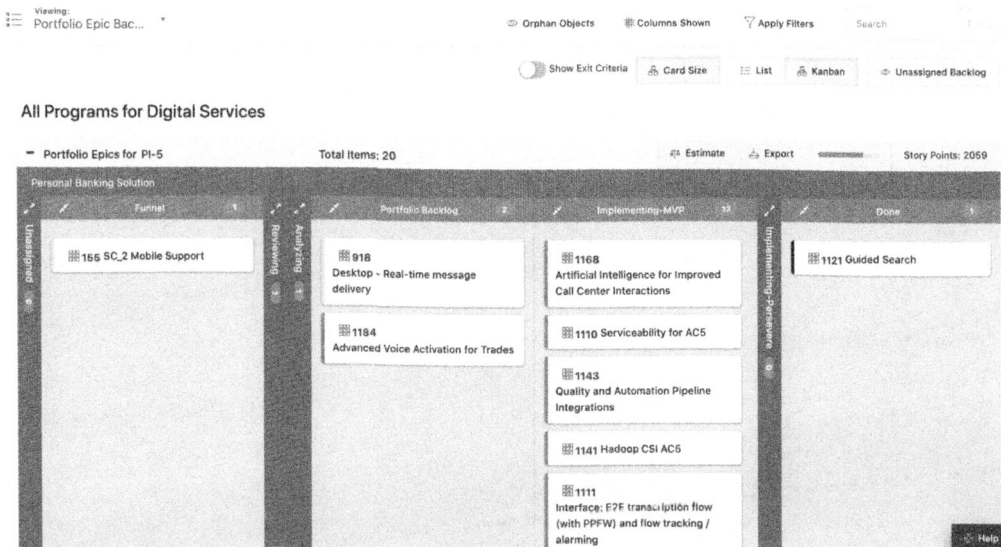

Figure 2.32 – Portfolio-level epic funnel

The portfolio team can periodically prioritize epics using **weighted shortest job irst (WSJF)**, which Jira Align calculates after you enter a score for the four parameters: Business Value, Time Value, Risk Reduction/Opportunity Enablement Value, and Job Size. The following screenshot shows the WSJF parameters used to calculate the score:

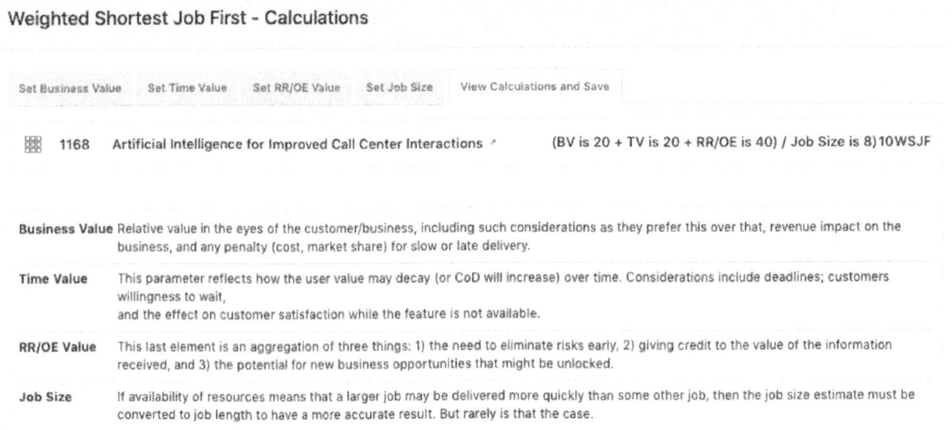

Figure 2.33 – Calculated WSJF based on parameter scores

The following screenshot shows the portfolio epic backlog ranked by WSJF:

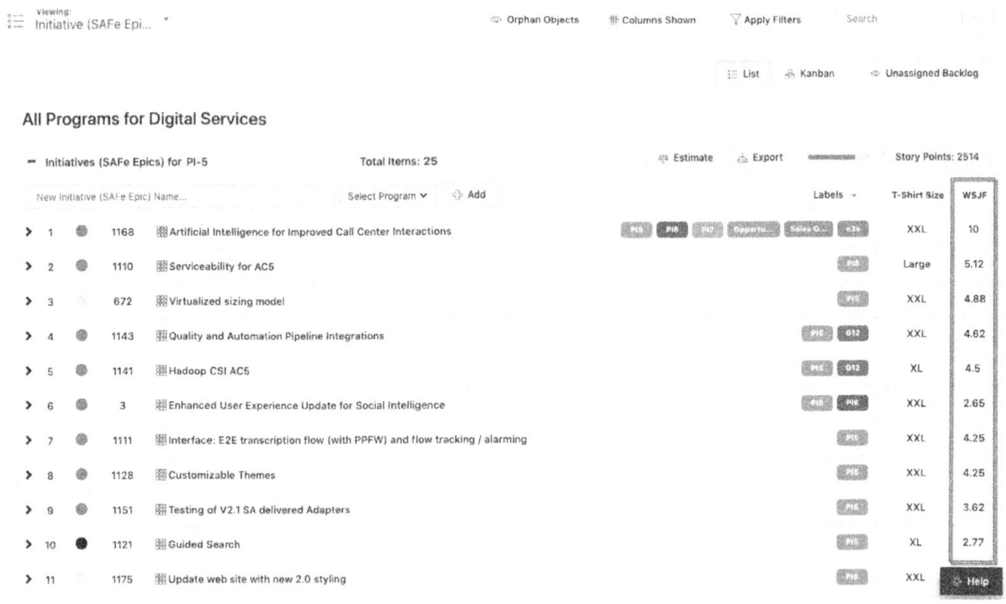

Figure 2.34 – Portfolio epic backlog ranked by WSJF

The portfolio team can also use Jira Align's Value Engineering functionality to determine whether work items are worth building, and later, based on collected metrics, whether to pivot or persevere based on the *build-measure-learn* approach popularized by Eric Ries in *The Lean Startup*:

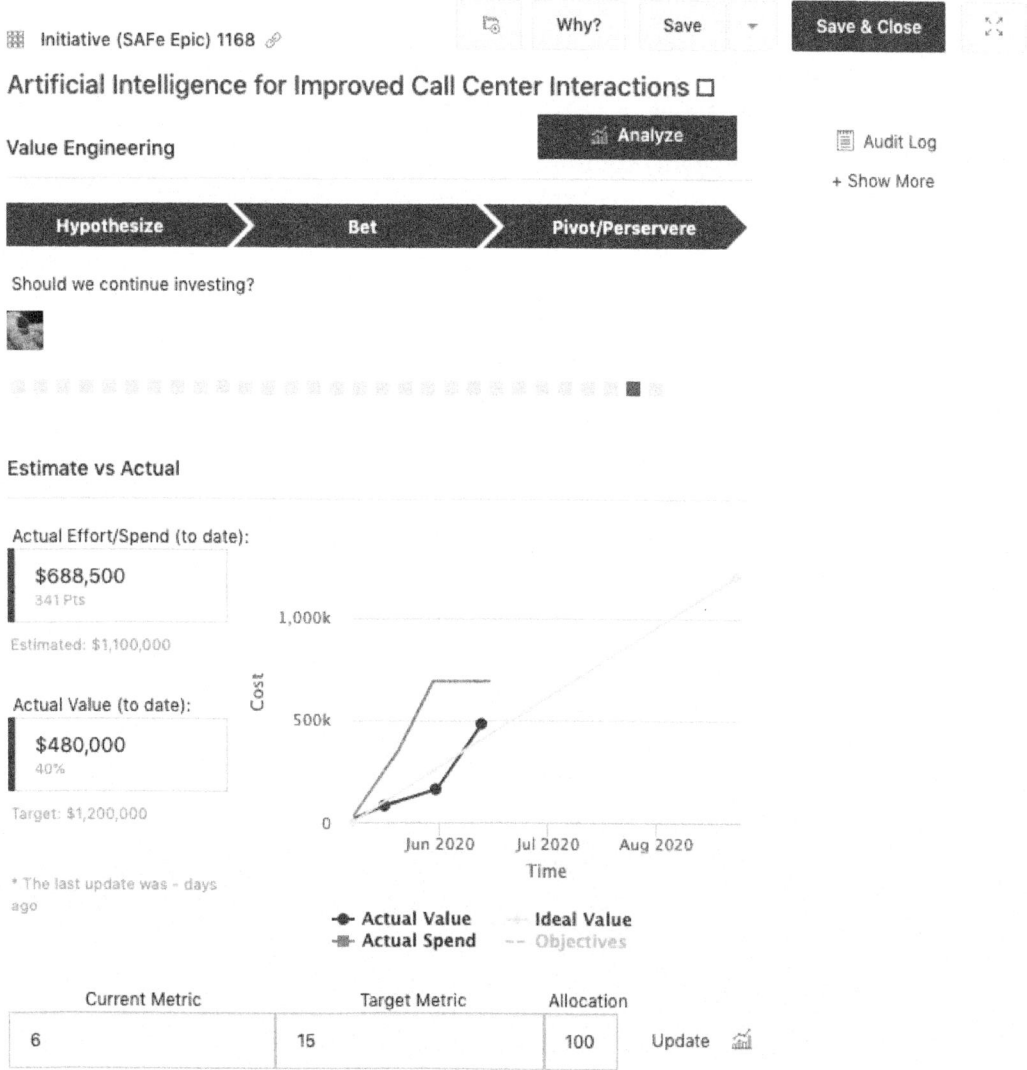

Figure 2.35 – Value engineering data shown on the epic details panel

The rise in popularity of establishing the portfolio in Jira Align earlier in the implementation makes sense as organizations wish to connect strategy with execution, from themes to portfolio epics to features, to stories and tasks. Referring again to *Figure 1.1*, the sooner you connect strategy with execution, the sooner you achieve the ripple effect leading from alignment to business transformation. Once the levels are connected in Jira Align, the organization has visibility into key financial reports, such as investment by theme and investment versus actuals, as well as real-time status from live product roadmaps and progress bars for work item rollups in the work tree.

There are, however, considerations as to whether an organization is ready to extend Jira Align to the portfolio. Those who achieve the greatest success at the portfolio level adopt the practices discussed in the following sections.

Establishing a portfolio vision and roadmap

You cannot connect execution with strategy if the latter is ill-defined. Jira Align provides canvas templates to help the portfolio team define its vision statement and value proposition. The following screenshot shows a template for the portfolio vision canvas:

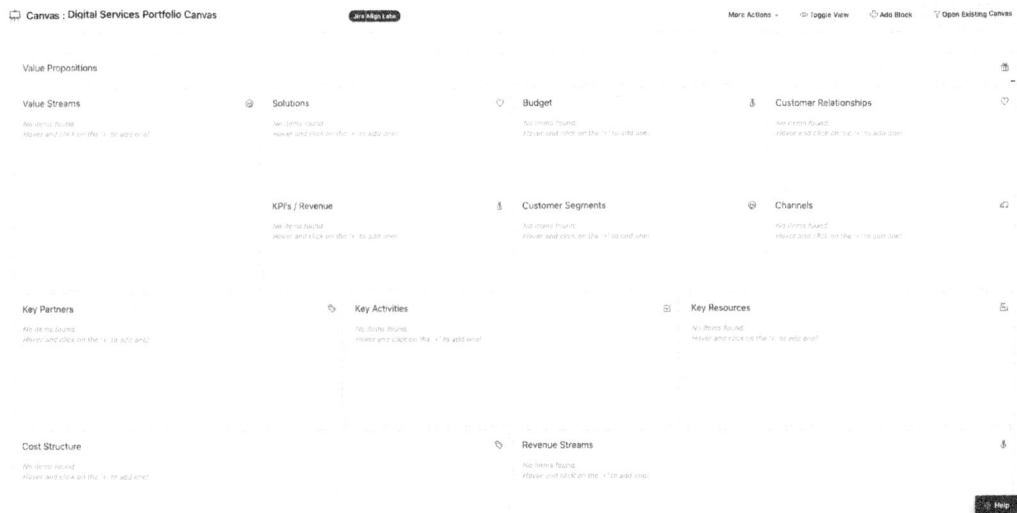

Figure 2.36 – Portfolio canvas template

The portfolio team can then define high-level directional roadmaps, such as epics grouped by theme, spanning across business quarters. The following screenshot shows the portfolio roadmap:

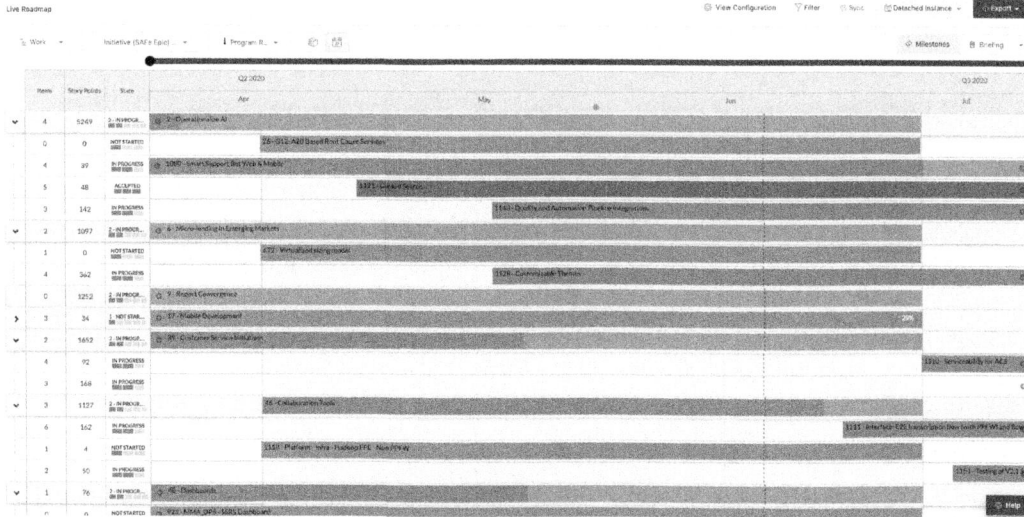

Figure 2.37 – Roadmap of portfolio epics by theme

Funding value streams and teams, not projects

In agile budgeting, you fund persistent teams and bring the work to them, as opposed to traditional budgeting, where you fund projects and assemble teams to deliver them. If following SAFe, you will have value stream budgets that remain fixed each quarter and adjust the allocation of funding across value streams about twice a year. The persistent teams then develop work items to deliver upon these value streams. Each quarter, work is funneled to the teams who break down higher-level work items into features that can be delivered within the quarter and stories that can be delivered within sprints. The group of sprints comprising the quarter, usually five or six of them, is called a Program Increment in SAFe, but whether following SAFe or not, the practice remains generally the same when operating at scale.

An important aspect of agile budgeting is that it relies on the average cost of a story point based on a blended rate. The financial reports in Jira Align, such as the investment by theme and investment versus actuals reports, rely on this approach. Organizations that leverage this approach have found it to be lighter and less burdensome than traditional budgeting and have even obtained **capital expense (CapEx)** and **operating expense (OpEx)** costs in this manner. However, while the average point cost approach often closely matches other methods, it is important to note that Jira Align is not meant to be the organization's financial system of record.

The rise in interest in establishing the portfolio level early in a Jira Align implementation also coincides with the launch of SAFe's Lean Portfolio Management certification in Fall 2019. More and more organizations are moving toward funding and managing value streams. Indeed, 78% of respondents to the 14th Annual State of Agile survey stated that their organization has implemented, is implementing, or has expressed interest in, approaches focused on value streams.

Connecting the enterprise

In this modern software and digital age, you will find that most organizations are starting, or have started, their transformation journey. But those achieving the best outcomes have taught us that business and technology teams alike need to be connected, aligned, and stay in sync. Attaining business agility requires connecting the entire enterprise.

It is important that your non-technical teams, such as HR, procurement, compliance, and finance, embrace and understand the value of agile to propel an organization forward in achieving goals such as accelerating the time to market. Any and all functions of the business required to deliver value to customers must be onboard and engaged at the right levels to keep the flow of value delivery consistent and unblocked. When the entire enterprise knows the product roadmap and required support for the teams (staffing, tooling, security reviews, and suchlike), organizational silos are reduced while business agility increases.

If you are yet to extend your team-level execution to the portfolio, then you may face challenges regarding transparency, consistency, and predictability. The best way to bridge this gap is for teams at all levels to gain visibility to work, measure outcomes, and continually optimize investments to maximize value – in short, get them onboarded and acquainted with Jira Align. We'll now help you get oriented with the tool, beginning with basic navigation.

Summary

In this chapter, we discussed the fundamentals of implementing Jira Align. We learned the importance of analyzing existing programs, aligning the organizational language, and mapping people, work, time, and outcomes. We then looked at a quick setup to connect team-level execution in Jira with programs and strategy in Jira Align. Lastly, we covered the importance of extending to the portfolio sooner rather than later when implementing Jira Align.

Now you know how to analyze the underlying data and prepare Jira Software for Jira Align. You know the technical requirements to set up and connect Jira Align with Jira. Lastly, you've seen three proven practices on how to extend agile practices to the portfolio level.

In the next chapter, we move beyond implementation to the actual use of Jira Align, beginning with the basics of navigation.

Questions

1. Why is it important to align the organizational language and reflect it in Jira Align?
2. What are the most critical health checks when analyzing existing programs in Jira?
3. How do you organize projects/boards in Jira to map with teams in Jira Align?
4. What is the integration mapping between Jira and Jira Align?
5. What are the three practices adopted by organizations that have achieved success at the portfolio level?

Further reading

- *Jira 8 Essentials – Fifth Edition*, by Patrick Li (Packt, 2019)
- *Hands-On Agile Software Development with Jira*, by David Harned (Packt, 2018)

3
Navigating Jira Align

In this chapter, we will master basic user interface navigation and core functionality to provide a solid foundation for making the most out of Jira Align. We will explore how Jira Align facilitates onboarding by enabling alignment and continuous learning. We will then learn how to create and refine a backlog. This involves creating, linking, importing and exporting, ranking, estimating, deleting, and searching for work items. Lastly, we will discuss team collaboration and keeping everyone informed through notifications and alerts in Jira Align.

In this chapter, we will cover the following topics:

- Getting around Jira Align
- Facilitating onboarding
- Creating and refining backlogs
- Collaborating in Jira Align

Technical requirements

Make sure you've done the quick setup that we covered in *Chapter 2, Implementing Jira Align.*

Getting around Jira Align

Jira Align is a web-based application accessed via a web browser. It is compatible with the latest version of most popular browsers, including Google Chrome, Mozilla Firefox, Apple Safari, and Microsoft Edge. You will sign in to Jira Align by navigating to your Jira Align URL, `https://ORGANIZATION-NAME.jiraalign.com`, where `ORGANIZATION-NAME` is replaced by your organization's subdomain.

Jira Align supports SSO integration, which can bypass the login page shown here and take you straight to the landing page. We have already covered this in *Chapter 2, Implementing Jira Align*, where you learned how to set up SSO in Jira Align with your chosen SAML 2.0 supported Identity Manager:

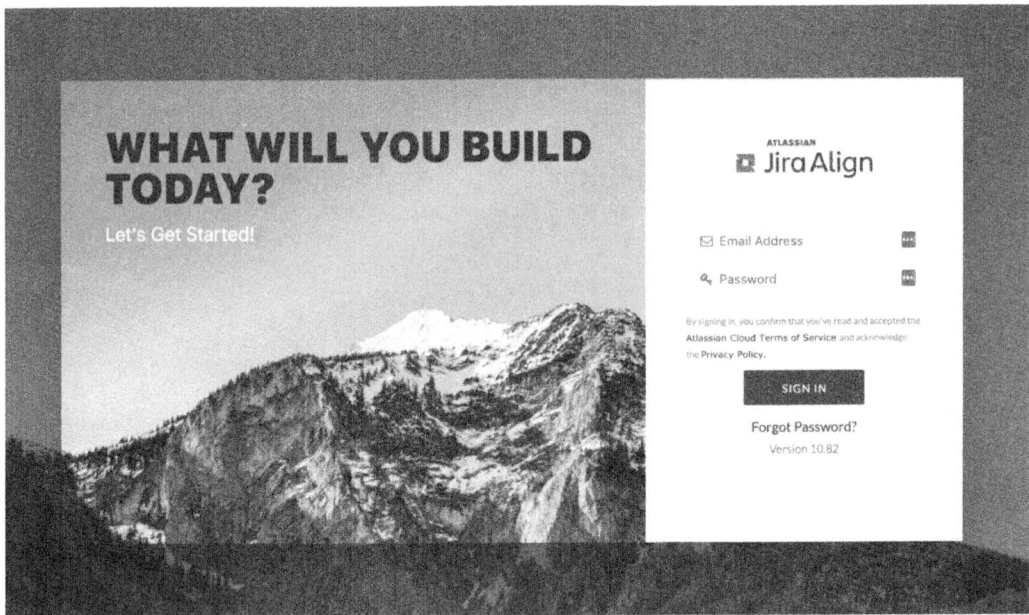

Figure 3.1 – Jira Align login page

Once you sign in to the application, you will see the following home page:

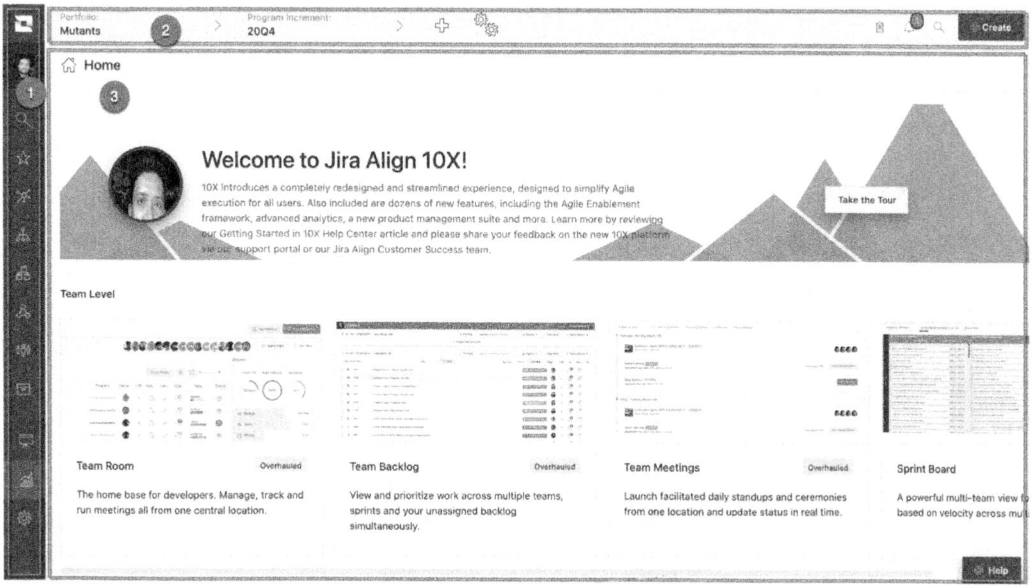

Figure 3.2 – Jira Align home page

The following are three key areas to master in Jira Align:

1. **Navigation menu**: This is located on the far left and expands when you click on a menu item. It allows you to navigate modules for displaying and editing work items at each level of scale.

2. **Configuration bar**: This is located at the top of each page and allows you to set the context configuration for filtering your work items based on people, time, and other dimensions, such as product and organization.

3. **Workspace**: This is located in the center and is the main hub for all information displayed in Jira Align. The information is based on the levels of scale you select from the navigation menu and the context filter you set in the configuration bar for the people, time, and other dimensions.

Let's explore each of these three key areas.

Navigation menu

The navigation menu is organized methodically to group modules at the corresponding levels of scale: enterprise, portfolio, solution, program, and team. For example, when you hover over the primary menu and select **Program**, it expands to display the associated modules grouped by meaningful categories, such as Program, Manage, Track, and Transform. As shown in the following screenshot, you can access the program backlog under **Program | Backlog** and the feature grid under **Manage | Features**:

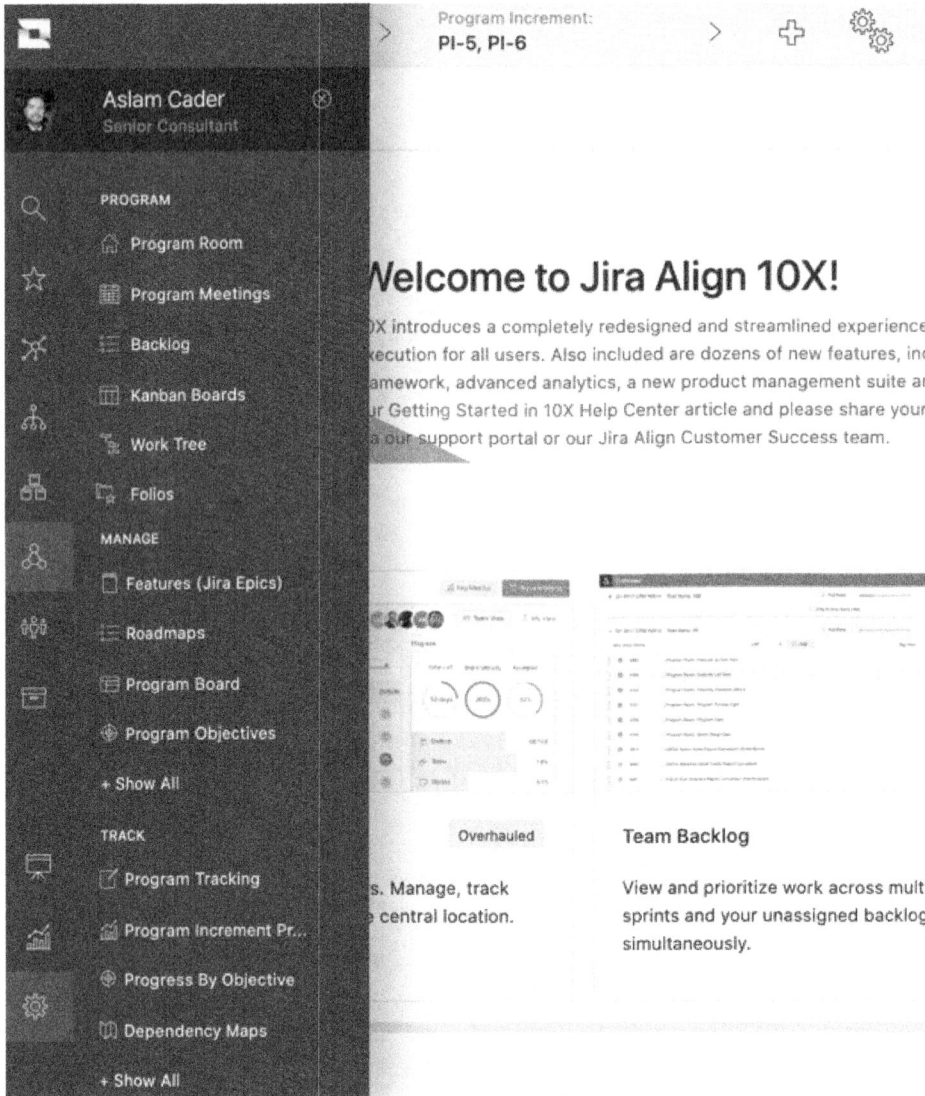

Figure 3.3 – Jira Align program menu

If you can't remember where a module is located in the navigation menu, you can click on the search icon (magnifying glass) to find the module. You can access your frequently used modules by clicking on the star menu icon. To add a new favorite, click on the encircled plus sign to favorite the current page, as shown in the following screenshot. You can also see recently accessed modules by clicking on **Recents**:

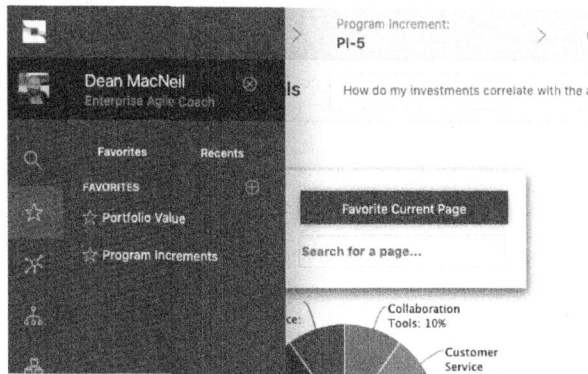

Figure 3.4 – Jira Align favorites

If you are unable to find a module, speak with your Jira Align administrator. Module access is controlled via Jira Align roles and your administrator can help to ensure that your role has access to the right modules. They will do this by simply toggling module access on or off under **Administration | Access Controls | Roles**, as shown in the following screenshot:

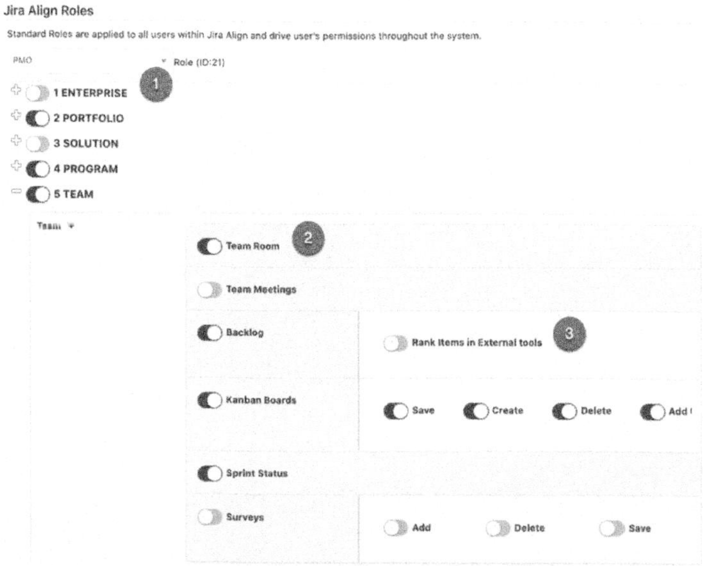

Figure 3.5 – Jira Align role permissions

The role permissions are organized into three levels:

- **Level 1**: Controls access to navigation menu items corresponding to the levels of scale and additional verticals, such as administration, products, collaboration, and additional options. For example, you can choose to toggle off the solution menu if the solution level is not in use at your organization or if it does not apply to the selected user role.

- **Level 2**: Controls access to the modules within each main level menu. You can toggle on or off modules in submenus, for example, the **Roadmaps** module appearing under **Manage** in *Figure 3.3 – Jira Align program menu.*

- **Level 3**: Controls the module-specific actions that are directly linked to permissions. You can grant a user permission to perform an action by toggling on or off the module-specific actions, such as save, create, or delete.

Tips and tricks

We recommend starting with the default roles in Jira Align. The default roles include Super Admin, PMO, Executive, Product Owners, Team Leads, Team Member, Kanban Users, and External User.

If you need to create a new role, we recommend that you copy an existing role that maps closely to your intended new role. This will copy permissions from the existing role, which you can then adjust to meet the needs of the new Jira Align role.

Now that you've got the right level of access for your role, let's review the reports that you have available. You can access the reports dashboard by clicking on the reports menu icon, which is second from the bottom in the following screenshot:

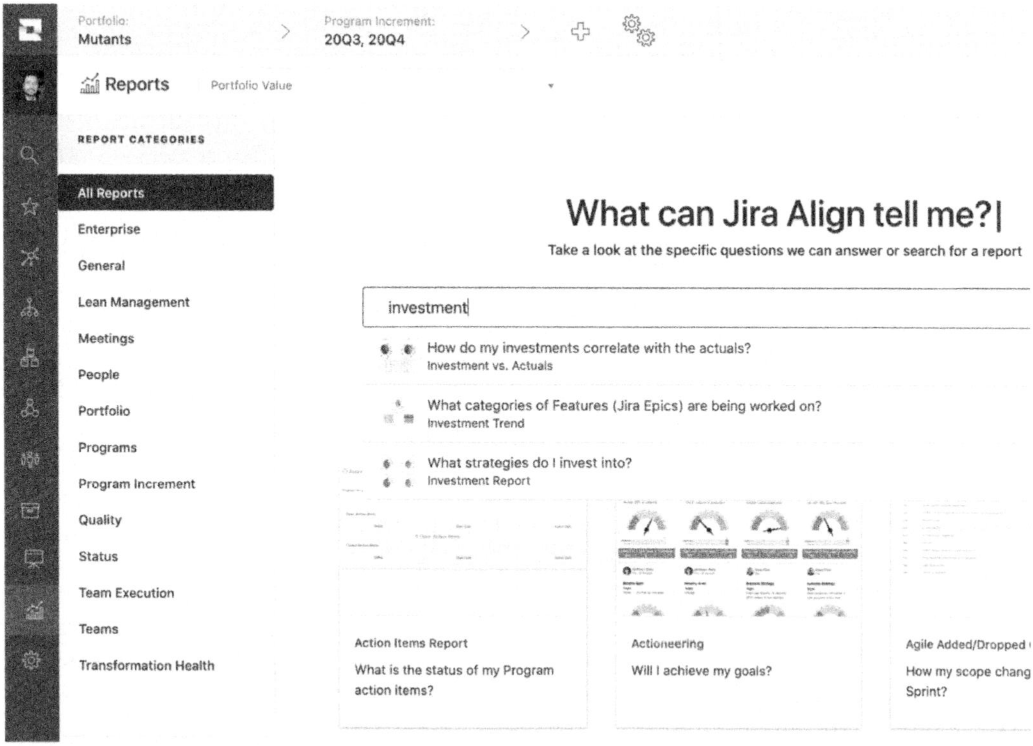

Figure 3.6 – Jira Align reports dashboard

Here you will see a list of report categories and a search box. These enable you to explore over 165 reports that will help you track and analyze work and outcomes at every level of scale. As with modules, access to reports is controlled via Jira Align roles, so speak with your administrator regarding any additional reports you may need.

Now that you know how to find reports and modules, let's explore some user profile and preferences settings that will optimize your experience. These can be found under the user menu:

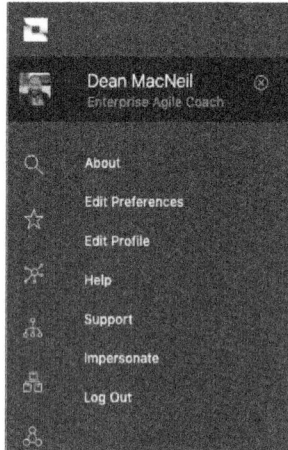

Figure 3.7 – Jira Align user menu

To access this menu, click on the **User Menu** icon at the top of the navigation bar, just below the Jira Align icon. The first item we'll look at is where you can add your photo in order to put a more human face to your work and interactions with fellow coworkers. To do that, click on **Edit Profile** to display your user profile data, as shown:

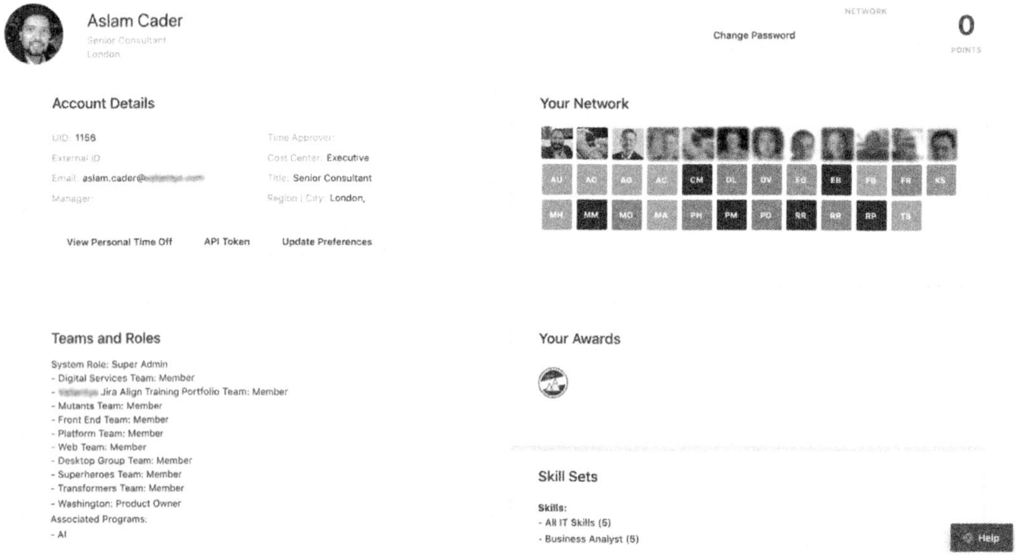

Figure 3.8 – Jira Align edit profile

If you haven't already uploaded a photo or you wish to change your photo, you can do so by hovering over the area to the left of your name and clicking on the pencil icon. You can change your password by clicking on the button to the top right. In the area below, you can generate an API token, view personal time off, and see a complete summary of your work environment, including your connected user network, awards, skills, associated teams, and roles.

> **Tips and tricks**
>
> If you want to make any changes to your account details, speak with your Jira Align administrator, who will be able to assist you. The user accounts are managed under **Administration | Access Controls | People**. This topic has been covered in *Chapter 2, Implementing Jira Align*, where you learned the details for creating and managing a user account.

Now that your profile is complete, let's make a few recommended settings in your preferences. To do so, either click on the **Update Preferences** button shown in the previous edit profile screenshot, or click on the user menu icon, which is your photo at the top on the navigation menu, and then on **Edit Preferences**, to bring up the following page:

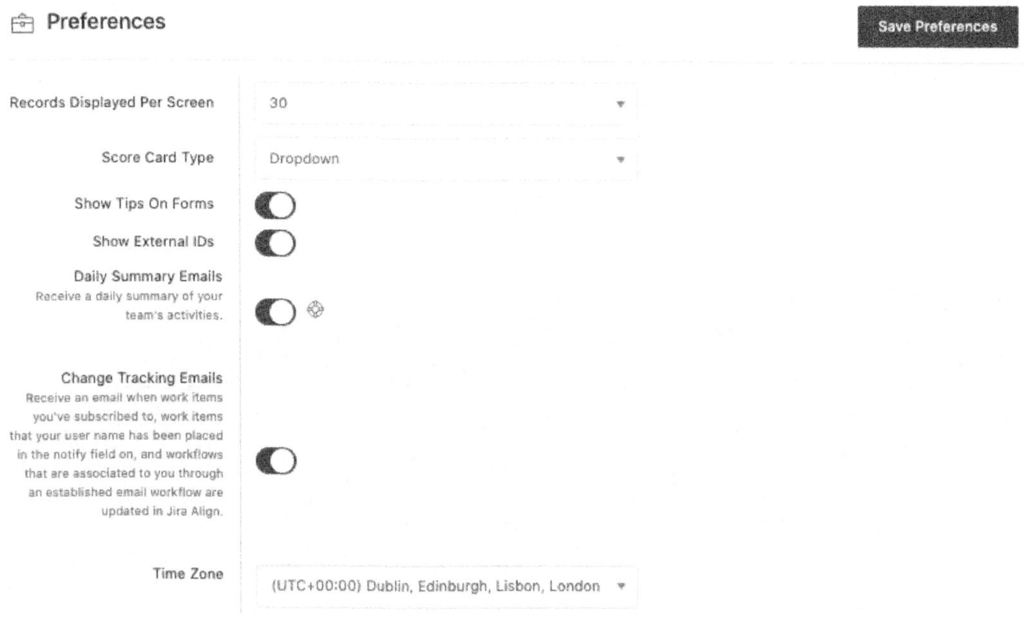

📋 Preferences   Save Preferences

Records Displayed Per Screen	30
Score Card Type	Dropdown
Show Tips On Forms	⬤
Show External IDs	⬤
Daily Summary Emails Receive a daily summary of your team's activities.	⬤
Change Tracking Emails Receive an email when work items you've subscribed to, work items that your user name has been placed in the notify field on, and workflows that are associated to you through an established email workflow are updated in Jira Align.	⬤
Time Zone	(UTC+00:00) Dublin, Edinburgh, Lisbon, London

Figure 3.9 – Jira Align edit preferences

The recommended settings, as shown in this screenshot, are as follows:

- **Records Displayed Per Screen**: Set the records per screen to **max 30** to display more records in the workspace.

- **Show External IDs**: Toggle on this option to show the Jira issue keys for work items that bi-directionally sync with Jira.

- **Time Zone**: Set your time zone to ensure that the time is converted and displayed according to your local time.

In addition to these recommended settings, you can toggle on or off daily summary and change tracking emails and the display of tips when filling out forms (helpful for new users). You can also specify whether you want to use sliders or a drop-down menu for scoring epics and capabilities on their **Value** tabs.

Now that we've set preferences, let's see where to find Jira Align's application version, build details, and release notes. It's important to check the release notes in order to learn about the latest feature updates. Jira Align is improving continually, with releases every 2 weeks. Simply go to **User Menu | About** to access this information.

There are a few more important items under the user menu. Clicking on **Help** will direct you to the public knowledge base where you will find a wealth of Jira Align articles and FAQs. Clicking on **Support** will direct you to the Jira Align support channels, for example, if you think you've encountered a bug. Lastly, you can sign out of the application by clicking on **Log Out**, which will direct you back to the login page.

Tips and tricks

For Jira Align administrators, if you want to reproduce a Jira Align module access or functionality issue, you can use the **Impersonate** administration feature in the user menu to log on as another user without having to enter a password to authenticate. This helps with quick troubleshooting and is typically available only to Jira Align administrators. However, we recommend making this feature available for Jira Align core team members to reduce the burden on the administrator(s).

So far, we have seen how the navigation menu allows you to access work items at each level of scale. Now, let's see how to filter work items based on the people and time dimensions.

Configuration bar

The configuration bar allows you to configure the tool for your context, for what you want to see. For example, an agile program manager or **release train engineer** (**RTE**) would set the configuration bar for their particular program or team of teams (people dimension). They could further specify particular **program increment(s)** (**PIs**) that they would like to see (time dimension). In the following screenshot, the configuration bar is set for the Mutants portfolio and the 20Q3 and 20Q4 PI:

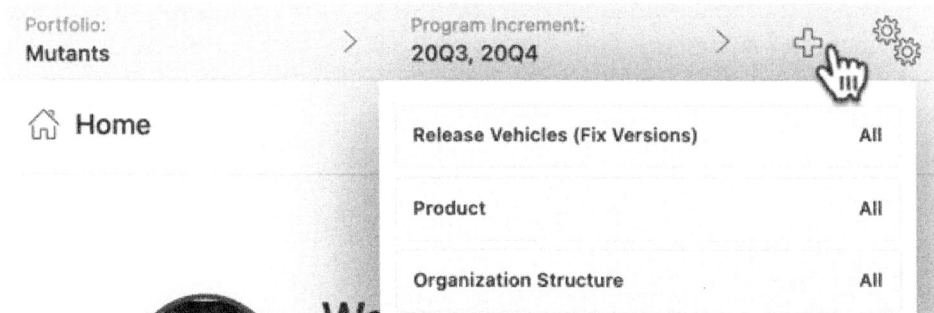

Figure 3.10 – Jira Align configuration bar

You can click on the plus icon to set additional configuration scope or use the gears icon to access and save advanced configuration filters. The configuration bar will retain your settings as you navigate through Jira Align and for future logins until you change them.

The parameters you can set and filter on in the configuration bar are as follows:

- **Portfolio structure**: Sets the scope for the people dimension based on the level of scale, for example, portfolio, solution, program, and team.

- **Program increment**: Sets the scope based on time; you can choose past, present, and future PI(s) or a specific date range, such as a year, a quarter, two quarters, or all time, as the scope.

- **Release vehicle**: Sets the release version, another element based on time; you can choose a specific release or delivery milestone.

- **Product**: Allows you to select products from the product tree; note that product is related to the work dimension, as features can be associated with products in Jira Align. Whether or not products are required for a given portfolio is set by the Jira Align administrator in **Administration | Settings | Platform | Portfolio | Portfolio Specific Configuration | Manage Products**. When set to **Yes**, the **Product** field will be required.

- **Organization structure**: Sets the scope based on your organizational structures, such as business unit and line of business.

- **Advanced configuration**: Allows you to set a granular scope based on additional filters, such as sprints, business driver, functional area, strategic snapshot, convention, defect suite, and tags.

If you will need to frequently use your custom configuration settings, you can simply click **Save as New** under the **Advanced configuration** filter to list it under **Saved Configurations**. You can return at any time to select your saved configuration filter and then click on **Apply**. Next to your saved configuration, you also have the option to delete or rename the saved configuration. If you need to make any changes to an existing saved configuration, simply select it, make the changes, and click on **Save Changes**. Alternatively, you can click **Apply Settings** to test the added changes to your custom configuration filter:

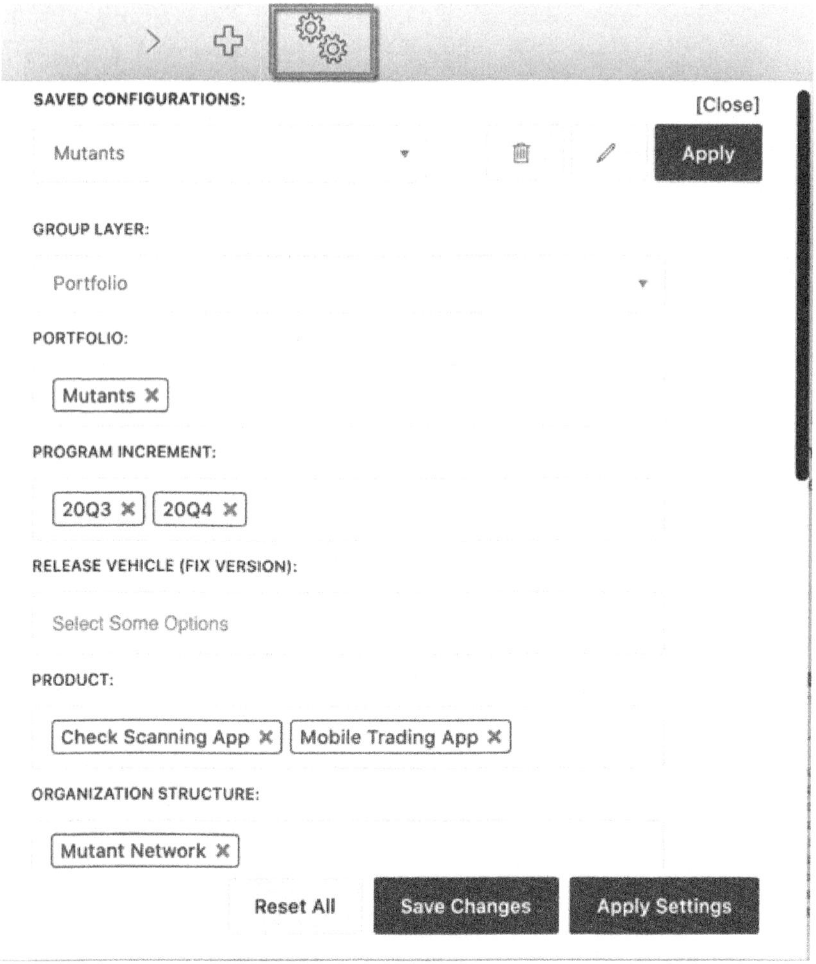

Figure 3.11 – Jira Align advanced configuration

Tips and tricks

If you want to clear values from the configuration filter, instead of removing the values one by one and applying the change, you can use the **Reset All** option under **Advanced configuration** to clear all filters, or you can choose the **Reset** option to clear a specific configuration filter setting. For example, if you reset the **Product filter** setting, it would clear the product-specific filter selections and display all work items.

We recommend resetting your configuration bar filter settings if you are experiencing issues with not being able to see work that is in the scope of your filter settings. To do so, click on the gears icon and then **Reset All**. This will clear any filters that could be set inadvertently, allowing all work items to be displayed.

Now you know how to set the scope for the work, people, and time dimensions. Next, let's see where you would find the information displayed in Jira Align.

Workspace

The workspace displays information based on your selected module from the navigation menu and your filters set in the configuration bar. You will typically see information arranged in grids, charts, and graphs. Note that in the lower right-hand corner of the workspace, there is a **Help** button. Clicking on this will open a panel on the right side of the workspace with contextual help based on what you are viewing in the workspace. For example, if you are viewing the feature backlog, the panel will display information explaining all the options and functionality available in the backlog, such as ranking.

In the upper-right corner of the workspace, you will find a **Columns Shown** button. Clicking on this allows you to configure the columns shown in grid views. For example, the feature grid allows you to add up to 12 columns to be displayed. You can access the feature grid by clicking on the Program icon in the navigation menu and selecting **Manage | Features**. In the following screenshot, we have configured the columns on the feature grid to display the developmental state, link to acceptance criteria, business driver, **MMF** (short for **minimum marketable feature**) indicator, release vehicle, and story points:

ID	Ext ID	Title	State	AC	Business Driver	MMF	Release Vehicle (Fix Version)	Story Pts
5505		Hadoop_E2E: Testing Hadoop flows in L3 environment (Split Part 2)	PENDING APPROVAL		Contractual	No		0
5504	JR-5	Application Mobile - PI Planning Epic Name (Split Part 1)	SPLIT		Standard Feature	No		15
5394	BAL-78	Ensure alert testing through to end client	IN PROGRESS		Standard Feature	No		48
5393	MOB-17	G12: Fast continuous integration	ACCEPTED		Contractual	No		8
5389	BAL-80	Large Data Set Collection & Testing	IN PROGRESS		Standard Feature	No		280
5387	MOB-16	G12: ESRs for AC5	ACCEPTED		Contractual	No		0
5386	MOB-12	G12 : AP2 machines stabilization	ACCEPTED		Contractual	Yes		0
4353		Interface: Diarization Stabilization	ACCEPTED		Standard Feature	No		16
4307	BAL-72	G13: Document A2BOW Suggest Features	ACCEPTED		Competitive Leap Frog	No	Green Emerald	8
4295	BAL-71	Hadoop: Purchase Order integration documentation	DEV COMPLETE		Standard Feature	No		8
4281	MOB-11	G12 : Hadoop E2E encryption	ACCEPTED		Contractual	Yes		3

Figure 3.12 – Jira Align feature grid

The first column shows the features' Jira Align IDs, which you can click on to open the details panel for a given feature. The next column displays the features' Jira issue keys and is present as a result of the **Show External IDs** setting that we made previously under **User Menu | Edit Preferences**.

While work item grids such as the feature grid may resemble a backlog, they are actually different. For example, the work item grid does not allow ranking. However, it does provide functionality not available in the backlog, which you can access by clicking on **More Actions** in the upper-right corner of the workspace. This will open a menu with additional actions, including mass move, import, and export, as shown:

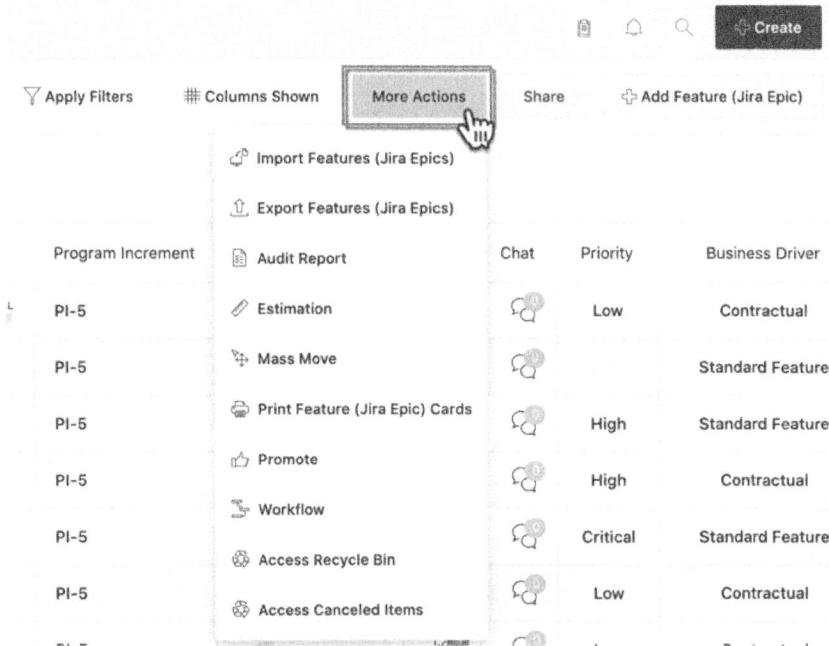

Figure 3.13 – Jira Align more actions menu

We will explore the import and export functionality later in the *Creating and refining backlogs* section.

Now that we know our way around the navigation menu, configuration bar, and the workspace, let's see how Jira Align can help orient our colleagues who are new to the application.

Facilitating onboarding

It is common practice to onboard users into Jira Align one program or team of teams at a time. When onboarding programs into Jira Align, a common challenge is aligning teams on practices and ways of working. A best practice for handling this is to train everyone on the team of teams together just before launching a program. Mapping your practices and ways of working to your tools and the modules within them can be another challenge. Jira Align solves this by offering a number of ways to get new users up and running in the platform as quickly as possible. Let's look first at its framework maps module.

Framework maps

Jira Align can facilitate aligning your team of teams with your selected scaling framework (see *Chapter 1*, *Introducing Jira Align*, in the *Selecting a framework* section). Frameworks such as SAFe include an overview illustration that summarizes the methods and practices for teams at each level of scale. You can simply add this illustration inside Jira Align and make it interactive so that when users click on a section in the illustration, they will be directed to a corresponding module within Jira Align or relevant external videos and training sources.

As an example, the following screenshot shows an interactive framework map set up to show the Portfolio SAFe Big Picture:

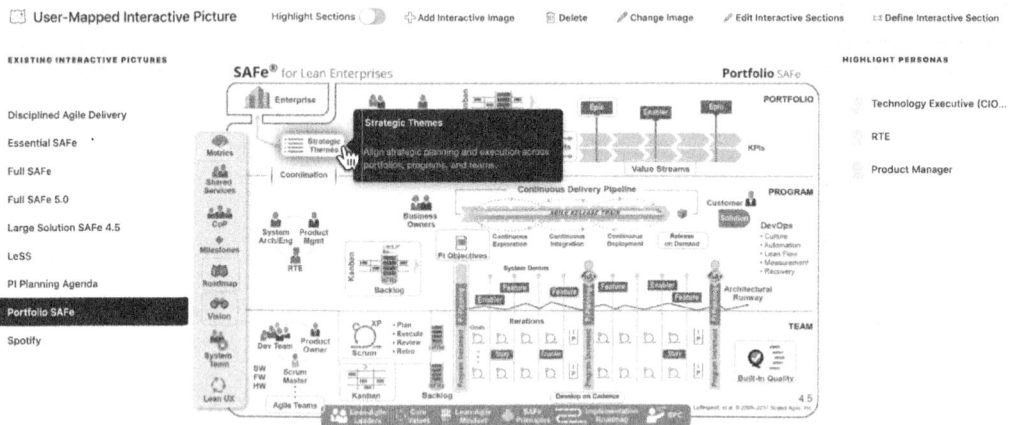

Figure 3.14 – Jira Align framework maps

In this example, the **Strategic Themes** section is linked to the **Strategy Room** module within Jira Align. This interactive approach is a great way for users to get familiarized with both practices and tools. It also serves as a resource for continuing education of teams at all levels.

To add a new interactive picture, perform the following steps:

1. First go to **Transform | Framework Maps** under the **Enterprise**, **Portfolio**, **Solution**, or **Program** menus of the navigation bar.

2. Click on the **Add Interactive Image** button and then provide a meaningful name for your new framework map and click on **Add**.

3. Next, select the image file to add as the new framework map and click on **Apply**. The supported maximum file size is 4 MB and the supported file types are as follows: *.gif, *.jpeg, *.jpg, *.png, and *.bmp.

4. Click on the **Define Interactive Section** button to simply click and drag to create interactive sections in the image. Next click on **Save Section** to confirm the defined sections.

5. Next, enter the following details for each interactive section:

   Name: Add a name to the interactive section, for example, `Strategic Themes`. Click on the pencil icon next to the name to rename it.

   Description: Add a description of the interactive section.

   Persona: You can optionally choose a persona for the interactive section that will allow a group of interactive sections to be highlighted for a given persona such as RTE.

   Step Link: Look up and add a Jira Align module.

   Use Video/Ext Link: You can toggle this on/off to add a video or external link to the interactive section.

6. Click **Save & Close** to save the changes, and then return to *step 4* to add details on all defined interactive sections. To confirm the updates, click on **Done**. If you need to return to make further changes to your interactive sections, you can click on the **Edit Interactive Sections** button.

The following screenshot shows an interactive section being edited:

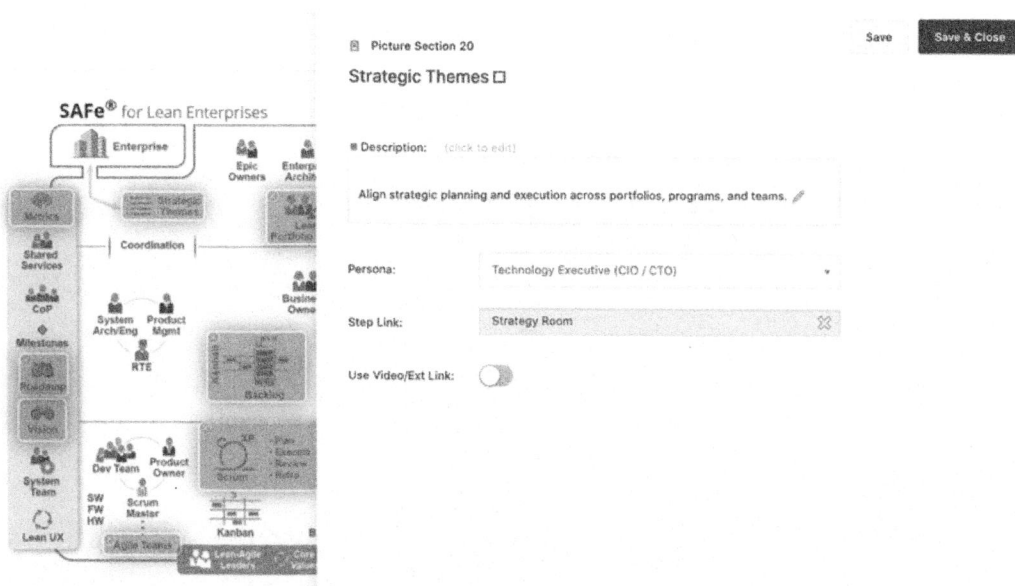

Figure 3.15 – Jira Align framework maps interactive section

Framework maps are one of the many cool features in Jira Align and the only limitation will be your imagination in making the most out of this module. Let's take a look at what other resources are available to facilitate user onboarding in Jira Align.

Training simulations

Jira Align provides pre-built training modules that are accessible from the configuration bar checklists icon, as shown:

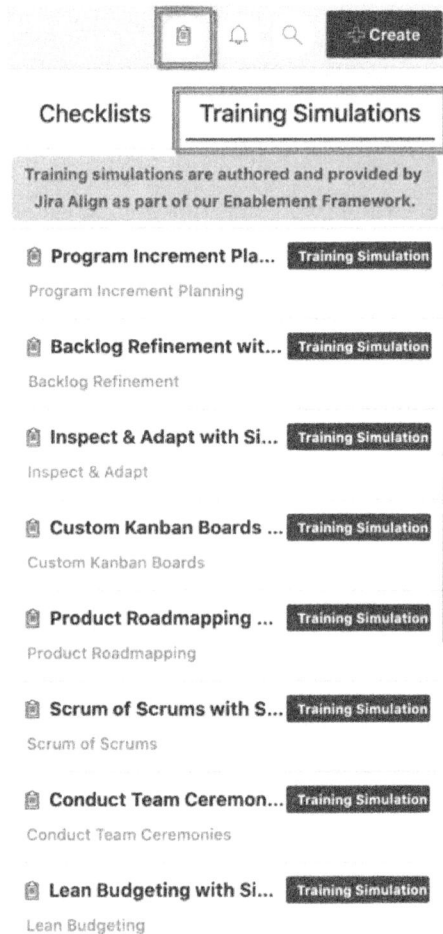

Figure 3.16 – Jira Align training simulations

Here you will find 8 hours of interactive videos on how the tool supports the following lean and agile practices: PI planning, backlog refinement, inspect and adapt, custom Kanban, product road mapping, scrum of scrums, conduct team ceremonies, lean budgeting, portfolio tracking, portfolio planning, time tracking, lean Kanban for essentials, Jira integration, product strategy, value engineering, and ideation. This wealth of knowledge can be accessed by any Jira Align user on-demand to learn more about the modules and how to practice lean-agile methods effectively.

Checklists

Another way to help get team members familiarized with Jira Align is to create a custom checklist with a sequence of steps to follow in order to complete specific tasks in Jira Align. You can build custom checklists specific to personas such as PMO or RTE, or practices such as backlog refinement and PI planning. Checklists are accessible from the configuration bar checklists icon, as shown:

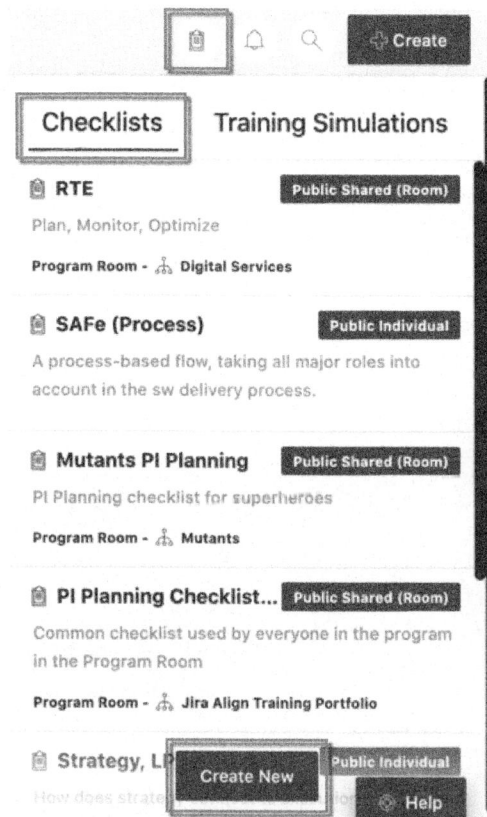

Figure 3.17 – Jira Align checklists

There are three types of custom checklists that you can create:

- **Private checklist**: You can create an individual checklist for your personal task tracking purposes. The checklist will only be available to you.

- **Public individual checklist**: You can create an individual shared checklist with others, but the steps will be tracked individually. For example, you can build a common checklist for scrum masters, but they could all be at different stages on the list.

- **Public shared checklist**: You can create a public shared checklist that multiple users can collaborate on. When one user checks an item on the list, other users associated with the checklist can see that that item has been checked. Public shared checklists are typically tied to rooms such as the program room to drive practices for large groups or efforts.

Let's see what it takes to build a PI planning custom checklist for our Mutants program. On the bottom of the checklist menu, click on **Create New** and then provide the following details:

- **Name**: Add a name to identify the checklist, for example, `Mutants PI Planning`.

- **Description**: Add a description, such as `PI Planning checklist for superheroes`.

- **View**: Choose the type `Public` to share this checklist with others. This option will expand the following additional details to be completed:

  a. **Usage**: Choose the `Shared` usage option to track the checklist as a team of teams.

  b. **Shared with**: Choose the `Room` option to share the checklist with everyone in the shared room. This option will expand the following two additional details.

  c. **Rooms**: Choose the type of room, `Programs Room`.

  d. **Portfolio**: Choose the applicable portfolio, `Mutants`.

  e. **Users and/or Roles**: You can specify additional users and/or roles with whom to share the checklist. When the checklist is shared, this information is optional.

Now that the required information is entered on the **Details** tab as shown, click on the **Save** button to create the checklist:

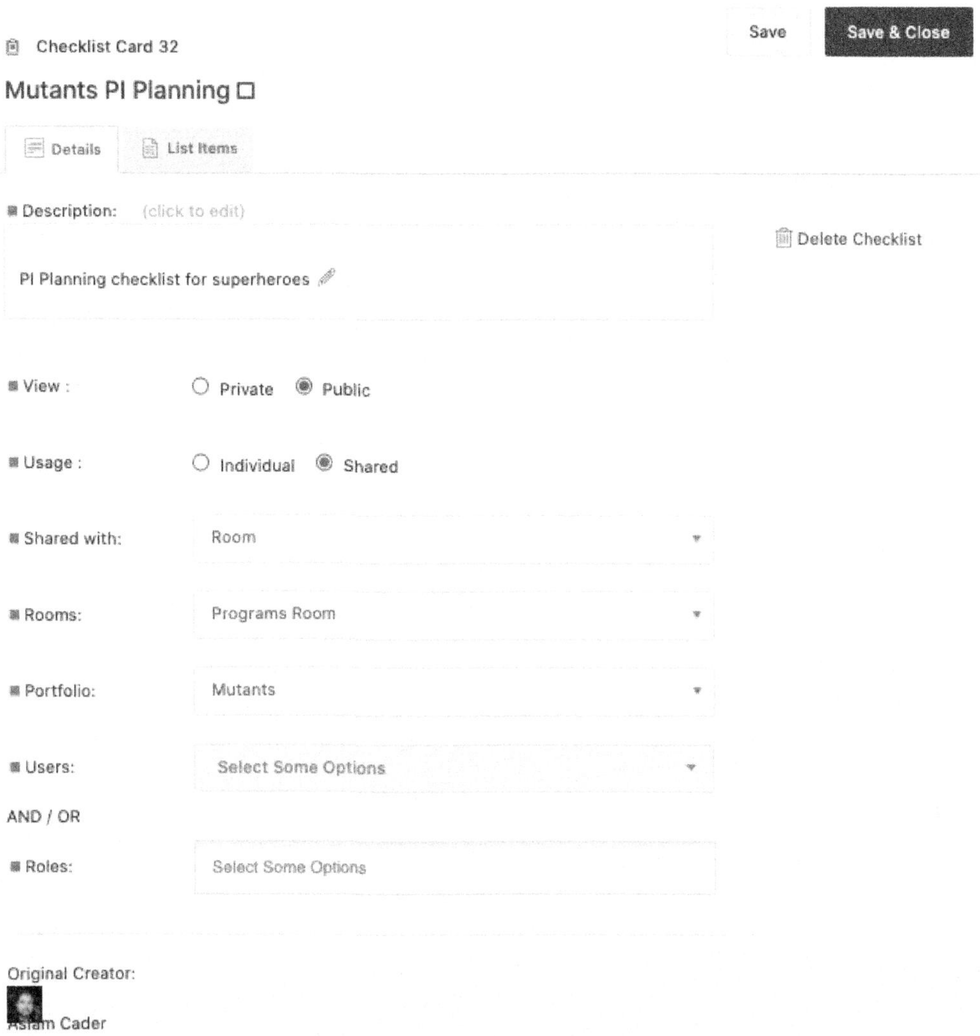

Figure 3.18 – Jira Align checklist creation

Next, click on the **List Items** tab as shown in the screenshot to add the checklist steps. For each step, provide the following details:

- **Step Name**: Add a step name, for example, `Get inspired`.

- **Step Description**: Add a step description, such as `Share the company's mission and vision`.

- **Search Step Link**: Map the checklist to a Jira Align module, in this case, `Strategic Snapshots`.

Now it's time to create the sequence of steps for the checklist by clicking on the **Add Item** button, as shown, and repeat as necessary:

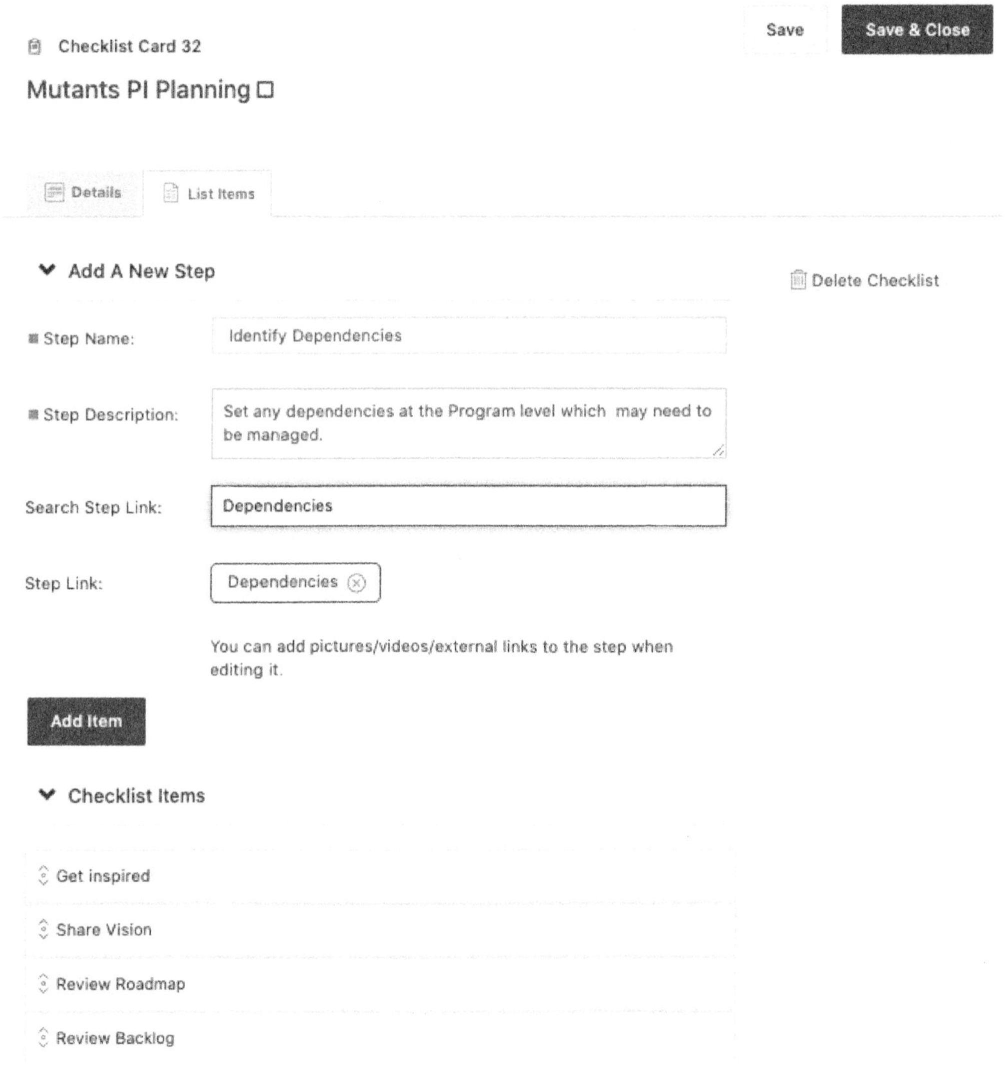

📄 Checklist Card 32

Save   **Save & Close**

Mutants PI Planning ☐

▦ Details   📄 List Items

❯ **Add A New Step**

🗑 Delete Checklist

▣ Step Name: Identify Dependencies

▣ Step Description: Set any dependencies at the Program level which may need to
                        be managed.

Search Step Link: Dependencies

Step Link: Dependencies ⊗

                        You can add pictures/videos/external links to the step when
                        editing it.

Add Item

❯ **Checklist Items**

⇕ Get inspired

⇕ Share Vision

⇕ Review Roadmap

⇕ Review Backlog

Figure 3.19 – Jira Align checklist items

If you want to link to external sources such as your corporate strategy video, simply edit the checklist item and toggle on the **Use Video/Ext Link** option. You can now upload a video still image and provide the link to the video source. Once the link and changes are added, click on **Save & Close**:

Save   **Save & Close**

🖹 Checklist Item 194

Get inspired ☐

📝 Checklist Card 32

▤ Description: (click to edit)

Share the companies mission and vision ✏

Search Step Link: Search (type name of the page you are looking for)

Step Link: Strategic Snapshots ⊗

Use Video/Ext Link: ⬤

▤ Video Still: Upload   Delete

▤ Video/Ext Link: https://www.youtube.com/watch?v=...

Figure 3.20 – Jira Align checklist item

Now, when you navigate to the **Checklists** menu and choose the `Mutants PI Planning checklist`, it will display in a panel on the bottom of the screen:

Figure 3.21 – Jira Align checklist display

Click on each step in a sequence to access the linked page with the information or module needed to complete the step. For checklist items with a video link, a play button will be displayed on the checklist item. Click on the checklist item's title, such as **Review Backlog**, to be directed to the Jira Align module that has been linked to that step. When the step is completed, click on the checkmark icon next to each step to signify its completion. When all the steps are checked, the checklist is complete.

When you hover over the checklist, it will display a menu along the top right, as you can see in the preceding screenshot. Here you can select the program or PI in order to track the progress for shared checklists. In addition, you will have the option to toggle the checklist size, edit the checklist, and close the checklist to exit.

Now that we've seen how to get teams up and running in Jira Align, let's look at how they can begin working with a key element of agile, the product backlog.

Creating and refining backlogs

A backlog is simply a prioritized list of work items with the most important items at the top signifying that they should be worked on first. There are six levels of backlog in Jira Align: theme, portfolio epic, feature (Jira epic), story, task, and defect, as well as an optional capability level. Typically, portfolio managers and epic owners manage the theme and epic backlogs, solution managers manage the capability backlog, product managers manage the feature backlog, and product owners manage the story backlog.

If you have connected to an existing Jira Software instance from Jira Align (as we covered in *Chapter 2, Implementing Jira Align*), then your Jira epics, stories, and sub-tasks will flow into Jira Align as features, stories, and tasks and then bi-directionally sync between the two applications.

If you have not yet connected to Jira, or if you want to import higher-level work items to connect to the lower-level work items from Jira, you can use Jira Align's file import functionality. But before we explore that, let's review how work items at each level are linked.

Let's assume that features, stories, and tasks have come in from Jira and that we now wish to connect these team-level work items to higher-level strategic themes and portfolio epics. Let's also assume, as is common in organizations new to Jira Align, that theme and epic information can be gathered and put into spreadsheets for import into Jira Align. This will allow for full linkage between strategy and execution, as we saw in *Figure 2.9*, in the previous chapter. Let's explore that linkage further from the top down.

Linking work items

At the highest level, the enterprise strategy is a long-term plan of action designed to achieve a set of goals or objectives. Below that comes themes, the highest-level work item in Jira Align, which link up to strategic goals. A theme is a long-term set of epics that connects a portfolio to an enterprise strategy. Each portfolio epic is a funded effort that spans several business quarters and requires new development to realize business benefits contributing to the theme to which it is linked in Jira Align.

Portfolio epics are comprised of either capabilities or features. A capability is an optional work item level representing a collection of features supporting the portfolio epic to which it is linked in Jira Align. Capabilities are typically sized to be delivered within a business quarter and are complex enough to require the coordinated effort of multiple programs. A feature is a service fulfilling a stakeholder need, supporting either the capability or portfolio epic to which it is linked, and sized to be delivered in one business quarter by a single program.

At the lowest level is the story, the fundamental unit of customer value supporting a feature and sized to be delivered in one sprint or iteration. The story is the basic building block and connected all the way up to top-level strategy in Jira Align. The beauty of this is that the full linkage from any work item is visible by clicking on the **Why?** button in the details panel. Thus, at a glance, any team member can see how their efforts are valuable to the mission of their company. For example, clicking the **Why?** button on a story shows information for its parent feature, epic, and theme, as well as any associated **WSJF (weighted shortest job first)** scores, success measurements, and business cases, as shown:

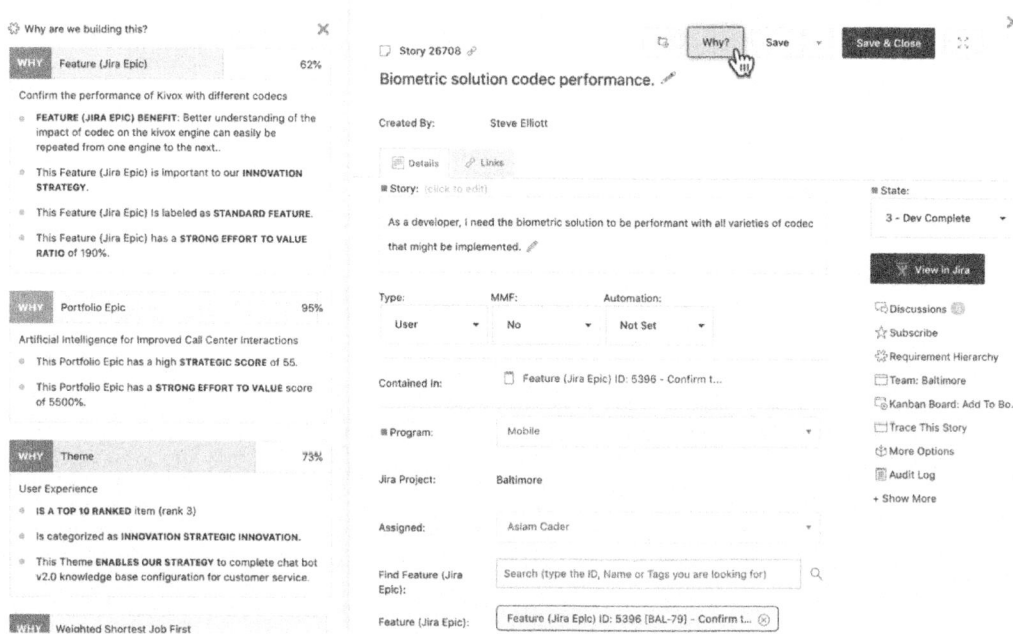

Figure 3.22 – Jira Align why? button

Here we see the **Why?** details panel to the left of the story details panel. The story is linked all the way up to a top-ranking theme connected to corporate strategy.

In the same story's details panel, let's now click on the **Requirement Hierarchy** link on the right, three positions down from the **State** dropdown. This provides a visual of the linkage up and down the chain from any work item, as shown:

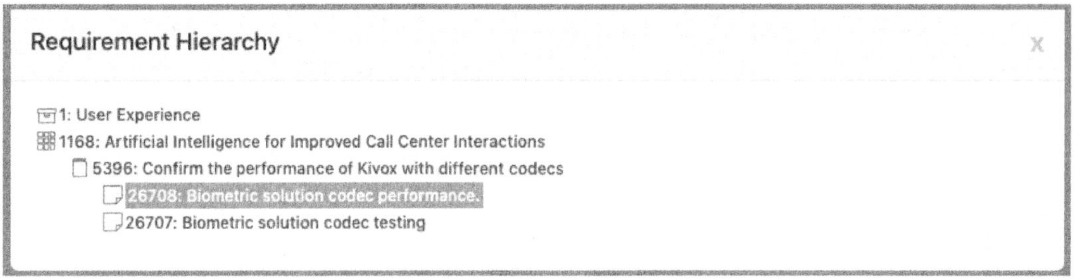

Figure 3.23 – Jira Align requirement hierarchy

Here we see the story in context with its sibling story, their parent feature, and the linked epic and theme above that. You can click on each item in the hierarchy to open its details panel. For example, let's click on the feature to open its details panel:

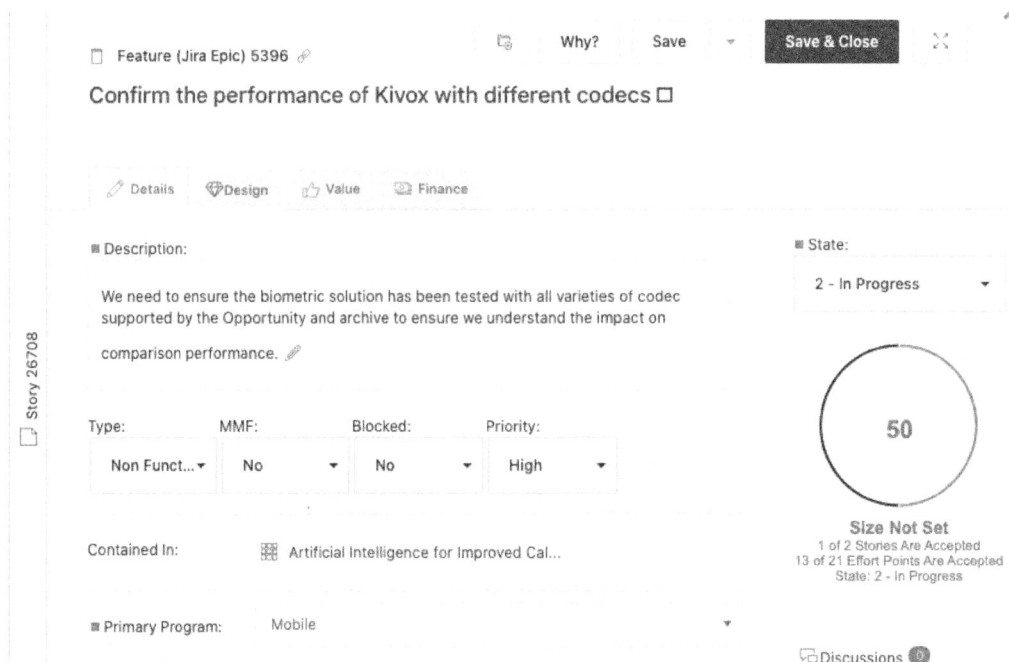

Figure 3.24 – Jira Align feature details panel

To then return to the original work item, in this case, Story 26708, simply click on the bar to the left of the panel. In this way, related work items can be explored from any level in the hierarchy.

In Jira Align, unlinked items are called *orphans*. It is common practice for team members at each level to review orphans and connect them up to higher-level items to promote visibility and tie execution to strategy. For this reason, each level of backlog in Jira Align has an **Orphan Objects** button near the top right of the workspace. For example, let's go to the story backlog and click on **Orphan Objects** to find stories not connected to features. These will be shown in a panel on the right side of the workspace:

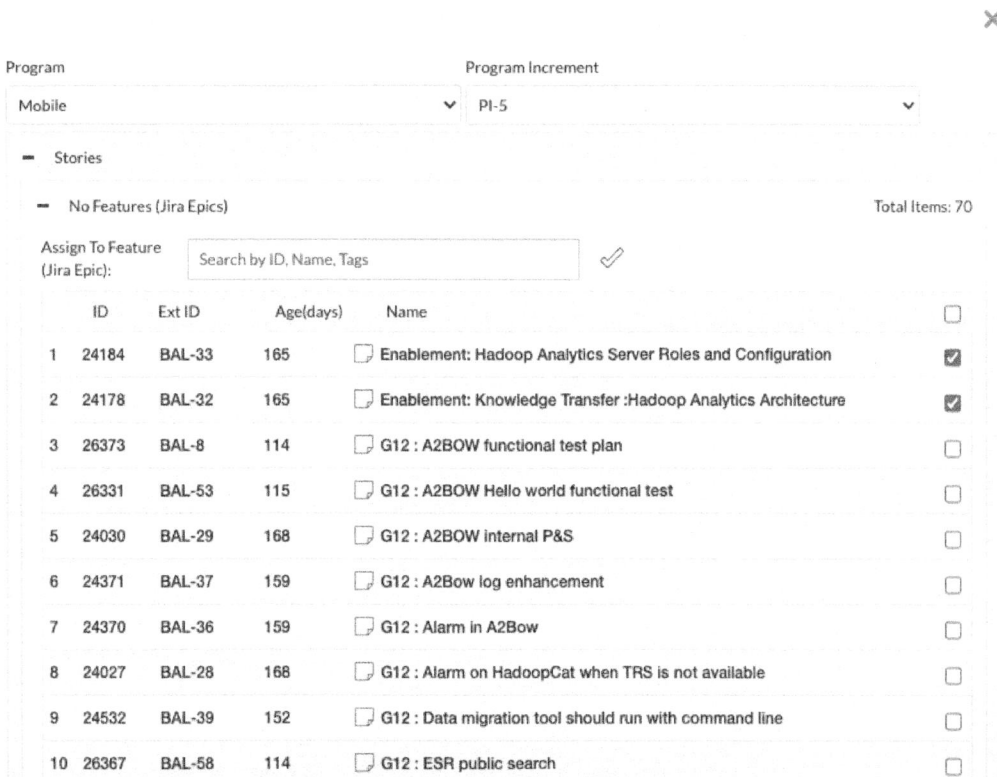

	Program				Program Increment	
	Mobile				PI-5	

— Stories

— No Features (Jira Epics)   Total Items: 70

Assign To Feature (Jira Epic):   Search by ID, Name, Tags   ✓

	ID	Ext ID	Age(days)	Name	
1	24184	BAL-33	165	Enablement: Hadoop Analytics Server Roles and Configuration	☑
2	24178	BAL-32	165	Enablement: Knowledge Transfer :Hadoop Analytics Architecture	☑
3	26373	BAL-8	114	G12 : A2BOW functional test plan	☐
4	26331	BAL-53	115	G12 : A2BOW Hello world functional test	☐
5	24030	BAL-29	168	G12 : A2BOW internal P&S	☐
6	24371	BAL-37	159	G12 : A2Bow log enhancement	☐
7	24370	BAL-36	159	G12 : Alarm in A2Bow	☐
8	24027	BAL-28	168	G12 : Alarm on HadoopCat when TRS is not available	☐
9	24532	BAL-39	152	G12 : Data migration tool should run with command line	☐
10	26367	BAL-58	114	G12 : ESR public search	☐

Figure 3.25 – Jira Align story backlog orphan objects panel

Here you can click on a story to see its details and use the checkboxes on the right to multi-select stories to assign to a feature, which you can search for by ID, name, or tags. This makes it easy to connect each level of backlog item to its parent item.

Now that we know the importance of linking work items at all levels to connect strategy with execution, let's go through the steps of importing. We will import portfolio epics in this example.

Importing and exporting

As mentioned previously in the *Workspace* section, work item grids at all levels allow for advanced actions, including importing and exporting. To access this functionality, go to the grid for any level work item. In this case, we are assuming that features and stories have come into a new Jira Align instance from the Jira connector and that we now need to import epics to which the features will be linked. To begin, go to the navigation menu and select **Portfolio | Manage | Epics**. Next, click on **More Actions | Import Epics**. This will display instructions and tips in the workspace, along with a drop-down list to select your program and a button to download the Excel workbook import template.

Once you've downloaded the template, select the tab for the work item you'd like to import and fill it out. Note that asterisks in the header indicate required fields and that it's important not to modify the four header rows. Next, save the file without changing its format. Return to the workspace and select your program from the aforementioned dropdown. Next, click on **Browse** to select the file and then click on the **Import Data** button. Finally, navigate to **Portfolio | Backlog** to see the results. Voilà! You've now got a backlog of portfolio epics!

Now you can go to **Program | Backlog** and click on **Orphan Objects** to multi-select features to assign to the newly imported epics in a similar manner to the assignment of stories to features shown in *Figure 3.25*.

Tips and tricks

As a guide in filling out the import template, it is helpful to refer to an exported file of real data you are familiar with for reference, since the layout of the import and export files are the same. To export epics, go to the navigation menu and select **Portfolio | Manage | Epics**. Next, click on **More Actions | Export Epics**.

It's advisable to do a test import of one or two rows before importing an entire spreadsheet of dozens or hundreds of rows.

If you need to adjust the associated metadata for several work items in Jira Align, you can export them, modify the spreadsheet, and then reimport them. This can be used, for example, to bulk change the parent capability or epic for numerous features.

When working remotely, it may be helpful to export your backlog to have as a backup in case of internet connectivity issues.

Creating work items

While viewing the epic and feature backlogs, you can quickly add new work items by entering a name and clicking on the **Add** button as shown in the following screenshot:

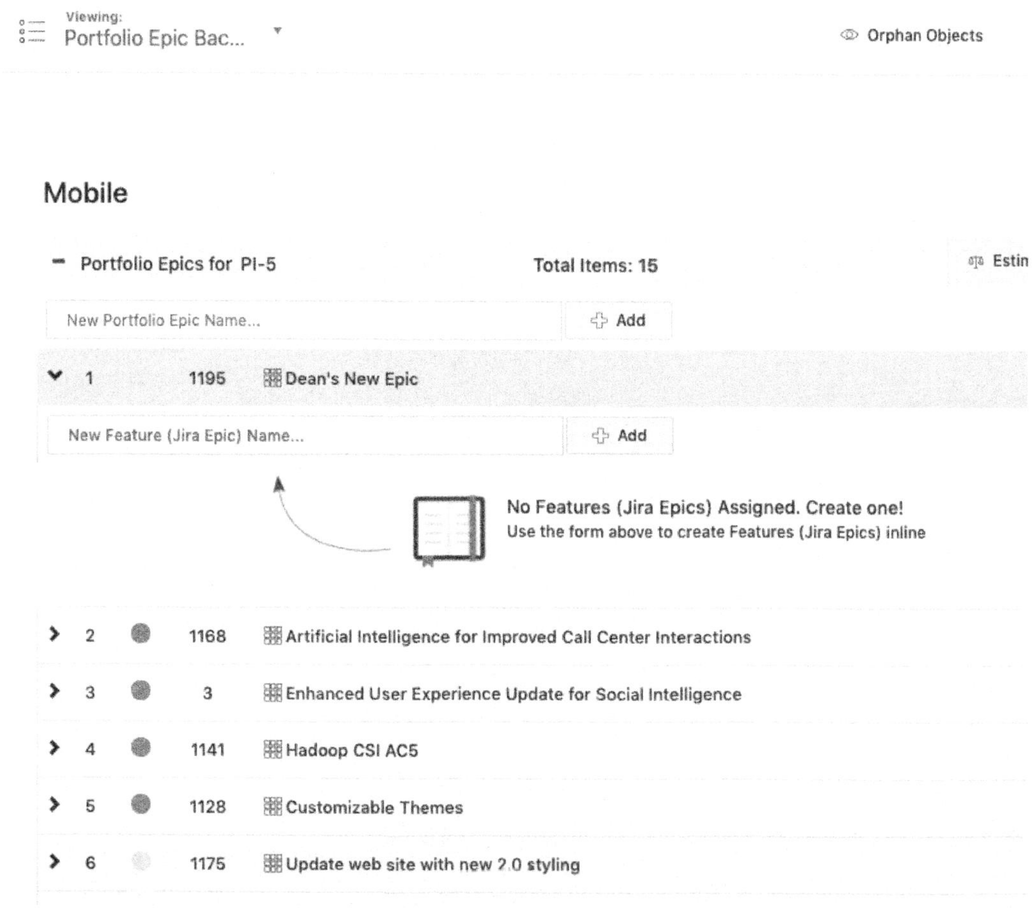

Figure 3.26 – Jira Align backlog add button

This allows for a quick add with only the essential elements. Here we've added a new epic. Note the prompt informing us that features can be quickly added under the epic by again entering a name and clicking on **Add**. Also, note that you can click on the pointing arrow symbol at the far left of any work item's row to expand it and show the children work items.

Let's now assume we want to go back and add more details to our epic. To do so, we click on the epic's name or ID in the backlog to open the details panel as shown:

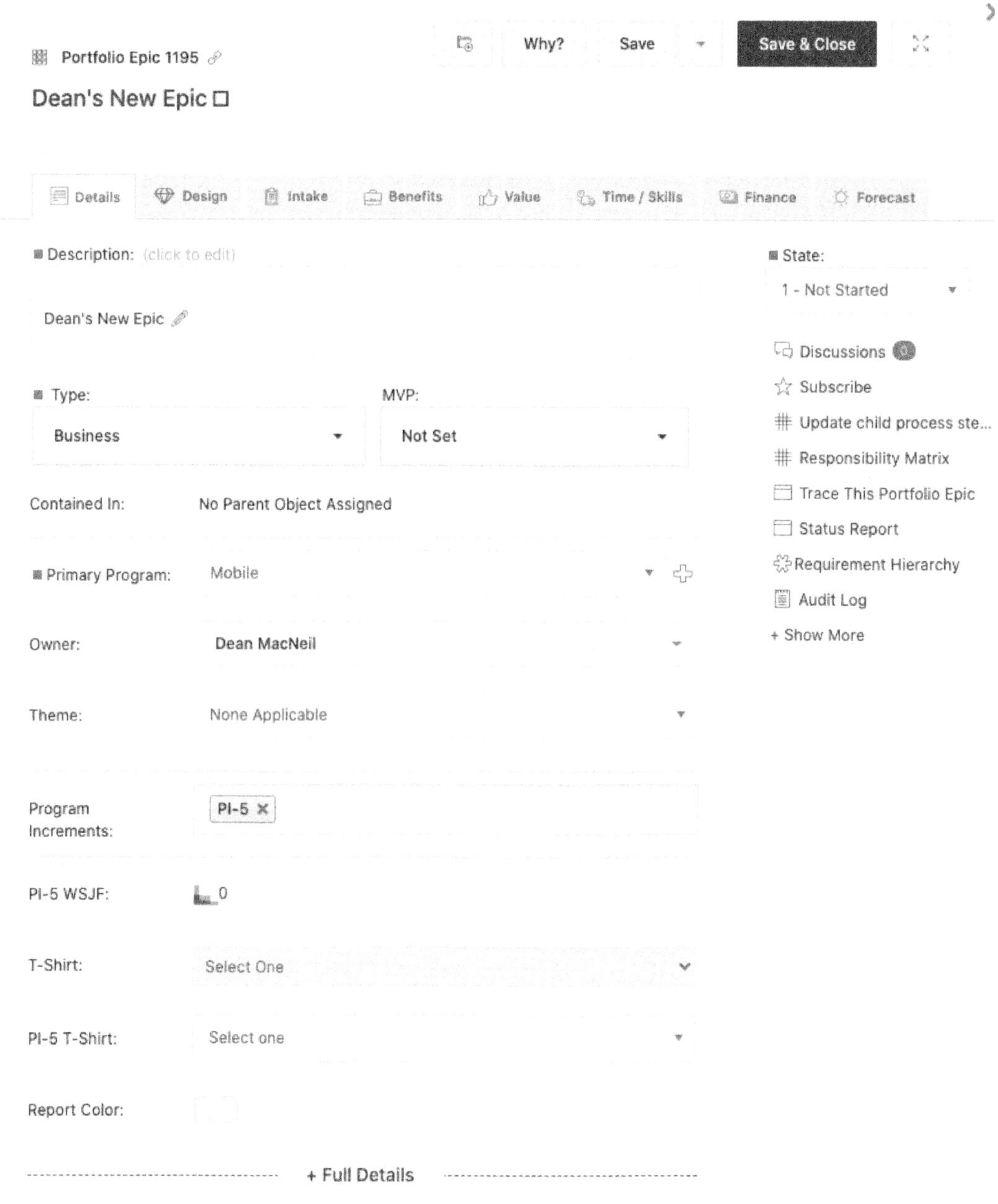

Figure 3.27 – Jira Align epic details panel

Here you will find several tabs for the entry of associated benefits, value, finance, and other data. Clicking on **Full Details** expands or hides additional fields for the entry of capitalization, investment type, strategic driver, and more. Note that the Jira administrator can set which fields are displayed and required in the details panel for each work item type under **Administration | Settings | Details Panel Settings**. These settings are per portfolio, so everyone in the portfolio, including its programs and teams, will have the same set of fields.

Scrolling down in the details panel, you will find where to associate features, acceptance criteria, risks, success criteria, dependencies, objectives, links, and attachments. Clicking on **Features** will expand that section to show the fields, as shown:

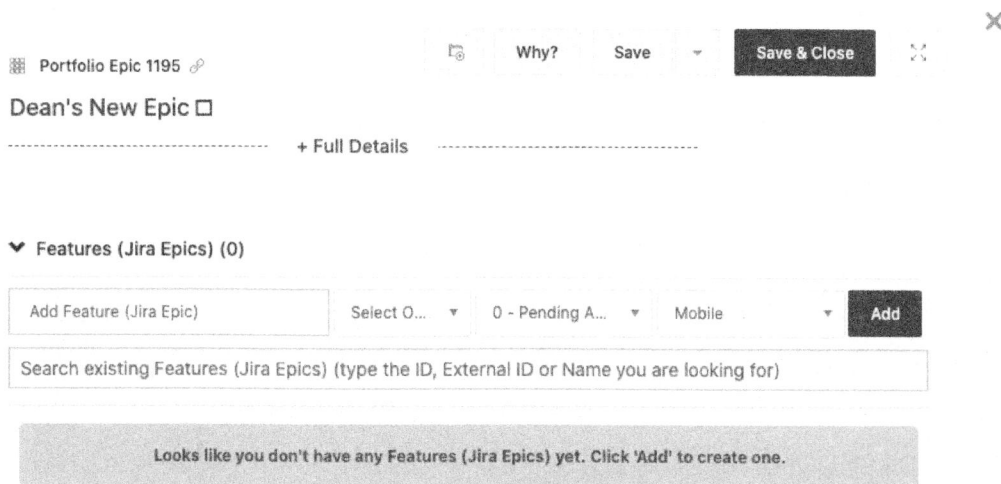

Figure 3.28 – Jira Align epic details panel, features section

Here you can either quick-add a new feature under the epic or search for an existing feature to link to it. In this manner, you'll be able to assign features that came in from Jira to the portfolio epics imported in our preceding example.

Note that you do not have to be in the backlog to add work items. Jira Align allows you to add work items of any level, as well as other types of items, at any time by clicking on the **Create** button at the far right of the configuration bar.

> **Tips and tricks**
>
> Product managers can add features to their backlogs without syncing them with Jira. This allows them to refine the features until they are ready.
>
> To keep a feature in Jira Align, the product manager would not make a selection from the Jira Project dropdown on the feature's details panel.
>
> Once the feature is ready for teams to see in Jira, the product manager can select a Jira project from the dropdown, allowing the feature to flow into Jira.

Now that you know how to import and create work items for your backlog, let's learn some basic refinement techniques.

Ranking work items

A well-refined backlog will be ordered by rank so that the team knows what to work on next. Note that while team-level backlogs of stories will be maintained in Jira, it's common practice for program, solution, and portfolio backlogs to be maintained in Jira Align, which is generally deemed to be the system of record for features, capabilities, and portfolio epics.

Jira Align provides two methods of ranking: manual and automated. The simplest way is to manually drag and drop the work item to a higher or lower position in the backlog list, which is in ranked order. You could also right-click on the work item and move it to the top, bottom, or a specified position in the backlog.

Automated ranking allows you to pull rank based on the ranking of higher-level work items. For example, if the portfolio team has ranked epics and you'd like to rank your features according to the rank of their parent epics, you can go to **Program | Backlog**, click on the **Pull Rank** button, and select **Use Epic**.

While manual and automated ranking are simple to do, there are a couple of important things to keep in mind. The first is that work items are always ranked relative to other work items of the same type. The second is that work items actually have several independent ranks based on how your configuration bar is set.

Global rank is the default ranking when the configuration bar is clear, meaning no specific portfolio, program, or PI is selected. If a PI is selected in the configuration bar, you will be viewing the rank for that particular PI. If a portfolio or program is selected, you will see the rank within that particular portfolio or program. If you select a portfolio and PI or program and PI, you will be viewing the rank within that portfolio or program for that specific PI. The lowest level is selecting a team and a sprint, for which you will see the ranking of items worked on by that team in a particular sprint.

There is another nuance regarding ranking. Earlier we noted that clicking on the pointing arrow symbol at the left of any row in a backlog list will expand the work item to show its children. Assuming there are several children, they can be dragged up and down under the parent to represent a sequence or rank; however, this is independent from the rank of those items when listed with all others of the same type. In other words, you can change the order in which features appear under a parent epic when its row is expanded, but that won't affect, for example, the program feature ranking you will see when you view the feature backlog and have a program selected in the configuration bar. This is where visibility of all work and rankings within the platform can drive discussions, for example, between epic owners and product managers, who must collaborate to ensure that their independent rankings of epics and features are aligned.

Lastly, we will note that Jira Align allows you to manually synchronize feature and story rankings between Jira Align and Jira. This option is only available in the feature and story backlogs when a program is selected in the configuration bar and no PIs are selected. Note that the Jira Align administrator must enable this option in **Administration | Connectors | Jira Settings | Jira Setup**. Here, the administrator must enter the Jira rank field ID under **Custom Fields** and set **Enable Rank Sync** to **Yes** under settings. Once these settings are made, you will have two additional options when you click on the **Pull Rank** button in the backlog, one to pull rank from Jira, and the other to push rank to Jira.

> **Tips and tricks**
>
> If, after pulling rank from Jira for your features, you'd like to apply that ranking to a particular PI, first add the PI to your configuration bar so that your program and PI are selected. Then use the **Pull Rank** button again, this time selecting **Use Program rank to sort Features**.

Estimating work items

Another facet of a refined backlog is that it's estimated. Estimates at all levels enable learning and predictability. For example, as a scrum team learns its average velocity (story points completed per sprint), it can estimate how many sprints it will take to complete a feature based on an initial point estimate for the feature. Later, when that feature is broken down into stories that are sized, the aggregate story points can be compared with the initial estimate for learning purposes.

While team-level story point estimates are typically done in Jira, Jira Align provides three options for how to size features, capabilities, and epics. They are, in order of popularity, t-shirt size, points, and team/member weeks. The last option may be useful in a bimodal environment where some portfolios are using waterfall development. The Jira Align administrator sets the estimation option for each portfolio in **Administration | Settings | Platform | Portfolio | Portfolio Specific Configuration**. This allows each portfolio to have its own estimation approach, which will be uniform throughout the portfolio, including its programs and teams.

If t-shirt size is the chosen estimation method, then Jira Align will convert t-shirt sizes to points for reports, grid views, and functionality, such as the PI load widget in the program room. The Jira Align administrator sets the conversion parameters in **Administration | Settings | Platform | Portfolio | Estimation Conversions**. Here is an example:

Estimation Conversions

T-Shirt Size for Initiatives	Team Weeks	Member Weeks	Hours	FTE/mo	Estimated Story Points	Sort	
X-Small	2	12	360	3	30	1	✖
Small	4	24	720	6	60	2	✖
Medium	6	36	1080	9	90	3	✖
Large	16	96	2880	24	240	4	✖
XL	26	156	4680	39	390	5	✖
XXL	80	480	14400	120	1200	6	✖

Add   Save Settings

Figure 3.29 – Jira Align estimation conversions example

There are two important considerations to note here:

- There is no accepted standard for the conversion of t-shirt sizes to team weeks and story points. Each organization will experiment and learn what works best for their context.

- The same conversion table applies to the entire Jira Align instance, including all portfolios.

Because portfolios may differ in terms of the conversion parameters, we recommend using points as the estimation method. This also ensures that reports and widgets are intuitive, as users could be confused by the t-shirt to point conversion.

Tips and tricks

Whether you choose t-shirt size or points as your default estimation method, you can still have a field to store the other estimation type. We recommend setting points as the default, with t-shirt size as the secondary field.

To have a secondary estimation field, ask your Jira Align administrator to add it as a custom field in **Administration | Settings | Details Panels Settings**. Here they would select the portfolio and work item and then click on **Add Custom Field**. They would then toggle the custom field on in **Details Panels Settings.**

You can view the original point estimate for features, capabilities, and epics alongside the sum of all story points rolling up from their children in your backlog and grid views. To do so, click on the **Columns Shown** button near the top right of the workspace, and then add both the **Points** (original point estimate) and **Story Points** (rollup of points as estimated by team members at the story level) columns.

Important note: the Jira Align administrator must toggle on both **Points** and **Story Points** in **Administration | Settings | Details Panels Settings** for each portfolio and work item type in order for the preceding to work.

To see work items without estimates, you can scan those columns in your backlog or grid views. You can also click on the **Orphan Objects** button in the backlog. Aside from showing unlinked items, as we saw in *Figure 3.25*, you can scroll down for more information, including items without estimates.

Deleting work items

Usually, only the Jira Align administrator has permission to delete. Other roles may be granted permission to move work items to the recycle bin. Note that if a work item that came into Jira Align from Jira is later deleted or archived in Jira, it will remain in Jira Align for audit purposes. It can be moved to the recycle bin if necessary. To view the recycle bin, go to a work item grid, for example, **Program | Manage | Features**, and then click on **More Actions | Access Recycle Bin**.

In rare cases, a Jira Align administrator may need to delete an entire team, program, or portfolio. If this is the case, for referential integrity, objects must be deleted from bottom to top of the hierarchy in this sequence: tasks, stories, features, epics/capabilities, themes, sprints, PI, teams, programs, portfolios, snapshot, and organization.

> **Tips and tricks**
>
> The Jira Align administrator can generate a report of items that were deleted in Jira by going to **Administration | Connectors | Jira Management | Jira Deleted Issues**. (This was already covered in *Chapter 2, Implementing Jira Align*, in the *Connecting to Jira* section.)

Searching for work items

Jira Align provides search boxes on all work item backlog and grid views so that you can find the exact item you are looking for within that view. Simply type the name or ID in the search box. You can also perform a global search for work items across all portfolios, programs, and teams to which you have access. To do so, click on the search icon (magnifying glass) near the right side of the configuration bar. This allows you to search by name or ID; however, note that here, an ID number must be preceded by the # sign, as shown here:

Figure 3.30 – Jira Align global work item search

Simply click on the item once it is found, in this case, a story with an ID of 26708, to open its details panel.

At this point, your backlog is built, ranked, and estimated. You know how to create, search for, and delete work items. Now it's time to begin collaborating with your fellow teammates on delivering those items.

Collaborating in Jira Align

As part of team collaboration, it is key that work is visible, tracked, and monitored. Jira Align supports this with sophisticated email and alert notifications on those work items that need attention. Notifications are a great way to receive info on specific events without being tied to your desk.

In order to receive notifications via email, you need the **Change Tracking Emails** preference option toggled on in your user preferences. This will enable you to receive emails for subscriptions, notifications, and workflow generated notifications:

Figure 3.31 – Jira Align change tracking emails preference

Tips and tricks

Jira Align administrators can set the default preference to be always turned on by going to the **Administration | Settings | Platform | Users** tab and setting the **Personal User Notification** dropdown to **Default To On**. They can select the **Reset All Users** button to push the default setting to all users.

Whether you choose to receive email notifications or not, you will also receive alert notifications via the bell icon near the right side of the configuration bar:

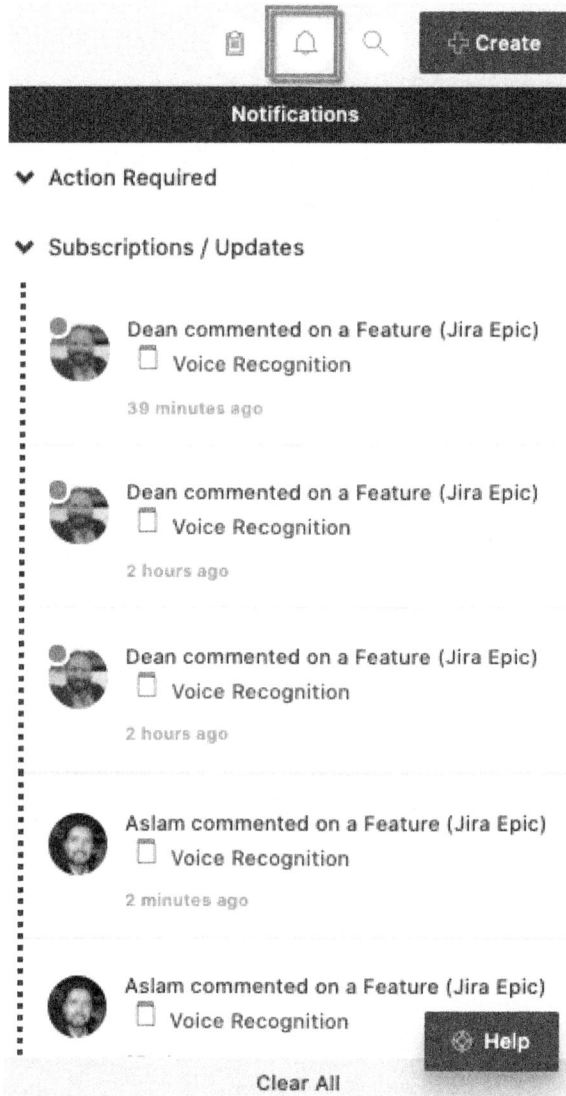

Figure 3.32 – Jira Align notification bell

These alerts are a great alternative to email notifications, as they keep team members informed within the Jira Align interface. The red dot signifies unread alert notifications. The **Action Required** section lists notifications that require actions such as approval, and the **Subscription/Updates** section lists notifications that require collaboration, including subscriptions, discussions, and workflow email notifications.

Alert notifications are heavily utilized by organizations that choose to turn off email notifications completely in order to reduce information overload. In order to receive these alerts, you must subscribe to work items in Jira Align, which we will learn about next.

Subscribing to notifications

You can choose to subscribe to notifications on work items by clicking on the **Subscribe** option. Once you subscribe, you will receive notifications. You can stop notifications by clicking on the **Unsubscribe** option at any time:

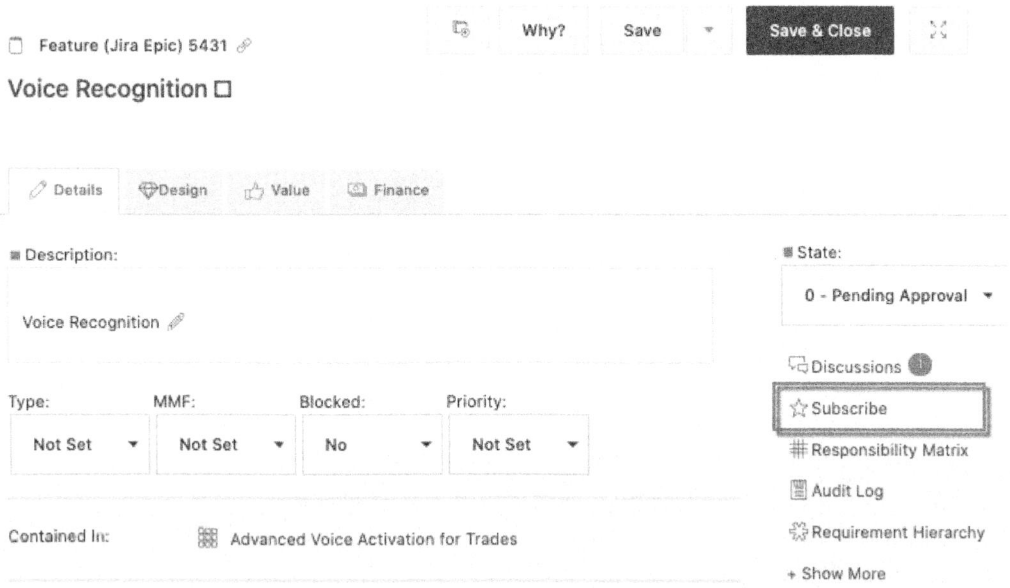

Figure 3.33 – Jira Align work item discussions and subscribing

Here are the work items, timeboxes, and planning artifacts that support the **Subscribe** function: themes, portfolio epics, capabilities, features, stories, tasks, defects, dependencies, risks, sprints, goals, specifications, brainstorming, success criteria, feeds, ideas, hotfixes, and UI designs.

Starting a discussion

You can start discussions for work items and @mention someone to generate a notification or alert. You will find the **Discussions** link within a work item's details panel. You can notify both individuals and teams to join a discussion, as shown here. As you @ mention, the helper will find the closest match to help autocomplete the recipient of the notification. Here is an example discussion:

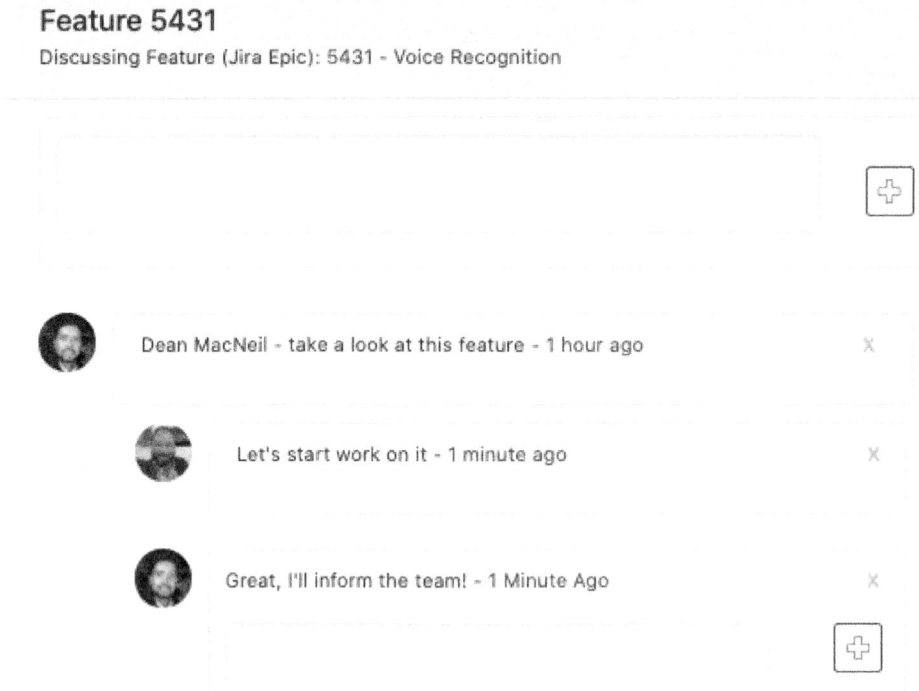

Feature 5431

Discussing Feature (Jira Epic): 5431 - Voice Recognition

Dean MacNeil - take a look at this feature - 1 hour ago   X

Let's start work on it - 1 minute ago   X

Great, I'll inform the team! - 1 Minute Ago   X

Figure 3.34 – Jira Align discussions

All communications will be highlighted using a red balloon annotation in the work item's details panel to indicate the number of discussions. For example, there is one discussion shown previously in *Figure 3.33*. You can also quickly access the discussions when the **Chat** column is displayed on a work item grid page. Here are the items that support notifications via the **Discussion** link: portfolio epics, capabilities, features, stories, defects, impediments, and brainstorming.

Configuring workflow emails

You can create email workflows to alert others and yourself automatically when a work item, team, or timebox is created, edited, or deleted. The workflow configurations are applied to an entire organization, including portfolios, programs, and teams. You can notify all roles within a program, agile team roles, or individual email addresses. You can configure the workflows under **Administration | Settings | Email** by selecting the workflow type and choosing the roles to notify:

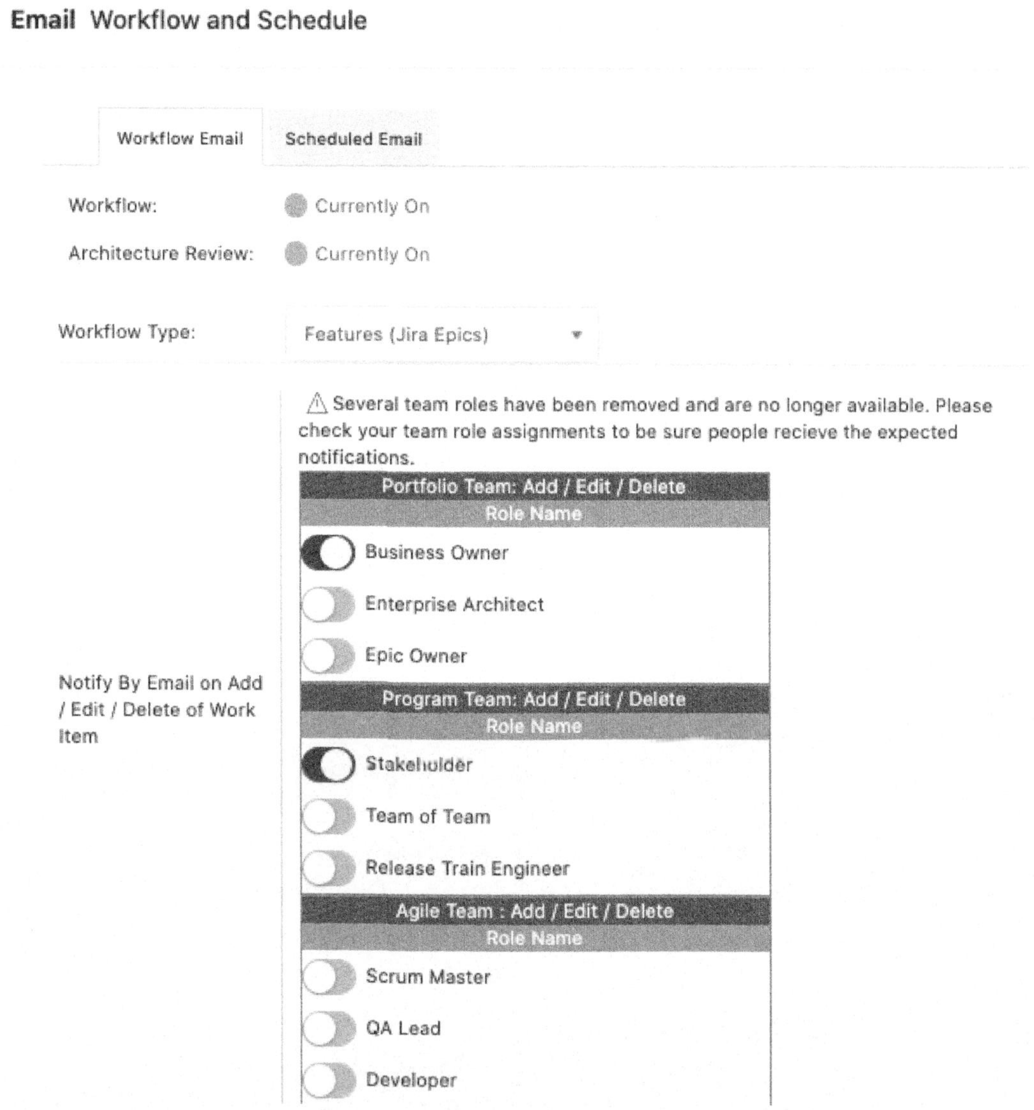

Email Workflow and Schedule

Workflow Email	Scheduled Email

Workflow: Currently On
Architecture Review: Currently On

Workflow Type: Features (Jira Epics)   ▼

⚠ Several team roles have been removed and are no longer available. Please check your team role assignments to be sure people recieve the expected notifications.

Notify By Email on Add / Edit / Delete of Work Item

Portfolio Team: Add / Edit / Delete
Role Name
● Business Owner
○ Enterprise Architect
○ Epic Owner

Program Team: Add / Edit / Delete
Role Name
● Stakeholder
○ Team of Team
○ Release Train Engineer

Agile Team : Add / Edit / Delete
Role Name
○ Scrum Master
○ QA Lead
○ Developer

Figure 3.35 – Jira Align email workflow

Several work items, timeboxes, and planning artifacts support email workflows, including portfolio epics, features, stories, defects, PI, release vehicles, and more. Some of these workflow types have additional attributes for configuring the workflow, some allow you to assign a role to be notified, and some allow you to add external emails to be notified.

There are specific work items in Jira Align that allow you to set up special workflows under certain conditions. For example, when creating a strategic snapshot, you can set up a notification for funding approval and funding change that emails individuals based on the workflow rules you set. The following screenshot shows how notifications are enabled for updates on strategic snapshots:

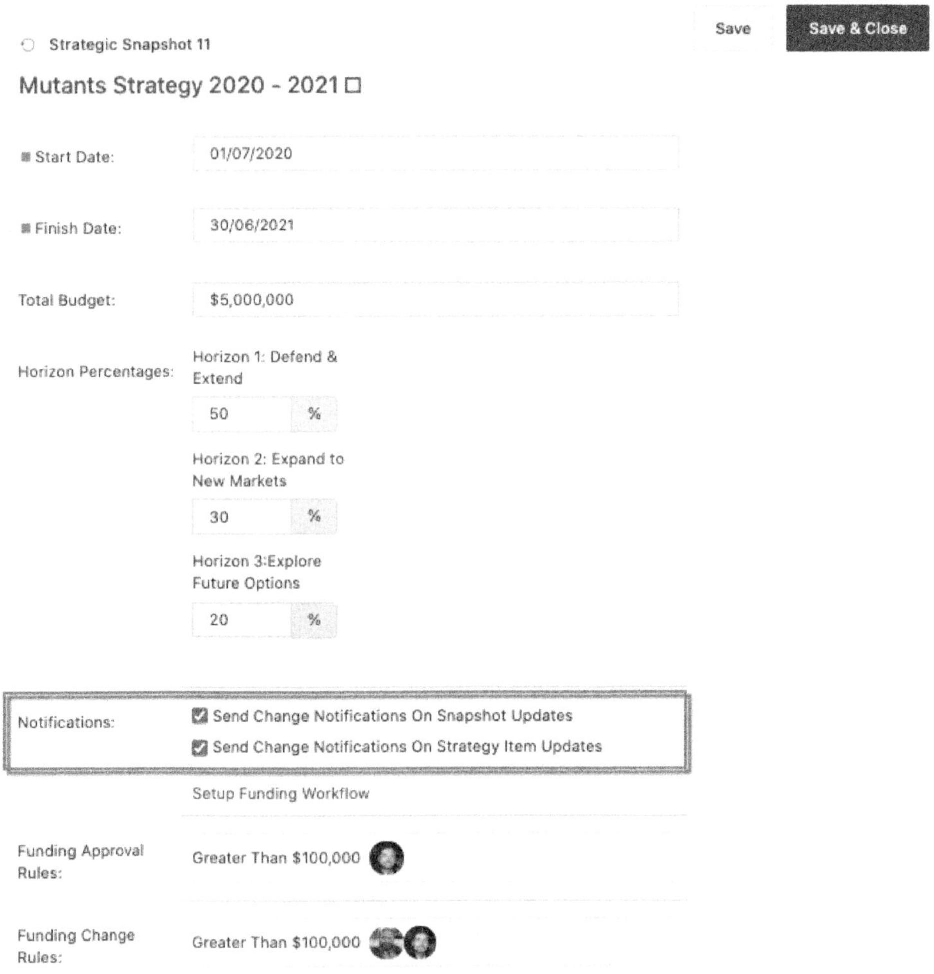

Figure 3.36 – Jira Align strategic snapshot notifications

You can also set up notifications for when a feature reaches a specific state in the workflow. To do so, go to **Program | Manage | Features | More Actions | Workflow**. Here is how you can set up the workflow states to notify one or more individuals:

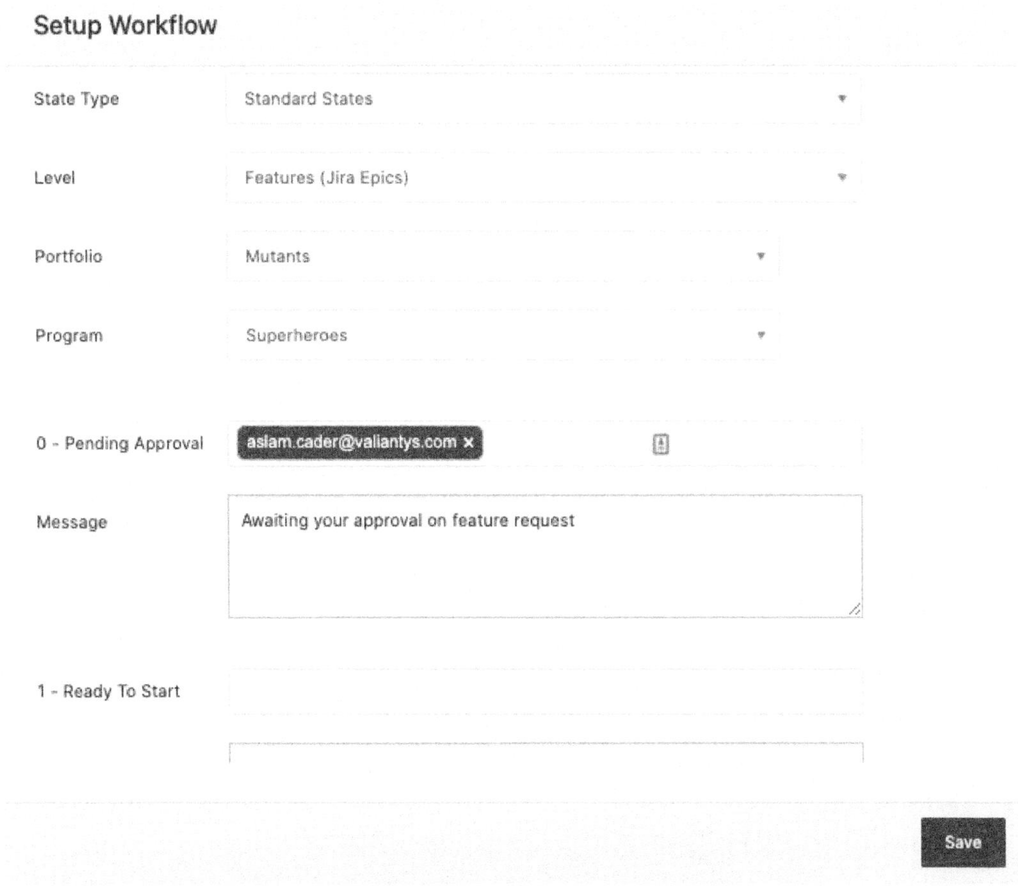

Setup Workflow

State Type	Standard States ▾
Level	Features (Jira Epics) ▾
Portfolio	Mutants ▾
Program	Superheroes ▾
0 - Pending Approval	aslam.cader@valiantys.com ✕
Message	Awaiting your approval on feature request
1 - Ready To Start	

Save

Figure 3.37 – Jira Align strategic workflow state notifications

You can also set up special workflow notifications on Kanban boards, value streams, defects, risks, PI status reports, and announcements.

Setting up scheduled emails

If you need to set up regular email communications, speak with your Jira Align administrator to schedule emails at a specific date/time. You can notify your teams to communicate reminders on deadlines and time-specific deliverables. The scheduled notifications are created by going to the **Administration | Settings | Email | Scheduled Email** tab and then clicking on the **Create New** button. Here are the details to add when creating a scheduled email:

- **Enable this message**: You need to check this box to activate the scheduled email. An unchecked box means it's inactive.

- **Send this message**: Choose the email send frequency, **Weekly** or **Monthly**.

- **Send Time**: Choose a time at which you want to send out the scheduled email.

- **Send Day(s)**: Choose the days on which you want to send out the scheduled email.

- **Start Date and End Date**: Add a start date to schedule the first email to go out. Optionally, you can add an end date for the scheduled emails to stop.

- **Recipients**: Choose the applicable roles as email recipients. Click on the **Advanced Recipient** filters to add a filter on the email recipients.

- **Region**: Choose **All Regions** or optionally choose the applicable regions for the notification scope.

- **Subject**: Set an email subject for the scheduled email.

- **Message**: Set an email body for the scheduled email.

- **Send Message Now**: Optionally, you can click on the **Send Message Now** button to send out the scheduled message.

- **Test**: Click the **Test** button to send out an email to yourself to validate that the scheduled email is working.

- **Report Association**: Click the **Report Association** button to associate a report to be linked to the scheduled email.

Click on the **Save** button to save the changes.

The following screenshot shows how you can set up a scheduled email reminder for weekly timesheet submission:

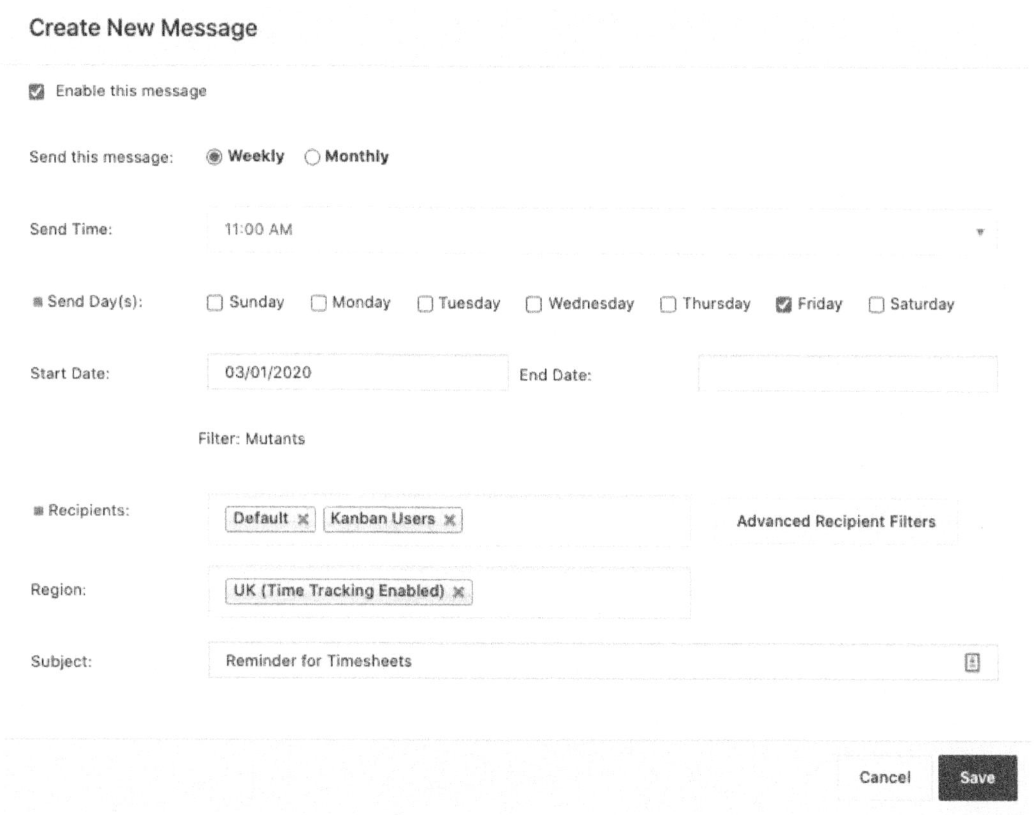

Create New Message

☑ Enable this message

Send this message: ◉ **Weekly**   ○ **Monthly**

Send Time: 11:00 AM   ▾

▣ Send Day(s):   ☐ Sunday   ☐ Monday   ☐ Tuesday   ☐ Wednesday   ☐ Thursday   ☑ Friday   ☐ Saturday

Start Date: 03/01/2020   End Date:

            Filter: Mutants

▣ Recipients: Default ✕   Kanban Users ✕   Advanced Recipient Filters

Region: UK (Time Tracking Enabled) ✕

Subject: Reminder for Timesheets   ⊞

                                                                    Cancel   **Save**

Figure 3.38 – Jira Align scheduled emails

You have now learned how to monitor and get notified of changes to work items in Jira Align. If you want to learn more about how Jira Align can facilitate collaboration for remote teams, read on to the next *Chapter 4, Team Challenges*.

Summary

In this chapter, we mastered basic Jira Align user interface navigation. We now know how to navigate and filter information across the people, work, and time dimensions. We explored how Jira Align facilitates user onboarding by providing tools for alignment and continuous learning. We learned how to create work items and refine the backlog. Lastly, we covered how to keep teams informed through notifications and alerts to promote collaboration.

Now that you know how to get around Jira Align, you are set free safely on the ground to further explore modules at each level of scale. The continuous circle of support, facilitation, and collaboration within Jira Align creates a fully connected knowledge environment that your organization can leverage to accelerate toward business agility.

In the next chapter, we will explore common team challenges that Jira Align can help solve.

Questions

1. What are the three key areas to master in Jira Align?

2. How does Jira Align facilitate onboarding and continuous learning?

3. What is the importance of the **Why?** button?

4. How do you link a work item to a higher-level work item?

5. What are the options for estimating features, capabilities, and portfolio epics?

Further reading

- *Hands-On Agile Software Development with Jira*, by David Harned (Packt, 2018)

Section 2: Problem-Solving with Jira Align

Here, you will learn common scaling challenges organizations face as they scale agility from the team to the program and then to the portfolio levels. Each chapter details a set of feature-based solutions available from Jira Align to support business agility and value delivery at every level of scale.

This section comprises the following chapters:

- *Chapter 4, Team Challenges*
- *Chapter 5, Program Planning Challenges*
- *Chapter 6, Program Execution Challenges*
- *Chapter 7, Enterprise and Portfolio Challenges*

4
Team Challenges

In this chapter, we concentrate on team-level agile, the foundation for scaling to the enterprise. Now more than ever, it's prudent to invest in your teams, their agile methods, and the tools that support them. Traditionally, teams have harnessed the power of colocation for effective face-to-face communication and collaboration (*Agile Manifesto*, Principle 6). One of the biggest challenges facing teams today is maintaining high performance and relentless improvement while fully remote and geographically dispersed due to various constraints, including the current global pandemic. Tools are now essential to support team planning, collaboration, and execution. Luckily, the Atlassian suite of products excels in this arena. While Jira Software is the central tool for team agility, Jira Align provides added features to help teams plan and collaborate, even when geographically dispersed. You will learn how teams connect and engage with Jira Align.

In this chapter, we will cover the following topics:

- Ensuring teams are connected
- Sizing stories with estimation games
- Loading sprints during remote planning
- Conducting ceremonies and meetings
- Reviewing sprints and giving shoutouts

Ensuring teams are connected

Agile teams are where the rubber meets the road, where the work of the connected knowledge enterprise gets done. Sprint after sprint, they focus with precision on delivering small batches of high-ranking user stories and shippable product increments of value to real customers. With Jira Software as their central collaborative workflow engine, they are able to hook into a variety of tools, including Bitbucket for version control and Bamboo for continuous integration and deployment. To put their work in context, teams can reference data like program increments and **Why?** button details pushed down from Jira Align while their work item statuses sync with Jira Align for rolled-up reporting.

Team members using Jira Software are considered *integrated users* of Jira Align, which allows their data to sync with Align and for them to access Align's team-level functionality. To ensure that team members flow in from Jira Software, the Jira Align administrator must first go to **Jira Settings | Jira Setup** and set **Allow Jira to add users to team if they belong to an issue** to **Yes** under the **Settings** section. Note, however, that this setting could result in a duplicate user record if an integrated user was previously set up in Jira Align. To prevent duplicates, the user's email address in Jira Software must be exposed so that Jira Align can combine the integrated and native user accounts. As of the time of writing, a security issue prevents this from happening automatically.

Tips and tricks

It is required to expose email addresses in Jira Software so that Jira Align can combine duplicate user accounts.

In Atlassian Cloud, Jira Software users can expose their email by clicking on their profile picture, selecting **Account settings**, and then setting their email address to be visible by **Anyone**.

In Jira Server/Data Center, the Jira administrator can set this globally by going to **Jira Administration | System | General Configuration** and then setting **User email visibility** to **Public**.

The Jira Align administrator can also set the default system role for integrated users by going to **Jira Settings | Jira Setup** and selecting a role for **Default System Role for New User(s)**. We recommend selecting the **Team Leads** role for slightly more access than the **Team Members** role, including the ability to use the Team Meetings module we will discuss shortly.

In addition to integrated user access, it is common good practice for product owners and often scrum masters to have full Jira Align licenses in order to access program-level functionality, which we will cover in *Chapter 5, Program Planning Challenges*. We recommend that both roles have full licenses because they often work closely with product managers and RTEs at the program level and we've found that the ability to access higher-level functionality allows them to easily pivot and fill any gaps between program and team. For example, POs may help product managers break portfolio epics down into features, align on cross-program dependencies, and manage program risks. Scrum masters represent their teams at scrum of scrums meetings, work to remove impediments, coordinate with the RTE, escalate issues and risks, and align on dependencies at the program level.

Both the PO and SM are emailed automatically when dependencies are requested of their teams. This ensures that they are in the loop even if the requesting team did not speak with them first, as would be expected. Note that this applies mainly to feature dependencies. Story dependencies are generally handled within Jira using the issue linking functionality.

Now that team-level users are connected, they have the option to log on to Jira Align to use team tools not available in Jira. We'll first explore how to size stories with estimation games.

Sizing stories with estimation games

Estimation, the process of predicting the most realistic effort required to deliver work items based on incomplete and uncertain input, is a typical challenge among development teams. Agile frameworks leverage relative estimating to mitigate this challenge. The power of relative estimating lies in accuracy over precision. If we were to ask you to look out the window and tell us how tall two buildings across the street are, chances are you couldn't give precise heights in feet or meters, but you could accurately state that one building is twice as tall as the other. Relative estimating allows teams to do the same thing with user stories. For reference, they start with a small, simple, and well-understood story (typically something that their team could build, test, and deploy in a day) and call it a 1-point story. They then estimate other stories relative to the 1-point story. For example, are they 2, 3, 5, or 8 times the volume, complexity, and uncertainty of the 1-point story?

Teams typically use the modified Fibonacci sequence to size stories, as it factors in the inherent uncertainty of larger work items: 1, 2, 3, 5, 8, 13, 20, 40, and 100. Think of the point sizes as buckets. If a story won't fit into a given size, try the next largest bucket. Note that it's best practice for teams to split any stories larger than an 8 or 13 into smaller stories before accepting them as ready to be worked on in a sprint.

Now is where the fun comes in. In his 2005 book, *Agile Estimating and Planning*, Mike Cohn popularized a game called planning poker, wherein each team member has a set of cards with Fibonacci numbers for voting on the size of stories. Facilitated by the SM, with story context and clarifications provided by the PO, teams vote, discuss the high and low votes, uncover new information, and revote until they converge on the team's estimate for each story.

Jira Align's estimation games module allows geographically dispersed teams to play planning poker remotely. While this can be done using the chat feature, we recommend that a voice conference bridge be open for these critical conversations. Note too that teams play planning poker at various times. We recommend, at a minimum, playing at a backlog refinement session in advance of sprint planning. The reason is that if you wait until sprint planning, there's not enough time for the PO to adjust priorities based on the latest size estimates.

To access the estimation games, go to **Team | Manage | Estimation** from the navigation menu. You can also access them by clicking on the **Estimations** button in the upper-right corner of the **Team Meetings** page. This will bring you to the following screen:

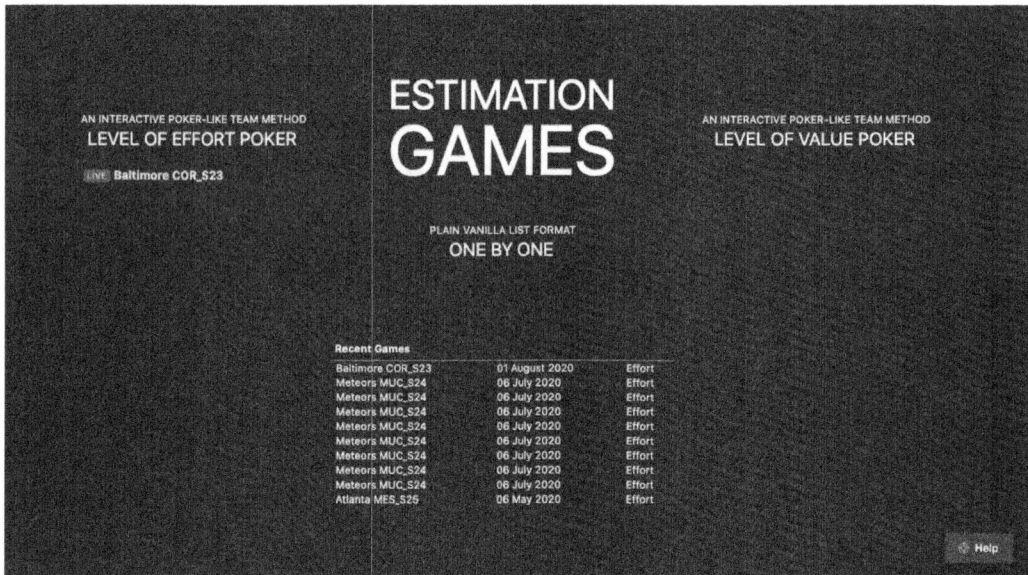

Figure 4.1 – Jira Align estimation games

Next, select the **Level of Effort Poker** option on the left to play traditional planning poker for sizing stories. There is also a **Level of Effort Poker** option and a simple list format option for quick entry of both effort and value.

It's important to note that the story points field is labeled **LOE** (**level of effort**) on story details panels in Jira Align. There may also be a field labeled **LOV** (**level of value**). Since value scores at the story level are not a standard agile practice, we recommend that the Jira Align administrator toggle off LOV under **Administration | Settings | Details Panels Settings**. The LOV functionality predates the current standard of capturing planned and actual business value at the program level, which we will cover in *Chapter 5*, *Program Planning Challenges*.

Once a game begins, it is shown with a red **Live** indicator so that other team members may join in by clicking on it. In *Figure 4.2*, planning poker for the `Baltimore COR_S23` sprint is live. There, you can see that recent games are also displayed.

To start a game, select the program increment, program, team, and the active team sprint to drive the set of stories to be estimated:

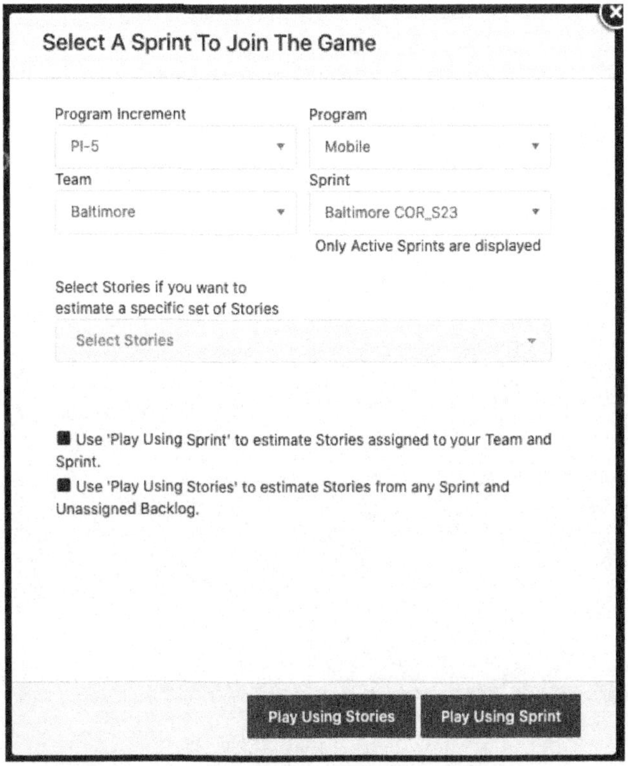

Figure 4.2 – Jira Align estimation games, sprint selection

Next, select one of two ways to play:

- **Play Using Stories**: Choose this option to estimate stories from any sprint, including the unassigned backlog. You will need to select a set of stories to start the estimation game.

- **Play Using Sprint**: Choose this option to estimate stories already assigned to your selected team and sprint. This will select all the applicable stories related to the chosen team sprint.

The individual who starts the planning poker game is called a **dealer**. The dealer has the following special game rights:

- The dealer can select a **Story** from the list on the left (see *Figure 4.3*). After the dealer selects a story, they discuss it with the team. The team members then vote with the cards at the bottom of the page or click on the **Pass** button. They can view assumptions, details of the story, discussions related to the story, or acceptance criteria by clicking the corresponding buttons at the top of the table, as shown in the following screenshot:

Figure 4.3 – Jira Align estimation games, story voting

The dealer can skip the voting round for a player by clicking **Pass** above a user's poker card. In the event that a team member's connection goes down or they get pulled away for any reason, this allows the dealer to maintain good housekeeping and keep the game rolling.

Once the team members have voted, the dealer can save the vote by clicking on the **Save it!** button on the table, as shown here:

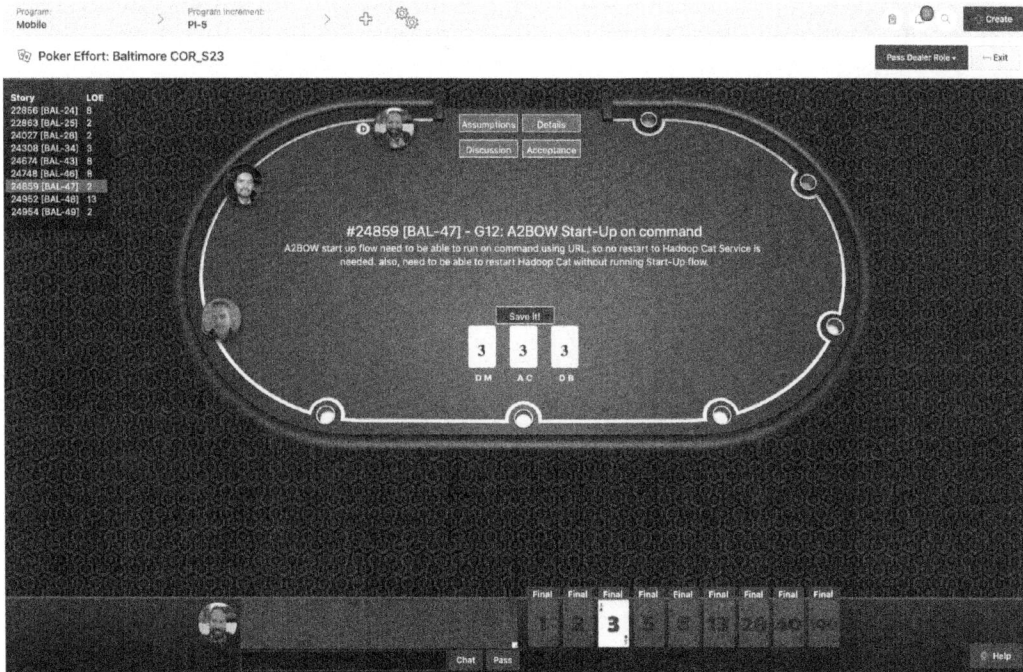

Figure 4.4 – Jira Align estimation games, saving the vote

If a consensus was not reached, the team can repeat the voting by clicking **Play Again** on the table. After the second or third round of voting, the dealer can set an estimation as final based on a discussion with the team by clicking **Final** above the card with the correct number.

During the game, the dealer role may be passed at any time to another team member attending the game. To pass the role, select the **Pass Dealer Role** button in the top right, and then select the name of the team member in the participant list that appears. To exit the game, click on the **Exit** button in the upper-right corner of the page.

Now that our stories are sized, the team is ready to load them into sprints during remote planning.

Loading sprints during remote planning

Another great feature to help with dispersed team planning is the backlog kanban, in sprint view. It provides scrum teams with an easy way to load sprints according to their capacity during PI planning team breakouts. Teams typically begin their first breakout by estimating their capacity for each sprint of the PI based on their historical velocity (visible in either Jira Align or Jira Software) and their availability during the PI, factoring in things such as holidays, vacations, and training. They then identify and size the work items likely needed to implement the program's top prioritized features and begin loading them into upcoming sprints.

Jira Align's backlog kanban in sprint view allows stories and tasks to be dragged from the unassigned backlog on the right into the program increment's sprint columns on the left, keeping track of load against the capacity for each sprint. To begin, select your PI in the configuration bar, then go to the navigation menu and select **Teams | Backlog**. Be sure that **Story Backlog** is selected in the **Viewing** dropdown at the top left of the workspace. Next, click on the **Kanban** button near the top right of the workspace and then select **Sprint View**, as shown in the following screenshot:

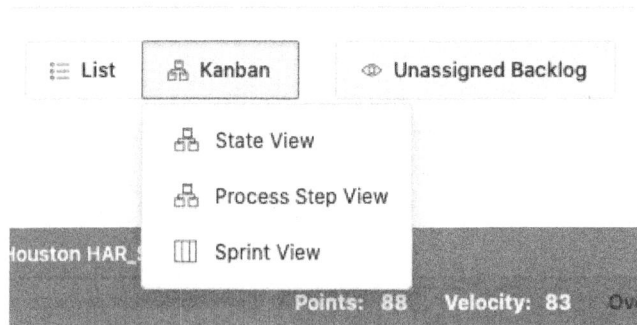

Figure 4.5 – Jira Align backlog kanban button

The backlog kanban in sprint view will now be displayed in the workspace. Next, click in the **Selected Sprints** box and add the sprints you wish to plan for the PI:

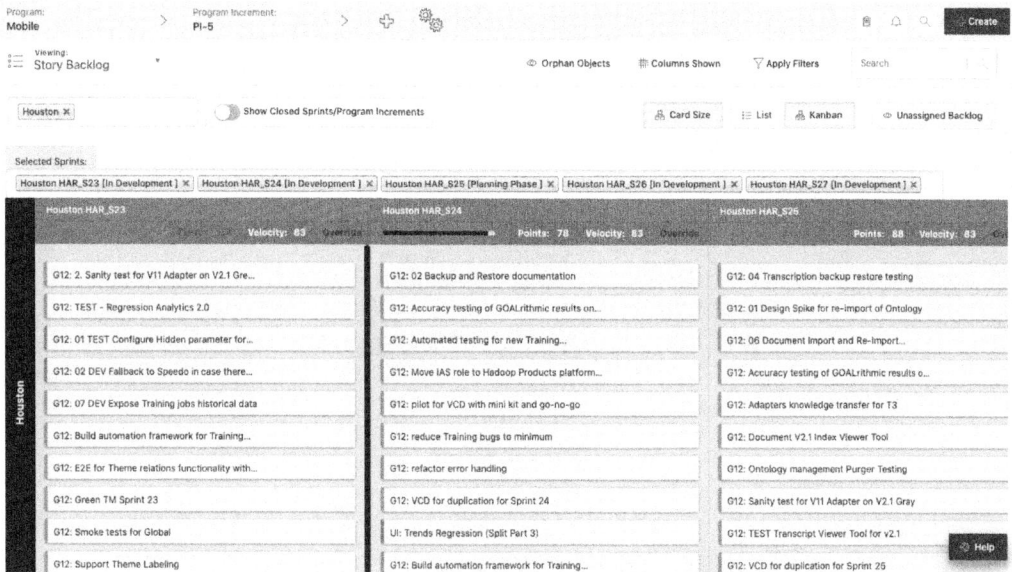

Figure 4.6 – Jira Align backlog kanban, sprint view

Here, we have selected five sprints in PI-5. Next, click on the **Unassigned Backlog** button near the top right of the workspace. This will open a panel on the right showing stories that are not yet assigned to sprints, as shown in the following screenshot:

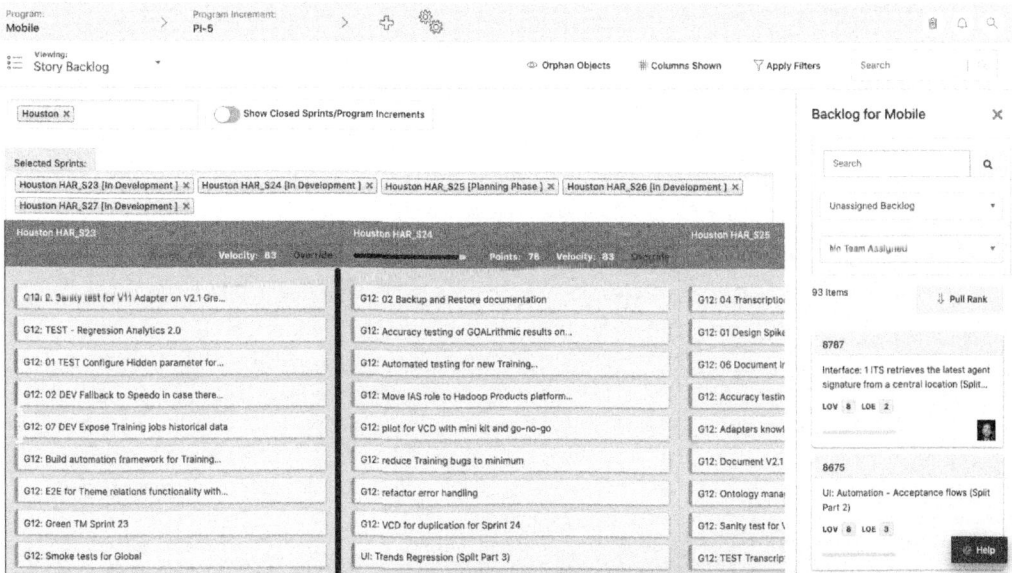

Figure 4.7 – Jira Align unassigned backlog panel

Now, team members can drag stories from the **Unassigned Backlog** on the right into the program increment's sprint columns on the left. The tops of the columns show the total story points loaded into the sprint next to the team's average velocity for the previous five sprints. This provides a good visual indicator of how realistic the load is for each sprint. In *Figure 4.7*, we see that the first sprint column has a red bar indicating an overloaded sprint. An **Override** button allows teams to overwrite the average velocity with the capacity figures they derived based on availability and other factors:

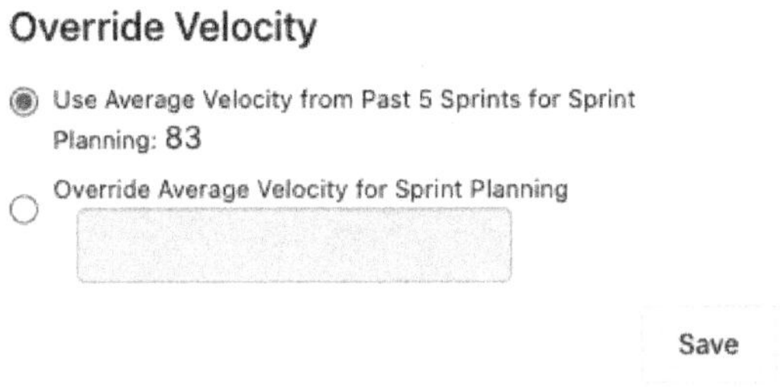

Figure 4.8 – Jira Align sprint capacity

Let's drag **Story 8787** from the unassigned backlog and add it to the second sprint column. Notice that the points loaded increased to **80**, still within the **83**-point average velocity for the past 5 sprints:

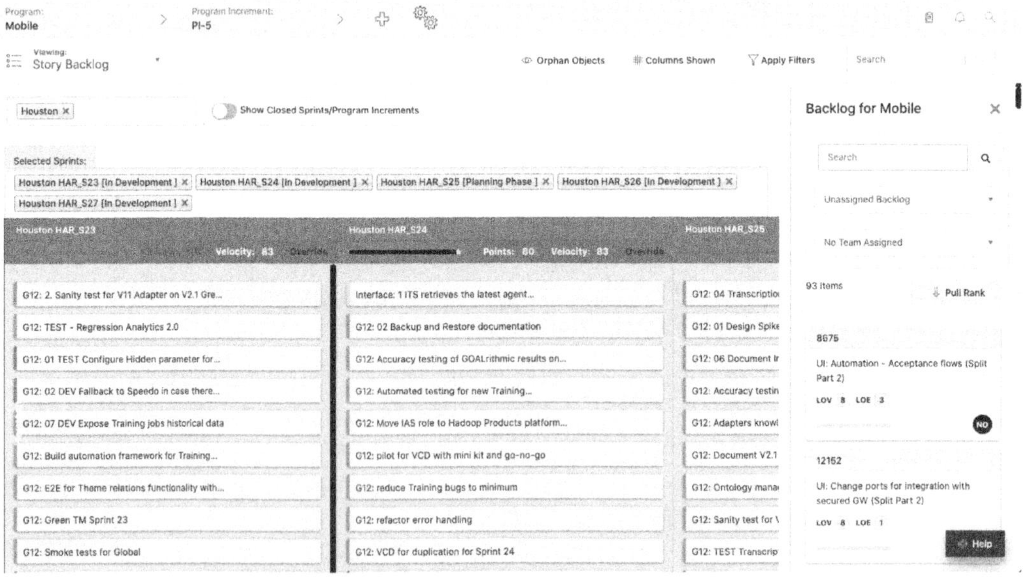

Figure 4.9 – Jira Align backlog kanban

In this way, each team can load their sprints for the program increment. Once the sprints are loaded and PI planning is complete, teams are ready to execute sprints and conduct ceremonies.

Tips and tricks

What does it take to work as a kanban team in Jira Align? High performing and disciplined agile teams often use kanban to deliver a steady stream of work items independent of size or timebox. Rather than velocity, these teams focus on cycle time and throughput as their performance measures.

Jira Align allows your programs to have a mix of scrum and kanban teams. While kanban teams may not size their work items (their metrics are based on item count regardless of size), it is recommended to apply a standard size to their items, such as one point each, for the purposes of roll-up reporting.

To connect a kanban team's board to Jira Align, the Jira Align administrator must add the kanban board under the **Administration | Connectors | Jira Management | Jira Boards** tab. This will create the Jira Align team as a kanban team type.

To set the default size for kanban teams' work items, go to **Teams | Manage | Teams** from the navigation menu and select the team to open its details slide-out panel. Next, enable the **Auto-populate Estimate** toggle and select a value to automatically apply to work items created and assigned to the team.

While kanban teams' work items are not tied to sprints, they are still connected to program increments via the features to which their stories are linked. They can also target features for delivery in a given sprint on the program board. In this way, they can communicate using the common sprint cadence of the program, even though they do not start and stop sprints during the program increment.

Conducting ceremonies and meetings

Predictability is a general delivery challenge that agile frameworks such as scrum seek to address. The cadence of sprints makes events such as planning and retrospectives predictable, and synchronization allows multiple perspectives to be explored and integrated concurrently. The key events that drive cadence and synchronization are known as *ceremonies* and they are integral to success as an agile team.

Jira Align provides tools to facilitate and conduct interactive meetings remotely. Simply go to the navigation menu and select **Team | Team Meetings** to open the Jira Align meetings workspace:

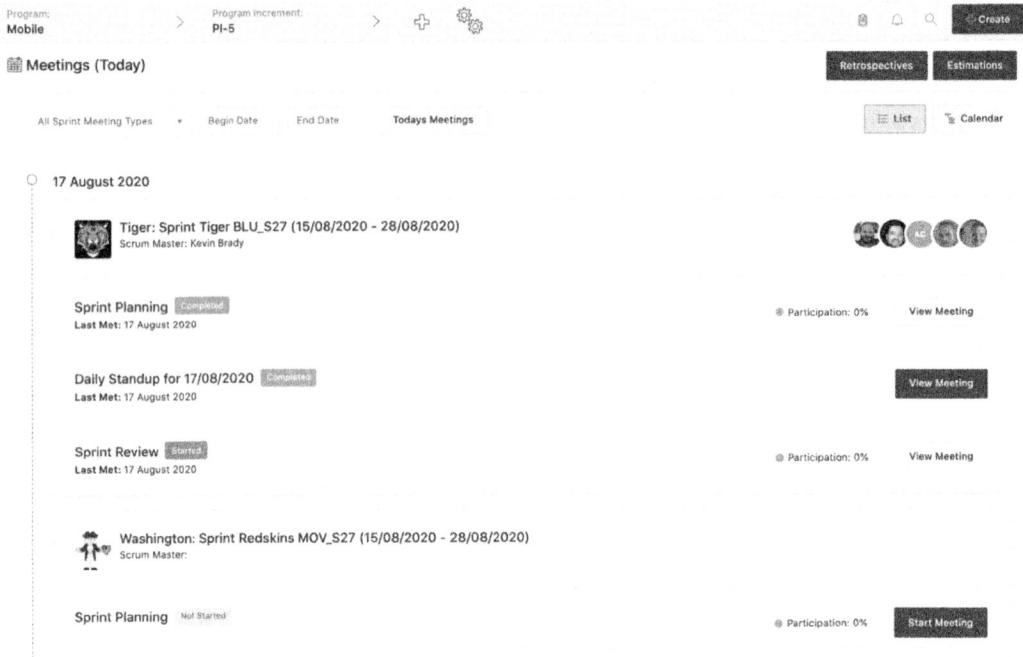

Figure 4.10 – Jira Align meetings

Here you can manage team meetings and launch retrospectives and estimation games. Once you set your program and program increment in the configuration bar, there are two meeting views available:

- **List**: Displays all team-level sprint meetings on a timeline. You can filter the list view further according to meeting types, a date range, or list only today's meetings.

- **Calendar**: Displays a standard calendar (view by month, week, or day) listing all planned team-level sprint ceremonies and holidays:

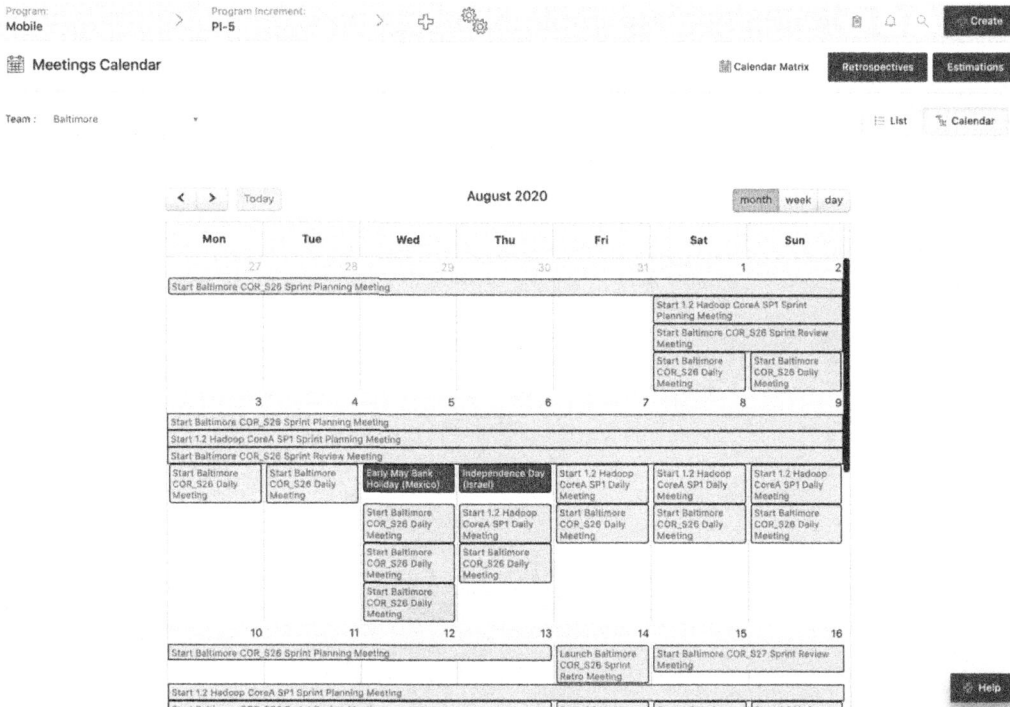

Figure 4.11 – Jira Align meetings calendar

In the preceding screenshot, meetings for the Baltimore team in the Mobile program during PI-5 are displayed on the calendar. To switch to a different team, simply select another team from the dropdown in the top left of the workspace. While in calendar view, you can also click on the **Calendar Matrix** button near the top right of the workspace to display a tracking grid of sprint planning, review, and retrospective ceremonies for the entire program.

Sprint planning

The sprint planning ceremony takes place at the inception of every sprint. It is a timeboxed, collaborative session for the entire team to define what will be delivered in the sprint and how it will be achieved.

To begin, locate the sprint planning meeting in the list or calendar view and then click on the **Start Meeting** button. For a meeting that has already started, you can click on the **Continue Meeting** button.

Once you click **Start Meeting**, it will open the sprint planning meeting page, as shown in the following screenshot:

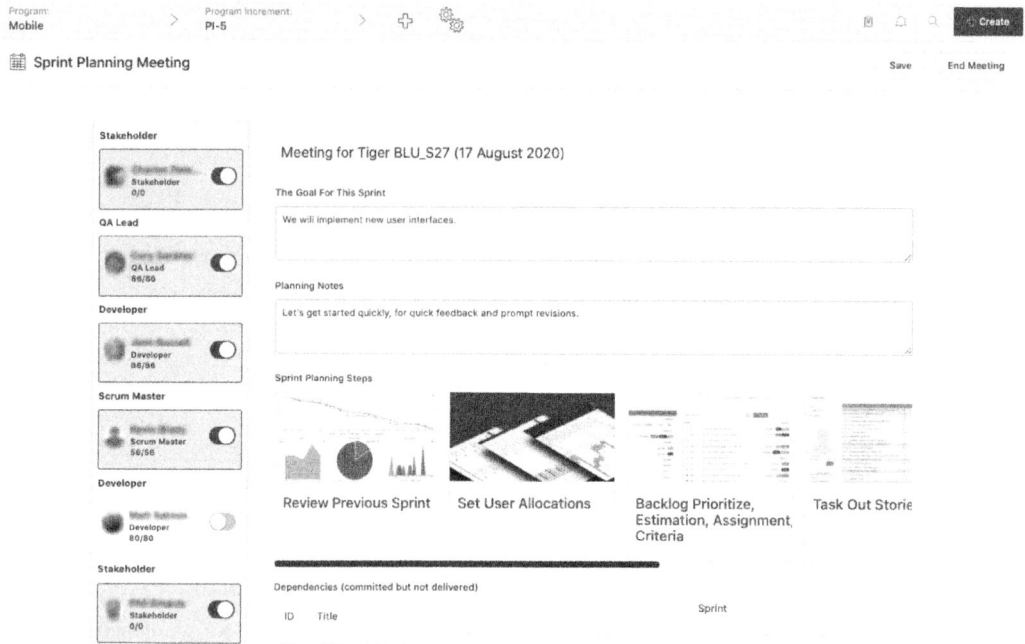

Figure 4.12 – Jira Align sprint planning meeting

Several details are available in the sprint planning meeting workspace. Note that you would need to scroll down in the workspace to see all of the following details:

- **Team**: Team members are shown on the left side of the workspace grouped by role. Here you can record team members' attendance using the toggle on option.

- **The goal for this sprint**: You can add a goal for the sprint. The goal completion will be tracked and validated during the sprint review meeting.

- **Planning notes**: You can add additional planning notes related to the sprint.

- **Sprint planning steps**: Displays a checklist to follow a set of actions to successfully run your sprint planning event.

- **Dependencies (committed but not delivered)**: Displays dependencies assigned to the team and sprint when they are due.

- **Team velocity over last 5 sprints**: When you scroll down, it lists the team's velocity over the last 5 sprints and the average velocity.

- **Sprint scope**: When you scroll down, it lists all the stories loaded in the sprint.

- **Capacity**: When you scroll down, it shows the number of tasks, task hours, sprint allocation hours, and under/over.

- **Team consensus**: When you scroll down, you can set the team consensus to ensure that the team has agreed to the sprint goal, tasks, and effort planned for the sprint.

You can complete the meeting by clicking on the **End Meeting** button in the top-right corner of the workspace. It will prompt you to end the meeting and, if required, you can send the sprint planning meeting notes via email.

Now that the sprint is planned, let's explore how the team drives sprint execution with a daily collaborative synchronization meeting.

Daily standup

The daily scrum, often called a standup, provides a daily opportunity for the team to synchronize on work activities. This meeting is for the team, not for managers to obtain status. Visitors may observe in the spirit of openness, one of scrum's five core values. The meeting is timeboxed with a recommended limit of 15 minutes. Each team member shares a quick update on what they completed yesterday, what they commit to completing today, and what issues are blocking them. The scrum master will note impediments and sometimes schedule a quick follow-on meeting for a deeper dive into urgent issues.

To begin, locate the daily standup meeting for a given date in the meetings list or calendar view and then click on the **Start Meeting** button. For a meeting that has already started, you can click on the **View Meeting** button. For a meeting that has ended, it will display a meeting summary.

Once you click **Start Meeting**, it will open the daily standup meeting page, as shown in the following screenshot:

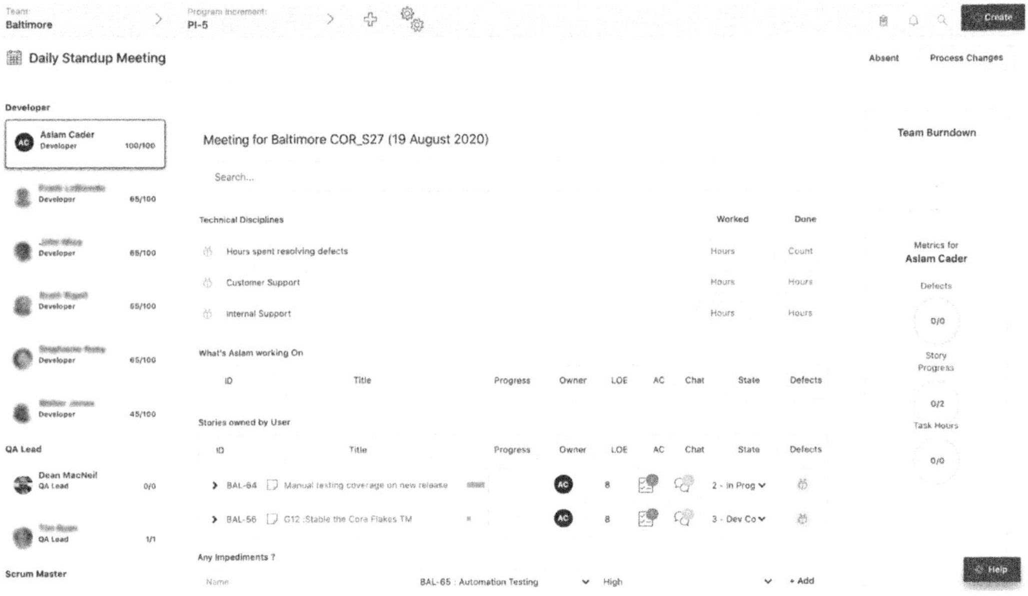

Figure 4.13 – Jira Align daily standup meeting

Several details are available in the daily standup meeting workspace. Note that you would need to scroll down in the workspace to see all of the following details:

- **Team**: Team members are shown on the left side of the workspace grouped by role. Clicking on each team member allows the facilitator to switch between team members for status updates. The meeting page displays information based on the selected team member. You can click on the **Absent** button in the top right of the workspace to record a team member's absence.

- **Team Burndown**: Click on the **Team Burndown** link to see the sprint status and burndown chart.

- **Metrics for user**: View the total defects closed, the total story points progress, and the total hours of logged time against tasks for the selected team member.

- **Technical disciplines**: Record time in hours against each technical discipline.

- **What's the user working on**: Display the stories assigned to the team member.

- **Stories owned by the user**: List the team member's stories for the current sprint.

- **Any impediments**: Add any impediments identified during the standup.

Click on the **End Meeting** button to end the daily standup meeting.

Now that the team has executed the sprint, it's time to review what they delivered.

Sprint review

The sprint review is a timeboxed meeting, generally between 1 and 4 hours, that takes place at the end of each sprint and is attended by the team and stakeholders. During the meeting, the PO or team members demonstrate the working product features completed during the sprint. The focus is on *what* they delivered, not *how* they delivered it.

To begin, locate the sprint review meeting in the meetings list or calendar view and then click on the **Start Meeting** button. For a meeting that has already started, you can click on the **View Meeting** button.

Once you click **Start Meeting**, it will open the sprint review meeting page, as shown in the following screenshot:

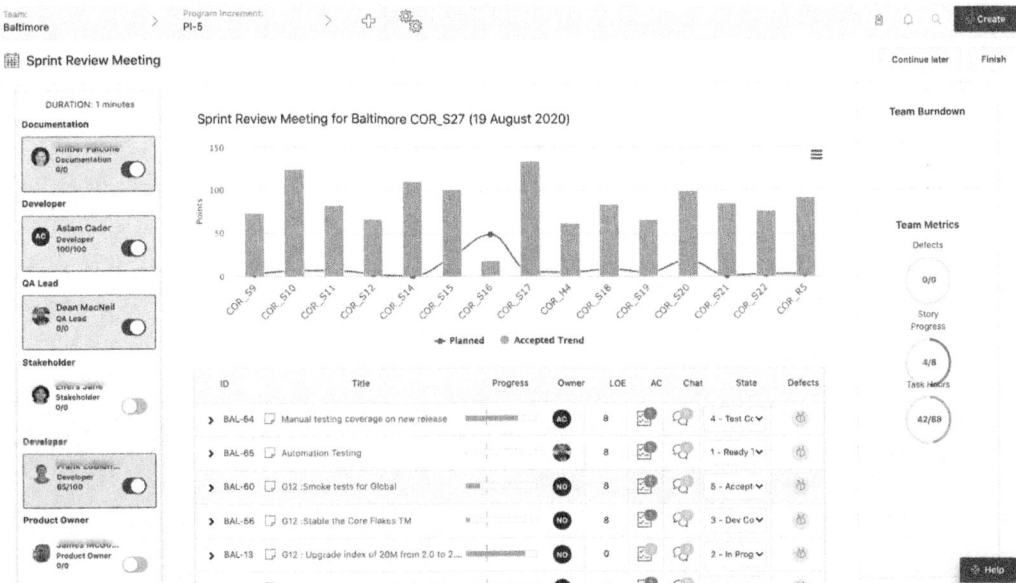

Figure 4.14 – Jira Align sprint review meeting

Several details are available in the sprint review meeting workspace. Note that you would need to scroll down in the workspace to see all of the following details:

- **Team**: Team members are shown on the left side of the workspace grouped by role. Here you can record team members' attendance at the meeting by using the toggle on option.

- **Planned vs Accepted Trend**: Shows planned versus accepted story points across several sprints.

- **Story List**: Displays stories planned for the sprint. You can click on the pointing-angle symbol to the left of a story to expand it and show its tasks. You can change a story's state, for example, to complete the story and accept it. Accepted stories will display with a light blue colored background.

- **Team Burndown**: Click on the **Team Burndown** link to see the sprint status and burndown chart.

- **Team Metrics**: View the team's metrics for total defects closed, total story points progress, and total hours of logged time against tasks.

- **Future Sprint Forecast**: Jira Align's sprint review meeting allows you to go beyond the traditional demonstration of what was delivered in the sprint to capture the team's general sentiment as they close one sprint and move to the next. This is known as the sprint forecast and resembles a weather report, as shown in the following screenshot:

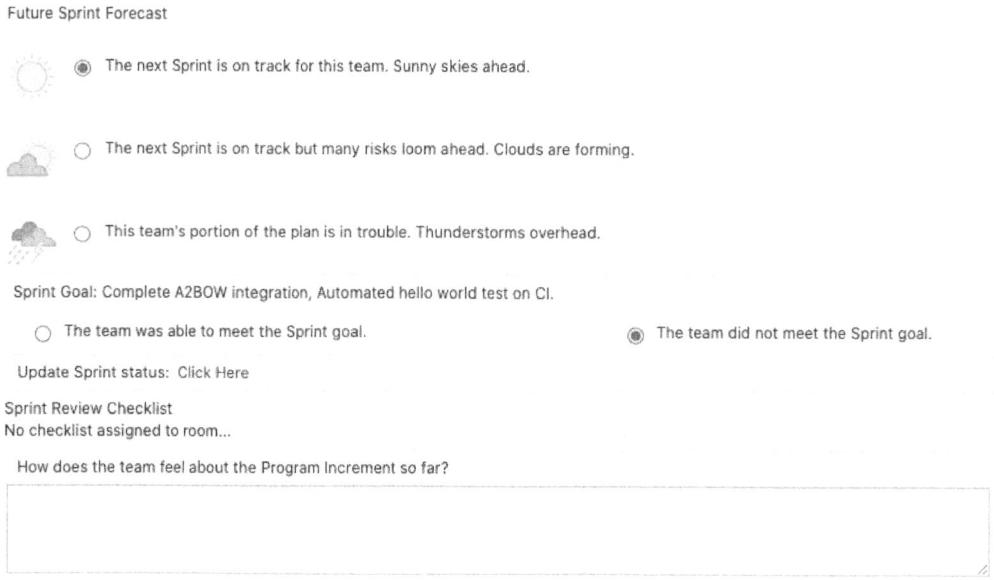

Future Sprint Forecast

⊙ The next Sprint is on track for this team. Sunny skies ahead.

○ The next Sprint is on track but many risks loom ahead. Clouds are forming.

○ This team's portion of the plan is in trouble. Thunderstorms overhead.

Sprint Goal: Complete A2BOW integration, Automated hello world test on CI.

  ○ The team was able to meet the Sprint goal.   ⊙ The team did not meet the Sprint goal.

Update Sprint status: Click Here

Sprint Review Checklist
No checklist assigned to room...

How does the team feel about the Program Increment so far?

Figure 4.15 – Jira Align sprint review, future sprint forecast

- **Sprint Goal**: Scroll down to record whether the team met its sprint goal.

- **Update Sprint status**: Scroll down to change the sprint status to **Completed**.

- **Sprint Review Checklist**: Scroll down to display a checklist to run your sprint review step by step.

- **Additional notes**: Scroll down to add additional notes, for example, to track team sentiment about the PI so far.

To end the sprint review meeting, click on the **Finish** button in the top-right corner of the workspace.

Now that the team has reviewed *what* they delivered during the sprint, it's time to reflect on *how* they delivered it, for continuous learning and improvement purposes.

Retrospectives

As part of the sprint cadence, teams take time to reflect on how to become more efficient and effective, openly sharing ideas for adjustments and improvements (*Agile Manifesto*, Principle 12). This takes place during a timeboxed sprint retrospective, occurring after the sprint review and prior to the next sprint planning event. In Jira Align, the retrospective is timeboxed to 1 hour and you may restart the meeting if more time is required. During the retrospective, the team will often create improvement backlog items to be implemented in the next sprint.

There are several retrospective formats and we recommend varying them to keep team engagement high and fresh ideas coming each sprint. The most basic retrospective format is for the team to discuss the following:

- What went well

- What could be improved

- What they commit to improving in the next sprint

To begin, click on the **Retrospectives** button in the top-right corner of the meetings workspace. This will open the team retrospective dashboard, as shown in the following screenshot:

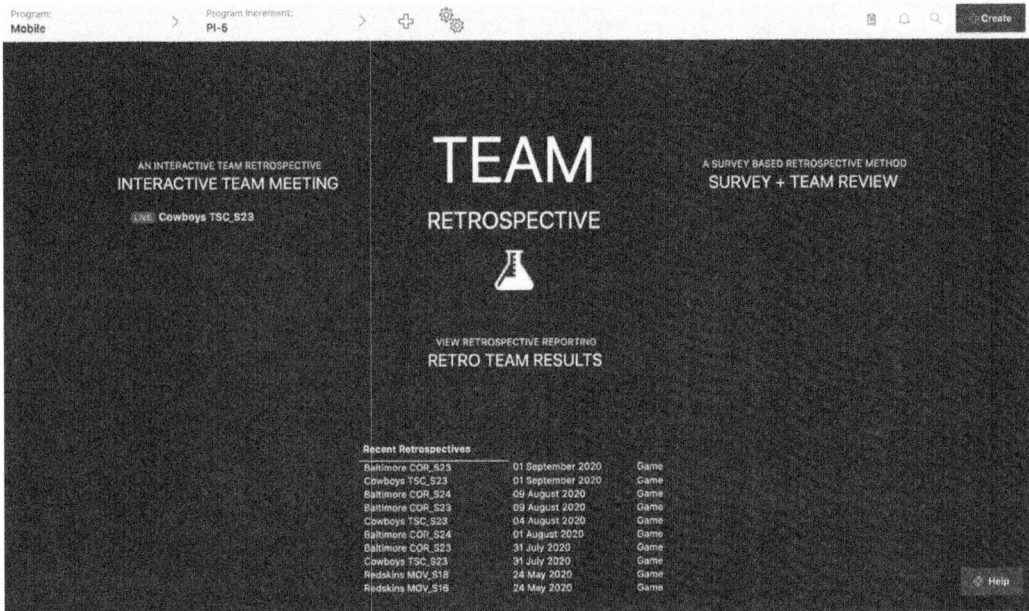

Figure 4.16 – Jira Align retrospective dashboard

To start the sprint retrospective, click on the **Interactive Team Meeting** link, which will open a prompt, as shown in the following screenshot:

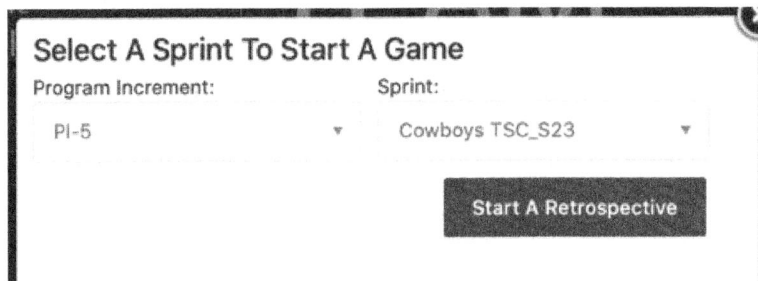

Figure 4.17 – Jira Align start a retrospective

Here, you will select the program increment and sprint, and then click on the **Start A Retrospective** button to launch the retrospective room shown in the following screenshot. The meeting is created with a series of time-boxed agenda items and allows team members to share and collaborate interactively:

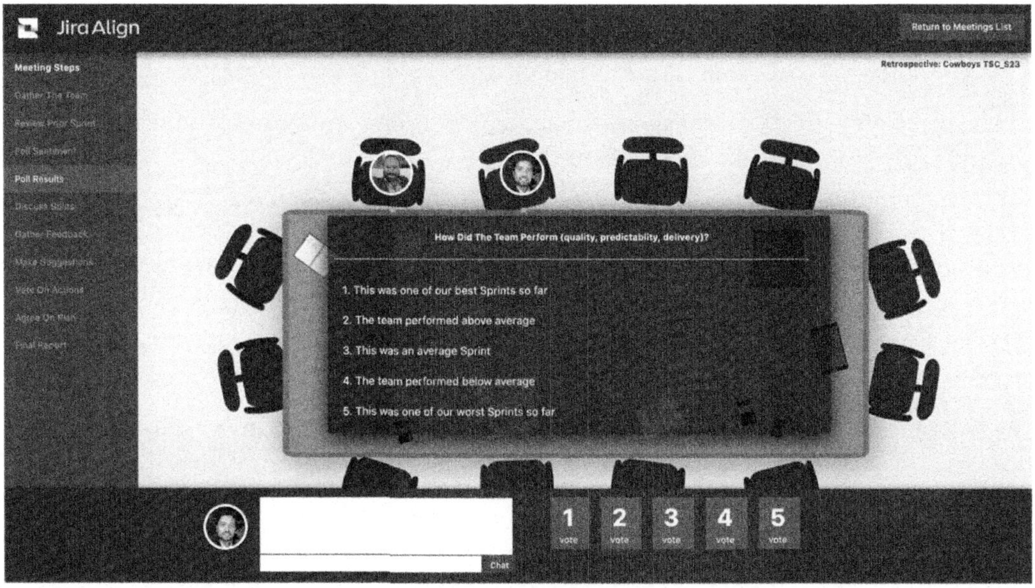

Figure 4.18 – Jira Align live team retrospective

Here are the retrospective meeting steps, as shown on the left side of the retrospective room:

1. **Gather the team**: Start the retrospective meeting once the team joins.

2. **Review prior sprint**: Displays action items from the previous sprint retrospective. The facilitator marks them complete if done.

3. **Poll sentiment**: The team votes on how they felt about the sprint (covering teamwork, attitude, and improvement). The scale is 1 to 5, where 1 is the best and 5 is the worst.

4. **Poll results**: The team votes on how they performed (covering quality, predictability, and delivery). The scale is 1 to 5, where 1 is the best and 5 is the worst.

5. **Discuss splits**: Discuss the reasons for stories being split during the sprint (for example, due to underestimating the size) and ideas on how to avoid splits.

6. **Gather feedback**: Collect feedback on what went well and what did not go well during the sprint.

7. **Make suggestions**: Explore and share ideas that the team could implement in the next sprint to improve performance and overall team satisfaction.

8. **Vote on actions**: The team votes on action items for improvement. The scale is 1 to 10, where 10 is awesome and 1 is bad.

9. **Agree on plan**: The team agrees on action items for improvement in the next sprint. As a minimum, 1, and up to 3 items, will be selected.

10. **Final report**: End the retrospective and share the meeting summary notes.

At the end of the meeting, Jira Align generates a retrospective summary report. You can access this by clicking on the **Retro Team Results** link on the retrospective dashboard. You can also access the team review meeting and survey results by clicking on the **Survey + Team Review** link.

Now that we have learned how to facilitate ceremonies in Jira Align, let's explore how to produce measures of the teams' delivery and predictability and how to celebrate teams and individuals for their great work.

Reviewing sprints and giving shoutouts

When reviewing team performance, some key metrics to consider are team happiness, committed versus delivered, and predictability. While burndowns and velocity are important for teams to review in Jira, the Jira Align sprint metrics (M1) report provides scrum masters, RTEs, team leads, and others with a way to see sprint-by-sprint metrics for an entire program increment. It's a useful report to review with teams during sprint planning or retrospectives. It helps teams see how they are progressing toward team and program goals for the PI. The focus of the report is on team delivery and predictability, not on velocity or comparing teams to one another. To get the most out of this report, teams must use the ceremonies within the Jira Align meetings module, as discussed earlier.

To begin, go to the navigation bar and select **Teams | Track | Sprint Metrics (M1)**. This will open the M1 report, as shown in the following screenshot. The report can be run for a single team by clicking on the **Extra Configs** button in the top right of the workspace, or for all teams in the program. The report can be saved and shared outside the tool by clicking on the **Capture** button in the top-right corner, as can be seen in the following screenshot:

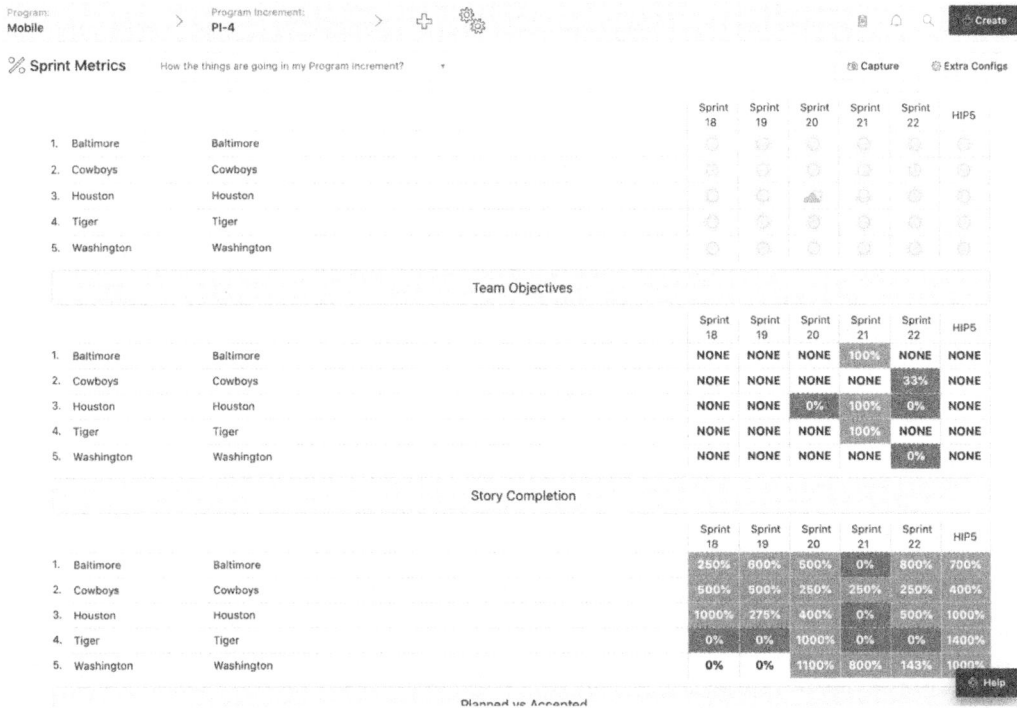

		Sprint 18	Sprint 19	Sprint 20	Sprint 21	Sprint 22	HIP5
1. Baltimore	Baltimore						
2. Cowboys	Cowboys						
3. Houston	Houston						
4. Tiger	Tiger						
5. Washington	Washington						

Team Objectives

		Sprint 18	Sprint 19	Sprint 20	Sprint 21	Sprint 22	HIP5
1. Baltimore	Baltimore	NONE	NONE	NONE	100%	NONE	NONE
2. Cowboys	Cowboys	NONE	NONE	NONE	NONE	33%	NONE
3. Houston	Houston	NONE	NONE	0%	100%	0%	NONE
4. Tiger	Tiger	NONE	NONE	NONE	100%	NONE	NONE
5. Washington	Washington	NONE	NONE	NONE	NONE	0%	NONE

Story Completion

		Sprint 18	Sprint 19	Sprint 20	Sprint 21	Sprint 22	HIP5
1. Baltimore	Baltimore	250%	800%	500%	0%	800%	700%
2. Cowboys	Cowboys	500%	500%	250%	250%	250%	400%
3. Houston	Houston	1000%	275%	400%	0%	500%	1000%
4. Tiger	Tiger	0%	0%	1000%	0%	0%	1400%
5. Washington	Washington	0%	0%	1100%	800%	143%	1000%

Planned vs Accepted

Figure 4.19 – Jira Align sprint metrics M1 report

The M1 report displays a series of metric grids. Here we describe each metric, color indicators if applicable, and any prerequisites for populating the grid. Some metric grids, as noted, allow you to open the sprint coaching report, which highlights variances between what was committed for the sprint versus what was delivered, a useful tool for scrum masters in their role as agile coaches. Note, you would need to scroll down to see all grids.

- **Team emotion**: Displays an indicator of team happiness during each sprint using the analogy of a weather report (sunny, partly cloudy, or cloudy). Prerequisite: Team emotion captured during the sprint review.

- **Team objectives**: Displays a percentage metric (# objectives completed / # objectives planned per sprint). Prerequisites: The team created sprint objectives during sprint planning and voted on sprint objective completeness during the sprint review. Green = 100% or greater, orange 85% to 99%, and red < 85%. Click any colored cell to open the sprint coaching report.

- **Story completion**: Displays a percentage metric (# stories completed / # stories planed per sprint). Green = 100% or greater, orange 85% to 99%, and red < 85%. Click any colored cell to open the sprint coaching report.

- **Planned vs accepted**: Displays a percentage metric (# points completed / # points planned per sprint). Green = 100% or greater, orange 85% to 99%, and red < 85%. Click any colored cell to open the sprint coaching report.

- **Splits and drops**: Displays the sum of all splits (when stories are split, usually due to incompleteness at the end of a sprint) and drops (when stories are dropped from the sprint by moving them to the backlog or next sprint). White = 0 splits or drops, orange = 1 split or drop, and red > 1 split or drop. Click any colored cell to open the sprint coaching report.

- **Team defects**: Displays the sum of defects regardless of state. White = 0 defects, orange = 1 defect, and red > 1 defect. Click any colored cell to open the sprint coaching report.

- **Goal state**: Indicates whether the sprint goal was met. Prerequisites: The team defined the sprint goals during sprint planning and voted on whether the goal was met during the sprint review. The sprint goals themselves are displayed in a grid below the goal state metric grid.

- **Sprint completion**: Indicates whether the sprint was marked as complete. Prerequisite: Team marked the sprint as complete during the sprint review.

Now that we know the data captured in the M1 report grids, let's take a look at the Sprint Coaching report (also known as the Sprint Wrap-Up report) that is accessible by clicking on the cells in many of the grids as noted above. This report is beneficial to scrum masters, product owners, and team members for assessing if the overall goal of the sprint was achieved. It details the team plan at the beginning of the sprint in contrast with the final result, and may be helpful to review with stakeholders during the Sprint Review. Click on the colored indicator cells on the M1 report or go to the navigation menu and select **Teams | Track | Sprint Coaching** to open the report, shown in the next screenshot.

Program: Program Increment:
Mobile   >   PI-5   >   ➕   ⚙️   📋 🔔 🔍 |

↱ **Sprint Coaching**   How did our team do against the goals we set for this S... ▾

Sprint: Baltimore COR_S24   ▾

🔲 Sprint Goal / Objectives

"Complete A2BOW integration, Automated hello world test on CI."

This Team did not run a Sprint Review Meeting for this Sprint

3495   SA - A2BOW integration done with poTestl and training - SA - A2BOW integration done with poTestl and training   Baltimore   Sprint 24

⚏ The Committed Plan

Committed Work	Task Breakdown	Plan Efficiency	Total Effort	Total Value	Acceptance
13 User Stories	**0** Task Hours	**31** Buffer Hours	**102** Effort Points	**208** Value Points	**30** Tests
13 at the start of the Sprint			102 at the start of the Sprint	208 at the start of the Sprint	

🏃 The Core Team

The Statistics

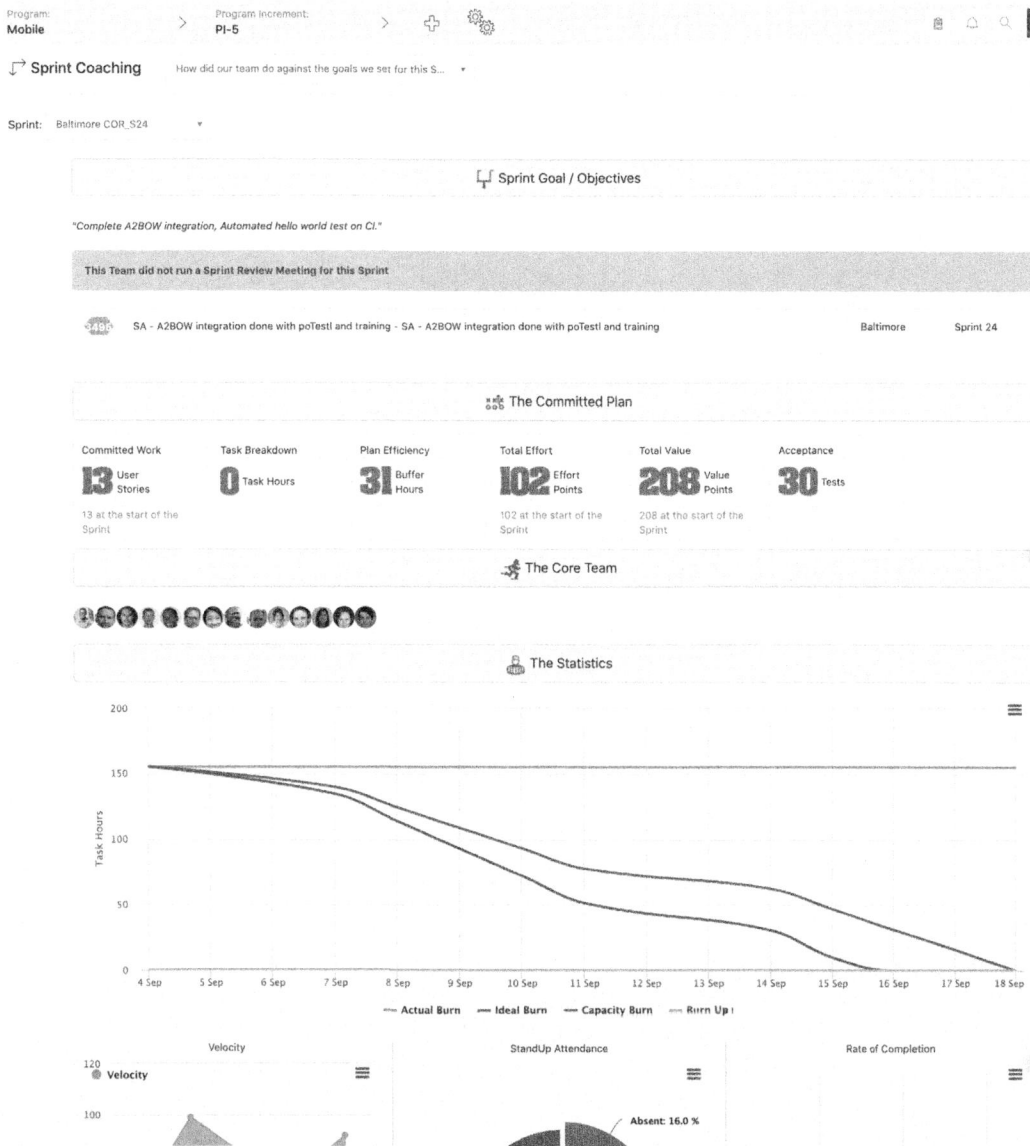

Figure 4.20 – Jira Align sprint coaching report

Here we see sections for the following information. Note, you would need to scroll down to see all the sections.

- **Sprint Goal/Objectives**: Displays the sprint goal and objectives.

- **The Committed Plan**: Details the commitments made during sprint planning, including the number of user stories, initial Development and QA task hours, and effort and value points.

- **The Core Team**: Lists the team members. Click or hover over a photo to see the team member's name and role.

- **The Statistics:**

    Burndown chart shows how task hours are burned down in the sprint compared to the ideal. If the sprint is not yet complete, the Estimated Remaining Burn is shown.

    Velocity chart displays the velocity for the team over the past several sprints.

    Standup Attendance displays the attendance at the interactive meetings available within Jira Align.

    Rate of Completion shows the Dev Complete stories in orange and the Test Complete stories in blue.

    Sprint Story Progress: Click on **Show Details** to view the overall sprint story progress. You see the progress bars, story health, and acceptance criteria. Value points, effort points, and the total number of hours spent are also shown here.

- **Final Score**: Shows what was delivered in terms of stories, quality metrics, and unburned task hours.

- **Weather Forecast**: Shows how the team feels about upcoming sprints. The weather prediction is set using the interactive Sprint Review meeting within Jira Align.

The report paints an overall picture of the sprint: Were commitments met? What was delivered? How is team velocity tracking? How is the team emotion trending? Having the various charts and graphs handy can enable the team to make adjustments in the upcoming sprint. For example, you may need to adjust the amount of points/task hours in future sprints or add more resources to increase velocity.

Tips and tricks

Teams will generally refer to the Velocity Chart in Jira Software, which shows actual versus committed velocity across several sprints. For an alternate visualization that shows velocity variance (velocity of a sprint divided by the velocity of the previous sprint) over time, try Jira Align's Velocity Variance report by going to the navigation menu, clicking on the search icon (magnifying glass), and then searching for "Velocity Variance."

Now that we've reviewed how the team delivered in the sprint, let's acknowledge the collective and individual contributions that stood out. An important part of team synergy and collaboration is acknowledging individual and team accomplishments such as company anniversaries and performance awards. This is done in the Shout Out module. To access it, go to the navigation menu and select **Team | Manage | Shout-Outs**.

On the left side of the workspace, as shown in the next image, you will see three sections to view awards: **Shout-outs** lists the awards by the name of the award, **People** lists the awards by recipient, and **Year** lists the awards by year. At the top of the workspace, there are three buttons to display awards: The **Feed** button displays the most recent awards, **My Shout-Outs** displays all awards earned by you, and **Leaderboard** displays a hall of fame for award recipients ordered by award points earned. You can view all available awards by clicking on the **Shout-Out Awards** List link in the top left corner:

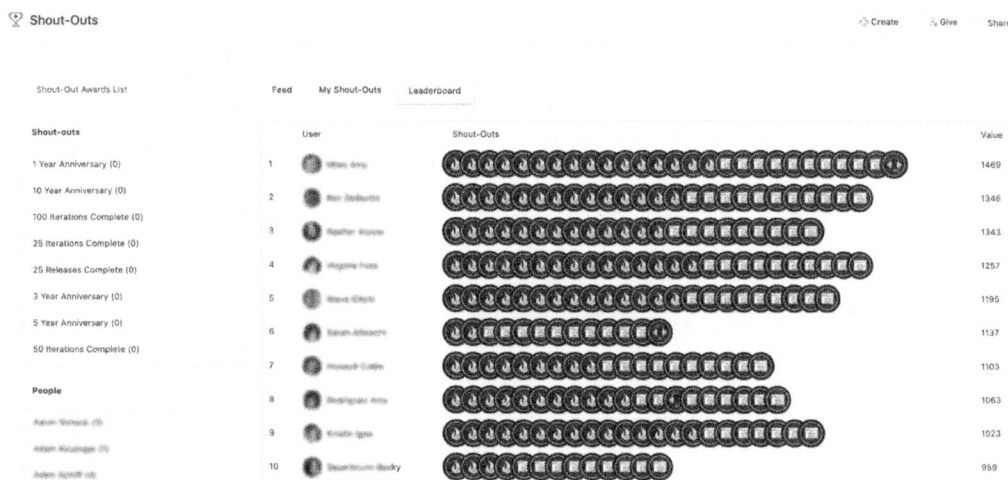

Figure 4.21 – Jira Align shout-out leaderboard

Let's award a teammate for going the extra mile in delivering a high-quality shippable product increment. To do so, click on the **Give** button in the top-right corner of the workspace and a panel will open on the right so you can select an individual or members of a team. Next, choose the award for each individual. Here we choose the **Extra Mile Award**:

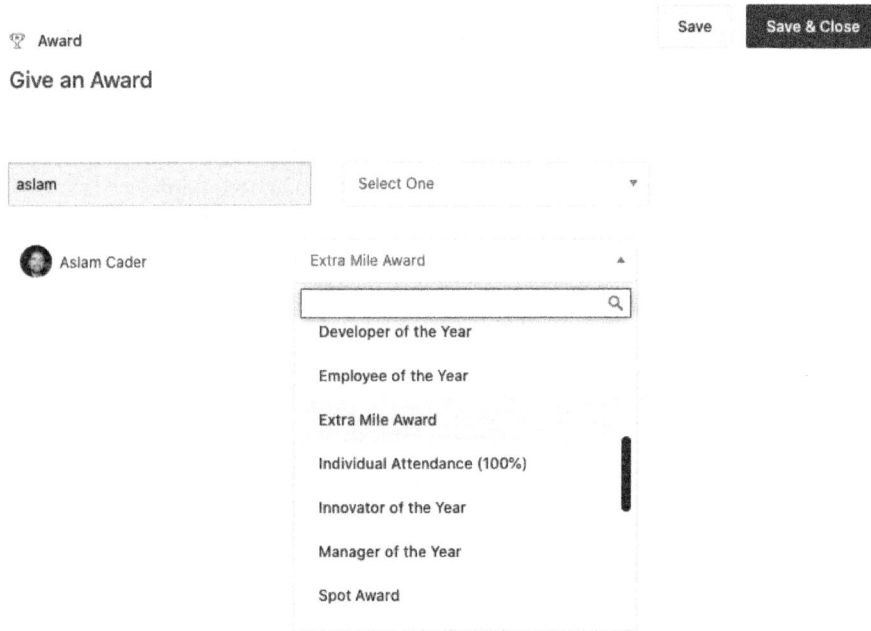

Figure 4.22 – Jira Align give an award

The award is applied to the team member's profile. To see it there, go to **User Menu | Edit Profile | Your Awards**. The team member will also receive an alert notification as follows:

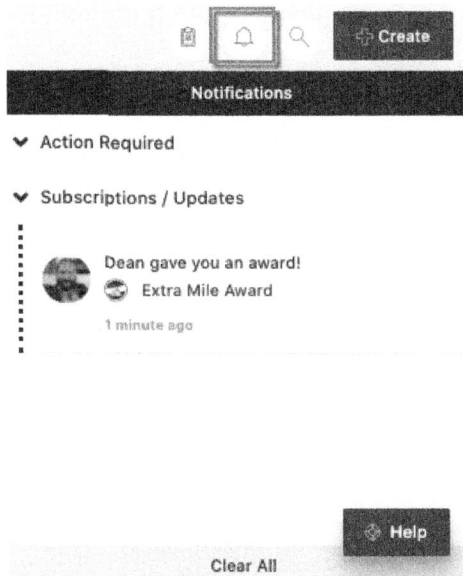

Figure 4.23 – Jira Align new award notification

You can create new awards by clicking on the **Create** button to open the window shown in the next image:

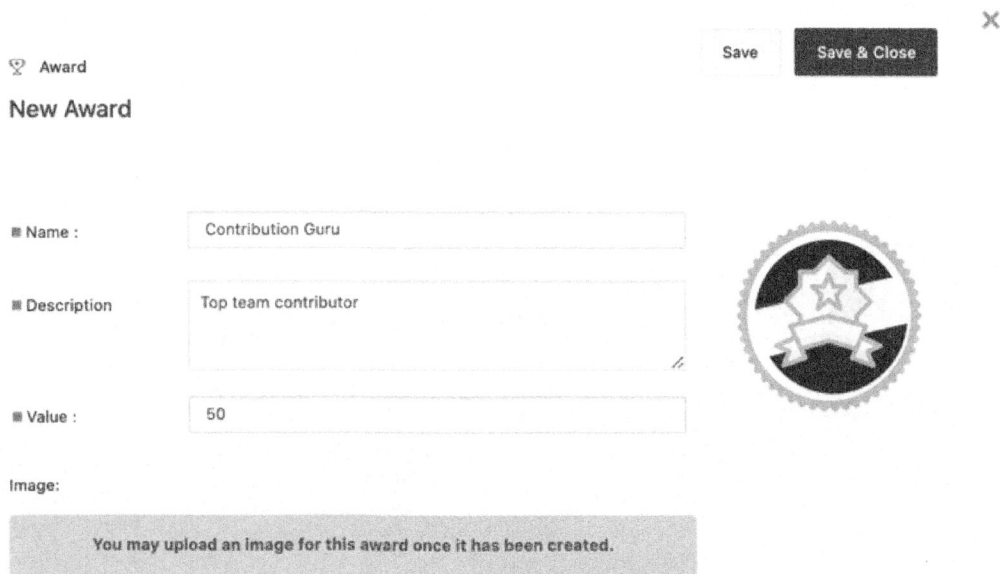

Figure 4.24 – Jira Align new award creation

Here you will need to provide the following details:

- **Name**: Add a meaningful name to your award, such as `Contribution Guru`.
- **Description**: Add a description to the award, such as `Top team contributor`.
- **Value**: Add a points value to the award. The points will be used for the leaderboard.
- **Image**: Upload an image or add a badge to present the award.

Shout-outs create a sense of gamification and encourage teams to strive and do better. As illustrated in *Figure 1.1, Alignment toward transformation by connecting strategy with execution*, shout-outs further shape the culture and contribute to a continuous learning organization.

Summary

In this chapter, we discussed common challenges faced by geographically dispersed teams in today's world and how Jira Align can help keep teams connected through collaborative team tools. We looked at some key features that aid team agile practices, such as remote planning poker, sprint planning, and other ceremonies. We then explored how these ceremonies drive sprint execution and the resulting metrics that help guide delivery and predictability. Lastly, we learned how to recognize individuals in Jira Align for their contributions and give shout-outs to increase team morale.

In the next two chapters, we shift from teams to teams of teams. There we will unfold common challenges faced at this higher level and how Jira Align answers them by enabling effective agile planning and execution at the program level.

Questions

1. What do you call the Jira Software users synced in Jira Align?
2. What are the two types of estimation games in Jira Align?
3. What are the key measures produced in the sprint metrics (M1) report?
4. What are the agile ceremonies you could facilitate within Jira Align?
5. How do you award team members in Jira Align for their great work?

Further reading

- *Jira Software Essentials*, by Patrick Li (Packt, 2018)
- *The Professional ScrumMaster's Handbook*, by Stacia Viscardi (Packt, 2013)

5
Program Planning Challenges

In this chapter, we focus on the common problems that organizations face when planning at the program level, which is considered the *sweet spot* of both agile at scale and Jira Align. Agile frameworks such as scrum work well for a single product development team or a handful of teams that sync up regularly via a scrum of scrums meeting. But what if you've got 5 to 12 agile teams working together on a set of features each business quarter? The general term for a group of teams delivering in this manner is a *program*. Now, what if you have several programs? The effort to coordinate teams has now leveled up to coordinating teams of teams. This is where agile scaling frameworks and the tools that support them come into play. Regardless of the scaling framework you choose, Jira Align helps solve this coordination challenge.

While a team delivers stories in sprints, a program delivers features within business quarters. Features are the middle-sized work item between portfolio epics and stories. While stories are the basic building block of value delivery, features are sized appropriately for display on roadmaps and program boards, and to be associated with release vehicles and products in Jira Align. This chapter will prepare you for the next chapter, where we cover program-level execution.

In this chapter, we will cover the following topics:

- Building product roadmaps
- Planning for value delivery as a program
- Organizing around value to reduce dependencies
- Visualizing program velocity for planning and predictability

The key construct we explore in this chapter is program-level planning, that is, planning to deliver business value as a coordinated team of teams. By the end of the chapter, you will know how to build live product roadmaps of work items and objectives, utilize the program board for quarterly planning, capture planned and delivered value, measure value delivery predictability, manage risks and dependencies, and measure program velocity for better planning.

Building product roadmaps

We begin our discussion of program-level planning with Jira Align's live product roadmaps, which can run the gamut from aspirational, long-range product planning roadmaps to more definitive, feature-level roadmaps for the next PI. Unlike traditional static roadmaps, these are connected to the actual work items to provide real-time insights and statuses.

An essential tool for product managers, roadmaps provide a timeline of key milestones and delivery targets to communicate product direction and align stakeholder expectations. Roadmaps can strengthen the relationship between the organization and its customers and suppliers, enabling transparency and collaborative planning for future value delivery.

To view a roadmap, first set your context in the configuration bar and then go to the navigation menu and select **Program | Manage | Roadmaps**. The Jira Align roadmap module has three views: **Work**, **Program Increment**, and **Release Vehicle**. These are selected from the view dropdown in the upper-left corner of the workspace, as shown in the following screenshot:

Live Roadmap

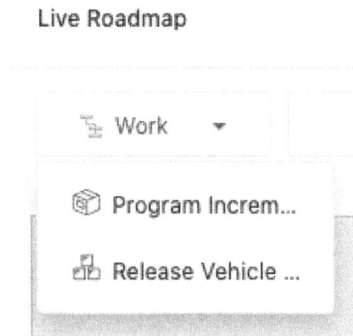

Figure 5.1 – Jira Align roadmap views

We will first explore the functionality of the work view before learning how to configure three particular work view roadmaps suggested by **SAFe**. In the next chapter, we will explore the program increment and release vehicle views.

Work view roadmap

The work view roadmap is a timeline that displays a list of planned and/or unplanned work items. There are two options for the timescale: **sprints by program increment** and **month by quarter**. Click on the cube button to select the former or the calendar button for the latter:

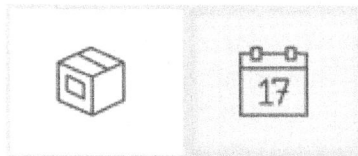

Figure 5.2 – Jira Align roadmap timescale options

The work items displayed are features, portfolio epics, or themes. Work items can be rolled up under their parent by selecting either **feature by portfolio epic** or **portfolio epic by theme** from the context dropdown. In the following screenshot, we've selected **feature by portfolio epic** and set the timescale to show **sprints by program increment**:

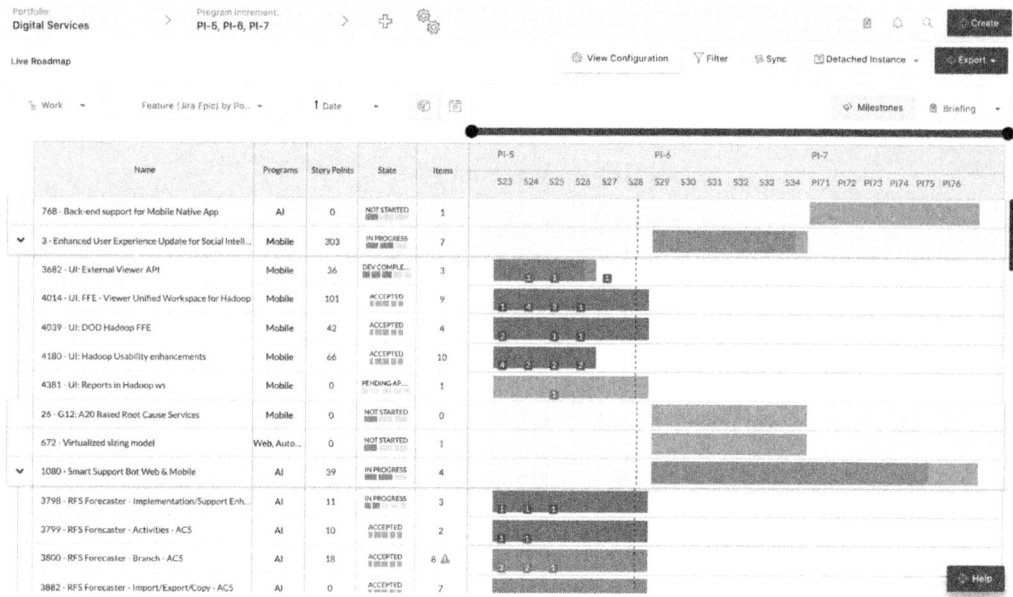

Figure 5.3 – Jira Align roadmap work view

Note that the feature rows are shown under the portfolio epic rows. A downward-pointing arrow symbol at the far left of each portfolio epic row indicates that it is expanded to show child work items. Click on the arrow symbol to collapse the child rows and show only portfolio epics.

Next, we note that the list of work items can be ordered by the earliest or latest start dates, best or worst health, or program rank. To select one of these options, click on the dropdown to the left of the timescale options to see the list shown in the following screenshot:

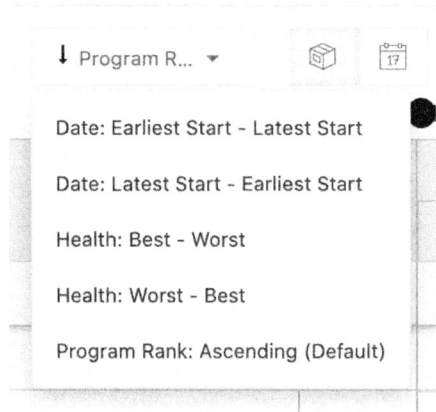

Figure 5.4 – Jira Align roadmap order by options

Simply click on one of the options to order the work items accordingly.

The next option we will explore is how to include unplanned work items, which are not associated with a PI. By default, the roadmap shows all planned work items assigned to a PI. To show unplanned work items alongside the planned, click on the **View Configuration** button near the top of the workspace to the right of center to open the window shown in the following screenshot:

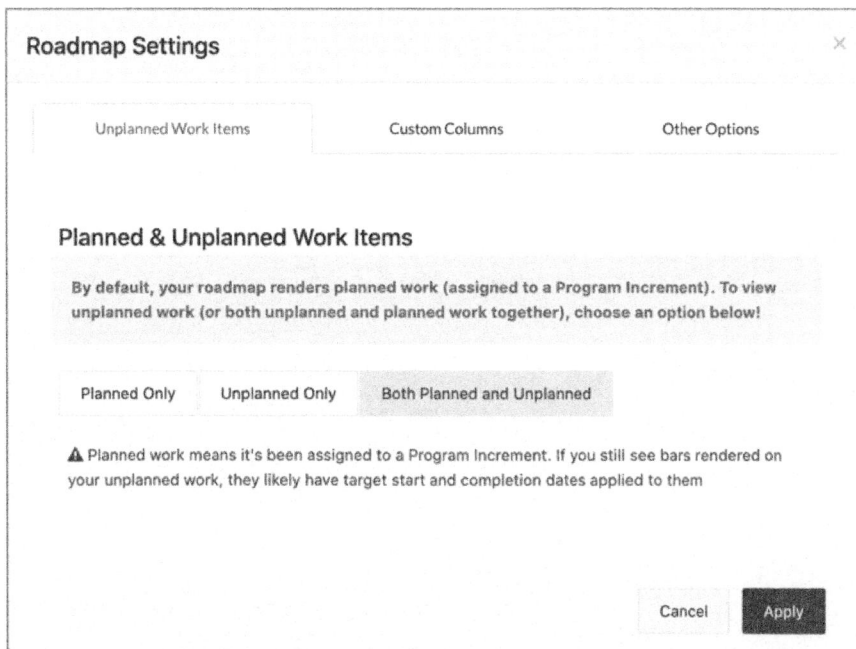

Figure 5.5 – Jira Align roadmap unplanned work

Here, on the **Unplanned Work Items** tab, click on the **Both Planned and Unplanned** button and then on the **Apply** button. Note that unplanned work items, by definition, will not have progress bars on the timeline. You can set target dates for an unplanned work item by clicking and dragging on the timeline to set a progress bar for the item.

Next, let's add up to six columns to be displayed on the roadmap by clicking on the **View Configuration** button, and then on the **Custom Columns** tab. Displaying additional columns on the roadmap can enable faster decision making without the need to drill down into an item. It is recommended to start with the defaults and then add or remove columns as needed. For example, the **Story Points** default column displays the sum of all story LOE points rolled up under parent work items. Select the checkboxes for the additional columns you'd like to add to your roadmap and then click on the **Apply** button, as shown in the following screenshot:

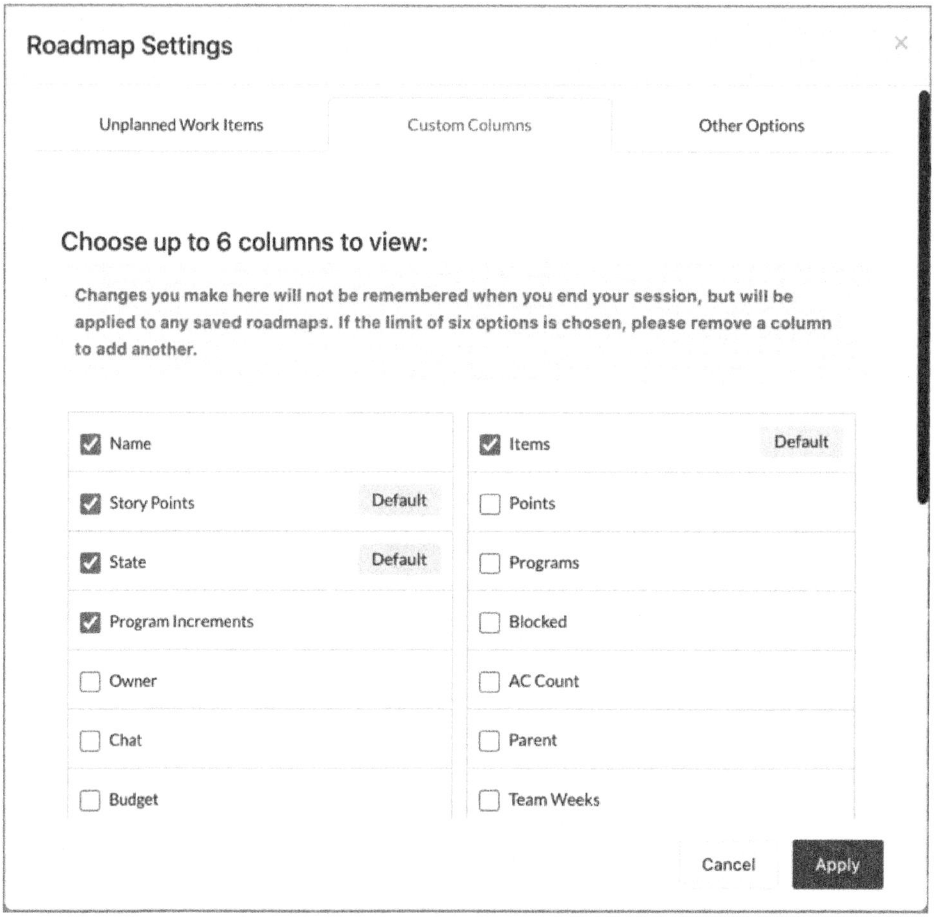

Figure 5.6 – Jira Align roadmap custom columns

Next, let's add additional display options to the roadmap by clicking on the **Other Options** tab. Here you will find toggles that allow you to display the percentage complete on progress bars and group work items by owner, parent, theme, business driver, primary program, product, state, objective, team, and strategic driver. These are shown in the following screenshot:

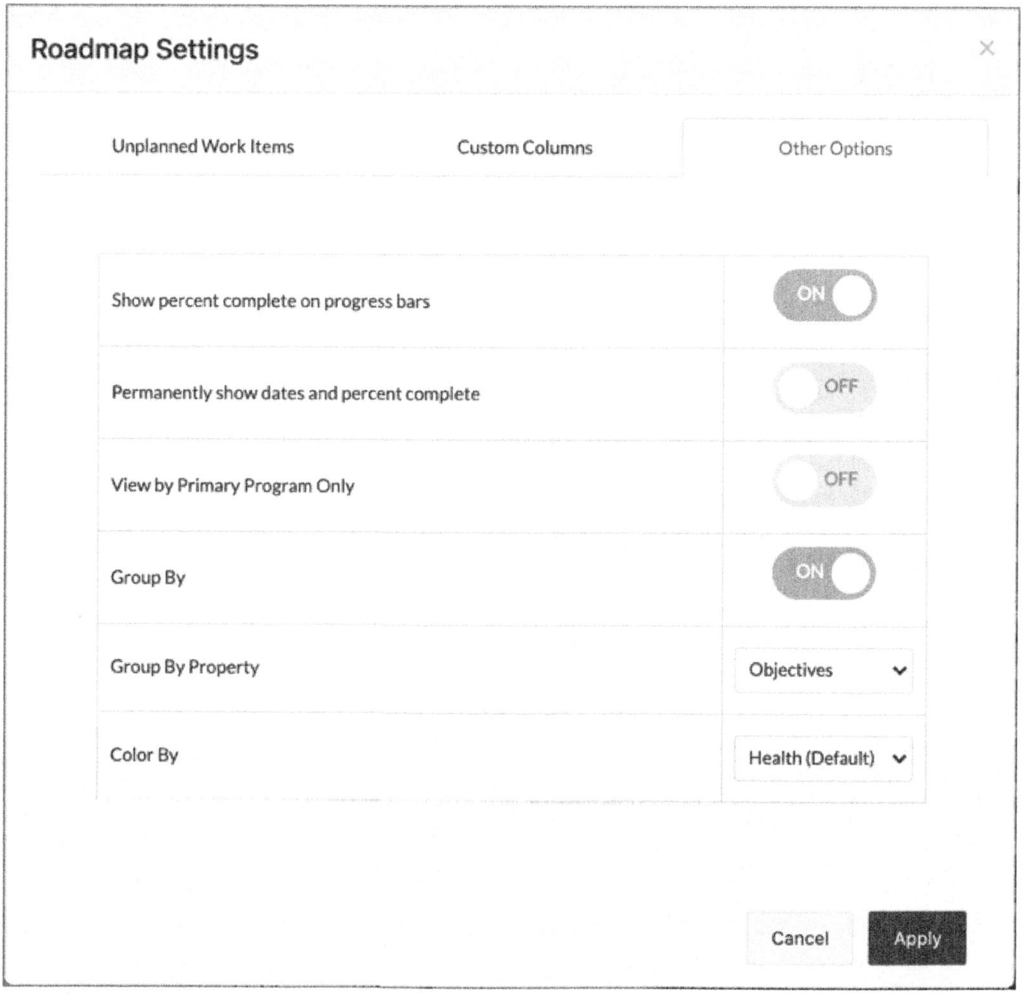

Figure 5.7 – Jira Align roadmap other options

Note that the **Group By** option only works for a single-level roadmap, not for a two-level one such as the **feature by portfolio epic** roadmap shown in *Figure 5.3*. It is a popular option for grouping features or portfolio epics by their associated objectives or **OKRs** (**objectives and key results**). Lastly, there's an option to color the roadmap items by health, state, owner, product, primary program, parent, theme, or business driver.

Now that we've modified the roadmap's columns and appearance, let's further refine the scope of items shown on the roadmap. To do so, click on the **Filter** button near the top right of the workspace to open the window shown in the following screenshot:

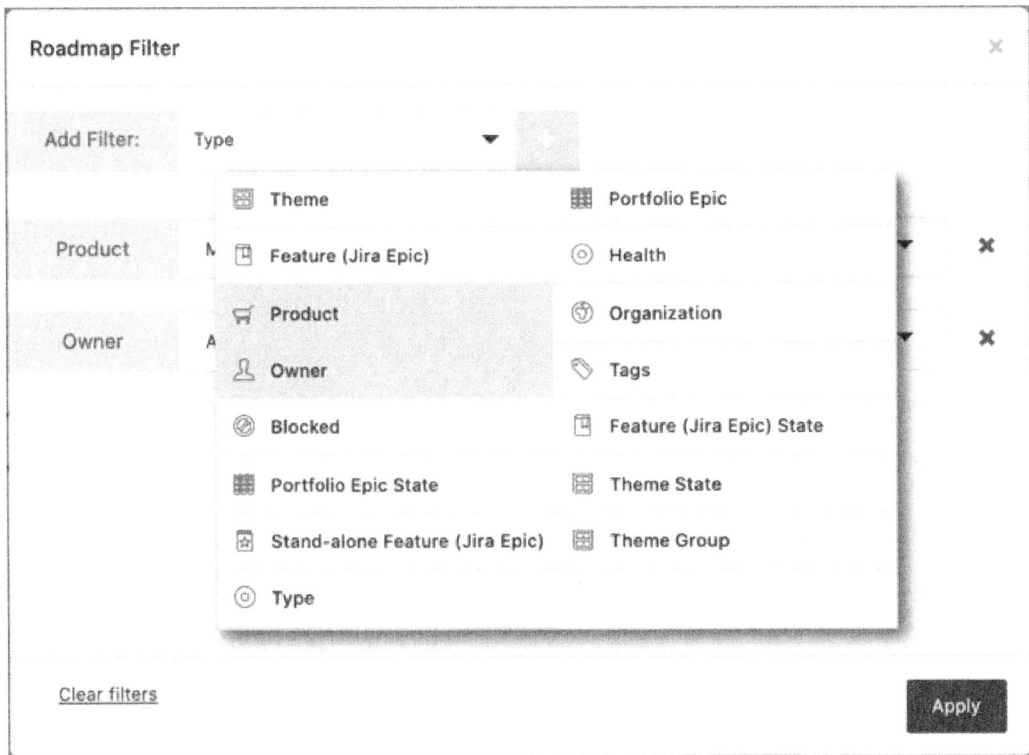

Figure 5.8 – Jira Align roadmap filter

Here we can select attributes to add and specify values to refine the roadmap scope. For example, we can narrow the roadmap scope to a specific product and product owner. In order to remove the filter, click on the **Clear filters** link in the lower-left corner of the window.

Jira Align makes it easy to create a customer-centric roadmap by setting the scope to a specific customer. To do so, click on the **Briefing** button located in the top-right corner of the workspace, as shown in the following screenshot:

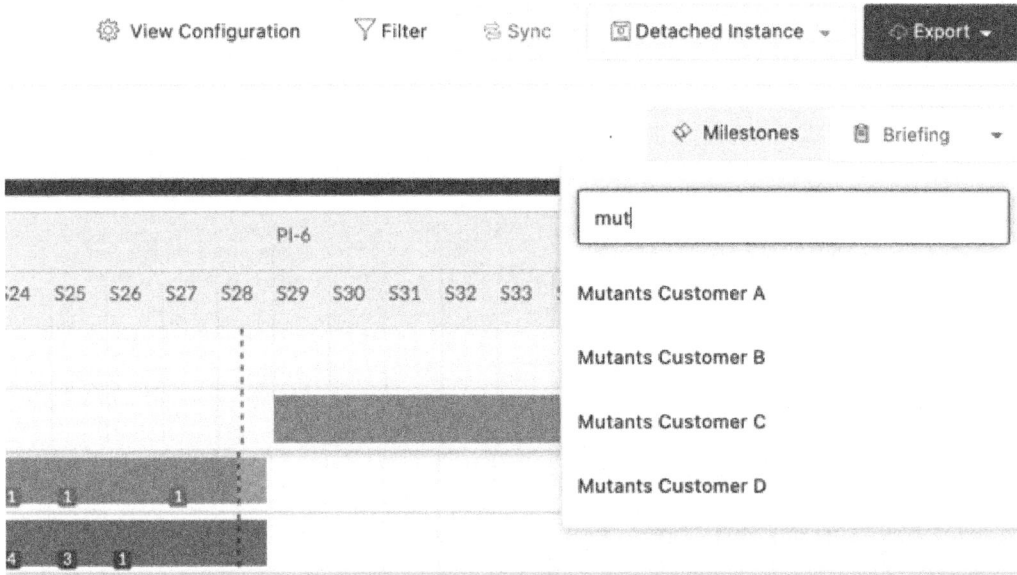

Figure 5.9 – Jira Align roadmap briefing

Next, select a customer from the list to generate the roadmap. This is a quick and easy way to generate a roadmap view of the functionality to be delivered for a specific customer that includes real-time work item status.

> **Tips and tricks**
>
> As a prerequisite to using the **Briefing** option, customers must be associated with features and/or portfolio epics in the customer field on the work items' details panel.
>
> Note that the customer list is managed under **Administration | Setup | Customers**. There, the Jira Align administrator can add a new customer by clicking on the **Add Customer** button, typing the customer name, and then clicking on the **Save & Close** button.

Now that we have learned how to set the scope and display options for a roadmap, it's important to discuss the fact that a work view roadmap is essentially a *sandbox* where you can safely make adjustments without worrying about changing the underlying data. This enables you to review and commit the changes you wish to reflect in the underlying data by clicking on the **Sync** button near the top right of the workspace. This will open a window displaying any changes made to the roadmap, as shown in the following screenshot:

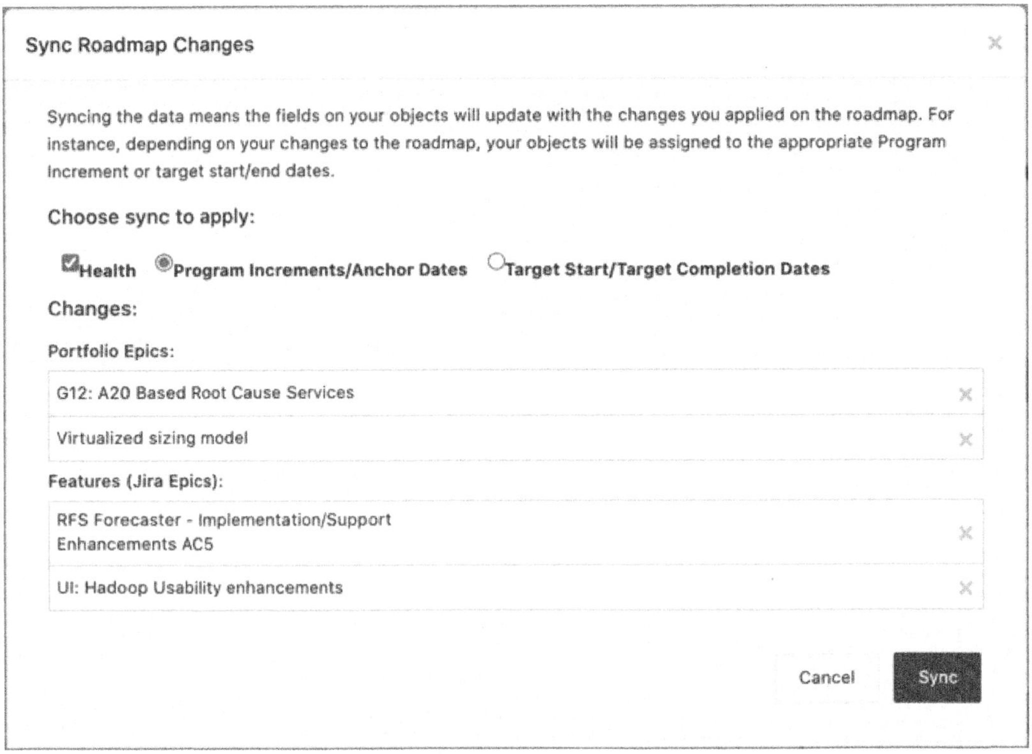

Figure 5.10 – Jira Align sync roadmap changes

Here you can review the list of changes to your roadmap data and then click on the **Sync** button to push the changes down to the underlying objects permanently. If there are changes you wish to remove, click on the **X** to the right of the particular object before you sync changes. The **Health** checkbox enables you to sync the object health you set on the progress bar. The **Program Increment/Anchor Dates** radio button allows you to sync the PI and sprint data, while the **Target Start/Target Completion Dates** radio button allows you to sync those dates. These sync options will populate the respective values down to the actual objects in the database, thus setting the status according to the specified parameters.

Jira Align does not require that you push changes down to the underlying objects in the database. In fact, you can create various *what if* analysis roadmaps and save them for consideration. To do so, create a detached instance of the possible roadmap changes that can be saved and shared with other Jira Align users using a unique URL. This allows product managers and product owners to experiment with different scenarios and versions of the roadmap. Simply select the **View My Instances** menu near the top right of the workspace and then click on the **Create New Instance** option, as shown in the following screenshot:

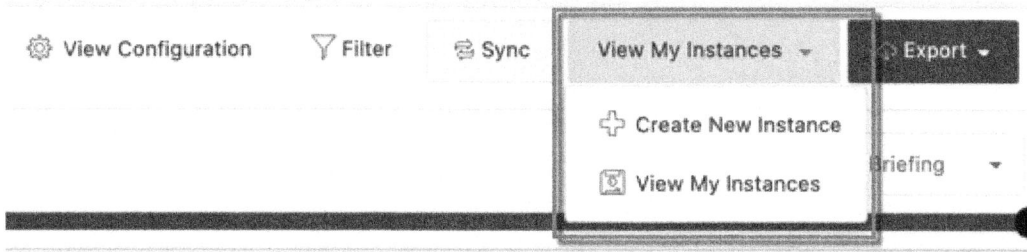

Figure 5.11 – Jira Align roadmap instances

Next, add a meaningful snapshot name to the new detached instance of your roadmap and then click on the **Create Instance** button. You can access the saved detached instances by clicking on the **View My Instances** option, as shown in the preceding screenshot.

At this point, there are other important attributes to consider. Namely, you can display key events on your roadmap by clicking on the **Milestones** button near the top right of the workspace, as shown in the following screenshot:

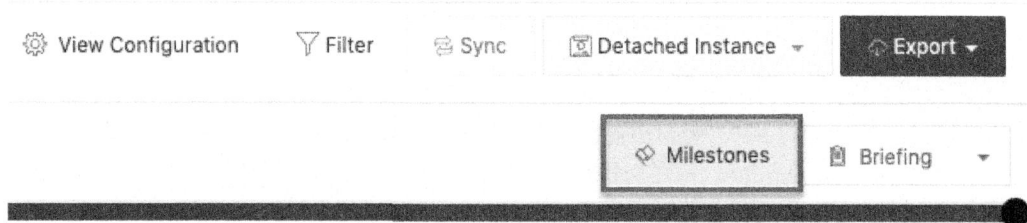

Figure 5.12 – Jira Align roadmap milestones button

This opens the **Work-View Milestones** window shown in the following screenshot:

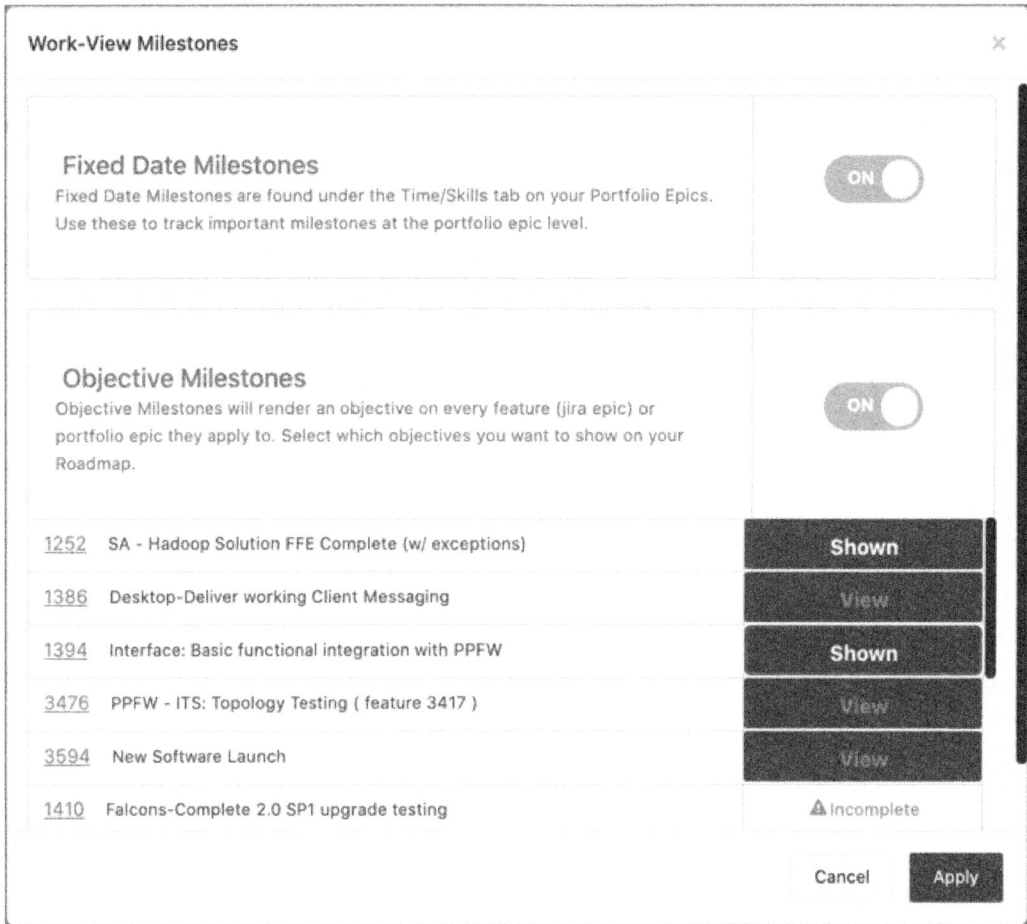

Work-View Milestones   ✕

Fixed Date Milestones
Fixed Date Milestones are found under the Time/Skills tab on your Portfolio Epics.
Use these to track important milestones at the portfolio epic level.   ON

Objective Milestones
Objective Milestones will render an objective on every feature (jira epic) or
portfolio epic they apply to. Select which objectives you want to show on your   ON
Roadmap.

1252	SA - Hadoop Solution FFE Complete (w/ exceptions)	Shown
1386	Desktop-Deliver working Client Messaging	View
1394	Interface: Basic functional integration with PPFW	Shown
3476	PPFW - ITS: Topology Testing (feature 3417)	View
3594	New Software Launch	View
1410	Falcons-Complete 2.0 SP1 upgrade testing	⚠ Incomplete

Cancel   Apply

Figure 5.13 – Jira Align roadmap milestone settings

Here you can slide the **Fixed Date Milestones** toggle on to show key dates associated with portfolio epics. Note that these dates are added to the **Time/Skills** tab of a portfolio epic's details panel. The dates are color-coded and displayed using stars on the progress bar, as shown in the following screenshot: **Start / Initiation** is displayed in cyan, **Portfolio Ask** is displayed in purple, and **Target Completion** is displayed in yellow:

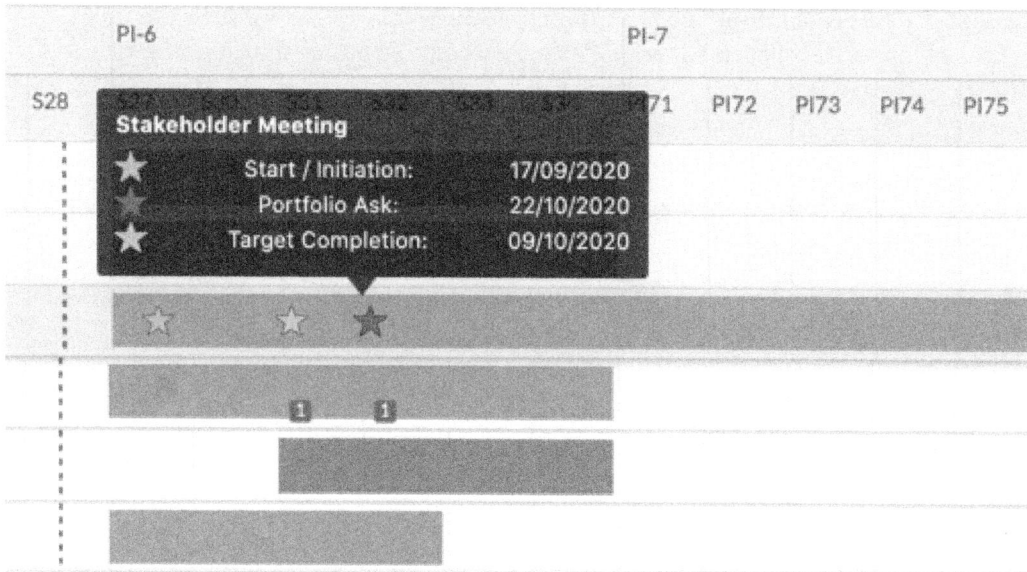

Figure 5.14 – Jira Align roadmap milestones

Next, you can slide on the **Objective Milestones** toggle to show objective dates for features and portfolio epics. Note that you must click on the **View** button next to each listed objective in order to display the objective milestones on your roadmap. Any objectives with missing target completion dates are shown here as incomplete. After clicking on the **Apply** button, the selected objective milestones are displayed as flags on the roadmap timeline. These can be seen in *Figure 5.16*.

There are a few other important aspects of the roadmap to point out:

- The dotted line on the timeline indicates today's date.

- The count of stories associated with each feature is displayed along the progress bars. Story counts are positioned in the columns corresponding to their scheduled delivery sprints, enabling you to monitor the flow of stories for each feature.

- If you hover over the story count, a popup displays the story IDs and names. Click on the ID or name to open a story's details panel.

Once you've gathered information in this manner, you can set a feature's health by right-clicking on its progress bar and selecting one of the options shown in the following screenshot:

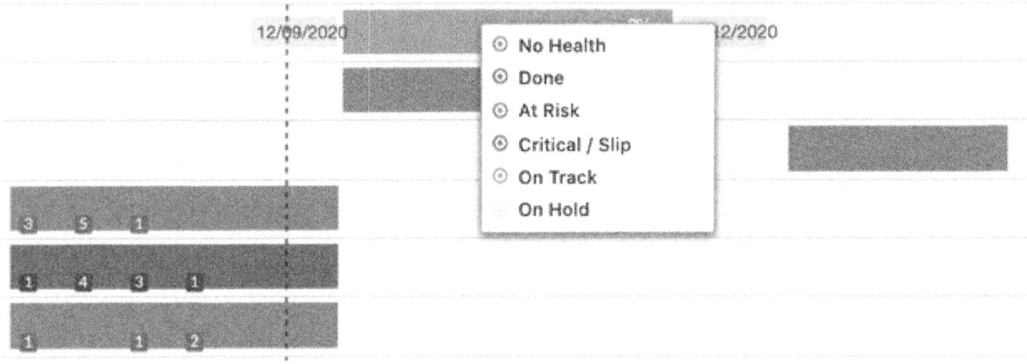

Figure 5.15 – Jira Align roadmap object health

Note that the health of the work item is subjective and set manually. Now that you've updated your roadmap, you can export and share it with external stakeholders who don't have access to Jira Align. Simply click on the **Export** button in the top-right corner of the workspace and choose a **PNG** image or **CSV** file. At this point, we are ready to learn how to create roadmaps defined by **SAFe**.

SAFe defines three types of roadmaps: the **near-term PI roadmap**, **long-term solution roadmap**, and **portfolio roadmap**. We will explore them in that order.

Near-term PI roadmap

The near-term PI roadmap displays commitments for a program ART or solution train for the planned and upcoming PIs. As shown in the following screenshot, the near-term PI roadmap offers a forecast into the fixed date and objective milestones for the next two to three PIs:

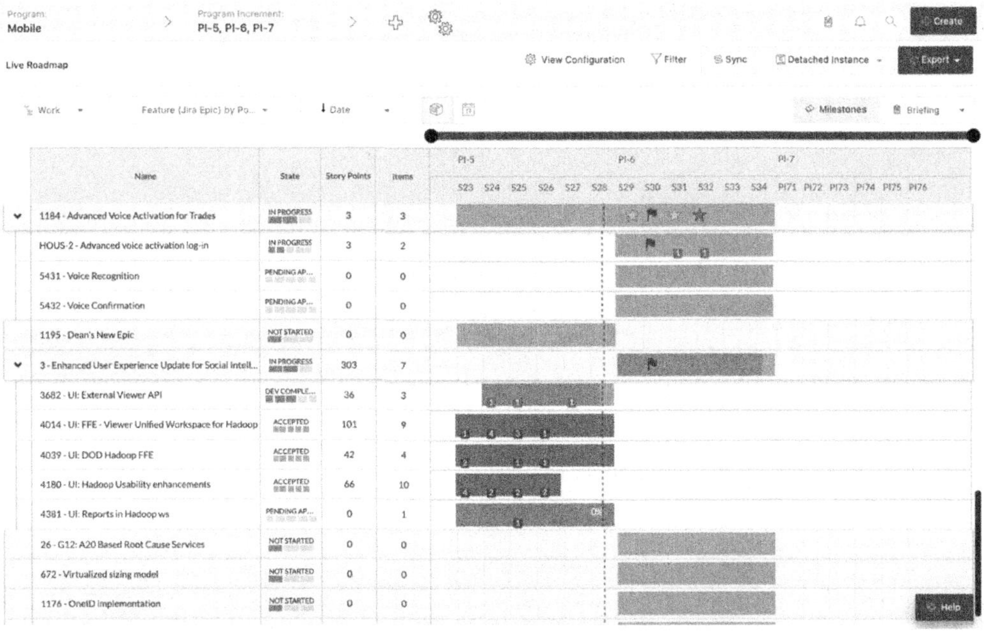

Figure 5.16 – Jira Align near-term PI roadmap

To create a near-term PI roadmap, we will use what we've already learned about the work view roadmap and configure it as follows:

- **Set the configuration bar context**: Select a program and choose the planned and two upcoming PIs for the context. Here we have chosen the `Mobile` program and the following three PIs: `PI-5`, `PI-6`, and `PI-7`.

- **Set the roadmap objects context**: Select **Features** or **Features by Portfolio Epics** to display the work items.

- **Set the order of the objects**: Select **Program Rank: Ascending** or **Date: Earliest Start - Latest Start** to order the work items accordingly.

- **Set timescale view**: Click on the cube symbol button to set the timescale to display **Sprint by Program Increment**.

- **Set the view configuration**: Click on the **View Configuration** button to add the default or other columns to the roadmap.

- **Set the milestones**: Click on the **Milestones** button, toggle on the **Fixed Date** and **Objective Milestones** options, and select objectives to show on the roadmap by clicking the **View** button.

Now that we know how to configure a roadmap of near-term PIs, let's see how to configure a long-term solution roadmap.

Long-term solution roadmap

The long-term solution roadmap displays commitments for a solution train over the course of multiple program increments and often multiple years. As shown in the following screenshot, it displays the key fixed date and objective milestones needed to achieve the solution vision over time:

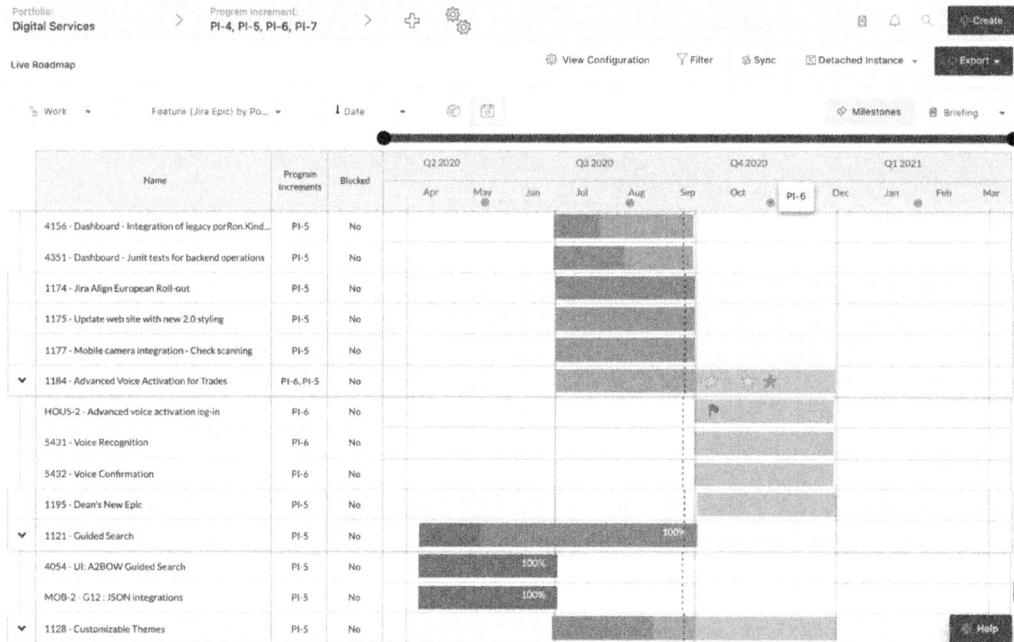

Figure 5.17 – Jira Align long-term solution roadmap

To create a long-term solution roadmap, configure the work view roadmap as follows:

- **Set the configuration bar context**: Select the portfolio and choose the past, planned, and two upcoming PIs from the configuration bar. Here we have chosen the Digital Services portfolio and the following PIs: PI-4, PI-5, PI-6, and PI-7.

- **Set the roadmap objects context**: Select **Features by Portfolio Epics** to display these work items.

- **Set the order of the objects**: Select **Date: Earliest Start - Latest Start** to order the work items accordingly.

- **Set timescale view**: Click on the calendar button to set the timescale to display **Month by Quarter**.

- **Set the view configuration**: Click on the **View Configuration** button to add the default columns to the roadmap. In addition, you can add the **Program Increment** column to see the PIs for the work items and the **Blocked** column to identify any blocked work items. Note that if a child feature is blocked, meaning the **Blocked** field is set to **Yes** on its details panel, then the parent portfolio epic will also be blocked.

- **Set the milestones**: Click on the **Milestones** button, toggle on the **Fixed Date** and **Objective Milestones** options, and select objectives to show on the roadmap by clicking the **View** button.

Now that we've configured a long-term solution roadmap, we're ready to explore the third and final roadmap recommended by **SAFe**, the portfolio roadmap.

Portfolio roadmap

The portfolio roadmap displays commitments for a portfolio over the course of multiple PIs and often multiple years. As shown in the following screenshot, it displays the key fixed date and objective milestones needed to achieve the portfolio vision across the portfolio's value streams over time:

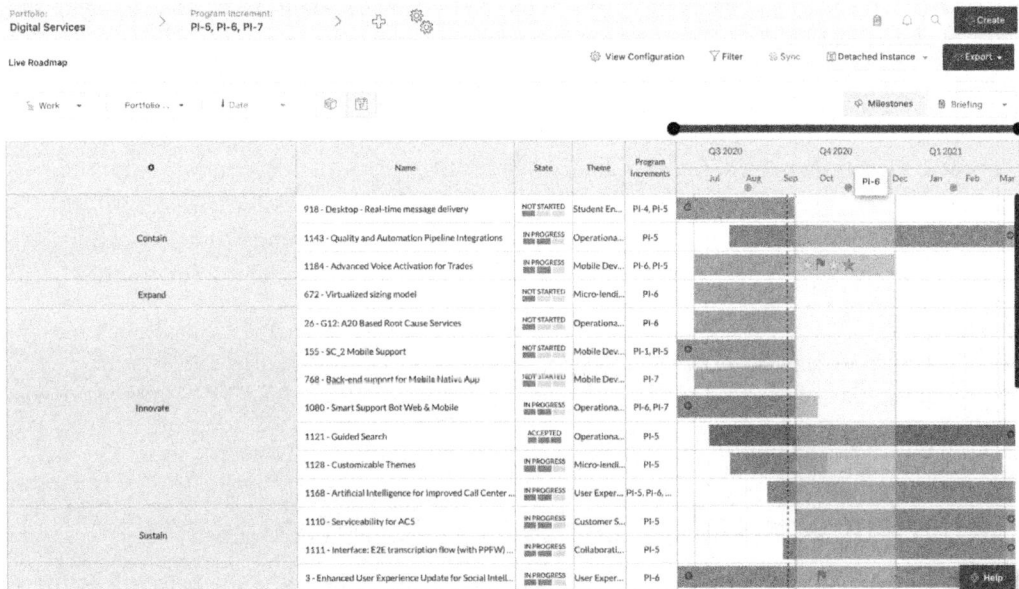

Figure 5.18 – Jira Align portfolio roadmap

To create a portfolio roadmap, configure the work view roadmap as follows:

- **Set the configuration bar context**: Select the portfolio from the configuration bar. You can choose one or more portfolios as the context. Here we have chosen the `Digital Services` portfolio and the following PIs: `PI-5`, `PI-6`, and `PI-7`.

- **Set the roadmap objects context**: Select **Portfolio Epics** to display these work items.

- **Set timescale view**: Click on the calendar button to set the timescale to display **Month by Quarter**.

- **Set the view configuration**: Click on the **View Configuration** button to add columns to the roadmap. For example, add the **Theme** column to display the linked parent theme work item, the **Status** column to display the portfolio epic status, and optionally the **Owner** column to display the epic owner.

- **Set the group by property**: Go to **View Configuration | Other Options**, toggle on the **Group By** option, and choose **Strategic Driver** as the **Group By** property.

- **Set the milestones**: Click on the **Milestones** button, toggle on the **Fixed Date** and **Objective Milestones** options, and select the objectives to show on the roadmap by clicking the **View** button.

Note that the portfolio epics are grouped by their strategic drivers, such as **Expand**, **Innovate**, and **Sustain** in *Figure 5.18*. The portfolio roadmap provides a strategic and long-term directional view of epic delivery over multiple business quarters. While this is a valuable long-term view, it must be balanced with the goal of enterprise agility and flexibility to respond quickly to market rhythms and events. Therefore, it is important for product managers, epic owners, and C-level execs to meet regularly to update the portfolio roadmap based on continuous learning and market changes.

Now that we have learned how to build work item roadmaps, including those recommended by **SAFe**, let's examine how to quantify the planned and actual value that those work items deliver to customers.

Planning for value delivery as a program

A best practice for delivering business value as a coordinated team of teams is to capture the planned and actual business value at the program level. Programs typically select a dozen or so of the highest-ranking features from the product backlog to deliver each business quarter. Teams will then break features down into stories, load the stories into sprints, and determine target sprints for feature completion.

Teams also take note of, discuss, and agree upon dependencies, for example, when one team needs to deliver a story for a feature primarily developed by another team. Note that while the program itself owns the features, it is common for a particular team to take the lead and be the primary team for feature delivery. Jira Align supports these standard dependencies among teams in the program as well as external dependencies, for example, when a feature relies on a component being delivered by an outside vendor.

Each team then decides on their objectives for the quarterly program increment, and ideally, these objectives are **SMART**: **specific**, **measurable**, **achievable**, **realistic**, and **time-bound**.

There are several key outputs of quarterly planning that Jira Align helps to facilitate. Here we will discuss the program board, the centerpiece of program-level delivery, followed by objectives, program predictability, risks, and dependencies.

Program board

The program board serves as a single source of truth for what the program commits to delivering throughout the PI. It's a living document that is critical for both planning and execution. It has columns for the sprints in the PI and rows for teams in the program. It shows critical information, such as when features and objectives are targeted for completion and dependencies across teams. To access the program board, go to the navigation menu and select **Program | Manage | Program Board**. Be sure to set your context in the configuration bar. In the following screenshot, we've set the `Mobile` program and `PI-5` as our context:

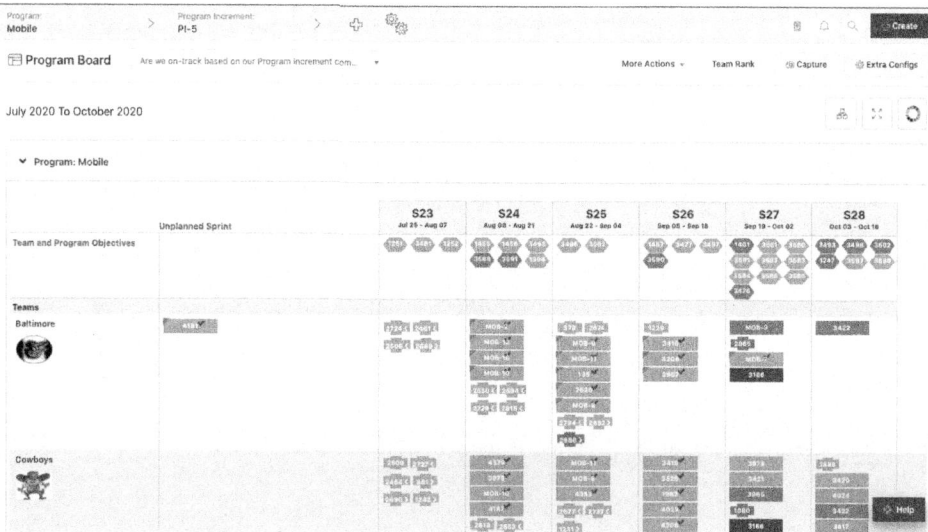

Figure 5.19 – Jira Align program board

Notice how the program board visualizes the target delivery sprints of features, shown as rectangles, and objectives, shown as hexagons. Unlike a physical board with red strings for dependencies, which can get cluttered, Jira Align represents dependencies by showing bowtie symbols in the swim lanes of teams upon which others (including teams from other ARTs) depend.

The colors are important indicators used throughout the PI to track status. For example, red means that an item is blocked, and orange signifies scheduling issues, as shown in the report legend. To access the legend, click on the **color wheel** button near the top-right corner of the workspace, as shown in the following screenshot:

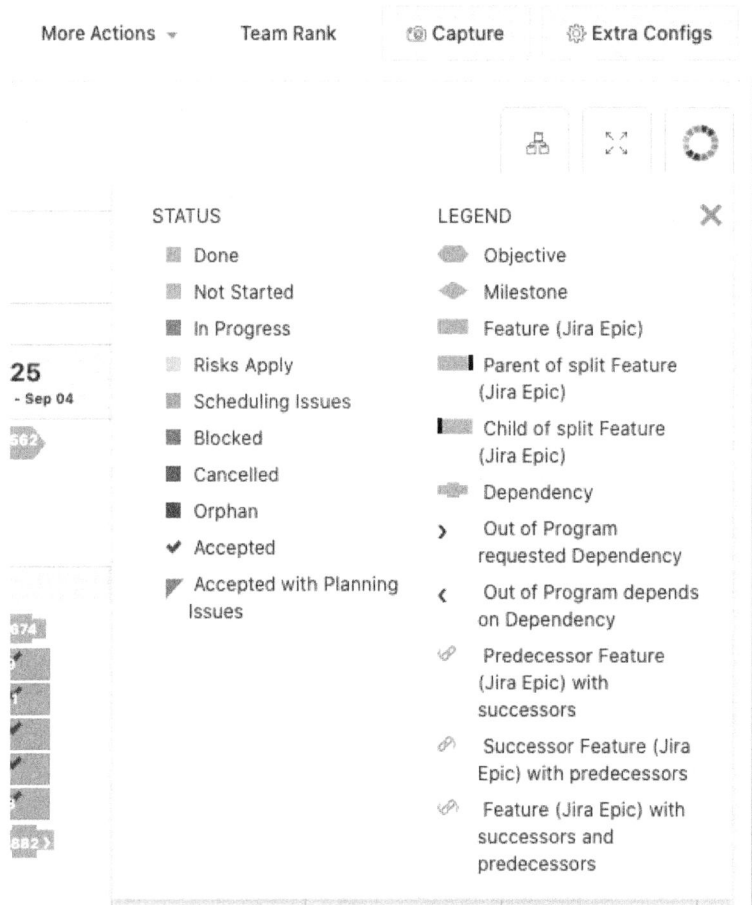

Figure 5.20 – Jira Align program board legend

While the colors provide quick visualizations of status, you can hover over an item on the board to see more details displayed in the bottom-left corner of the screen. If applicable, any planning issues will be indicated by the presence of red or orange color blocks, as shown in the following screenshot:

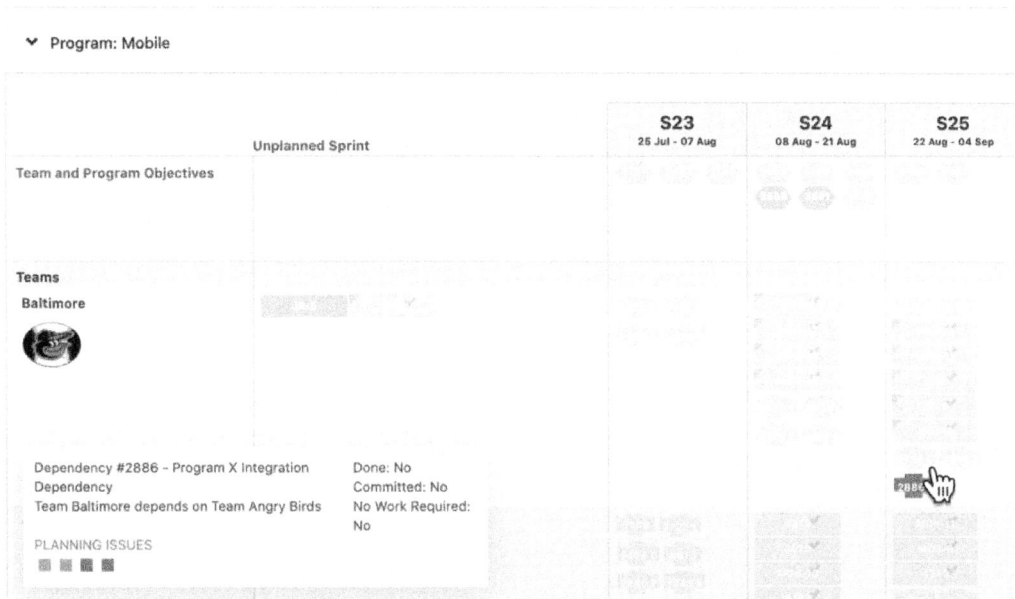

Figure 5.21 – Jira Align program board item details

You can click on any item on the board to open a quick view panel with key information such as its child work items and associated risks. Clicking on the IDs for those items in the quick view will open their details panels, allowing you to drill down for more information. For full details of the item on the board, click on its ID and title at the top of its quick view panel to open its details panel for the complete set of information.

You can change the program board view by clicking on the **card tree** button, the second button to the left of the color wheel. This will present three options for displaying items on the program board with varying levels of detail:

- **Normal View**: Items are displayed on the board as cards containing their IDs, titles, and report legend symbols, including the rectangle, hexagon, and bowtie.

- **Small View**: Items are displayed on the board in the shape of their report legend symbols with their IDs. This is the most popular view used by most organizations.

- **Heat Map View**: Items are displayed on the board as scaled-down versions of their report legend symbols with IDs.

You can present the program board in full screen by clicking on the **Expand** button next to the color wheel. The full-screen presenter view hides the configuration bar and navigation menu to maximize the information displayed when presented on the big screen during planning.

> **Tips and tricks**
>
> When displaying the program board during planning events, we recommended using a browser-based add-on or extension to auto-refresh the board at 30-second intervals. This ensures that up-to-date information is displayed. The add-on or extension you choose may vary based on the operating system and/ or web browser used. You can speak with your Atlassian solution partner for recommendations.

The next set of display options is found by clicking on the **Extra Configs** button in the top-right corner of the workspace. This will present a series of option toggles, as shown in the following screenshot:

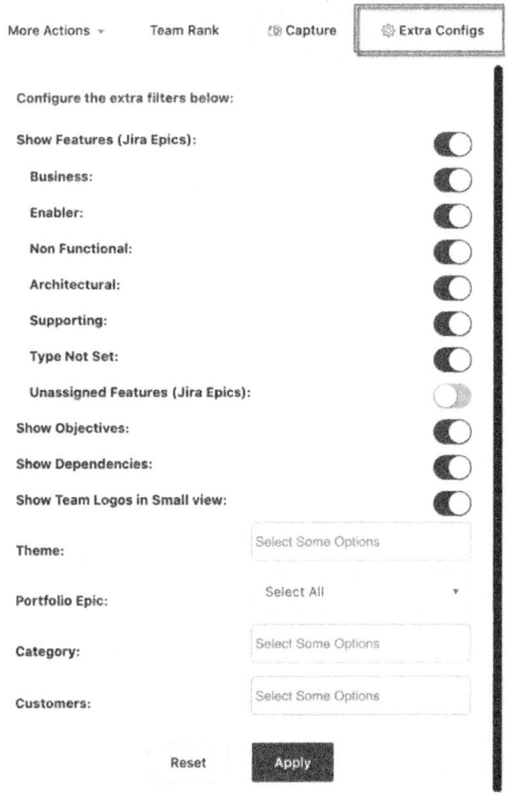

Figure 5.22 – Jira Align program board extra configs

Here you can slide the toggles on to display specific types of features, unassigned features, objectives, dependencies, and further filter the program board according to a selected list of themes, portfolio epics, strategic driver categories, and/or customers. After setting the toggles to your liking, click on the **Apply** button to see the configured options displayed on the program board.

During planning, as product owners write stories for features, those features will land in their teams' swim lanes. However, features with no associated stories can still be shown in teams' swim lanes on the program board. To do so, click on the **More Actions** button near the top right of the workspace and select the **Orphans** option to open the window shown in the following screenshot. Note that Jira Align uses the term **orphans** to apply both to parent items without children (as is the case here) and children without parents:

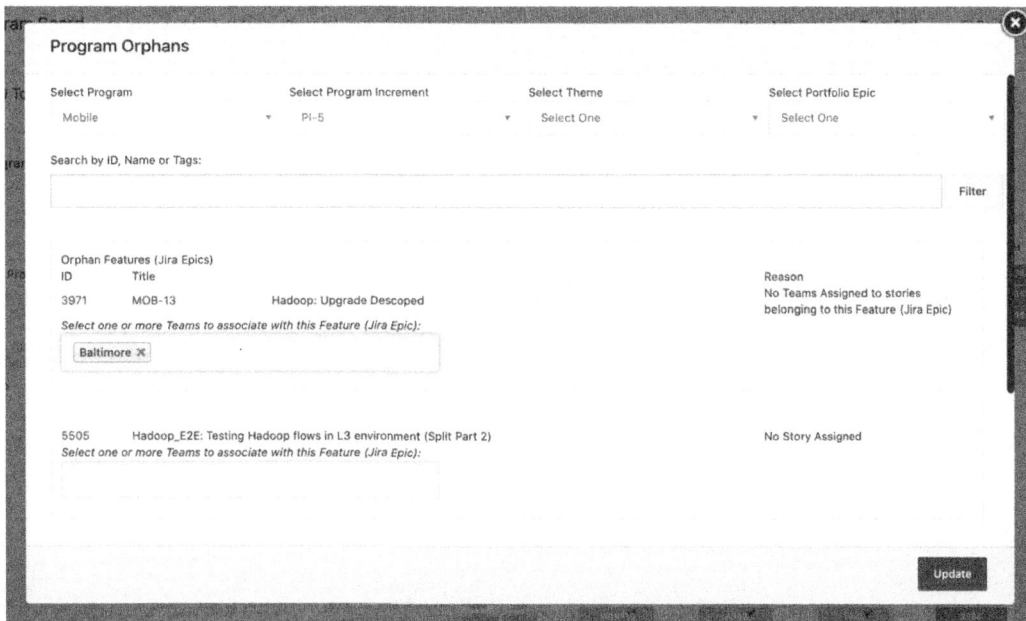

Figure 5.23 – Jira Align program orphans

Next, select a team or teams to associate with a given feature and it will display in gray in the unassigned column to the left of the sprint columns on the program board. In the preceding screenshot, we have selected team `Baltimore` to associate with feature ID `3971`. Associating an orphan feature in this manner allows the team to target a delivery sprint for the feature even if stories aren't written yet. This can provide a window for advance planning so that teams can start thinking about interdependencies while stories are being written.

> **Tips and tricks**
>
> If the **Orphans** menu option is not available under the **More Actions** menu, be sure to toggle off the **Unassigned Features** option from the **Extra Configs** menu. Note that the **Unassigned Features** option is toggled off by default, as shown in *Figure 5.22*.

Now that we've seen how orphan features can be displayed on the program board, let's see how to generate a history report showing all scheduling edits made to features on the board. Simply click on the **More Actions** button and select the **History** option to open the report shown in the following screenshot:

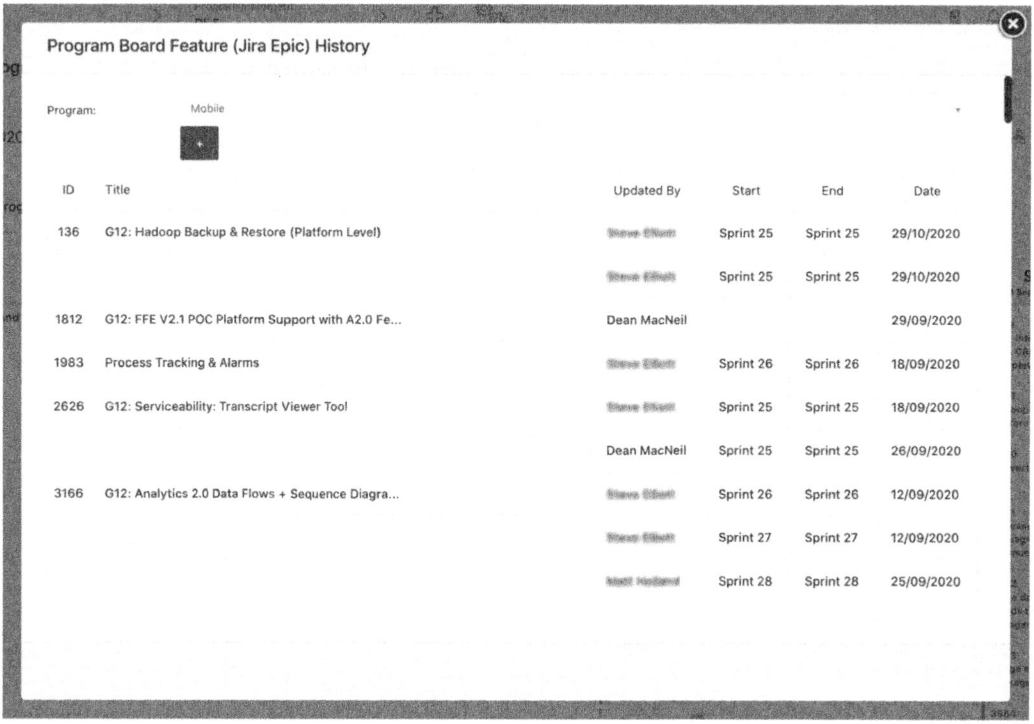

Figure 5.24 – Jira Align program board history

When a feature's schedule is modified, the report indicates the user who made the update, the start sprint, end sprint, and timestamp when the modification was made. Any unplanned features will show the start and end sprints as empty. You can filter the report by clicking on the blue plus + icon to display all available filters, including programs, date ranges, program increments, portfolio epics, and tags.

Programs typically have up to 12 teams. You can change the order in which teams are displayed on the program board by clicking on the **Team Rank** button near the top-right corner of the workspace, as shown in the following screenshot:

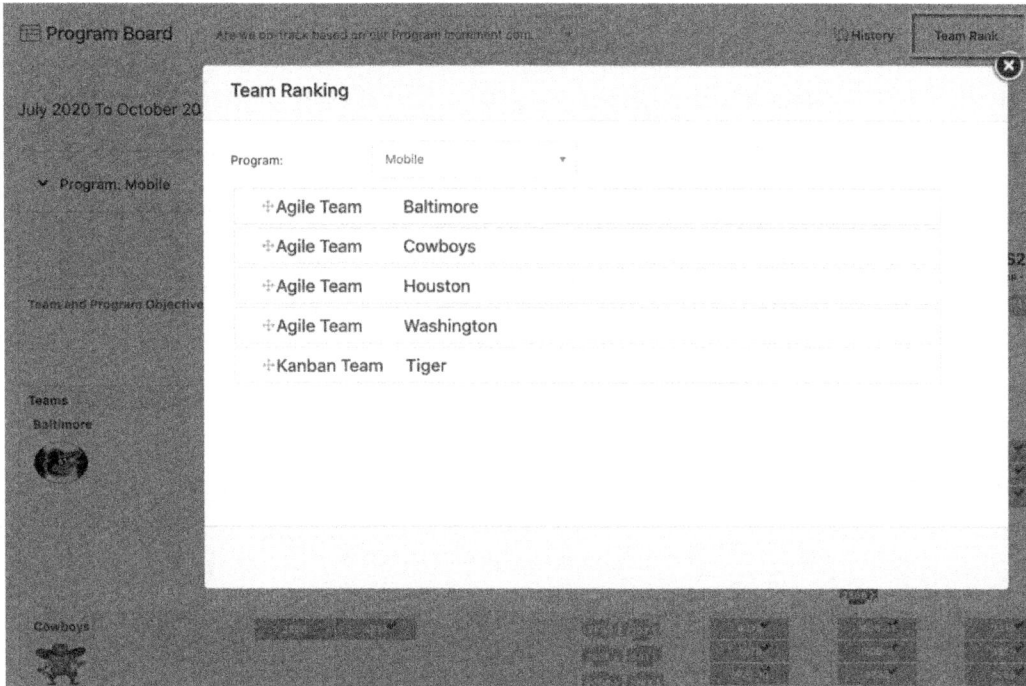

Figure 5.25 – Jira Align program team rank

Here you can select a program to list its teams and then drag and drop to adjust the teams' display order on the board. Lastly, you can export the program board by clicking on the **Capture** button to generate an image.

The Jira Align program board may require some getting used to for those accustomed to a physical board where sticky notes and string make features and dependencies tangible. Yet companies, especially larger ones, have long been using Jira Align's program board, even during in-person PI planning. One reason is that it saves time entering physical board data into the tool. Another is that Jira Align's dependency functionality enforces a contract between teams that is documented, trackable to resolution, and provides visualizations that can serve as inputs to the management review and problem solving session. For example, a plethora of dependencies upon a single team may warrant the redistribution of team members to reduce knowledge silos. Dependencies are so important that we'll discuss them in their own section later in this chapter.

Objectives

Another key output of quarterly planning is a list of several agreed-upon PI objectives per team. These are often linked to one or more features because they represent the business outcomes achieved as a result of delivering the features. If you are following **SAFe**, PI objectives receive special attention. Business owners, who are the stakeholders of what is to be delivered in the quarterly increment, assign a business value score to the teams' PI objectives on a scale of 1 to 10, with 10 being the highest level of value.

The release train engineer or program-level scrum master then summarizes the team objectives into the program's PI objectives in a format suitable for management communication. According to **SAFe**, PI objectives help shift the program's focus from output to outcomes, from delivering work to delivering value. If not following **SAFe**, you may associate key results with these objectives, thus turning them into quarterly OKRs for the program.

In Jira Align, you can add objectives at the team, program, solution, and portfolio levels. Here, let's see how the RTE can view team objectives for the PI and create higher-level program objectives for management reporting purposes. To see the program's team objectives for the PI, set the program and PI in the configuration bar, and then go to the navigation menu and select **Team | Manage | Team Objectives**.

To see the planned and actual business value, click on the **Columns Shown** button at the top of the workspace to the right of center and then select the **Planned Value** and **Delivered Value** columns. In the following screenshot, we see the `Mobile` program's team objectives for `PI-5`, sorted by planned value:

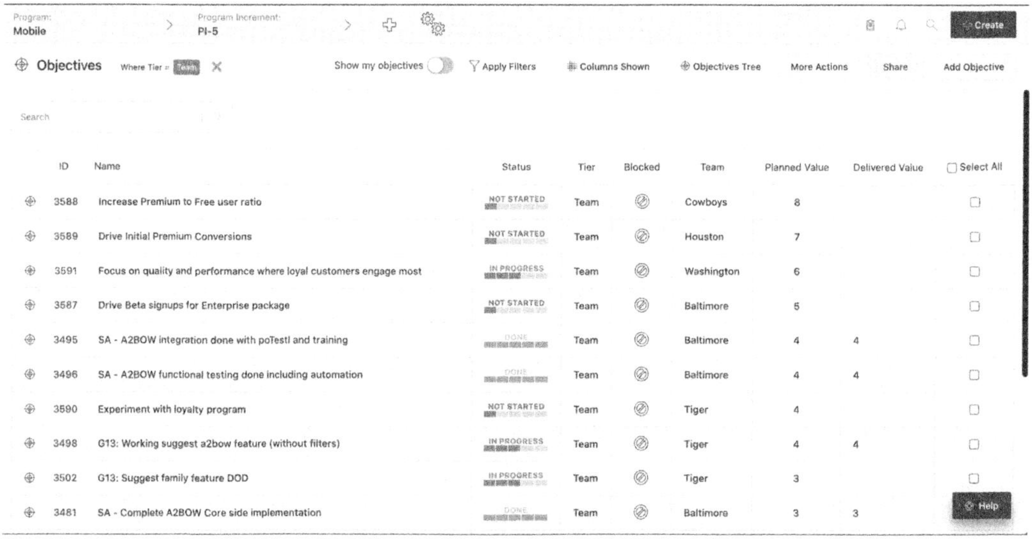

Figure 5.26 – Jira Align team PI objectives

To create an objective, click on the **Add Objective** button in the top-right corner of the workspace and enter the following details:

- **Tier**: Select one of the objective levels: **Team**, **Program**, **Solution**, or **Portfolio**.

- **Name**: Add a meaningful objective name.

- **Description**: Add additional details to describe the objective.

- **Program**: Select an applicable program.

- **Program Increment**: Select a program increment.

- **Owner**: Select an objective owner.

- **Primary Team**: Select a primary team from the program that will be responsible for the objective.

- **Target Sync Sprint**: Select the target delivery sprint for the objective.

- **Find Parent Objective**: Select a parent objective if applicable. For example, select a program objective as the parent when creating a team objective.

- **Dates**: Select dates for the following, if applicable: **Portfolio Ask**, **Start / Initiation**, and **Target Completion**.

- **Status**: Select a status for the objective: **Not Started, In Progress, Deferred, Cancelled, Missed,** or **Done**.

- **Health**: Select a color to indicate the health of the objective: **Red, Orange, Green, Yellow, Gray,** or **Blue**.

- **Blocked**: Select **No** or **Yes** to indicate whether the objective is blocked.

- **Category**: Select **Critical Path** or **Stretch Goal** if applicable. Note that in **SAFe**, stretch objectives are planned, but not committed to, by the team because of too many unknowns or risks.

- **Type**: Select a type, if applicable: **Feature Finisher, Incremental Delivery, Non-Code,** or **Roadmap Milestone**.

- **Planned Value**: Select a value from low (**1**) to high (**10**), as scored by the business owners during the PI planning event.

- **Delivered Value**: Select a value from low (**1**) to high (**10**), as scored by business owners following the PI system demo.

- **Notes**: Add additional notes.

At the end of the program increment, usually during the *Inspect* and *Adapt* event if you are following **SAFe**, business owners apply the actual business value delivered to the objectives created during PI planning. Note that this is a list of PI objectives per team, not the summarized view created by the RTE, which will often roll up many similar objectives into a single one. The comparison of actual to planned value serves as a predictability metric, which is the percentage of planned value points delivered. **SAFe** advises that this metric be captured at the team level and then rolled up to determine predictability at the program level. Predictability is a common challenge for teams that is only compounded at the program level, so it's an important metric to consider.

While Jira Align supports the earlier-described **SAFe** practice, you have the option to apply business value to both team and program objectives. To see the list of program-level objectives for the PI, go to the navigation menu and select **Program | Manage | Program Objectives**.

Jira Align also makes it easy for the RTE to group team objectives into program objectives by assigning a parent objective in a team objective's details panel. The relationship between the objectives can then be viewed by going to the navigation menu and selecting **Enterprise | Objective Tree**. This module provides a visual representation of the hierarchy between related objectives and their higher-level strategic goals. In the following screenshot, we've clicked on the first button to the right of the blue oval **Jira Align Labs** icon to display the popular list view. There is also a tree hierarchy view available by clicking on the other button:

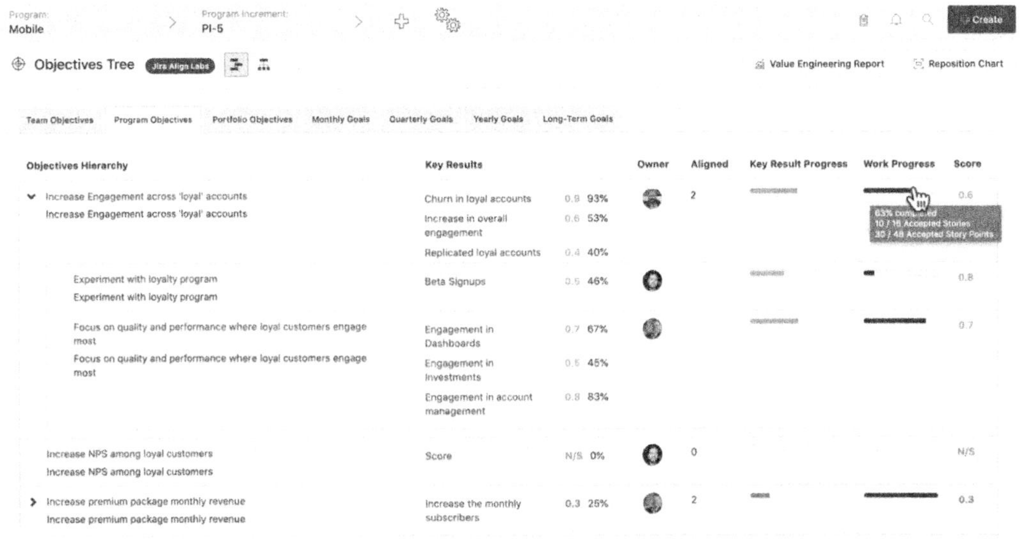

Figure 5.27 – Jira Align objectives tree list view

Note that we've set the `Mobile` program and `PI-5` as our context in the configuration bar and then selected the **Program Objectives** tab to show that objective level. We've also clicked on the pointing angle symbol to the left of the first objective in the list to expand and display its child objectives. The columns in this view display the following objective and goal information:

- **Name and description**, shows the objective details.
- **Key Results**, shows scores and percent of target achieved.
- **Owner**, the person responsible for the objective.
- **Number of aligned objectives or goals**, meaning the number of child items.
- **Key Result Progress**: Color-coded bar displaying the percentage of completed key results.
- **Work Progress**: Color-coded bar displaying the percentage of completed stories related to the objective or goal.
- **Score**: Displays the score for the objective or goal. Objectives that haven't had a baseline value set or progress recorded on key results will display a score of **N/S** (not scored).

Note that progress and scores are applied at each level, so higher-level objectives don't roll up the metrics below them. Click on the name of an objective, goal, or key result to view and edit details. By displaying the relationship between objectives and goals at different levels of your organization, this report helps RTEs and others ensure that the child items align with and properly inform the next level up. The progress bars at each level provide quick status indicators, useful for program/portfolio leadership and enterprise executives to get a read on value delivery.

> **Tips and tricks**
>
> At present, the **Objectives Tree** is a **Jira Align Labs** module. If you don't see it, speak with your Jira Align administrator to enable it for your role.
>
> The Jira Align REST API 2.0 supports the creation, reading, and updating of objectives and key results. Speak to your Atlassian solution partner to enable the REST API in your instance. You can read more about the REST API by going to the user menu and selecting **Support | Documentation | Knowledge Base | Integrations**.

Now that we've learned how to capture planned and delivered values for PI objectives, let's take a look at one of the reports that help visualize value delivery.

Program predictability

Examining the percentage of completed objectives achieved during a selected time period can help provide a better understanding of the program's ability to deliver business value. The program predictability report makes this easy. To access it, go to the navigation menu and select **Program | Transform | Program Predictability Report**. As shown in the following screenshot, it displays a line chart by team/program with an average for all selected teams/programs:

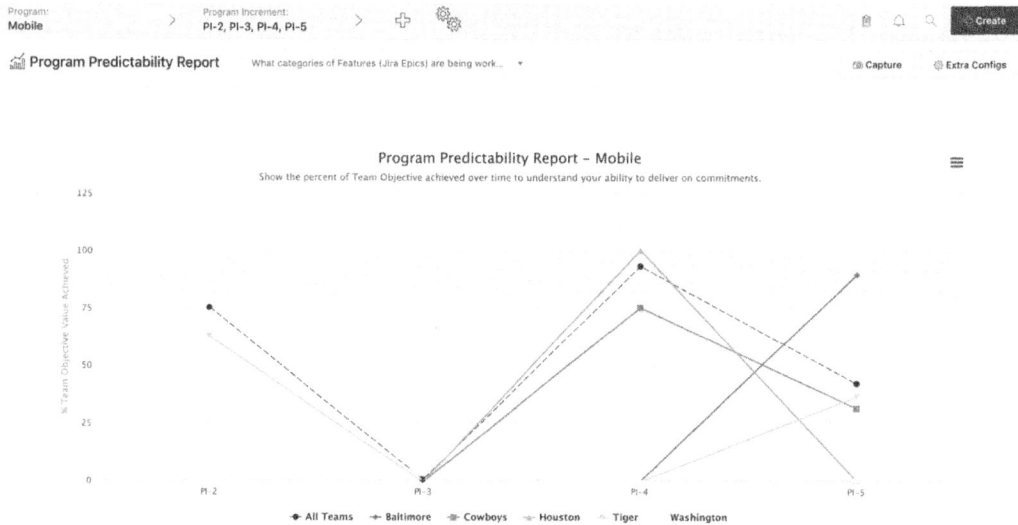

Figure 5.28 – Jira Align program predictability report

Here we are looking at team objectives, so teams appear on the *x* axis. You can run the report for other objective levels by clicking on the **Extra Configs** button in the top-right corner of the workspace. For all other levels, programs appear on the *x* axis.

This report is useful during PI planning to enable teams to compare committed objectives with their historical average of completed objectives to help ensure delivery capability. The report can be displayed in fullscreen or downloaded by clicking on the three bars at the top of the chart to the right of the title.

Now that we've explored how to create, measure, and visualize objectives and their value metrics, let's learn how to record risks that could impact the delivery of work items and outcomes.

Risks

Tracking and reporting risks are important activities irrespective of whether you are following **SAFe** or not. In **SAFe**, program risks are key outputs of PI planning. During breakouts, teams identify program-level risks and impediments that could impact their ability to meet objectives. These are reviewed openly and honestly together as an ART, facilitated by the RTE, and categorized as follows onto a **ROAM** board, available in Jira Align:

- **Resolved**: The teams agree that the issue is no longer a concern.

- **Owned**: Someone on the program ART takes ownership of the item since it cannot be resolved at the meeting.

- **Accepted**: Some risks are just facts or potential problems that must be understood and accepted.

- **Mitigated**: Teams can identify a plan to reduce the impact of an item.

The following screenshot is an example ROAM board in Jira Align:

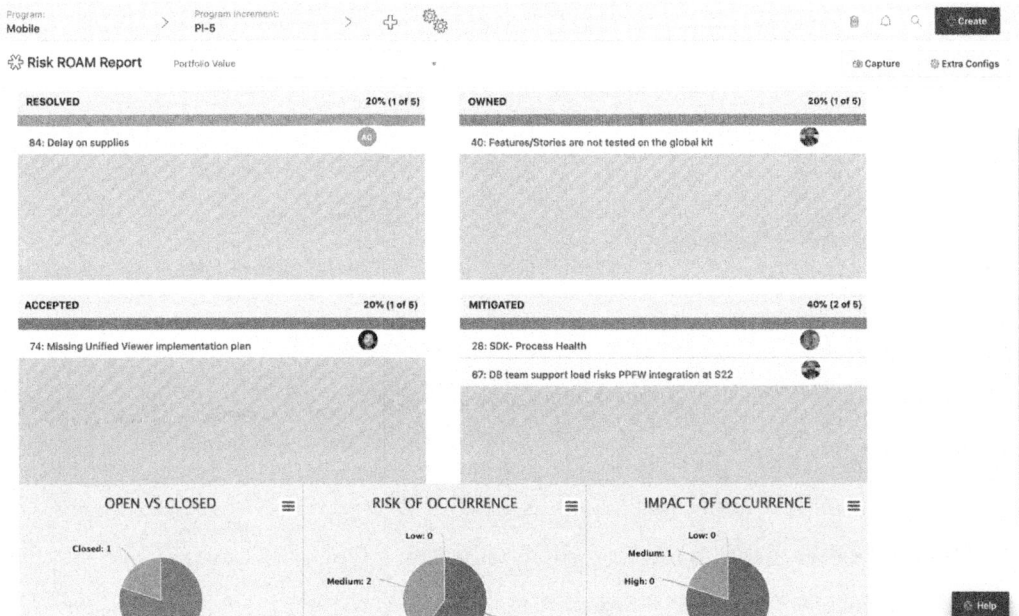

Figure 5.29 – Jira Align ROAM board

Note that risks appear under their given ROAM category, and pie charts provide summarized risk data.

To add a risk, go to the navigation menu and select **Program** | **Manage** | **Risks** to open the risk grid. To filter risks for your context, select the program and PI in the configuration bar. Next, click on the **Add Risk** button in the top-right corner of the workspace to open the risk details panel, as seen on the right in the following screenshot:

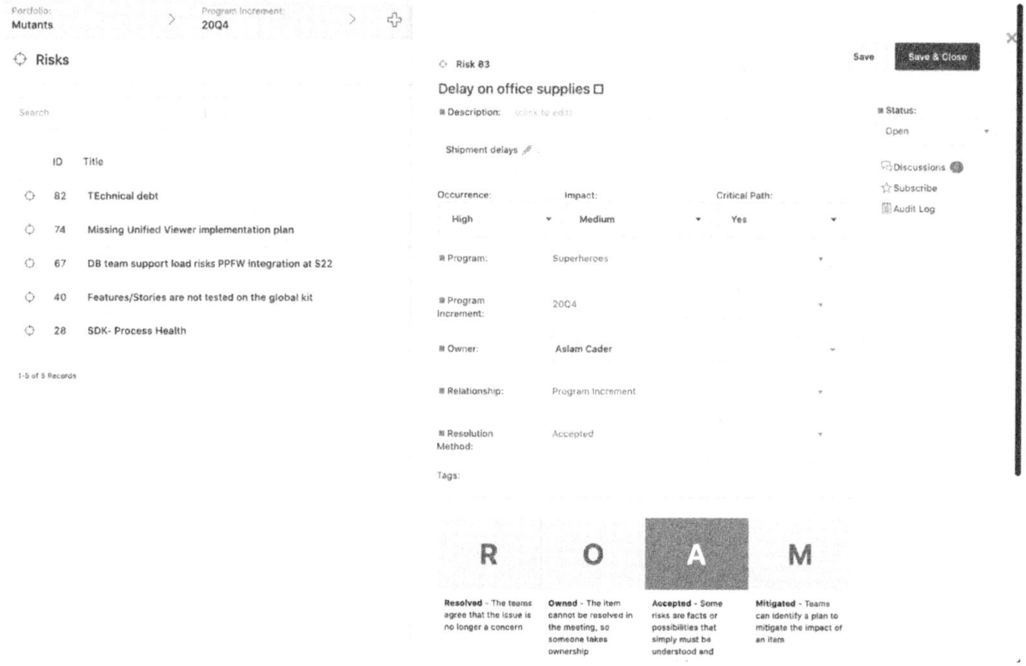

Figure 5.30 – Jira Align risks details panel

Use this panel to enter and track the following risk details:

- **Name**: Add a risk summary.

- **Description**: Add additional details to describe the risk.

- **Status**: Select a status to identify whether the risk is **Open** or **Closed**.

- **Occurrence**: Select a probability of the risk occurring using the following scale: **Critical**, **High**, **Medium**, or **Low**.

- **Impact**: Select an impact of the risk using the following scale: **Critical**, **High**, **Medium**, or **Low**.

- **Critical Path**: Select **Yes** or **No** for whether the risk affects the critical path of program increment execution.

- **Program and Program Increment**: Select the affected program and PI for the risk.

- **Owner**: Assign an owner to the risk to set responsibility.

- **Relationship**: Select how the risk relates to the program. You can choose the program increment or a work item (feature, portfolio epic, or theme). Selecting a work item will enable an additional attribute to link the impacted work item.

- **Resolution Method**: Select a resolution method by applying **ROAM: Resolved, Owned, Accepted**, or **Mitigated**.

- **Consequence**: Add details related to the consequence of the risk if it were to occur.

- **Contingency**: Add details related to the risk contingency plan on how to handle the risk if it were to occur.

- **Mitigation**: Add details related to risk mitigation steps to reduce the risk impact.

- **Resolution Status**: Add details on how the risk was resolved at the time of risk closure.

Now that all details are captured, the risk will appear on the ROAM board. To access this board, click on the **More Actions** button near the top right of the risk grid workspace and select **Risk ROAM Report**. As shown in *Figure 5.29*, it displays risks by ROAM category, and you can click and drag risks across the board from one category to another. The board also displays pie charts showing open versus closed, the risk of occurrence, and the impact of occurrence.

You can further filter the ROAM board by clicking on the **Extra Configs** button in the top-right corner of the workspace. This allows you to filter by work item type (feature, portfolio epic, or theme) or a specific item within a type. Lastly, to share it with external users, you can export the report by clicking on the **Capture** button to generate an image.

To see how risks impact PI execution, refer to the program board by going to the navigation menu and selecting **Program | Manage | Program Board**. Any item with an associated risk will appear in yellow, as indicated in the report legend. Click on the item to open its quick view panel, where you can then click on the associated risk for full details.

Note that while risks are usually associated with work items, you can also associate risks with objectives. To do so, open an objective's details panel, scroll down to the **Risks** section, and either use the search box to select an existing risk or click on the **Add** button to add a new risk.

Now that we've captured features, objectives, and risks on the program board, let's return to the important concept of dependencies. Paying attention to dependencies during planning can help set the program up for successful execution.

Organizing around value to reduce dependencies

Programs or ARTs are virtual teams of teams, organized around value delivery. It's therefore important to identify your value streams upfront in order to set these teams up for efficient and effective value delivery. That's why the **SAFe Implementation Roadmap** has the *Identify Value Streams and ARTs* step soon after the decision to *Go SAFe*.

Each ART should be able to deliver features independently with minimal dependencies on other ARTs. This may take a few PIs to get right, so hold off on making any organizational changes around ARTs. In fact, the traditional hierarchy can remain intact while the ARTs are a virtual overlay. While the traditional hierarchy is geared toward stability, the virtual team of teams overlay is meant for nimble pivoting and agility. The two can work hand in hand in achieving your business' sought-after outcomes.

A common pitfall is to structure ARTs along functional lines – this will create numerous dependencies that impede the effective flow of value delivery. Luckily, Jira Align visualizes team and program dependencies as a matrix or wheel that allows you to click on them to take action. The wheel view, in particular, has helped organizations adjust their ART structures to reduce dependencies and improve delivery flow. If the wheel view resembles a spider web, it may be time to reevaluate team structure. We will explore dependency visualizations in the next chapter.

In Jira Align, you can create dependencies between teams and programs, either within a portfolio or across portfolios. You can also create dependencies on external entities. To begin, access the dependencies grid by going to the navigation menu and selecting **Program | Manage | Dependencies**. Be sure to set your context in the configuration bar. In the following screenshot, we have selected the Mobile program and PI-5:

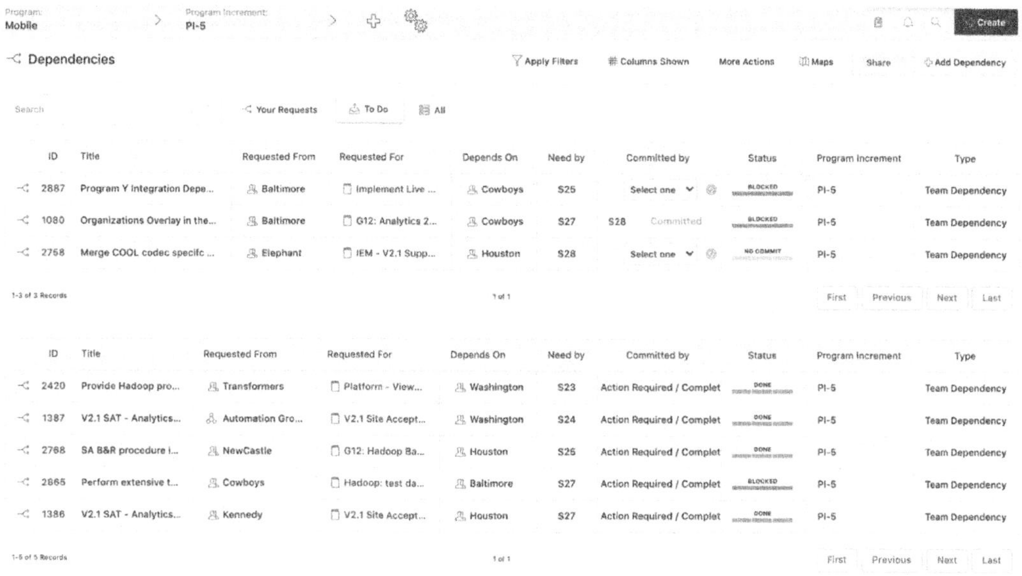

Figure 5.31 – Jira Align dependencies grid

Note that the dependency grid is split, displaying dependencies that require action from you at the top and all others at the bottom. At the top left of the workspace is a search box where you can search for dependencies by ID or keywords. You can also click on the following quick filter buttons to refine the list of dependencies shown in the grid:

- **Your Requests**: Displays dependencies that were raised by you and are awaiting a commitment

- **To Do**: Displays dependencies that require attention and action to be taken by you or your team

- **All**: Displays all dependencies that are relevant to you and your team

You can customize the dependency grid by clicking on the **Columns Shown** button to add or remove columns and then clicking on the **Save** button. Click on the **Apply Filters** button to refine the dependency list based on several selectable parameters. Once the dependency grid is configured and filtered to your liking, you can share a link by clicking on the **Share** button.

You can further explore dependencies by clicking on the **More Actions** button at the top of the workspace to open the menu shown in the following screenshot:

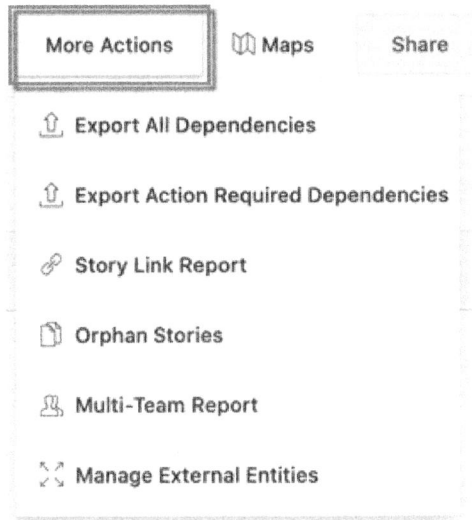

Figure 5.32 – Jira Align dependency grid, more actions menu

Here you can select from the following options:

- **Export All Dependencies**: Export all of your dependencies to an Excel file, allowing you to email or review the data.

- **Export Action Required Dependencies**: Export only the dependencies requiring action to an Excel file, allowing you to email or review the data.

- **Story Link Report**: Generate a report of all story links in Jira Software for the purpose of converting them to dependencies in Jira Align. Note that this requires configuration by your Jira Align administrator under **Administration | Jira Settings | Manage Projects | Manage Custom Fields**. Furthermore, we recommend that team-level dependencies remain in Jira Software where teams manage them locally using Jira's issue linking functionality, while Jira Align is reserved for the program level on up.

- **Orphan Stories**: Generate a report of all stories from multi-product features with no related dependency.

- **Multi-Team Report**: Generate a report showing the status of dependencies that horizontally affect multiple teams.
- **Manage External Entities**: Manage the list of external stakeholders and internal contact responsible.

We now know how to view, customize, and share information from the dependency grid. We will explore Jira Align's sophisticated dependency workflow in the next chapter. Now, let's examine how to visualize velocity for better planning as a program.

Visualizing program velocity for planning and predictability

Velocity is key for team level predictability. Let's say that a feature is sized at 80 points and the team's average velocity is 40 points per 2-week sprint. We can then predict that the feature can be delivered in 2 sprints or 1 month. Just as it's important for a team to know its velocity in order to predict when a work item can be delivered, so too is it important for a team of teams to know its program velocity. Jira Align has several visualizations for this. Here we highlight three of them: the Program Increments Velocity, Program Increments Burnup, and Velocity Trend reports.

Program Increments Velocity

This report shows the overall velocity for the teams participating in the selected program and PI. The format is a bar graph with sprints on the horizontal axis and story points on the vertical axis. The report provides portfolio managers, RTEs, and others with a high-level understanding of whether the work relating to a PI is on track.

It is beneficial to review the report during pre- and post-PI planning meetings and retrospectives. The report is based on the program and PI selected in the configuration bar. In the following screenshot, we have selected the `Mobile` program and the `PI-5` program increment:

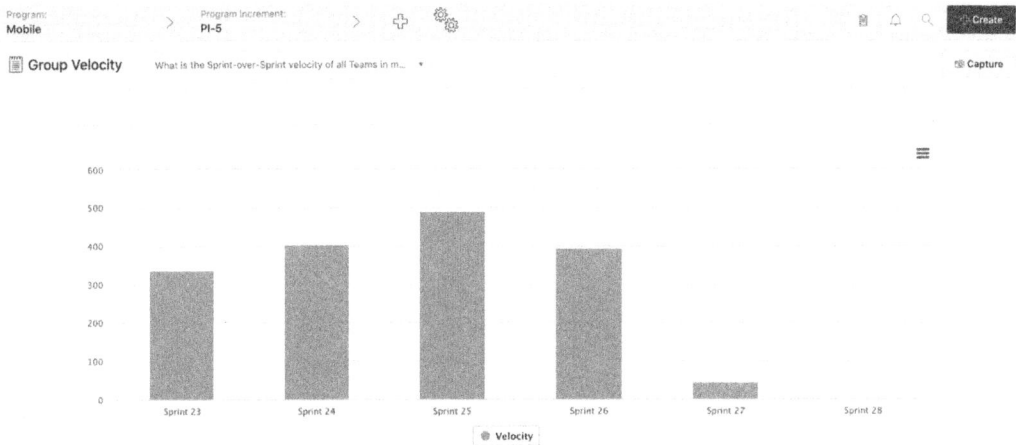

Figure 5.33 – Jira Align program increments velocity report

You can access the report by going to the navigation menu, clicking on the search icon (magnifying glass), and then searching for `Program Increments Velocity`. It is a common misconception that velocity should continually increase. The sign of a healthy, stable development organization is that velocity, and thus predictability, remains consistent. If you see many peaks and troughs, this may point to team instability, a high interrupt environment, inaccurate work estimation, or the early stages of agile maturity. Note that you can quickly export the data by clicking on the **Capture** button in the top right of the workspace.

Program Increments Burnup

The Program Increments Burnup report shows the burnup of story points for the PI. Additionally, for teams that size defects in story points, it displays a defect burnup. Depending on the context, environment, industry, company size, and other variables, teams may or may not treat their defects like user stories.

This report is especially useful for portfolio managers and RTEs to gain insight into the teams' ability to deliver stories as planned. As shown in the following screenshot, the format is a combined chart, including the plotting elements of a line graph with a bar chart displaying sprints on the horizontal axis and story points on the vertical axis:

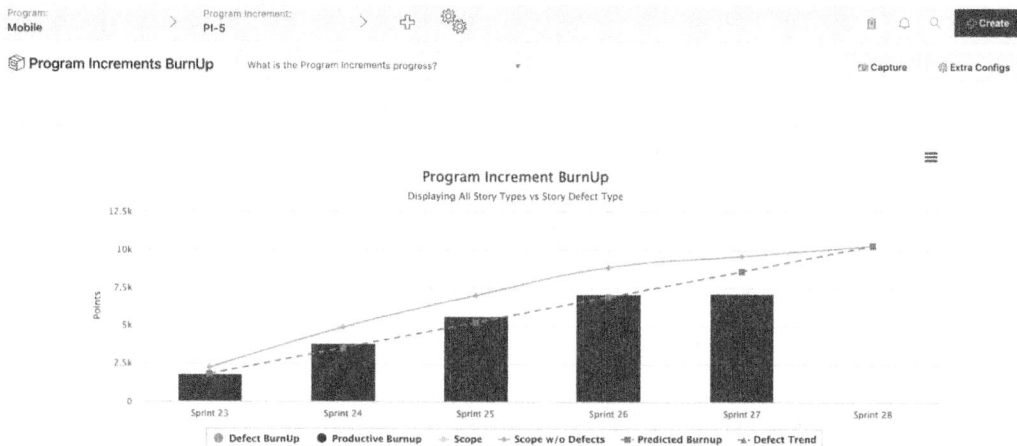

Figure 5.34 – Jira Align program increments burnup report

You can access the report by clicking on the search icon (magnifying glass), and then searching for Program Increments Burnup. The display can be filtered by PI, release vehicle, and team by clicking on the **Extra Configs** button.

This report is useful for assessing the maturity and stability of product development teams. Organizations new to agile will have fluctuations in sprint velocity that will even out over time as program teams shift from *doing* agile to *being* agile aided by coaching, inspecting, and adapting. Lastly, note that you can quickly export the data by clicking on the **Capture** button at the top right of the workspace.

Velocity Trend

The Velocity Trend (planned versus actual velocity variation by team) report highlights the planned and actual velocity by team over a specified period. As shown in the following screenshot, the format is a bar chart grouped by team and time period on the horizontal axis, with story points on the vertical axis:

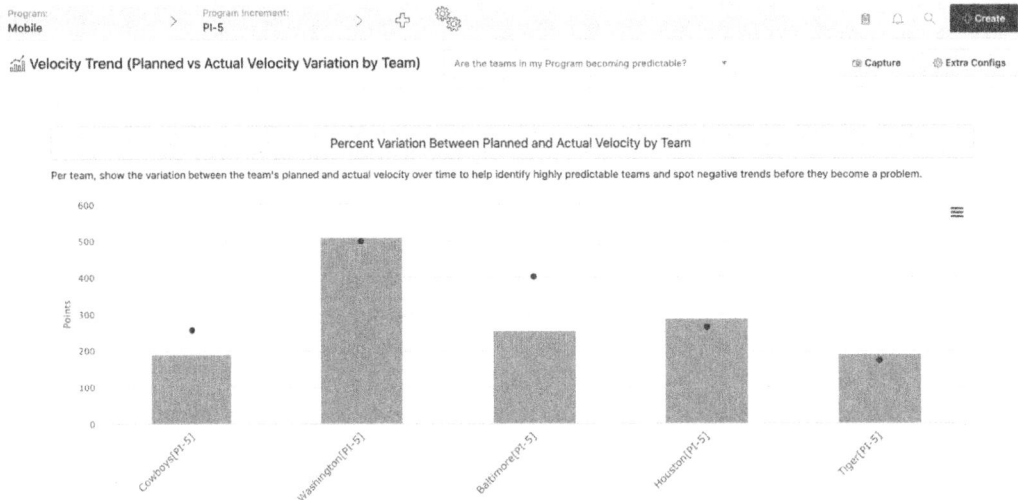

Figure 5.35 – Jira Align velocity trend by team report

Note the dots that show committed or planned velocity and bars that show actual velocity per team for the program and PI selected in the configuration bar. To access the report, go to the navigation menu and select **Program | Transform | Velocity Trend**. Click on the **Extra Configs** button to configure the report view for years, quarters, or program increments. It's beneficial to review the report regularly to identify highly predictable teams, help make realistic work commitments, and spot any negative trends early. Lastly, you can quickly export the data by clicking on the **Capture** button at the top right of the workspace.

Now that we've learned how to leverage Jira Align's reporting for better planning and predictability, let's see how it can help with other key concerns of the program in the next chapter.

Summary

In this chapter, we learned how to overcome planning and coordination challenges at the program level. We began by learning how to build product roadmaps for the near-term, long-term, and portfolio. We then explored how to effectively plan and deliver as a program, including the use of the program board, objectives and OKRs, and risk management. Next, we introduced Jira Align's rich dependency functionality and how it can help programs align toward value delivery. Lastly, we covered various program velocity views to assist with planning and predictability.

In the next chapter, we will focus on execution challenges at the program level. We will introduce the program room, the control center for program execution. We'll then continue the discussion on dependencies, including workflow and visualizations, and then explore ways to reduce unnecessary work, manage scope, and communicate PI and release progress.

Questions

1. What are the three roadmap types recommended by SAFe?
2. Which report allows you to predict the ability to deliver business value?
3. Which risk model do SAFe and Jira Align use for managing risks?

Further reading

- *Scaling Scrum across Modern Enterprises*, by Cecil Rupp (Packt, 2020)

6
Program Execution Challenges

In this chapter, we will continue the discussion of program-level agile with a focus on execution. Planning and execution go hand in hand. Indeed, as we saw in the previous chapter, key planning tools such as roadmaps and the program board are living documents that support ongoing execution since they are connected to the actual work items being delivered. This chapter rounds out the previous one, providing essential tools for scaling agile team execution to the program. Program-level execution is so important for business agility that the **Scaled Agile Framework (SAFe)** calls it **Essential** in **SAFe 5.0**. In other words, you are not following **SAFe** if you are not delivering at the team of teams level.

In this chapter, we will cover the following:

- Overseeing the program room
- Negotiating and visualizing dependencies
- Reducing waste, managing scope, and communicating progress

Overseeing the program room

Jira Align provides a dashboard for teams at each level of scale called a **room**. The dashboard for program teams is the Program Room. It's a one-stop-shop for all things related to program-level execution. Here, the release train engineer (RTE), scrum masters, and other program members have a bird's-eye view of what's happening in the program increment. To access it, select your program and PI in the configuration bar, then go to the navigation menu and select **Program | Program Room**.

The program room is highly configurable, but there are two data sections that always display sprints and work items. These are shown in the middle of the following screenshot:

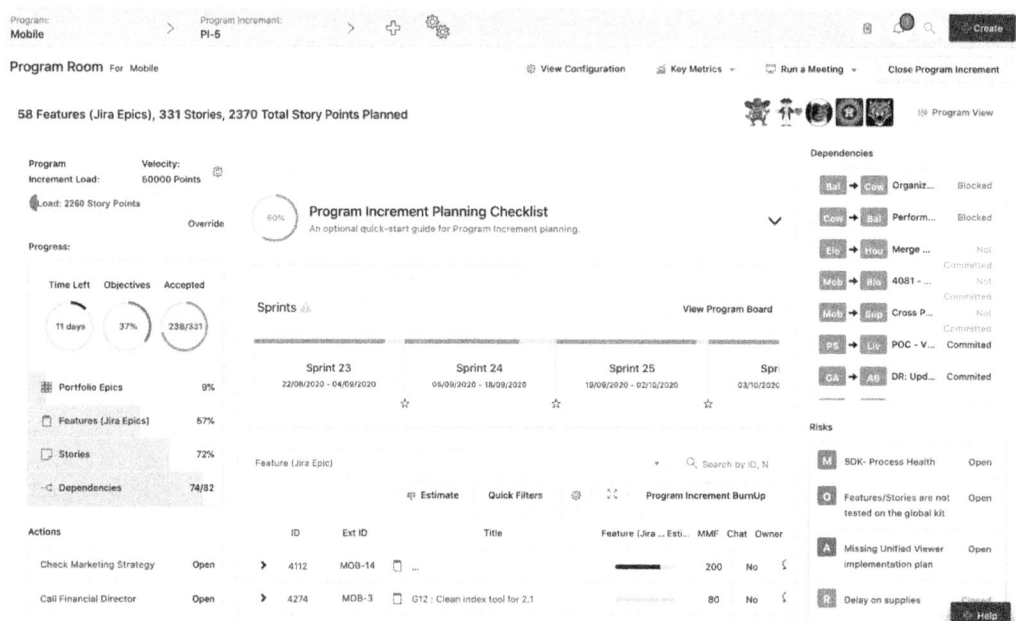

Figure 6.1 – Jira Align program room

The **Sprints** section displays the following information:

- Each sprint in the PI has a green bar indicating the completion percentage based on accepted story points. Hover over the bar to see the numerical percentage. Stories must be assigned to the sprint to be included, but don't need to be accepted within the sprint.

- The diamond icon indicates a release vehicle ship date. Hover over the diamond to see the name of the release vehicle and the completion percentage.

- The star icon indicates milestone and objective target completion dates. Hover over the star to see the name of the objective or milestone.

The work items list displays the following information:

- All features, capabilities, and portfolio epics assigned to the selected program and PI.

- You can select the **Feature view**, **Feature by Portfolio Epic** view, or, if capabilities are enabled, the **Feature by Capability** view. Do this by clicking on the header of the work items list.

- Note that the data for portfolio epics reflects the portion pertaining to the selected PI.

The program room is configurable with over a dozen widgets that can be toggled on by clicking on the **View Configuration** button at the top of the workspace to the right of the center. Widgets can be repositioned in the room by clicking and dragging them. In the previous screenshot, we toggled on the progress, program increment load, team progress, and team load versus capacity widgets and positioned them to the left of the sprints and work items sections. We toggled on the actions, dependencies, and impediments widgets and positioned them to the right.

The following are descriptions of the various widgets:

- **Progress**: Displays the time left for the PI; the percentage of objectives completed; the number and percentage of accepted stories versus total stories; the percentage of accepted portfolio epics, capabilities, features, and stories; and the number of dependencies completed out of the total number of dependencies.

- **Actions**: Displays open and closed meeting action items for the selected program and PI.

- **Chat**: Provides an area for chat and discussions on any work item in the PI.

- **Dependencies**: Displays dependencies where the selected program is a **Requesting** or **Depends On** program, dependencies between the program teams, and dependencies associated with the PI or that have a **Needed By** date within the PI.

- **Impediments**: Displays team impediments.

- **Objectives**: Displays PI objectives.

- **Program Increment Load**: Displays the program's average velocity over the previous two PIs, which you can manually change by clicking on **Override**, and the PI load, which by default is the estimated load based on total feature points. You can click on the gear icon to select the actual load based on total story points.

- **Release Vehicle**: Displays release vehicles with work items assigned to the PI (even if the release vehicle dates are outside of the PI) and to the program.

- **Risks**: Displays risks for the selected program that are assigned to the selected PI.

- **Team Load vs Capacity**: Displays the load versus capacity percentage for each team in the program, based on the total team story points loaded in the PI divided by the team's PI capacity. The PI capacity is the sum of the velocities of each sprint in the program increment. Click on a row to open the team's details panel for more information, including current and past sprints and the average team velocity over the previous five sprints.

- **Program Increment Planning Checklist**: Provides a configurable list of steps to complete before starting the PI.

- **Team Progress**: Displays the total story points accepted by the team within the PI as a percentage of the team's PI velocity. The team's PI velocity is their average velocity multiplied by the number of sprints in the PI.

- **Runway**: Displays the runway for portfolio epics, capabilities, features, and stories, which allows you to compare the amount of time needed to complete the work you haven't started with a goal you set. Click on the gear icon to enter the runway goal, which is measured in sprints for stories and months for features, capabilities, and portfolio epics, and the percentage deviation, which signifies how close you'd like to be to the goal.

You now know the key data sections and widgets of the program room, and they are only a portion of what the program room offers. Here are some other highlights:

1. Click on the **Key Metrics** button at the top of the workspace to see the PI burndown/burnup, group velocity, velocity by certainty, velocity by complexity, and PI defect trend.

2. Click on the **Run a Meeting** button to launch backlog refinement and scrum of scrums meetings. RTEs can start and stop PIs by clicking on the button in the top-right corner of the workspace.

3. Click on the **View Program Board** button to open that centerpiece of the program, which we covered in the previous chapter.

Now that you've been introduced to the program room, let's return to the all-important topic of dependencies.

Negotiating and visualizing dependencies

In the last chapter, we learned how to view, customize, and share information from the dependency grid. We'll now examine Jira Align's sophisticated dependency workflow. After that, we'll learn how to handle external dependencies. Lastly, we'll explore the various dependency visualizations beyond the basic grid view.

Dependency workflow

Jira Align's dependency functionality enforces a contract between teams supported by a collaborative workflow. The first step in the workflow is to create a dependency. To do so, click on the **Add Dependency** button in the top-right corner of the dependency grid workspace to open the **New Dependency** details panel, shown in the following screenshot:

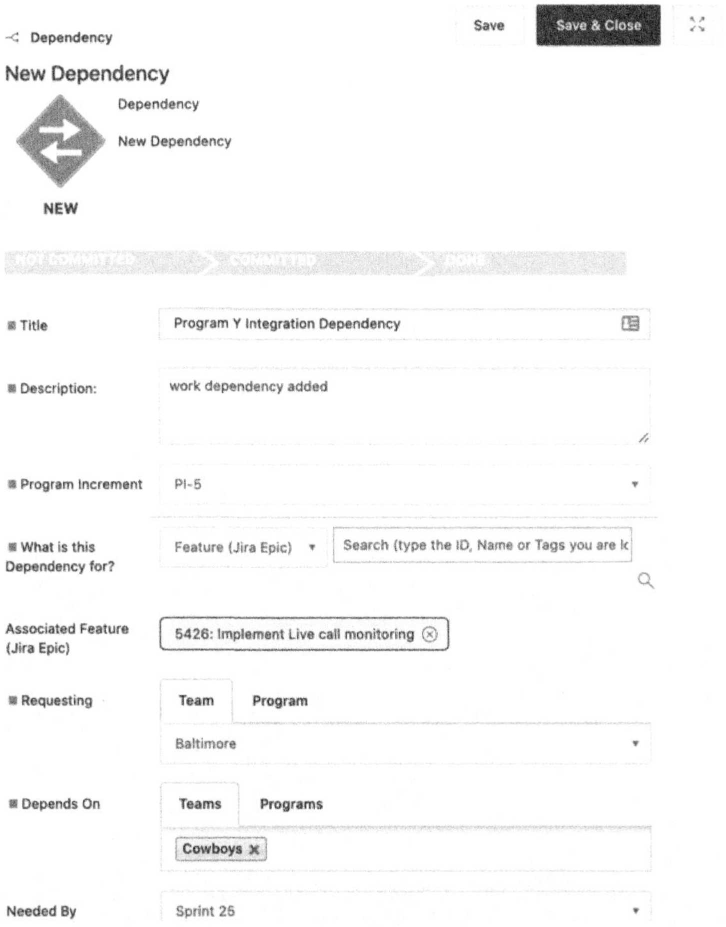

Figure 6.2 – Jira Align create a new dependency

Here, you can enter and track the following details for a dependency:

- **Title**: Add a meaningful title for the dependency.

- **Description**: Add further descriptive details about the dependency.

- **Program Increment**: Select the applicable program increment – for example, `PI-5`.

- **What is this Dependency for?**: Select the dependent work item (feature, capability, or portfolio epic). For example, select **Feature** and then associate a feature as the dependent work item. A dependent work item is one that depends on another team or program's work item.

- **Requesting**: Choose the requesting team or program – for example, team `Baltimore`.

- **Depends On**: Choose the team(s) or program(s) on which the requesting team depends – for example, team `Cowboys`.

- **Needed By**: Select the target delivery sprint for the requested work – for example, `Sprint 25`.

Next, click on the **Save** button. The dependency status will be set to **Not Committed**, as shown in the following screenshot:

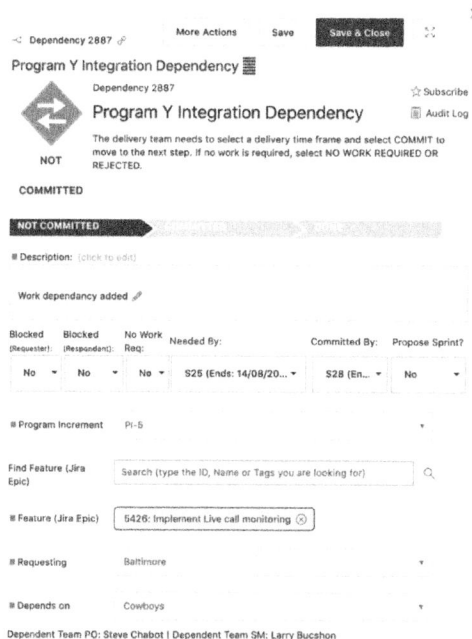

Figure 6.3 – Jira Align dependency not committed

The team on the receiving end of the request – in this case, Cowboys – should respond by selecting a **Committed By** sprint – for example, Sprint 24. If the respondent commits by or earlier than the **Needed By** sprint – for example, **Sprint 25** – then it will set the status to **Committed**, as shown in the following screenshot:

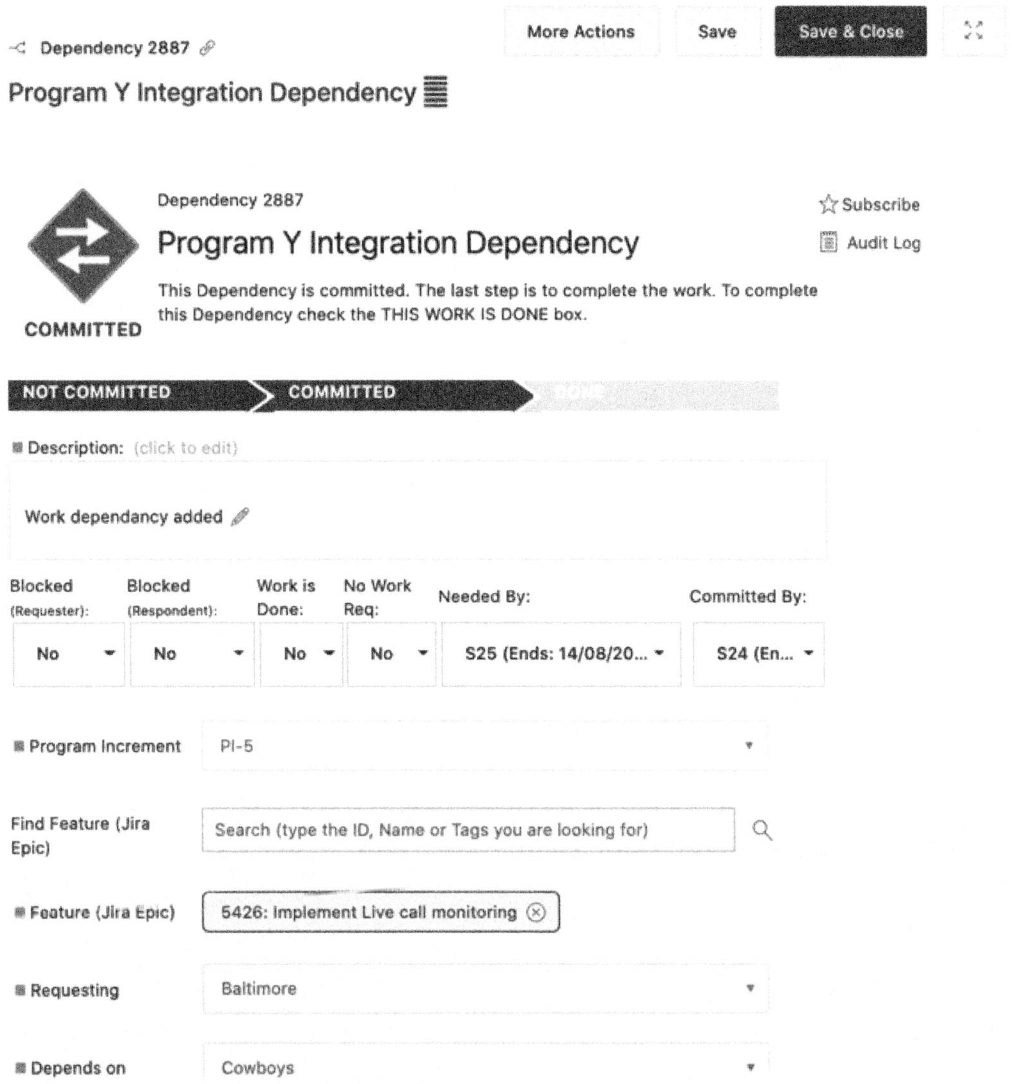

Figure 6.4 – Jira Align dependency committed

If the respondent chooses to commit to a later sprint – for example, by selecting `Sprint 26` as the **Committed By** sprint – then Jira Align creates a new proposal for the requesting team – in this case, `Baltimore` – to consider. This is shown in the following screenshot:

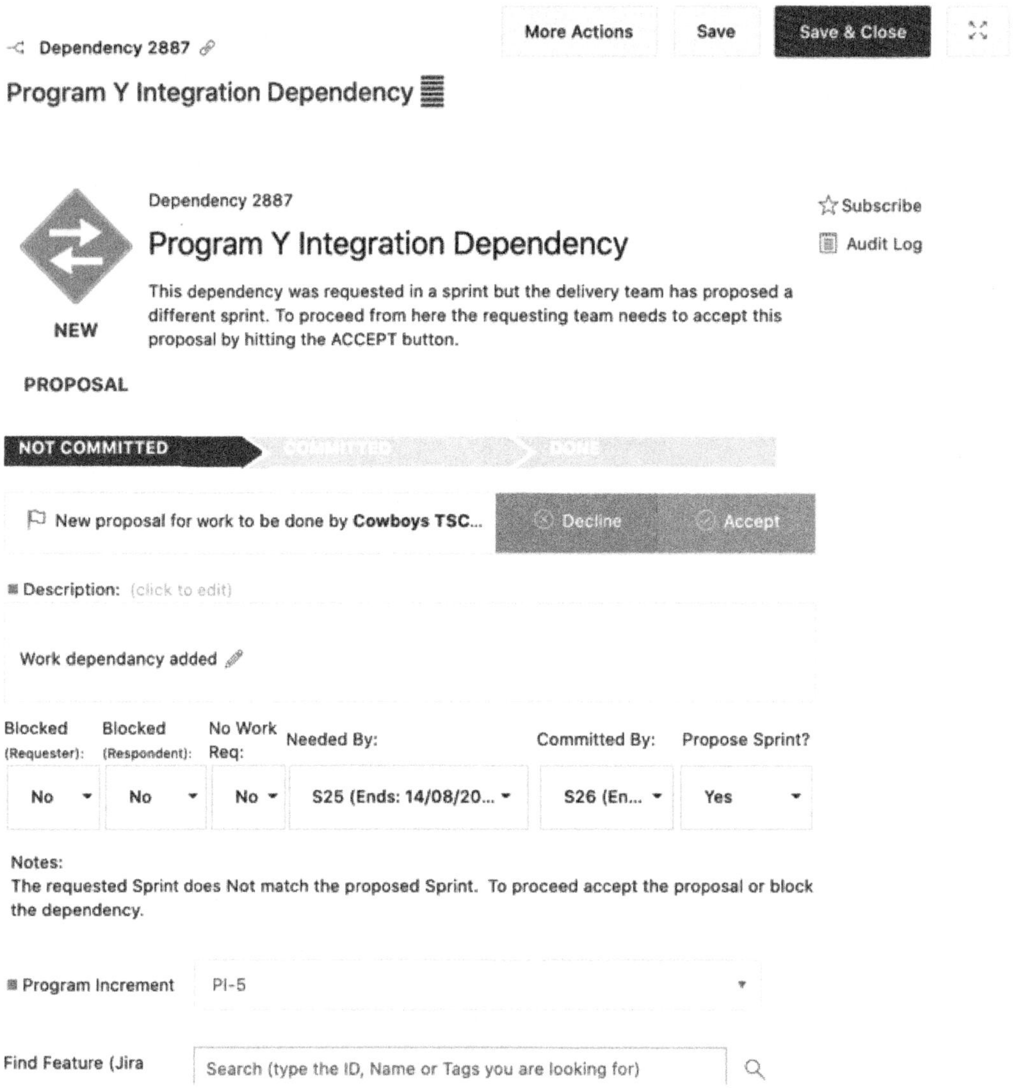

Figure 6.5 – Jira Align new dependency proposal

If the requester now clicks on the **Accept** button, this would set the dependency status to **Committed** and update the **Needed By** sprint to match the new **Committed By** sprint. If the requester clicks on the **Decline** button, then the status would be set to **NOT Committed**, as shown in the following screenshot:

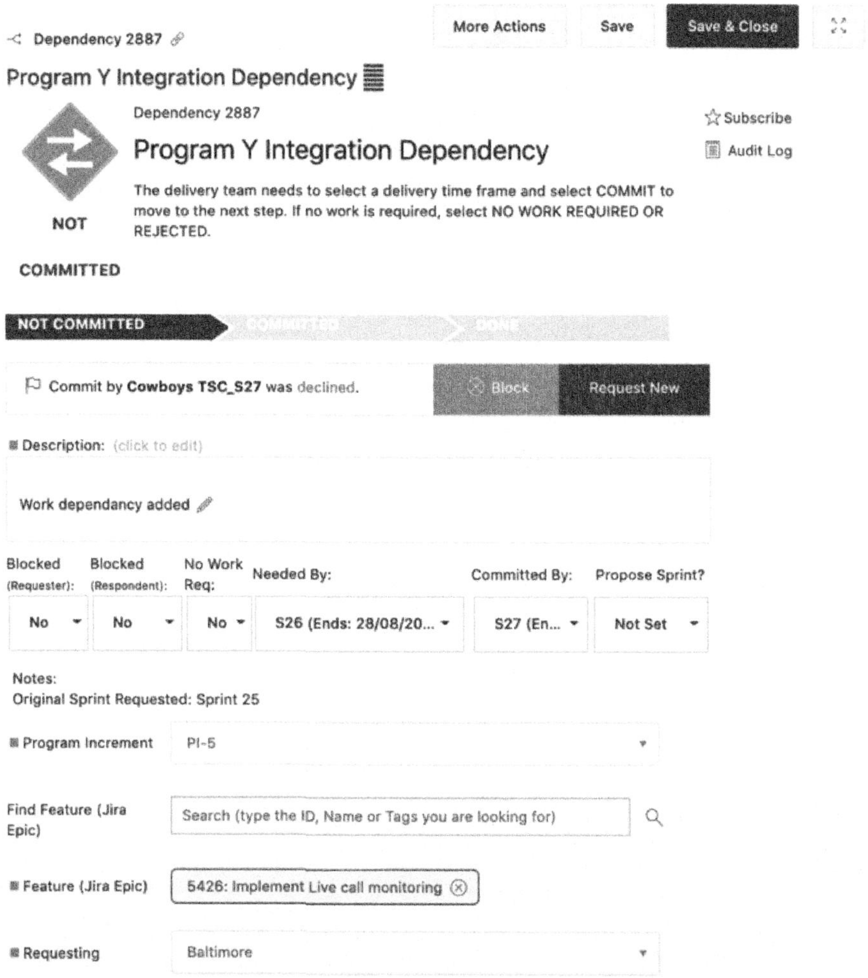

Figure 6.6 – Jira Align dependency proposal declined

> **Tips and tricks**
>
> It is important that the requester communicates with the respondent to negotiate a mutually agreeable commitment date. We recommend directly speaking with the other team to negotiate a suitable commitment date before formalizing the agreement in Jira Align.

Now that the requester has declined the new proposal, it's the respondent's turn to act. At this point, the respondent can indicate that their team is blocked by clicking on the **Block** button and providing a blocked reason, as shown in the following screenshot:

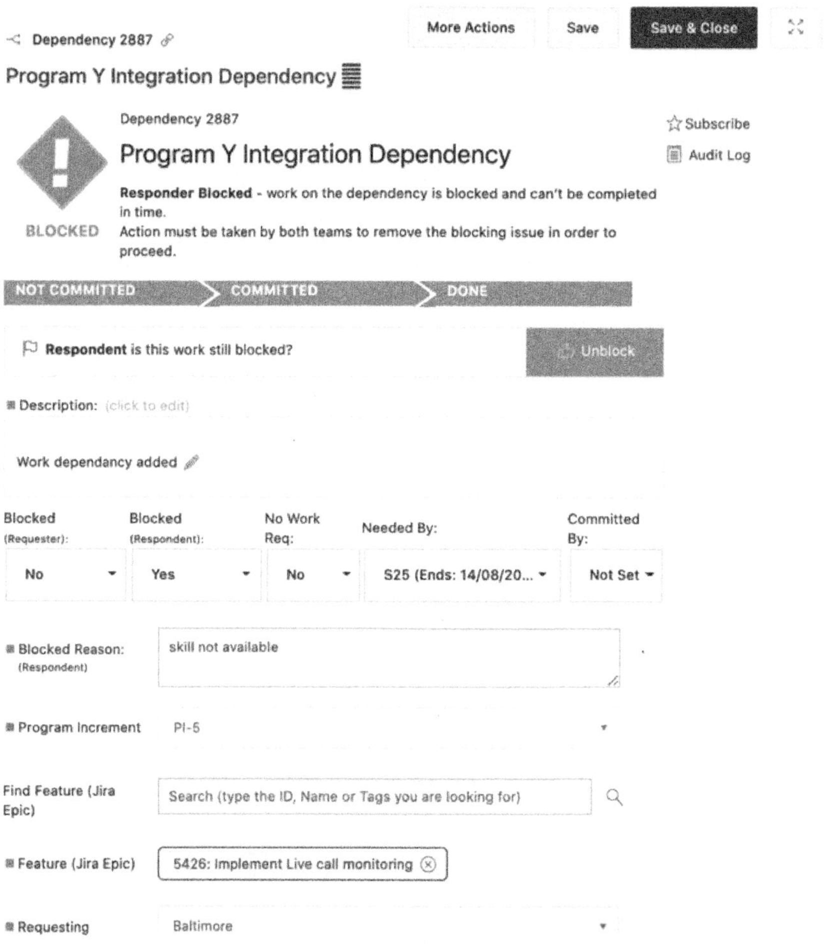

Figure 6.7 – Jira Align dependency blocked

Alternatively, the respondent can click on the **Request New** button and select a **Committed By** sprint on or before the **Needed By** sprint to set the dependency to **Committed** status. If this does not occur, it could take several volleys back and forth before both sides agree on a **Committed By** sprint. All of this activity can be viewed by clicking on the **Audit Log** link at the top right of the details panel. Clicking on the **Subscribe** link will notify you of changes to the dependency. Note that by default, the product owner and scrum master of the involved teams are automatically notified.

As work progresses, either the requester or the respondent can indicate that they are blocked at any time by setting the first or second field in the following screenshot to **Yes** and entering a blocked reason. This will set the dependency status to **Blocked**:

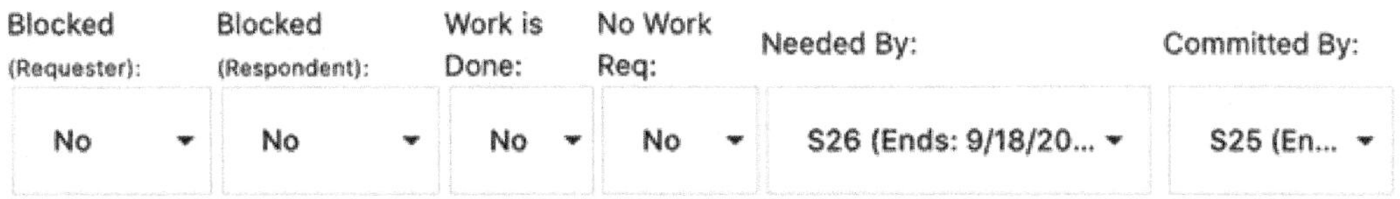

Blocked (Requester):	Blocked (Respondent):	Work is Done:	No Work Req:	Needed By:	Committed By:
No ▼	No ▼	No ▼	No ▼	S26 (Ends: 9/18/20... ▼	S25 (En... ▼

Figure 6.8 – Jira Align dependency work status

Once work is done, or if it turns out that no work is required to meet the needs of the dependent team, the third or fourth field in the previous screenshot can be set to **Yes**, which will update the status of the dependency to **Done**, as shown in the following screenshot:

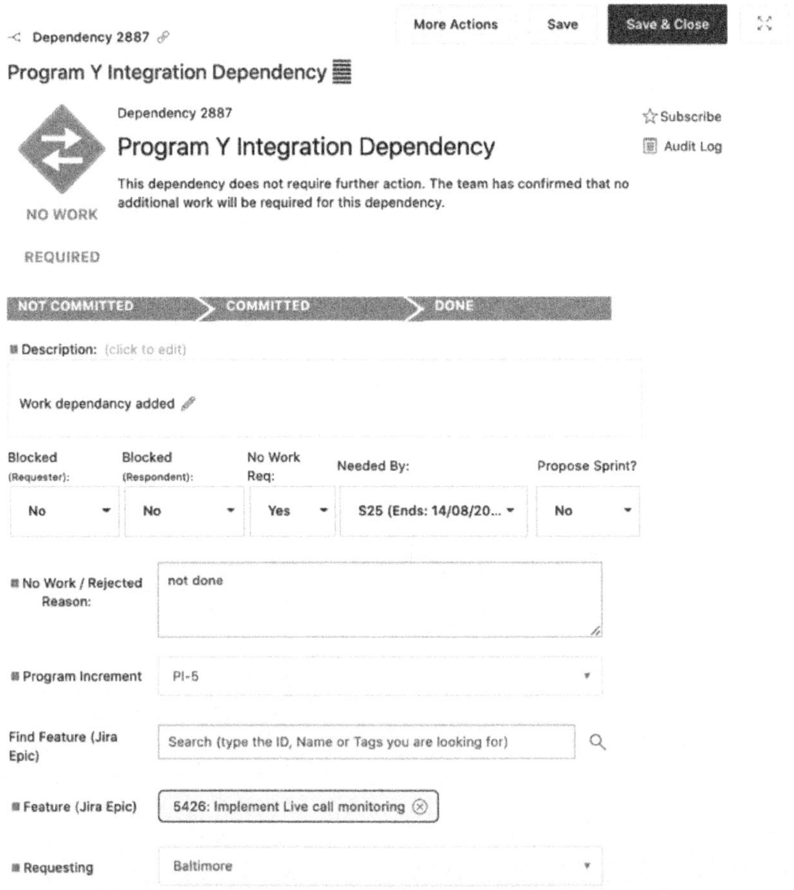

Figure 6.9 – Jira Align dependency with no work required

Note that aside from updating the **Work is Done** field (see *Figure 6.8*), it is best practice for the responding team to associate their work item – that is, the work item needed by the requesting team – with the dependency. This is done near the bottom of the dependency details panel. That way, the real-time status of the work item can be easily gathered when viewing the dependency details.

There are other actions you can take by clicking on the **More Actions** button at the top of the dependency details panel, as follows:

- **Delete**: Remove a dependency by deleting it.
- **Reject**: Cancel a dependency and mark it as **Rejected**.
- **Duplicate**: Clone a dependency to serve as the basis for a similar one.
- **Uncommit**: Move a dependency status back to **Not Committed**.

These options vary depending on the status of the dependency and your role permissions. Note that when a dependency is set to either **No Work Required** or **Rejected**, it will require **No Work / Rejected Reason** to be filled out, as shown in the following screenshot:

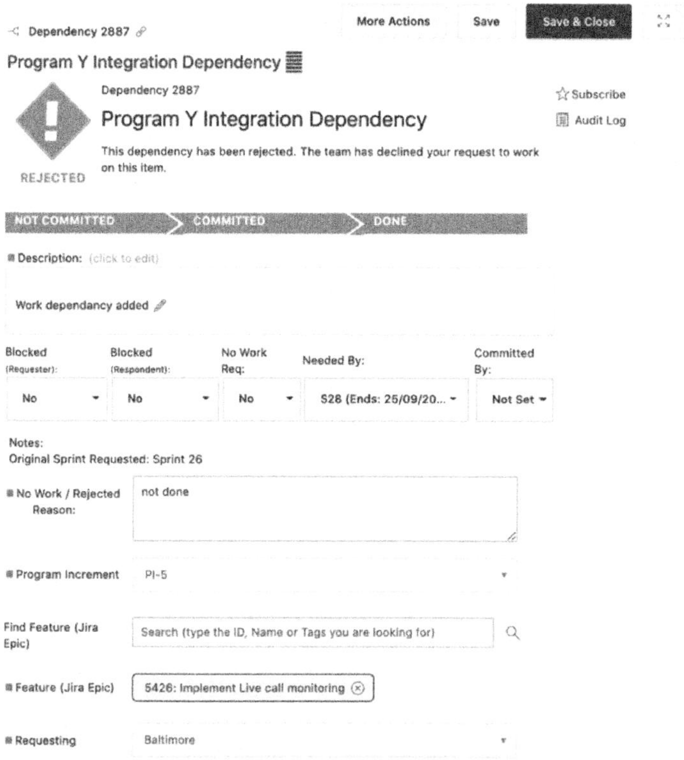

Figure 6.10 – Jira Align dependency rejected

Now that we've explored the dependency workflow, let's take a look at how to create external dependencies.

External dependencies

It is a common challenge for teams to track external factors that affect their delivery. In Jira Align, external dependencies are not enabled by default. The Jira Align administrator can enable them by going to **Administration | Settings | Platform** and clicking on **Manage Dependencies** in the **Team** tab. This will open the window shown in the following screenshot:

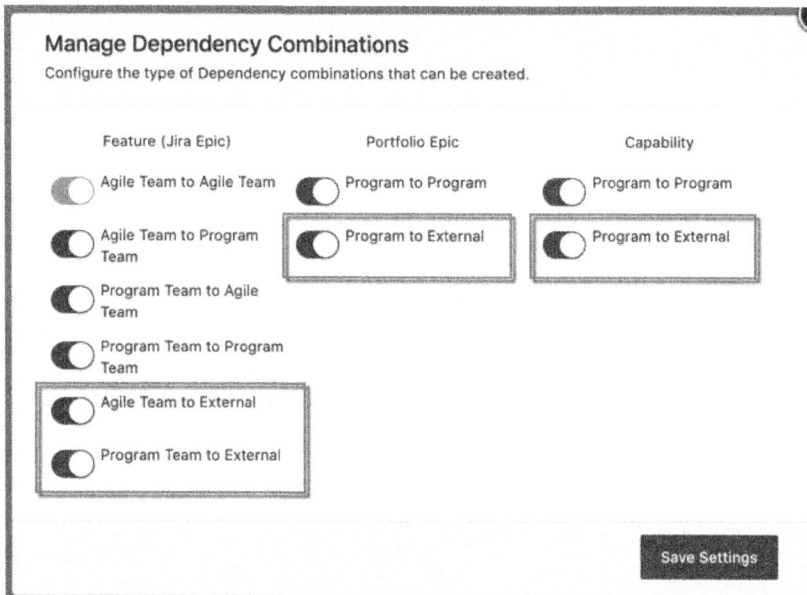

Manage Dependency Combinations
Configure the type of Dependency combinations that can be created.

Feature (Jira Epic)	Portfolio Epic	Capability
Agile Team to Agile Team	Program to Program	Program to Program
Agile Team to Program Team	Program to External	Program to External
Program Team to Agile Team		
Program Team to Program Team		
Agile Team to External		
Program Team to External		

Save Settings

Figure 6.11 – Jira Align manage dependency combinations window

Note the toggles shown for external dependencies at the feature, capability, and portfolio epic levels. The administrator can slide these on to enable external dependencies at those levels and then click on the **Save Settings** button to apply the changes.

Now that external dependencies are enabled, let's add external entities by going to **More Actions | Manage External Entities**. In the window that opens, add the external entity name and owner (a Jira Align user who will be the proxy for the external entity), and then click on **Add**. In the following screenshot, we are creating a new external entity called `Publishing House` and we assign an internal owner who will be responsible for communications with the external entity:

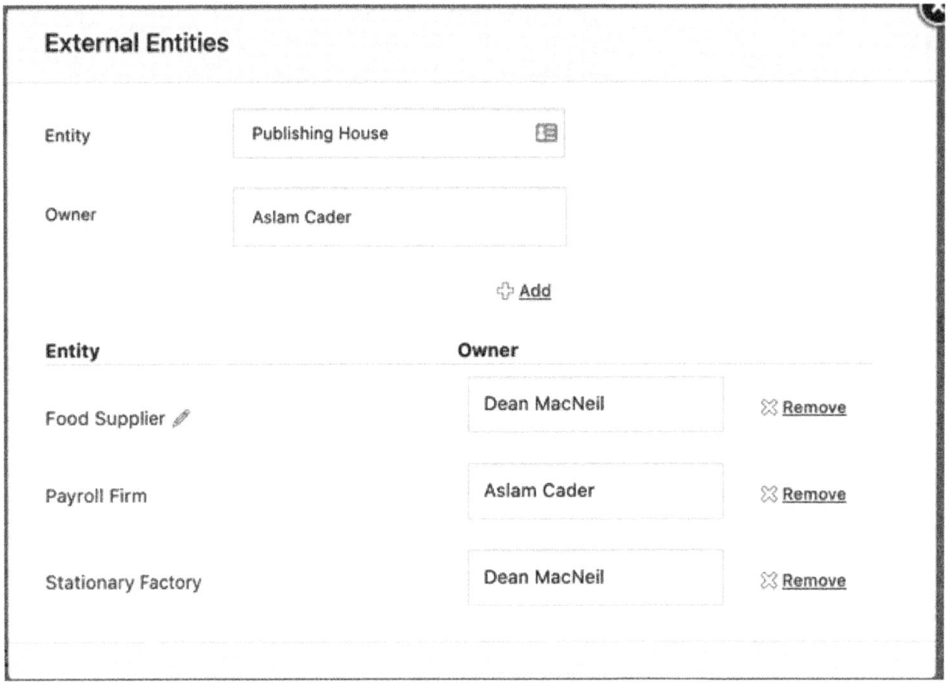

External Entities		
Entity	Publishing House	
Owner	Aslam Cader	
	✛ Add	
Entity	**Owner**	
Food Supplier 🖉	Dean MacNeil	✕ Remove
Payroll Firm	Aslam Cader	✕ Remove
Stationary Factory	Dean MacNeil	✕ Remove

Figure 6.12 – Jira Align external dependency entity creation

Now, when you close the window and create an external dependency, you will see the entities you added in the **External** dropdown list near the bottom of the following screenshot, in the **Depends On** section:

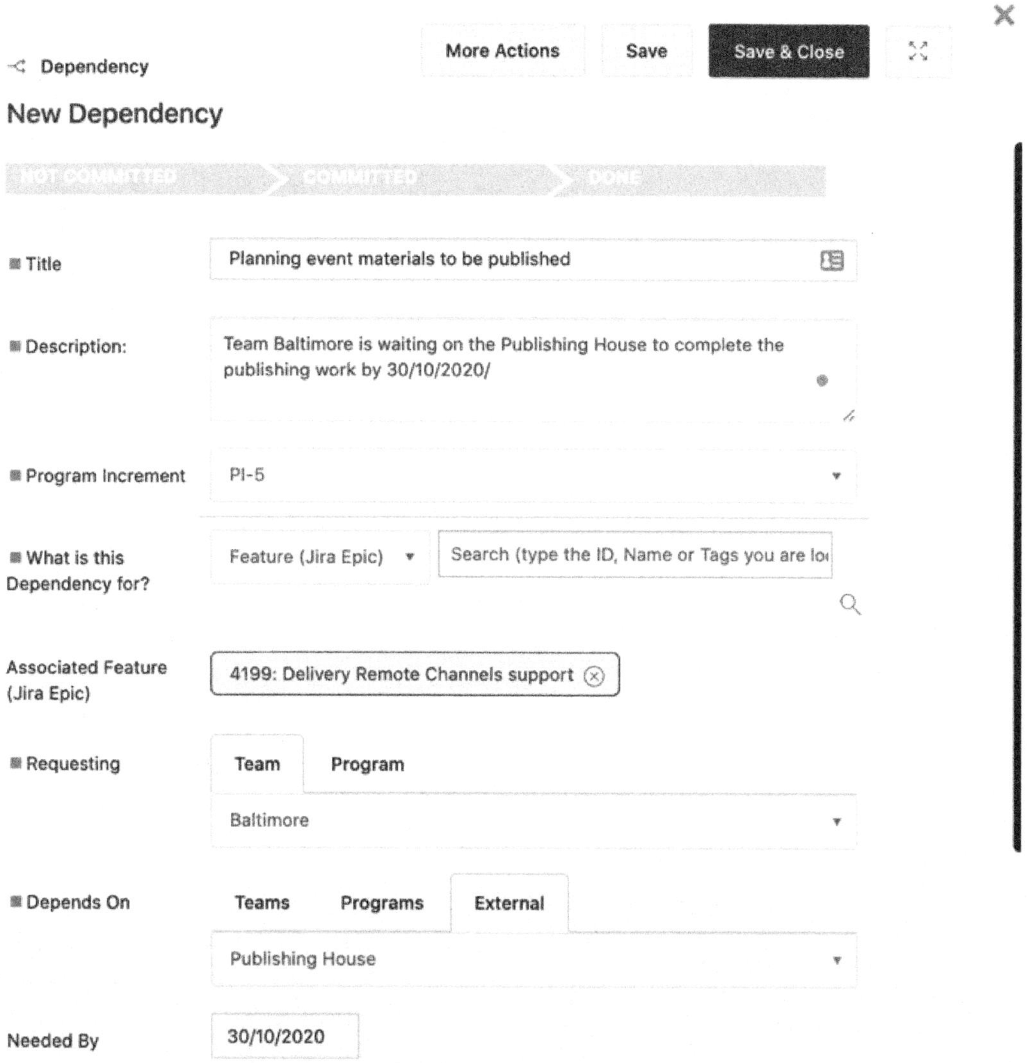

Figure 6.13 – Jira Align create an external dependency

Here, we are creating an external dependency in PI-5 for team Baltimore, which depends on the Publishing House external entity to complete work by 30/10/2020.

Now that we've explored the dependency workflow, including external dependencies, let's explore the various dependency visualizations.

Dependency maps

Jira Align calls its many helpful visualizations **dependency maps**. To access them, let's return to the dependency grid by going to the navigation menu and selecting **Program | Manage | Dependencies**. Next, click on the **Maps** button near the top right of the workspace to access the visualizations:

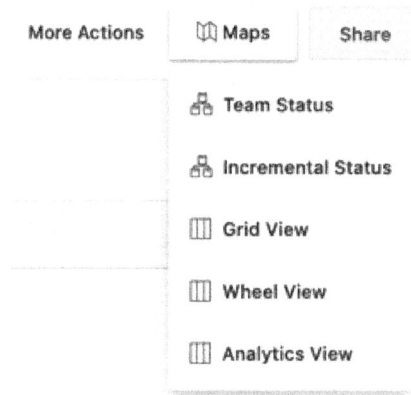

Figure 6.14 – Jira Align dependency maps

The options shown allow you to track, take action, and report on dependencies. Let's begin with the **Team Status** option.

Team status dependency map

This option allows you to view dependencies by team and prioritize them as needed. Be sure to set your team and PI context in the configuration bar. In the following screenshot, we have selected the Baltimore team and PI-5:

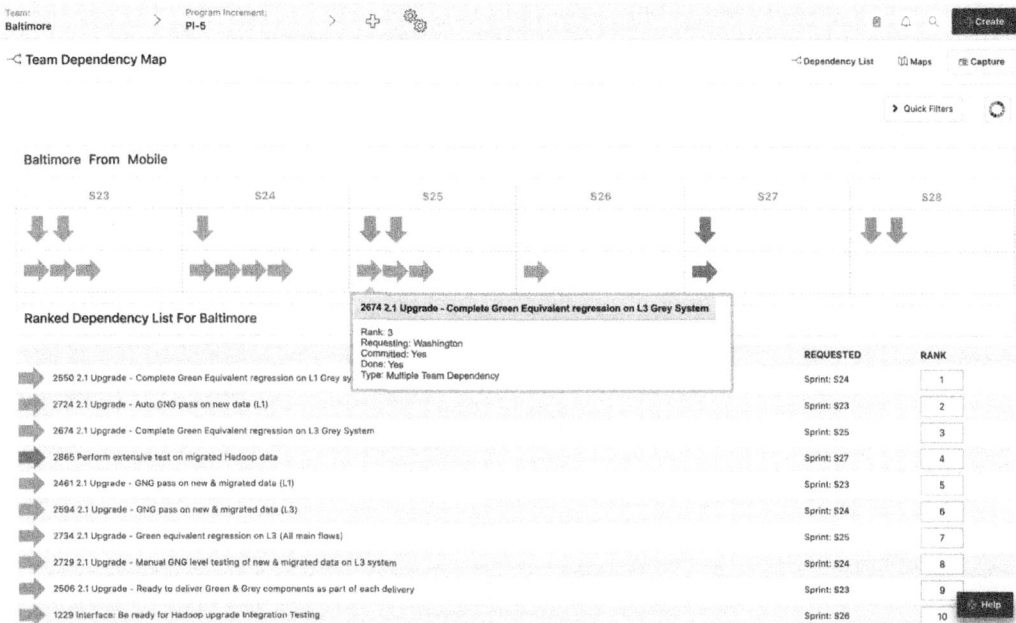

Figure 6.15 – Jira Align team status dependency map

The arrows on the dependency map indicate the following:

- **Right arrows**: Indicate outbound dependencies that the current team needs to deliver to another team.

- **Down arrows**: Indicate inbound dependencies that the current team needs from another team.

The color codes are shown in the report legend, which you can access by clicking on the color wheel button at the top right of the workspace. The dependencies are color-coded as follows:

- **Green**: Committed/delivered

- **Orange**: Not committed/not delivered

- **Blue**: Rejected or no work required

- **Red**: Blocked

Note that the dependencies are prioritized using the rank number and then ordered by clicking on the **Save** button at the bottom of the list. Click on the **Quick Filters** button to toggle on/off dependencies based on association (inbound or outbound) and status. Lastly, you can export a snapshot view of the dependency map by clicking on the **Capture** button. Let's now explore the **Incremental Status** option.

Incremental status dependency map

This option allows you to view dependencies by program to help coordinate the required work effort. As shown in the following screenshot, you can set the configuration bar context to include one or more programs with a program increment. Note that this is enabled by the best practice of programs within a portfolio sharing a common PI cadence:

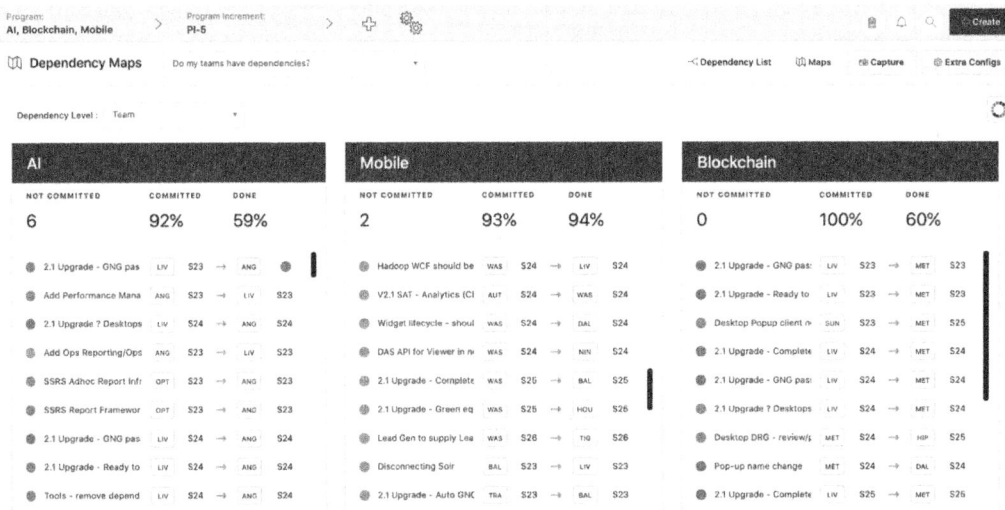

Figure 6.16 – Jira Align program increment status dependency map

Here, we've selected the AI, Blockchain, and Mobile programs and PI-5 as our context. Note the **Dependency Level** dropdown, where we've chosen to display **Team** dependencies. As with the previously discussed dependency map, statuses are color-coded to allow quick identification of dependencies that require attention and action. The color codes are shown in the report legend, which you can access by clicking on the color wheel button at the top right of the workspace. Additionally, you can click on the **Extra Configs** button to toggle on/off the dependencies based on status and/or target delivery sprint. You can export a snapshot view of the dependency map by clicking on the **Capture** button. Let's move on now to the **Grid View** option.

Grid view dependency map

This option displays the count of dependencies between teams and programs in the form of a matrix. The configuration bar context is set to include a program with a program increment. In the following screenshot, we've set the **Dependency Level** dropdown to **Program** to see a program dependency matrix:

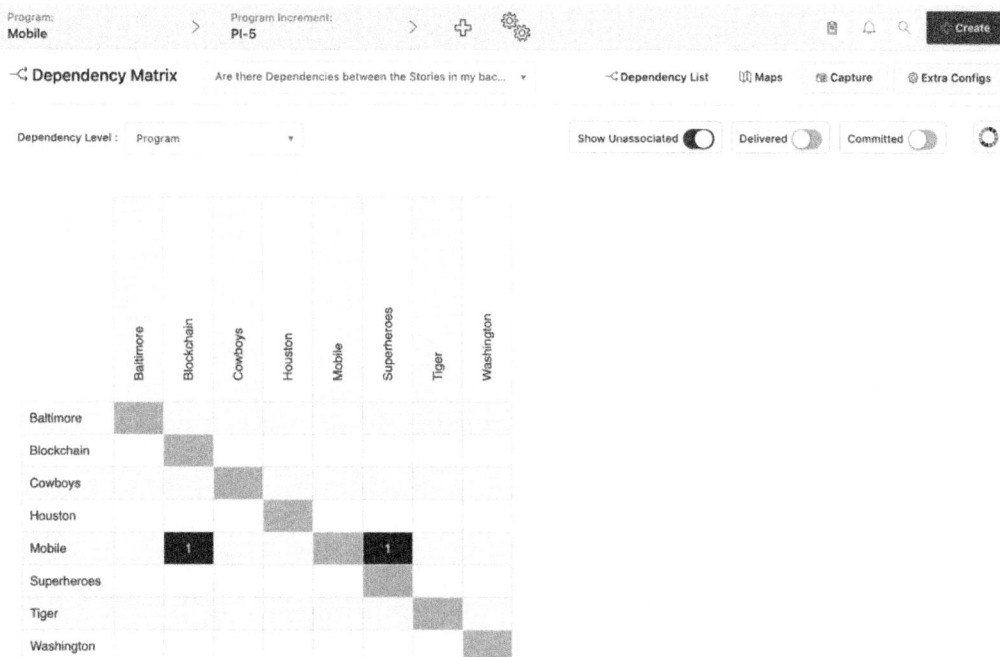

Figure 6.17 – Jira Align grid view dependency map

Note the toggle selections at the top right where you can choose to show unassociated teams/programs and dependencies that are delivered and committed. Click on the **Extra Configs** button to filter dependencies based on type – for example, team/program dependencies, multiple team/program dependencies, capability external dependencies, and external dependencies.

Next, click on any number in the grid to open a details panel on the right. For example, in the following screenshot, we've clicked on 5 in the `Baltimore` row to see the five dependencies that `Baltimore` needs from the `Cowboys` team:

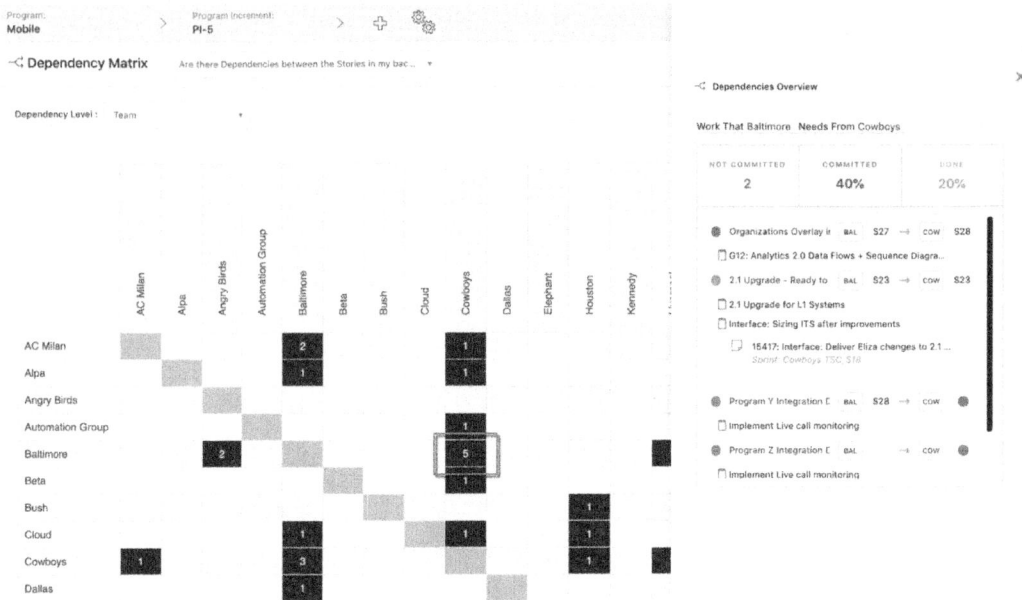

Figure 6.18 – Jira Align grid view dependency map details report

Note that dependencies are displayed with the dependent work item and that statuses are color-coded according to the report legend. You can export a snapshot view of the dependency map by clicking on the **Capture** button. We're now ready to explore the popular **Wheel View** option.

Wheel view dependency map

This option allows you to view dependencies as lines or strings between teams/programs. Green lines indicate delivered dependencies, blue ones indicate not delivered, and red ones indicate blocked or uncommitted dependencies. The configuration bar context is set to include a program with a program increment. Clicking on a team or a program on the wheel opens a details panel on the right. For example, in the following screenshot, we've clicked on **Cowboys** to see the dependencies they need from others and that others need from them:

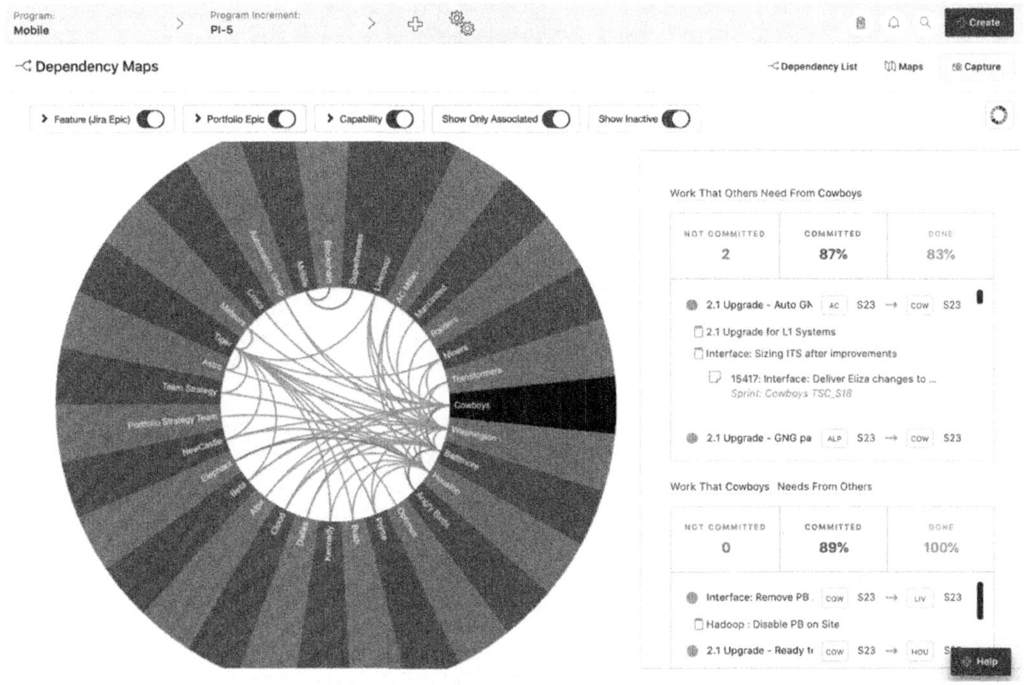

Figure 6.19 – Jira Align wheel view dependency map

Statuses are color-coded the same way as strings, and you can click on the color wheel icon in the top right for the color key. Note the toggle selections above the wheel, where you can show dependencies related to work items (features, capabilities, and portfolio epics), only associated dependencies, and inactive dependencies. You can further expand the work items to show specific levels of dependencies, as shown in the following screenshot:

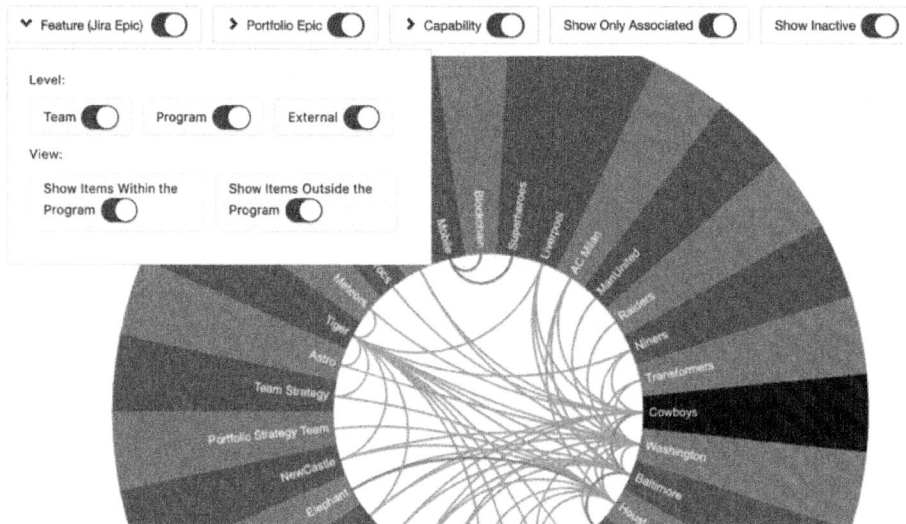

Figure 6.20 – Jira Align wheel view dependency map options

Here, we see that for dependencies associated with features, you can slide toggles on to display the team, program, and external dependencies. You can also toggle on the option to show items within or outside the program. For dependencies associated with portfolio epics and capabilities, you can slide on toggles to display program and external dependencies.

Lastly, you can export a snapshot view of the dependency map by clicking on the **Capture** button. We're now ready to explore the **Analytics View**.

Analytics view dependency map

This view allows you to analyze dependency clusters by showing which teams and programs have the highest quantity of dependencies. This way, you can find out where to focus your dependency reduction efforts. The configuration bar context is set to include a program with a program increment. You can set the **Dependency Level** dropdown to **Team** in order to see the team dependency trend, as shown in the following screenshot:

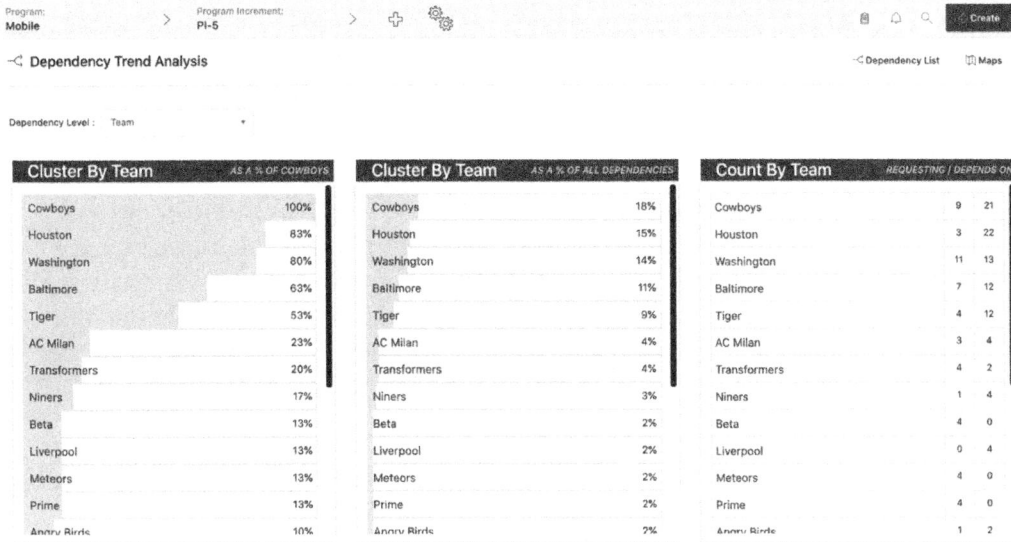

Figure 6.21 – Jira Align analytics view dependency map

The dependencies are grouped in the following way:

- **Cluster by team/program** as a percentage of the team/program with the most dependencies.

- **Cluster by team/program** as a percentage of all dependencies.

- **Count by team/program** for the PI.

Managing and reducing dependencies is critical for effective execution. Now that we've explored how to create, track, and visualize dependencies, let's examine how Jira Align can help with other key concerns of the program.

Reducing waste, managing scope, and communicating progress

In this closing section, we will explore how to get a handle on a program's scope of work for the PI, reduce duplicate work, and effectively communicate delivery status. We will begin with the popular **Work Tree** view, which has helped numerous organizations address these challenges. We'll then examine two reports, program increment progress and scope change, functionality for splitting features, and finally, the PI and release vehicle roadmaps. Together, these tools help ensure effective program-level execution.

Work tree

In the last chapter, we saw the benefits of real-time work status updates in the work view roadmap and program board. Another important visualization for real-time information is the work tree, which has the added benefit of showing how work items connect to one another from top to bottom and bottom-up. It is an important tool for analyzing work across the organization with an eye toward reducing work per *Principle 10* of the *Agile Manifesto*: *Simplicity—the art of maximizing the amount of work not done—is essential.* As a case in point, we've seen $750,000 in savings due to the avoidance of duplicate work for a single program ART in a single PI. Cost savings of this magnitude could not have been possible without full enterprise-wide visibility into all work happening across the organization.

To begin, go to the navigation menu and select **Program | Work Tree**. Be sure that your portfolio or program and PI context are set in the configuration bar. We have selected the `Mobile` program and `PI-5` program increment in the following screenshot:

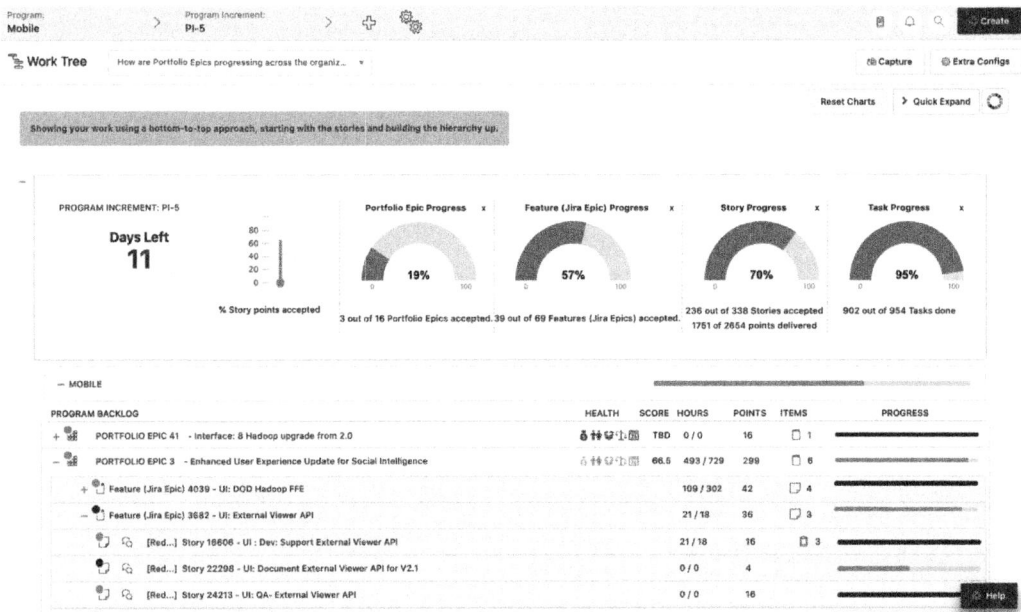

Figure 6.22 – Jira Align work tree

Next, click on the **Extra Configs** button in the top-right corner of the workspace to access the view dropdown list, as shown in the following screenshot. Here, we focus on two views: **Top-Down View from Portfolio Epic** and **Bottom-Up View from Story**:

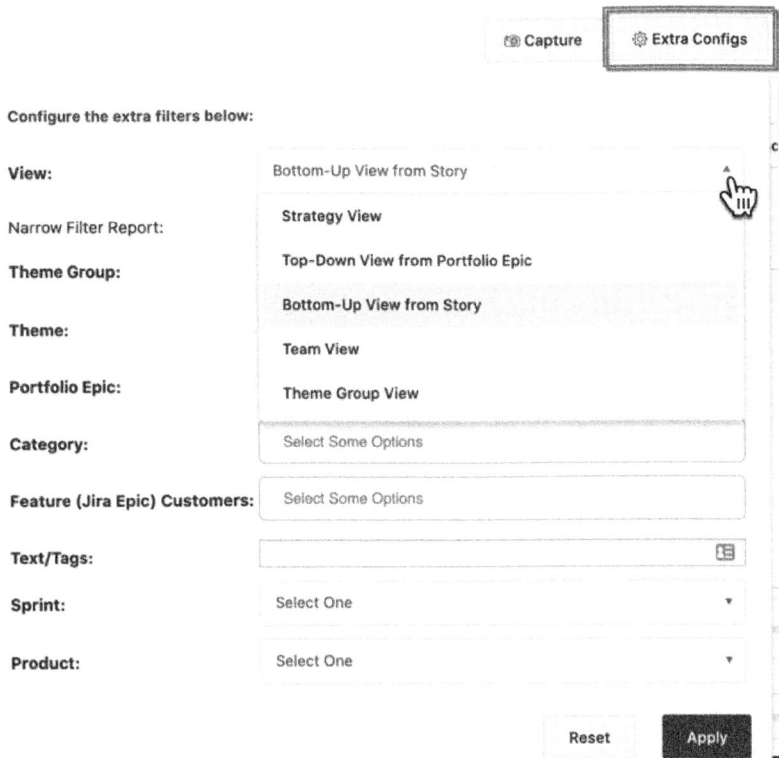

Figure 6.23 – Jira Align the work tree extra configs

For a broader-reaching view that could potentially help identify larger duplicate work items, choose the top-down view. It starts with portfolio epics associated with the selected PI, and then traces downward, including all child and grandchild work items that are attached to the epic, including those that fall outside the PI. This view shows fewer orphan stories and more of the larger-size work items.

If you are looking to identify more orphan stories with less attention to larger items, choose the bottom-up view. It starts with all stories associated with the selected PI and traces upward to the portfolio epics. It shows more orphan stories and fewer of the larger-size work items than the top-down view.

To limit the work items shown to only the selected PI, slide on the **Narrow Filter Report** toggle under **Extra Configs**. Note that the **Team View** option in the view dropdown is the same as the bottom-up view except that it allows you to filter the work tree for your team only. This is a good option for scrum masters and product owners.

Now that we've learned techniques for analyzing the interconnected work across the organization, let's explore two key reports for tracking the work of a PI as it progresses.

Program increment progress

The program increment progress report provides an understanding of whether the work for the selected PI is on track. It presents both burndown and burnup charts for features and stories. Burndown charts are useful for portfolio managers and RTEs to predict when all work of the PI will be completed. They display remaining work in story points on the vertical axis versus time on the horizontal axis. Burnup charts provide insight into the teams' ability to deliver features and stories as planned. They display completed work and the total amount of work in story points on the vertical axis versus time on the horizontal axis.

To access the report, go to the navigation menu and select **Program | Track | Program Increment Progress**. Be sure to set your context in the configuration bar. We've selected the `Mobile` program and `PI-5` program increment in the following screenshot:

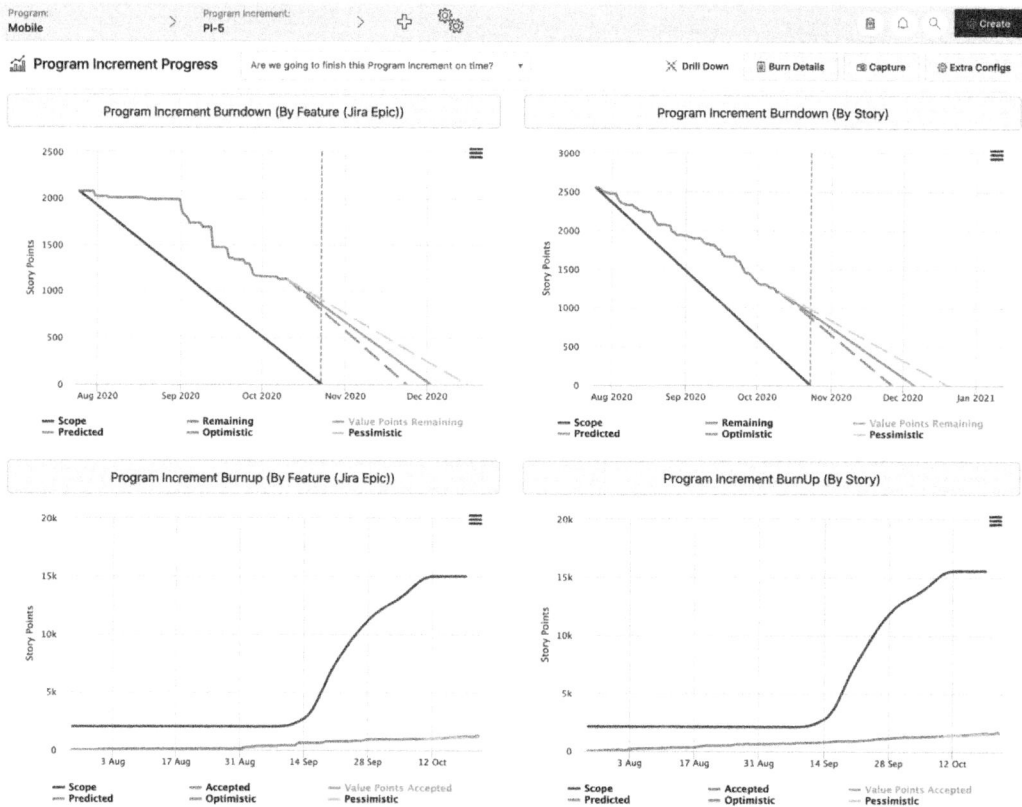

Figure 6.24 – Jira Align program increment progress report

Note the since `PI-5` is not yet finished, there are three projected lines continuing from the orange accepted line on the burndown charts at the top of the workspace. These predict the normal, optimistic, and pessimistic trends for acceptance of the PI's remaining work based on the current acceptance rate.

Click on the **Burn Details** button at the top right of the workspace to open a panel with the predicted daily burn rate and underlying team velocities used in the calculation, as shown in the following screenshot:

Burn Details

The Predicted line uses the daily Program burn rate to estimate when work will complete. Here, the daily Program burn is 21.2. This is a sum of the average velocities across all active scrum teams in the selected Program(s) divided by their average sprint days (275.6 / 13 = 21.2)

	End Date	Velocity
Baltimore		**82**
Baltimore COR_S18	3/18/2020	84
Baltimore COR_S19	4/8/2020	66
Baltimore COR_S20	4/29/2020	99
Baltimore COR_S21	5/20/2020	85
Baltimore COR_S22	6/10/2020	76
Washington		**76.2**
Redskins MOV_S11	9/4/2019	21
Redskins MOV_S12	9/25/2019	74
Redskins MOV_S13	10/16/2019	47
Redskins MOV_S21	5/20/2020	122
Redskins MOV_S22	6/10/2020	117
Houston		**72.2**
Houston HAR_S18	3/18/2020	48
Houston HAR_S19	4/8/2020	114
Houston HAR_S20	4/29/2020	65
Houston HAR_S21	5/20/2020	76
Houston HAR_S22	6/10/2020	58
Cowboys		**45.2**
Cowboys TSC_S17	2/5/2020	18
Cowboys TSC_S19	4/8/2020	50
Cowboys TSC_S20	4/29/2020	56
Cowboys TSC_S21	5/20/2020	52
Cowboys TSC_S22	6/10/2020	50

Figure 6.25 – Jira Align program increment progress report burn details

Note that scrum masters and product owners can easily filter the report for their teams by clicking on the **Extra Configs** button at the top right of the workspace and selecting their name from the dropdown list.

There are also various options for drilling down into data by clicking on the **Drill Down** button located near the top of the workspace to the right of center. Here, you can view the charts by programs or themes and then drill down to see the programs' teams or the themes' portfolio epics. In the following screenshot, we have drilled down to view the burndown charts for the teams in the program:

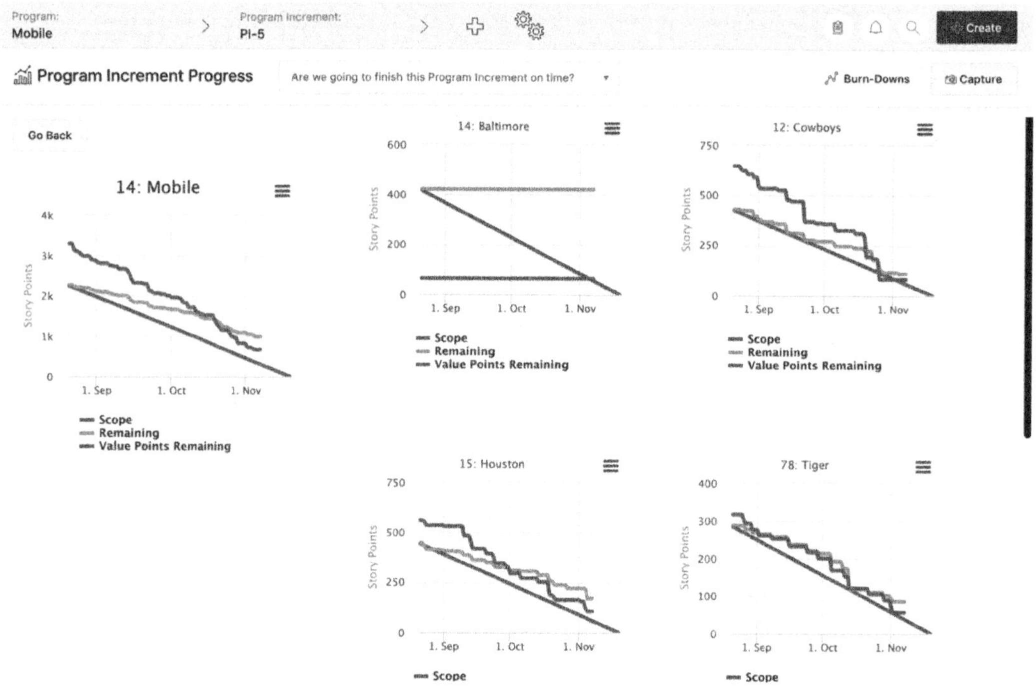

Figure 6.26 – Jira Align program increment progress report by teams

Lastly, note that any chart can be displayed in full screen or downloaded by clicking on the three bars at the top of the chart to the right of the title. Now that we've seen how scrum masters, RTEs, and others can monitor and predict work delivery, let's see how they can identify and review any scope changes impacting the selected PI.

Scope change

This report visualizes features that are added or removed during a PI and is useful for portfolio managers and RTEs to understand scope changes. To access the report, go to the navigation menu, click on the search icon (magnifying glass), and then search for Program Increments Scope. Be sure to set your context in the configuration bar. In the following screenshot, we have selected the Mobile program and the PI-5 program increment:

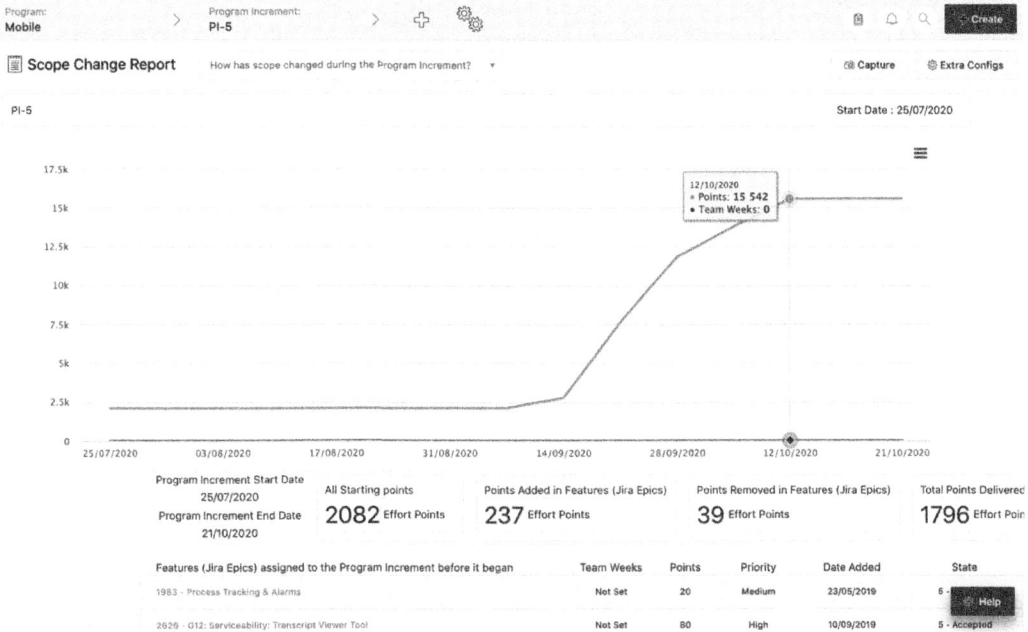

Figure 6.27 – Jira Align scope change report

The first section of the report is a line graph showing how the scope changed in terms of total story points on the vertical axis and PI date markers on the horizontal axis. Ideally, all scope should be added at the start of a PI. A slightly upward trend on the line graph or statistics is normal. However, a downward trend indicates that teams overcommitted and had to remove story points from the PI.

The next section shows a roll-up of scope change statistics for the PI, and the last section provides a list of features, broken down as follows: in scope at the start of the PI, added to the PI after it started, and removed from the PI after it started. The dates that features were added or removed are shown, along with their current state. This allows product managers and RTEs to evaluate the trade-offs made during the PI as inputs for continuous learning and better planning for future PIs.

Now that we've seen how to monitor scope changes during the PI, let's examine how RTEs can ensure that the PI is ready to be closed by using a PI cleanup report.

PI cleanup

The program increment cleanup is a comprehensive audit report showing all items due for completion in the selected PI that have not yet been closed, accepted, or delivered. It is useful for program leaders and RTEs to run the report toward the end of a PI, or even after a PI completes, to see what items are outstanding.

To access the report, go to the navigation menu, click on the search icon (magnifying glass), and then search for Program Increments Cleanup Report. Be sure to set your context in the configuration bar. In the following screenshot, we've selected the Mobile program and the PI-5 program increment:

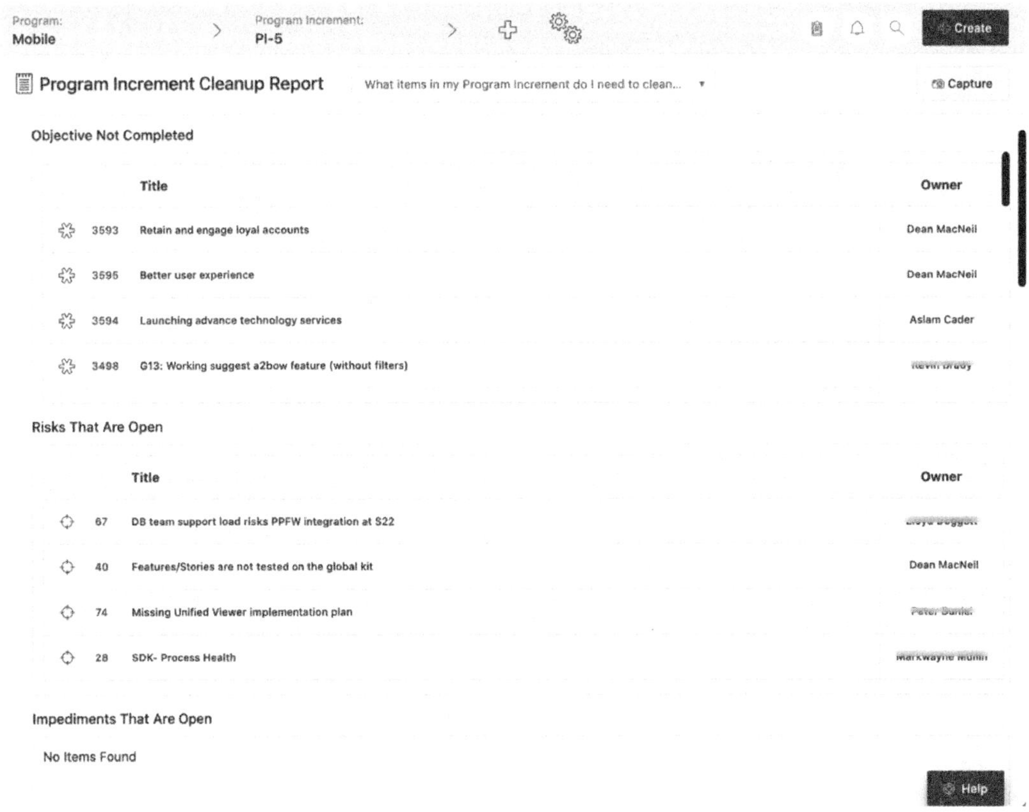

Figure 6.28 – Jira Align program increment cleanup

Here, you can click on any item's ID to open its details panel on the right. The report displays data in a series of scrolling sections, as follows:

- **Objective Not Completed**: All objectives due in the PI that are not yet completed

- **Risks That Are Open**: All risks that are not yet closed in the PI

- **Impediments That Are Open**: All impediments that are not yet closed in the PI

- **Stories Not Accepted**: All stories due in the PI that are not yet accepted

- **Features Not Accepted**: All features due in the PI that are not yet accepted

- **Open Action Items**: All action items that are not yet closed in the PI

- **Portfolio Epics Not Accepted**: All portfolio epics due in the PI that are not yet accepted

- **Dependencies Not Delivered**: All dependencies due in the PI that are not yet delivered

- **Stand-alone Features With No Epics Assigned**: All features due in the PI that are orphans and don't have a parent portfolio epic

- **Stories With No Features Assigned**: All stories due in the PI that are orphans and don't have a parent feature

An overall scan of the report will quickly provide a feel for the health of the PI for the selected program. It's especially useful to review the report toward the end of the PI so that outstanding items can be addressed before the PI is closed. In some cases, items may need to be moved to either the next PI or unassigned backlog, or split, a function we will explore next.

Handling unfinished work

Now that we've seen how the PI cleanup report brings attention to the program's unfinished work, we'll learn how best to handle it. Just as it's best practice for teams to split unfinished stories at the end of a sprint for a more accurate velocity metric, programs split unfinished features at the end of the PI. This practice ensures a more accurate program velocity and carries forward only the unfinished portion of the work.

Jira Align makes it easy to split unfinished features. Simply click on the feature in the backlog, program board, or elsewhere to open its details panel. Next, click on the **Split** link on the right, seven positions down from the **View in JIRA** button. This will open the window shown in the following screenshot:

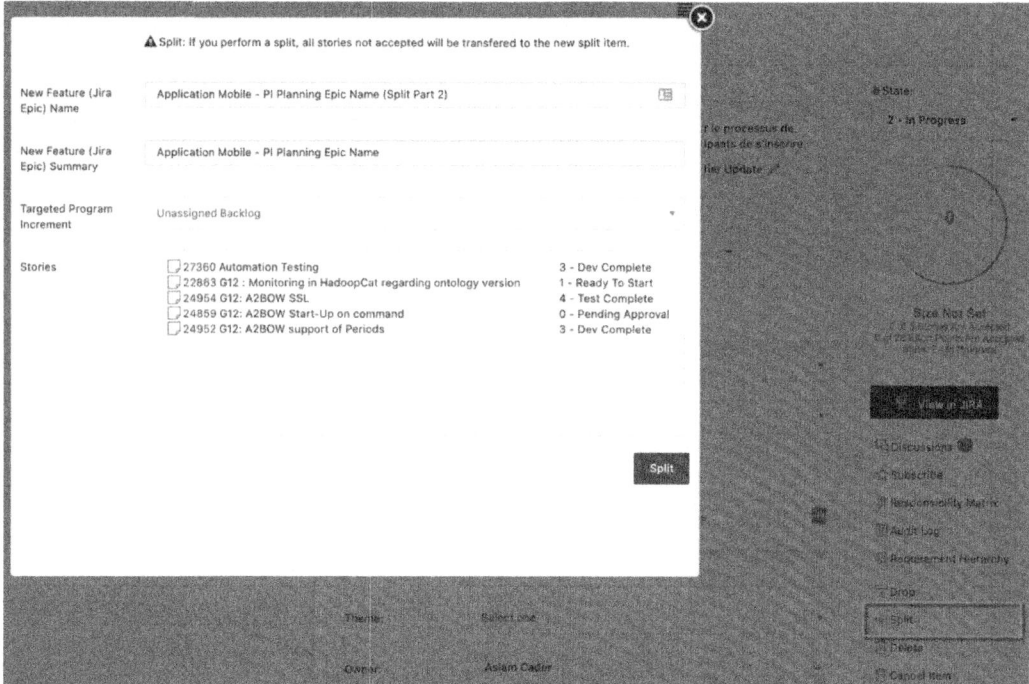

Figure 6.29 – Jira Align splitting a feature

Note that Jira Align adds a suggested (Split Part 2) suffix to the original feature name, which you can modify. Next, select a future PI or the unassigned backlog to which the new feature, along with the unaccepted stories from the original feature, will be moved. Lastly, click on the **Split** button to execute the feature split.

Once split, the original feature will display a link to the new feature, as shown in the following screenshot:

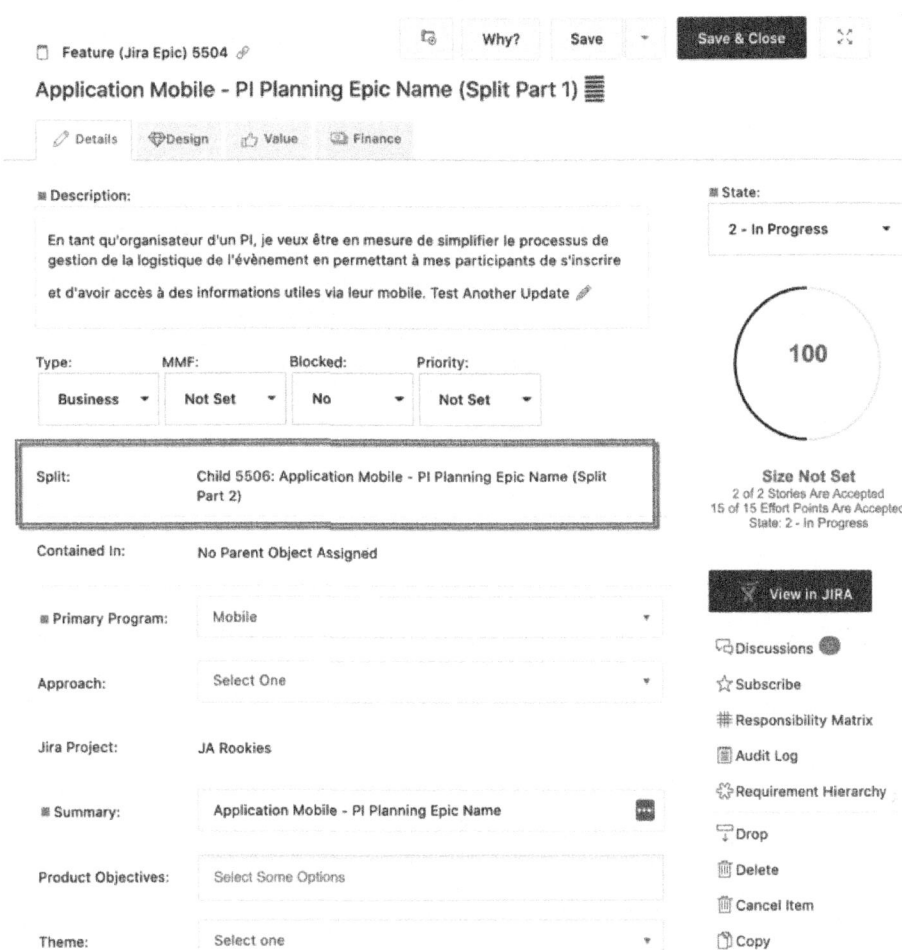

Figure 6.30 – Jira Align split feature link

Note that the original feature is identified as the parent and the new split feature as the child. You can click on the link to open the child from the parent and vice versa.

Now that we've seen some ways to better monitor scope and delivery for the PI, we'll return to the roadmaps module to see two effective ways for product managers, release managers, and RTEs to communicate delivery expectations by PI and release.

PI roadmap

The program increment view roadmap displays PI cards based on the context set in the configuration bar. To access it, go to the navigation menu, select **Program** | **Manage** | **Roadmaps**, and then select **Program Increments** from the dropdown at the top left of the workspace. Be sure to set your context in the configuration bar.

In the following screenshot, we have chosen the `Digital Services` portfolio and the following PIs: `PI-5`, `PI-6`, and `PI-7`:

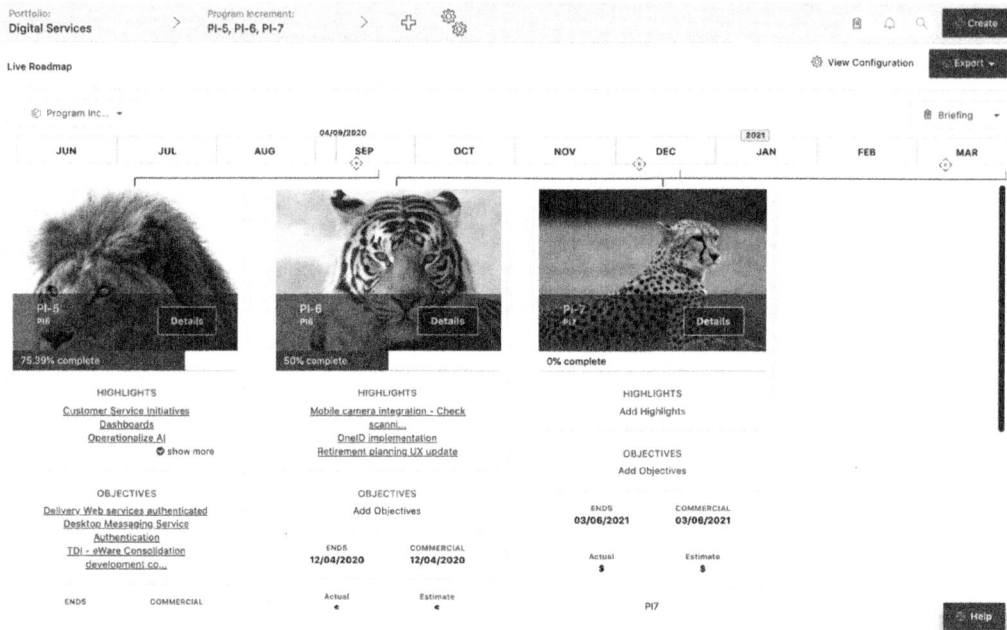

Figure 6.31 – Jira Align roadmap program increment view

Note that PI end dates are shown as diamond shapes along the timeline. Each PI card displays a progress bar based on the percentage of accepted story points for the PI along with several configurable details sections. To configure the PI cards, click on the **View Configuration** button to access the following options:

- **Photo**: Slide this toggle on to display an image for each PI card. To upload an image, hover over the card and click on the **Replace Image** button.

- **Dates**: Slide this toggle on to display either internal, external, or program increment dates.

- **Cost & value**: Slide this toggle on to display estimated and actual costs for the PI.

- **Description**: Slide this toggle on to display the PI description.

- **Highlights**: Slide this toggle on to enable the selection of themes, portfolio epics, or features to appear in the highlights section. Click on the **Add Highlight** link on a PI card to select the work items you'd like to draw attention to in this section.

- **Objectives**: Slide this toggle on to enable the selection of objectives to appear in the objectives section. Click on the **Add Objectives** link on a PI card to select the objectives you'd like to draw attention to in this section.

- **Show completed PIs**: Slide this toggle on to display stats for completed PIs.

Having the preceding information readily available on a live roadmap helps program-level staff such as RTEs to obtain and share the real-time status on PI execution and provide targeted delivery highlights. We'll now look at a roadmap geared toward release management staff.

Release vehicle roadmap

Release vehicles represent a set of features and/or stories released to actual customers. Releases can happen at any time following the agile practice of deploying continuously and releasing on demand. The release vehicle roadmap displays informative highlights based on the selected portfolio/programs and PIs. To access it, go to the navigation menu, select **Program | Manage | Roadmaps**, and then select **Release Vehicles** from the dropdown at the top left of the workspace. Be sure to set your context in the configuration bar. In the following screenshot, we have chosen the `Digital Services` portfolio and the following PIs: `PI-5`, `PI-6`, and `PI-7`:

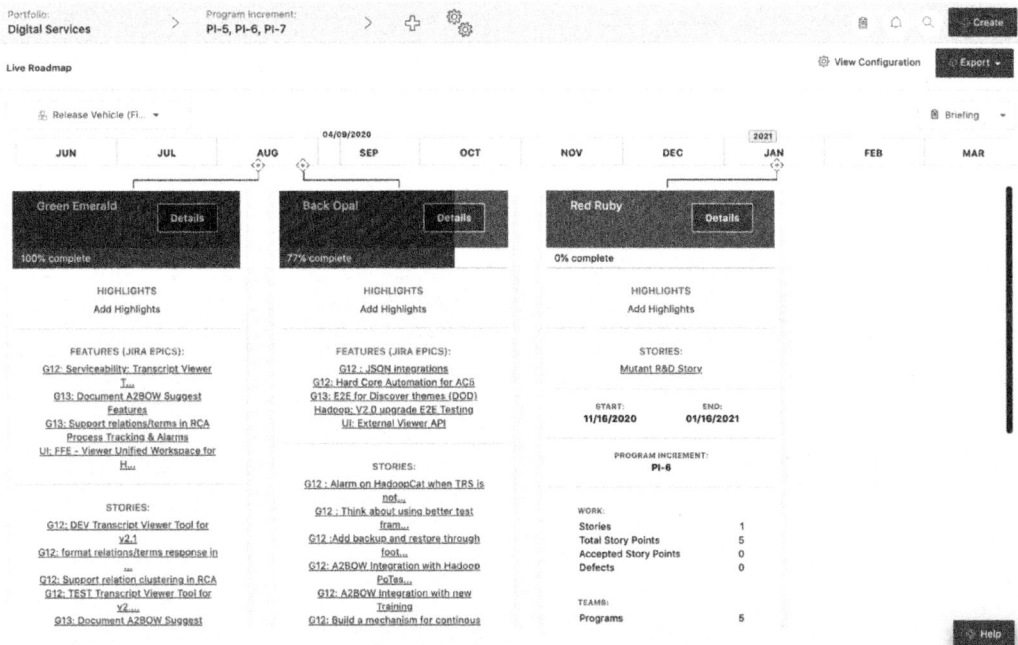

Figure 6.32 – Jira Align roadmap release vehicle view

Note that release dates are shown as diamond shapes along the timeline. Each card displays a progress bar based on the percentage of accepted story points for the release vehicle, along with several configurable details sections. To configure the release vehicle cards, click on the **View Configuration** button to access the following options:

- **Dates**: Slide this toggle on to display either internal, external, or program increment dates.

- **Program Increments**: Slide this toggle on to display the program increment during which the release is shipped.

- **Highlights**: Slide this toggle on to enable the selection of defects, stories, or features to appear in the highlights section. Click on the **Add Highlight** link on a release vehicle card to select the work items you'd like to draw attention to in this section.

- **Show completed**: Slide this toggle on to show stats for completed release vehicles.

Having the preceding information readily available on a live roadmap helps program-level staff such as release managers to obtain and share real-time insights on release readiness and provide targeted delivery highlights.

Congratulations, you've now learned how to build all varieties of roadmaps, from the work item roadmap at the start of the previous chapter to the PI and release vehicle roadmaps examined here. These, along with all that we learned in between, are sure to help you achieve alignment on all dimensions: people delivering work over periods of time to achieve outcomes.

Summary

In this chapter, we learned how to overcome the execution challenges at the program level. We began by looking at the command center for execution, the program room. We then learned about the dependency workflow and how to handle external dependencies and use dependency maps. Lastly, we explored ways to reduce unnecessary work, manage scope, and communicate PI and release progress.

In the next chapter, we will discuss common portfolio-level challenges, how **lean portfolio management** (**LPM**) shifts the mindset from project to product, and what it takes to connect business strategy with execution for organizational alignment.

Questions

1. Which program room widget displays the program's average velocity?

2. Which dependency maps allow you to visualize external dependencies?

3. How does the work tree module support reducing waste?

Further reading

- *Scaling Scrum Across Modern Enterprises* by Cecil Rupp (Packt, 2020)

7
Enterprise and Portfolio Challenges

In this chapter, we focus on the common problems and struggles faced at the highest levels of an organization: the enterprise and its portfolios. Depending on its size, an enterprise may have one or many portfolios. We'll learn how the enterprise sets the strategy and how portfolios play a crucial role in connecting strategy to execution. We'll then explain the benefits of the **lean portfolio management** (**LPM**) approach and how Jira Align supports it. Lastly, we will cover a number of ways in which to improve innovation.

In this chapter, we will cover the following topics:

- Connecting strategy to execution
- Implementing LPM
- Promoting innovation

By the end of the chapter, you will know how and why you'd access the strategy and portfolio rooms, create strategic snapshots, establish portfolio vision, create portfolio objectives and OKRs, use reports such as *Investment by Theme* and *Investment vs. Actuals*, leverage ideation functionality, and much more.

Connecting strategy to execution

Jira Align is purpose-built to connect strategy with execution and provide visibility and alignment. Often, connecting strategy with execution is a top-down, bottom-up, meet-in-the-middle approach. We've covered the basics from a bottom-up perspective in *Chapter 2, Implementing Jira Align*, beginning with connecting to Jira Software, where the tactical execution of team-level work items happens. Stories connect to features (Jira epics), then to capabilities, portfolio epics, and themes in Jira Align. Once these work item levels are connected, you can then harness the power of Jira Align's vast reporting capability. For example, you can view spend by theme with the help of the Investment vs. Actuals report or track budgets with financial status reports. We'll now examine the top-down perspective, beginning with the strategy room.

Strategy room

The strategy room is the highest-level module in Jira Align. It is where you model your organization's mission, vision, and values, and specify the long-term goals toward which the various work item levels and their associated outcomes align. It enables executives to ensure that execution aligns with corporate strategy while simultaneously empowering team members with an understanding of the value of their work and how it contributes to the enterprise goals.

To begin, go to the navigation menu and select **Enterprise | Strategy Room**. Next, choose a strategic snapshot from the dropdown to load associated work items and outcomes. Strategic snapshots are at the highest level of the time dimension in Jira Align. In practice, each snapshot comprises a set of program increments. In the following screenshot, we have selected the **Corporate Strategy 2020** strategic snapshot:

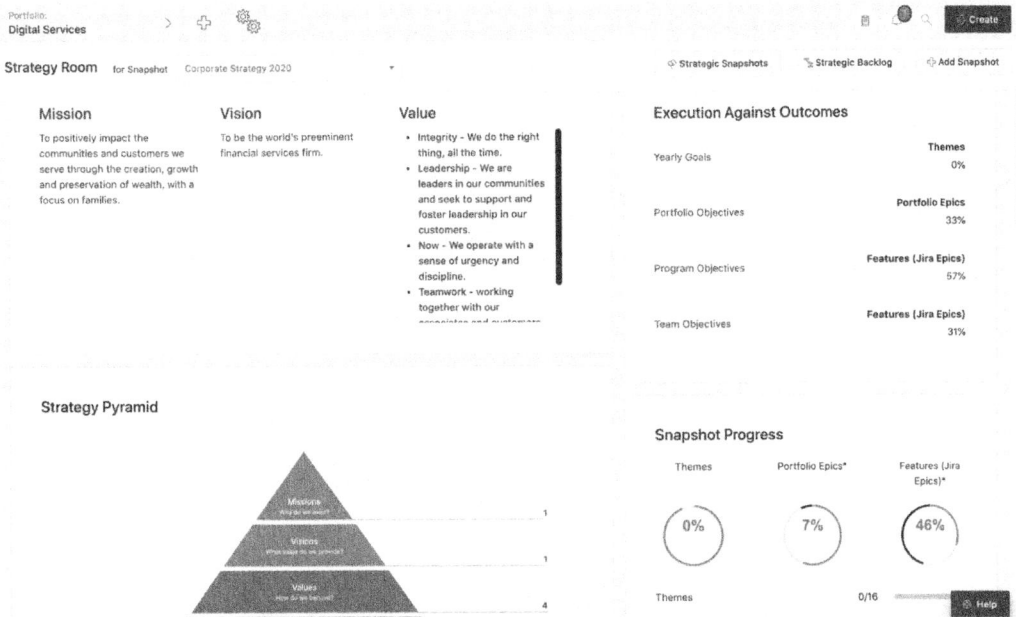

Figure 7.1 – Jira Align strategy room

Here, you can view or edit the mission, vision, and values by clicking on them in the top-left corner. The **Execution Against Outcomes** section in the top-right area shows the percent complete for each level of work item contributing to outcomes. Click on an outcome level such as **Yearly Goals** to view and edit items. The **Snapshot Progress** section below it shows the percent complete for each level of work item, regardless of whether or not they link and contribute to outcomes.

Next, let's view the **Strategy Pyramid** section to visualize strategic alignment. You may need to scroll down to view the whole pyramid, such as the one shown in the following screenshot:

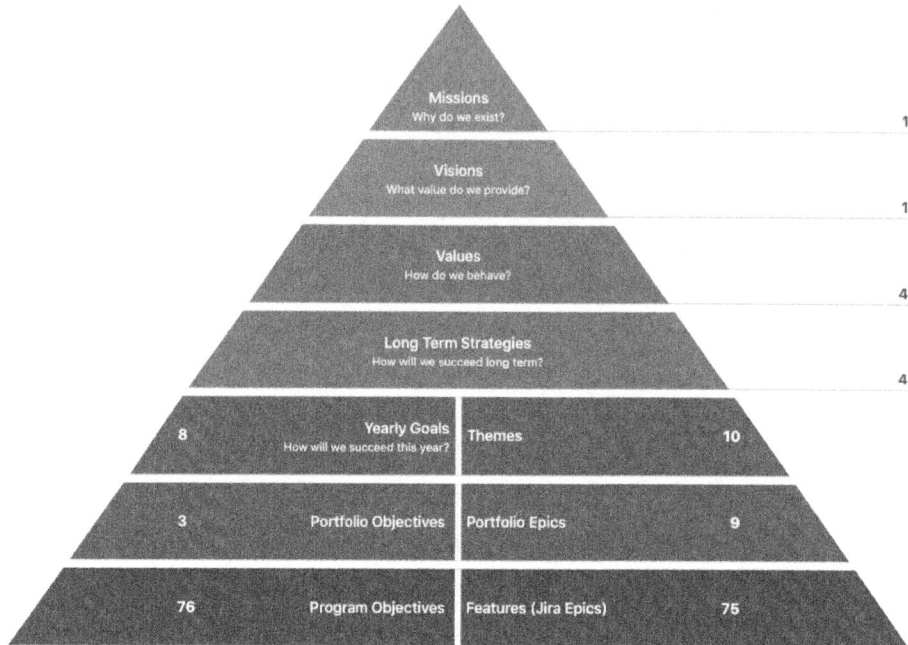

Figure 7.2 – Jira Align strategy pyramid

The pyramid shows the levels of your strategic hierarchy from the top down, as well as the count of each item type. For example, in the preceding diagram, there are four long-term strategy items. Note that the count of work items at the right of the lower levels represents the count of items linked and contributing to the outcomes shown on the left. For example, there are 10 themes connected to 8 yearly goals, but there may be other unconnected themes. Click on a strategy, goal, or objective type in the pyramid to create and edit those items.

Note that the pyramid is configurable, both in terms of the number of levels and the outcome names at each level. The Jira Align administrator can rename the outcome levels under **Administration | Settings | Platform Terminology** and scroll down to **Customize Pyramid Display** to toggle levels on or off.

By default, the pyramid has nine levels. However, in our experience, very few organizations require all nine levels of the strategic hierarchy. Therefore, we have toggled off two levels, **North Stars** and **Long-Term Goals**, in the Jira Align environment shown in our screenshots.

The strategy room focuses on outcomes over outputs. For example, OKR health can be gauged by scrolling down to see a heatmap located under the strategy pyramid, as shown in the following screenshot:

OKR Heatmap

PI-4	PI-5	PI-6	PI-7	Level	Item Count
65% 0.7 avg score				Long Term Strategies	4
42% 0.4 avg score				Yearly Goals	8
40% 0.4 avg score	78% 0.6 avg score	N/A	N/A	Portfolio Objectives	3
8% 0.1 avg score	5% 0.1 avg score	N/A	N/A	Program Objectives	76
4% 0 avg score	12% 0.1 avg score	N/A	N/A	Team Objectives	97

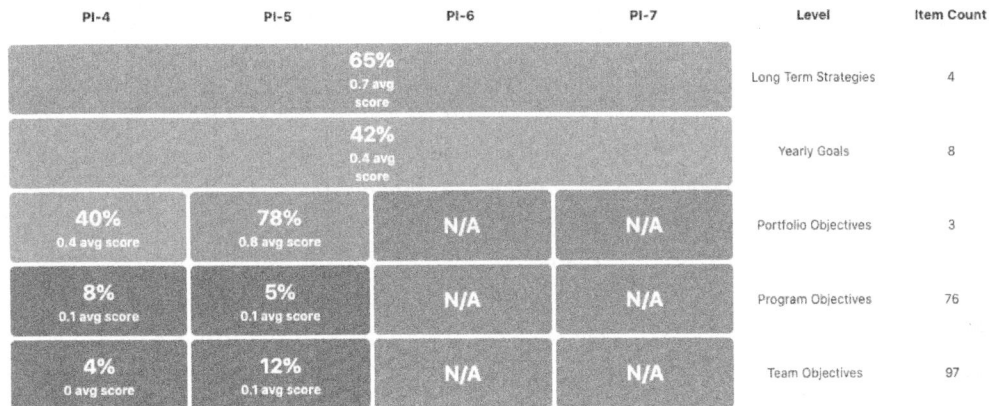

Figure 7.3 – Jira Align OKR heatmap

The heatmap's color indicators and statistics provide a quick visual representation of how you're doing in terms of achieving the different levels of strategic goals and objectives shown on the right along with their item counts. Clicking on the goals will direct you to the strategic backlog for that level and clicking on the objectives will direct you to the objectives grid.

The program increments associated with the strategic snapshot are shown along the top of the heatmap, and you can refine them further using the configuration bar. The heatmap's rows contain blocks with statistics for each outcome level during each PI in the snapshot. Since strategic goals aren't associated with PIs, they display as a single block that spans across all PI columns.

Each block displays the average percentage of progress made on the key results at the strategic goal or objective level. For the objective blocks in the lowest three levels, progress is only calculated for key results of objectives that are associated with PIs.

The blocks are color-coded according to the average key result score for objectives or strategic goals at that level (to the nearest 0.1), which displays at the bottom of the block, as follows:

- Gray = not scored (N/A). This indicates that none of the key results at the objective or goal level have been scored. If at least one key result has been scored, then the unscored key results will receive a score of zero in the average calculations.

- Red = 0.3 and below.

- Yellow = 0.4 to 0.6.

- Green = 0.7 and above.

Now that we've explored some of its key functionality, let's see how to create the strategic snapshots that drive the strategy room.

Strategic snapshots

The strategic snapshot provides the time dimension for the strategy room, allowing you to plan and track the progress of corporate strategy by month, quarter, or year. To manage snapshots, click on the **Strategic Snapshots** button near the top-right corner of the strategy room or go to the navigation menu and select **Enterprise | Manage | Strategic Snapshots**. This opens the strategic snapshots grid shown in the following screenshot:

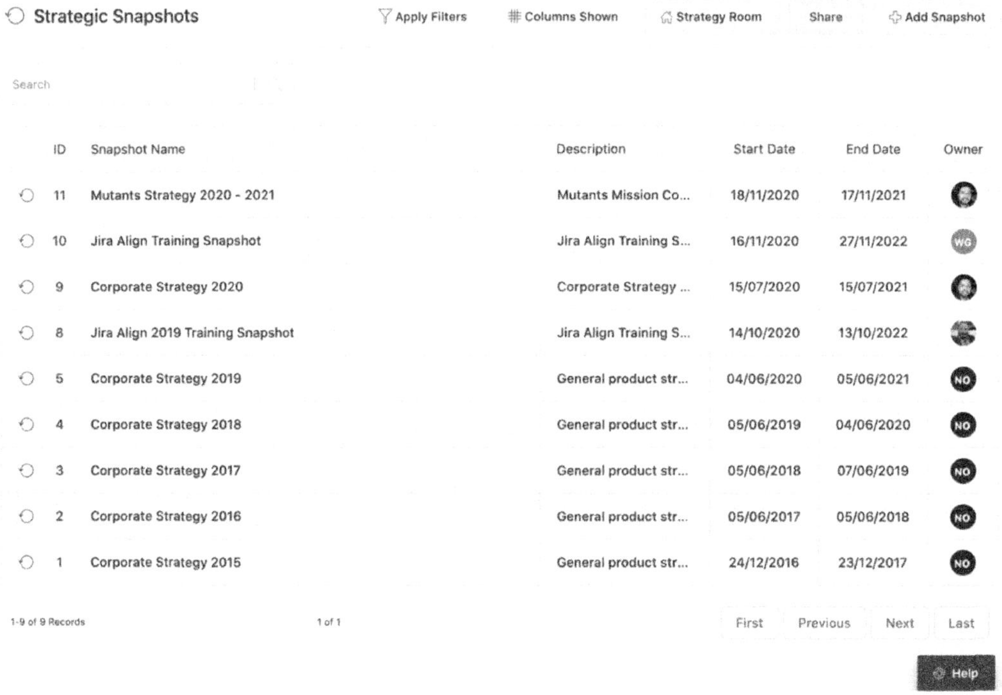

	ID	Snapshot Name		Description	Start Date	End Date	Owner
	11	Mutants Strategy 2020 - 2021		Mutants Mission Co...	18/11/2020	17/11/2021	
	10	Jira Align Training Snapshot		Jira Align Training S...	16/11/2020	27/11/2022	
	9	Corporate Strategy 2020		Corporate Strategy ...	15/07/2020	15/07/2021	
	8	Jira Align 2019 Training Snapshot		Jira Align Training S...	14/10/2020	13/10/2022	
	5	Corporate Strategy 2019		General product str...	04/06/2020	05/06/2021	
	4	Corporate Strategy 2018		General product str...	05/06/2019	04/06/2020	
	3	Corporate Strategy 2017		General product str...	05/06/2018	07/06/2019	
	2	Corporate Strategy 2016		General product str...	05/06/2017	05/06/2018	
	1	Corporate Strategy 2015		General product str...	24/12/2016	23/12/2017	

1-9 of 9 Records   1 of 1   First   Previous   Next   Last

Figure 7.4 – Jira Align strategic snapshots

To create a strategic snapshot, click on the **Add Snapshot** button in the top-right corner of the workspace to open the panel shown in the following screenshot:

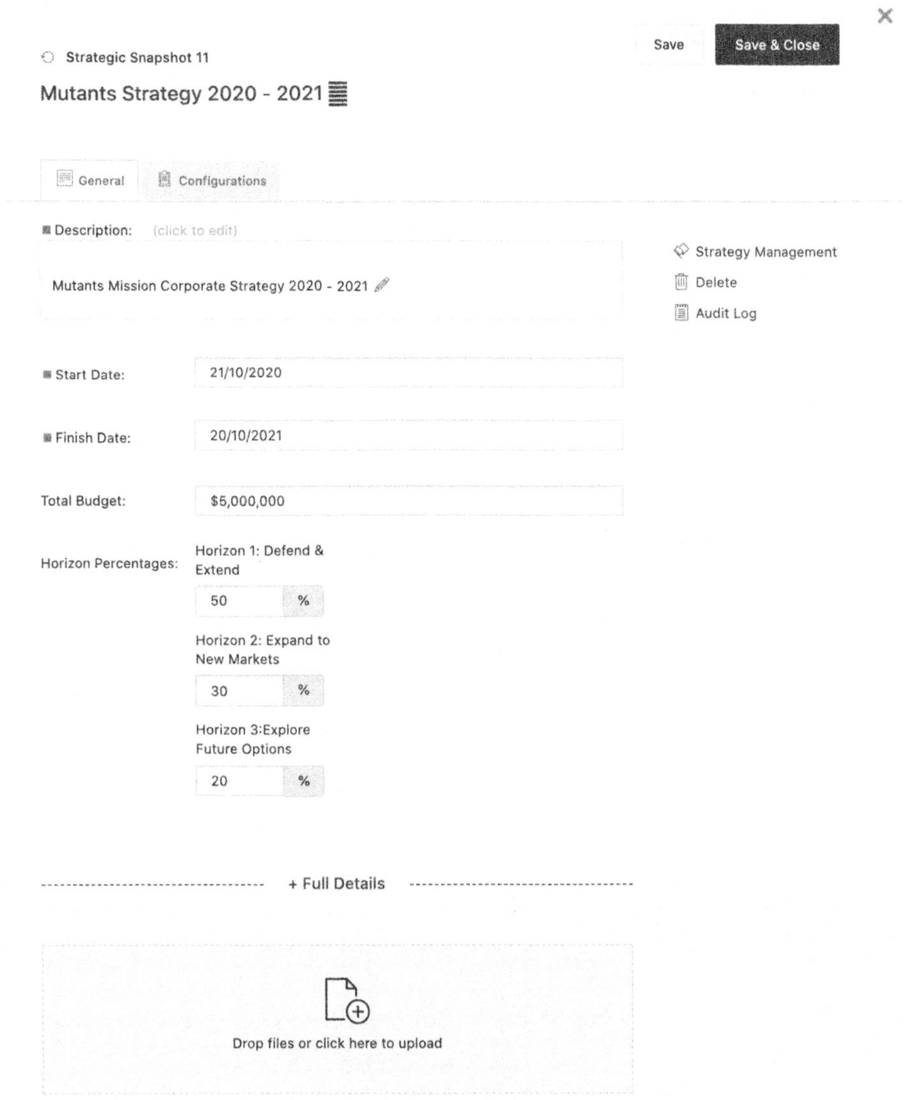

Figure 7.5 – Jira Align strategic snapshot details

Next, enter the following snapshot attributes. Note that red squares indicate required fields:

- **Snapshot Name**: Add a meaningful name to identify the portfolio and time period, for example, `Mutants Strategy 2020 - 2021`.

- **Description**: Add a detailed description of the strategic snapshot.

- **Start Date**: Add a start date for the snapshot.

- **End Date**: Add an end date for the snapshot.

- **Total Budget**: Optionally, add the total budget allocated for the duration of the snapshot.

- **Horizon Percentages**: Optionally, add a percentage allocation for the following three horizons: **Horizon 1: Defend & Extend**, **Horizon 2: Expand to New Markets**, and **Horizon 3: Explore Future Options**.

After entering the snapshot attributes, click on the **Save** button and then on the **Configurations** tab to provide the following optional details:

- **Strategy Team Members**: Add strategy team members, such as the **LPM** team.

- **Products**: Add the products associated with the snapshot, if applicable.

- **Program Increments**: Add the program increments associated with the snapshot. This is recommended, though not required.

- **Organization Structures**: Add the organization units associated with the snapshot, if applicable.

Click on the **Save** button to return to the **General** tab and then scroll down and click on **+ Full Details** to expand that section. Here you can set notification preferences, funding approvals, and distribute the total budget across each organization unit tied to the snapshot. Refer to *Chapter 3, Navigating Jira Align, Figure 3.36*, for details on how to set your notifications and funding approval rules.

Now that we've created the time dimension, let's learn how to manage the other elements that drive the strategy room. These are found in the strategic backlog.

Strategic backlog

Earlier, we mentioned the essential elements of mission, vision, values, and goals. These are part of the strategic hierarchy. To manage these and other elements, click on the **Strategic Backlog** button near the top-right corner of the strategy room or go to the navigation menu and select **Enterprise | Manage | Strategic Backlog**. Next, click on one of the hierarchy levels on the left. In the following screenshot, we clicked on **Yearly Goals** to see that level for the `Digital Services` portfolio:

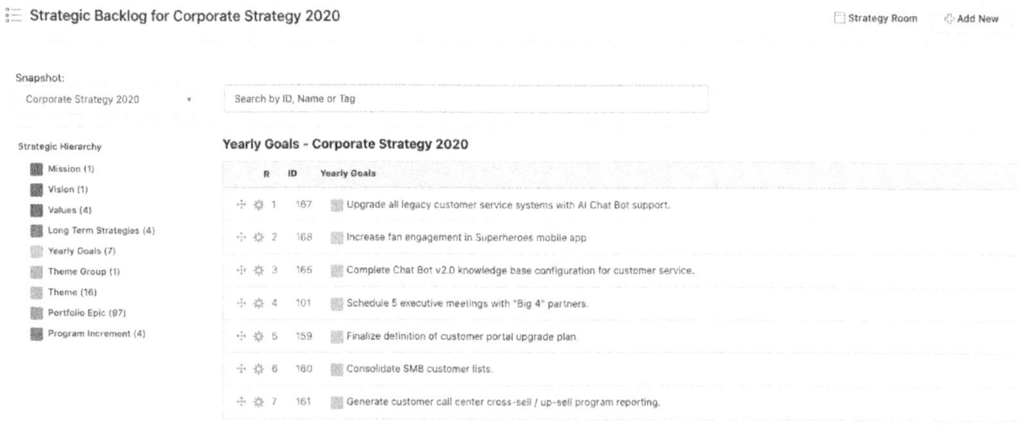

Figure 7.6 – Jira Align strategic backlog

Next, recall that a theme is the highest-level work item in Jira Align. By default, it is associated with the lowest-level strategic goal, the yearly goal. As noted earlier, your organization's Jira Align administrator can configure the number of levels of goals and their names.

> **Tips and tricks**
>
> While themes are the highest-level work item in Jira Align, they can be grouped into higher-level theme groups for use when filtering reports and views such as the work tree.
>
> As a prerequisite, this functionality must be enabled under **Administration | Settings | Platform | Portfolio Tab | Enable Theme Groups**.
>
> To create a theme group, go to the strategic backlog, click on the **Theme Group** level on the left, and then click on the **Add New** button. Alternatively, the Jira Align administrator can create theme groups under **Administration | Setup | Theme Groups**.

To add a new goal to the strategic backlog, click on a goal level on the left and then click on the **Add New** button to open the details panel shown in the following screenshot:

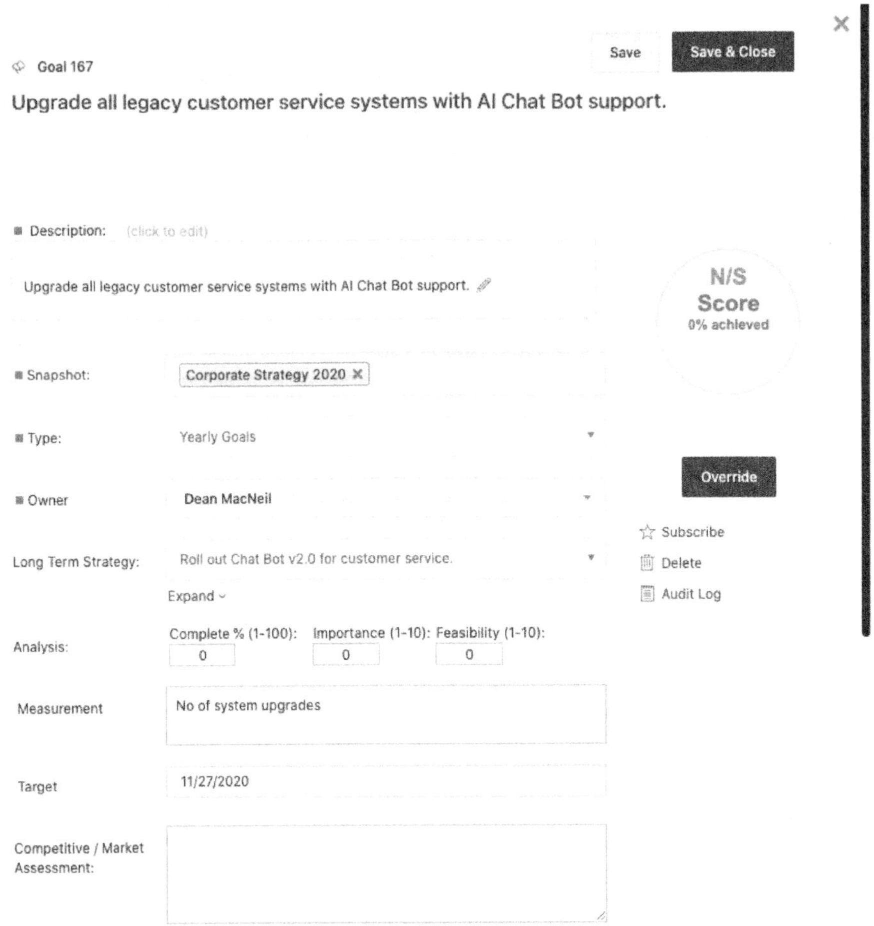

Figure 7.7 – Jira Align new goal

Here we add a yearly goal for the **Corporate Strategy 2020** snapshot by entering the following details. Note that red boxes in the screenshot indicate required fields:

- **Description**: Add a description to summarize your goal.

- **Snapshot**: Choose all applicable strategic snapshots that the goal will belong to; for example, Corporate Strategy 2020.

- **Type**: Select the type of goal you are documenting; for example, `Yearly Goals`.

- **Owner**: Assign the goal to an individual who will be responsible for monitoring status and progress.

- **Long Term Strategy**: Link the goal to a parent goal. In this case, the parent of a yearly goal is a long-term strategy.

- **Analysis**: Record the estimated **Complete %**, and, on a scale of 1 to 10, the goal's **Importance** to the organization, and **Feasibility**.

- **Measurement**: Add the success criteria that will be used to measure the completeness of your goal.

- **Target**: Add the target date for the goal's completion.

- **Competitive / Market Assessment**: Add the relevant competitive or market analysis.

- **Attachments**: Add any attachments related to the goal.

Once these details have been entered, click on the **Save** button to add the goal. Clicking on **Save** will also provide additional sections at the bottom of the details panel, where the following optional information can be added:

- **Key Results**: Add key results that will be used to measure the success of the goal. Note that you can associate key results with any level of goal or objective. By definition, a goal or objective with key results may be considered an OKR.

- **Themes**: Associate the goal with themes.

- **Links**: Add external links related to the goal.

Now that we've learned how to add goals, let's see how to manage portfolio objectives.

Portfolio objectives

Objectives represent work item outcomes at each level of scale: team, program, solution, and portfolio. You can access the objectives grid for each level via the navigation menu. We previously learned in *Chapter 5, Program Planning Challenges*, how team objectives reflect quarterly planning goals and are aggregated up to the program level. Here we explore portfolio-level objectives as a prelude to the next section, where we will cover key portfolio concepts in detail.

Let's begin by going to the navigation menu and selecting **Portfolio | Manage | Portfolio Objectives** to open the grid shown in the following screenshot:

Figure 7.8 – Jira Align objectives grid

Here we see portfolio objectives that are associated with the `Digital Services` portfolio and `PI-5`. Click on an objective's ID or name to open its details panel. Click on the **Add Objective** button in the top-right corner of the workspace to add a new objective.

Objectives are arranged in a hierarchy that is visible in the objectives tree. To access it, click on the **Objectives Tree** button above the objective grid to the right of center, or go to the navigation menu and select **Enterprise | Objectives Tree**. In the following screenshot, we see the hierarchy from the portfolio level down for the **Increase Customer Lifetime Value** portfolio objective:

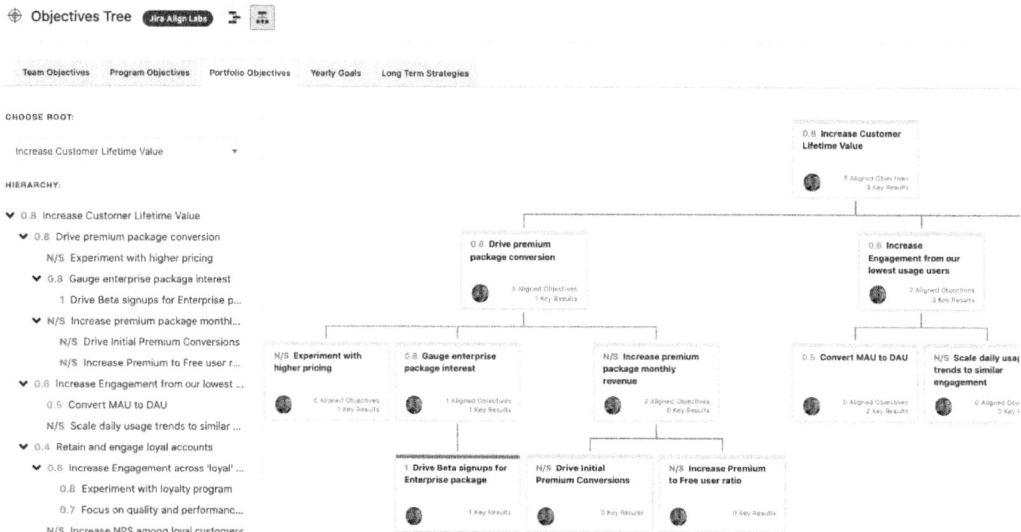

Figure 7.9 – Jira Align objectives tree

Here we see the selected portfolio objective at the top of the hierarchy, with its linked objectives at each level, from solution to program, down to the team level.

The blue bar on top of each card indicates the cumulative progress of associated key results. Hovering over a card and clicking on one of its sides allows you to collapse or expand neighboring cards to configure the objectives tree for your needs. You can switch from the tree hierarchy to a list view, as described in *Chapter 5*, *Program Planning Challenges, Figure 5.27*.

Now that we've seen how enterprise strategy is set in the strategy room and connects through the portfolio down to team-level execution, let's explore a modern approach to mitigating traditional portfolio-level challenges.

Implementing LPM

LPM is a core competency of SAFe that seeks to align strategy with execution by applying lean and systems thinking approaches to three areas: strategy and investment funding, agile portfolio operations, and governance. LPM has grown in popularity since SAFe introduced its LPM certification in fall 2019. It provides methods for overcoming the challenges of traditional portfolio management approaches, which are inadequate in this age of software and digital disruption when companies operate under greater uncertainty while driven to deliver more innovative solutions faster to market. In this section, we uncover several portfolio management challenges and how Jira Align supports LPM practices to overcome them.

Identifying value streams

A prerequisite for LPM is the identification of value streams. Generally speaking, SAFe defines a value stream as a long-lived series of steps used to create value, from concept to the delivery of a tangible result for the customer. Within this general definition, there are two kinds of value streams – operational and development. Operational value streams deliver end customer value, while development value streams build the systems and capabilities that enable operational value streams.

For example, one of the steps in a music company's operational value stream is to bring the music to market using traditional and digital marketing methods. We thus identified a development value stream for digital marketing aligned with a single program team that delivered systems for online fan engagement contests, social media marketing campaigns, delivery of digital marketing assets to business partners, and so on.

A word of caution about the phrase *value stream* – it can be ambiguous, as it is used in different ways in different contexts. Hereinafter, when we use the phrase, we are referring to development value streams. SAFe itself has complicated the issue by calling what is now the large solution level the "value stream" level in SAFe 4.0. Jira Align, too, adds to the confusion by referring to the process steps that drive kanban boards as a "value stream." Therefore, we have changed **Value stream** to **Process steps** in our platform terminology.

> **Tips and tricks**
> To avoid confusion over terminology in Jira Align, we recommend changing **Value stream** to **Process steps** under **Administration | Settings | Platform Terminology**.

In SAFe 5.0, value streams exist at the portfolio level and are broad-reaching. In this sense, they are akin to themes, although they are not objective-based, like SAFe themes, nor are they work items, like Jira Align themes. Even so, since a value stream object doesn't exist, at least currently, in Jira Align, reporting based on themes, such as the Investment by Theme report, could serve as a reasonable substitute for value stream budgeting in Jira Align. It's admittedly a workaround, but it allows you to capture broad budget allocations and apportion budget by percentage across multiple items. We will examine this report shortly.

Now that we have a handle on value streams, we can discuss the group that manages them – the portfolio.

Defining the portfolio

A typical portfolio management challenge is that people are organized in functional silos, creating excessive dependencies and lag time. LPM organizes people around value and applies cadence-based planning to improve the flow of value and innovation. It shifts the approach from functional silos and temporary project teams to long-lived program teams delivering a continuous stream of value. In short, it brings the work to the people, not the people to the work.

In SAFe, a portfolio is a collection of development value streams, each of which builds, maintains, and supports solutions delivered to either internal or external customers. A helpful tool when discovering and defining value streams is the value stream canvas. Jira Align makes creating them easy. To create a value stream canvas, go to the navigation menu and then select **Enterprise | Canvas**. Next, give your canvas a name and select **Value Stream Canvas** from the template dropdown, as shown in the following screenshot, before clicking on the **Create new Canvas** button:

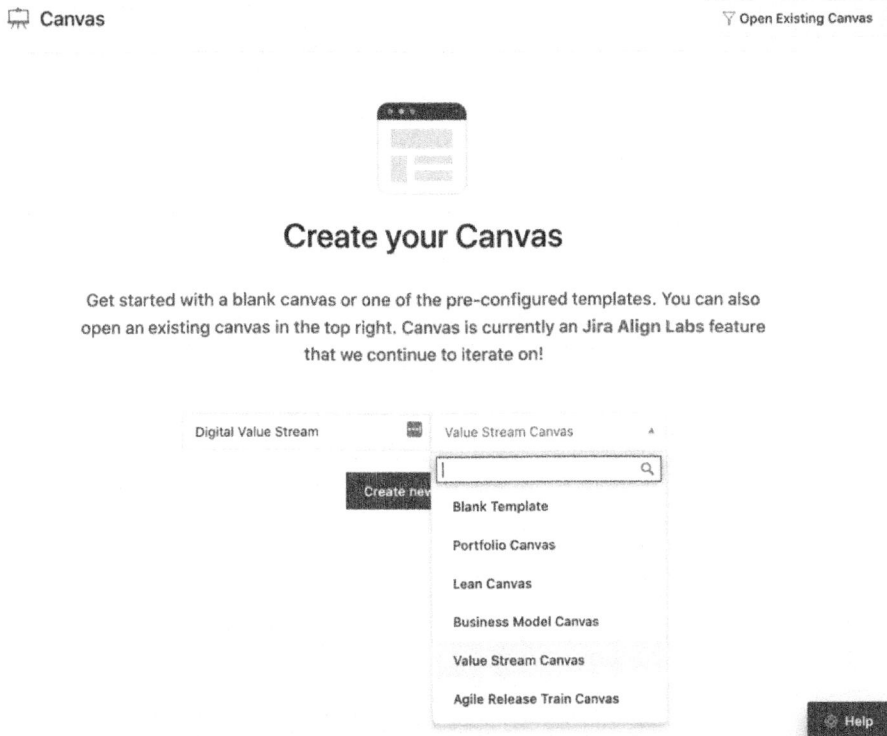

Figure 7.10 – Jira Align create your canvas

There are three variations when organizing people around value: one value stream per program, many value streams per program, and many programs per value stream. From a tooling perspective, the first is the easiest, since you can simply use program budgets as value stream budgets, whereas the other two require the tracking of additional attributes in order to allocate budget across value streams.

To see program budgets in Jira Align, open the portfolio room financials view by going to the navigation menu and then selecting **Portfolio | Portfolio Room**. Next, click on the **Extra Configs** button in the top-right corner of the workspace and then select a strategic snapshot. The right panel of the portfolio room will then display key information, including program budgets, as shown in the following screenshot:

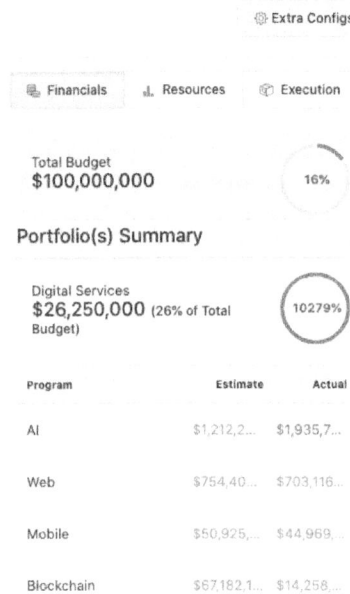

Figure 7.11 – Jira Align portfolio room, right panel

Here we see the following information:

- **Total Budget**: Displays the value set in the **Total Budget** field of the selected strategic snapshot. The circle graph displays the actual spend to date, calculated from points on accepted stories, as a percentage of the total snapshot budget.

- **Portfolio(s) Summary**: Displays the rollup of PI budgets tied to programs in the portfolio as a percentage of the total snapshot budget.

- **Program summary**: Displays the sum of the budgets in each program of the portfolio, in terms of story-level estimates and actuals, converted to dollars based on team velocity and a blended rate.

This is just one facet of the portfolio room. For more information, refer to
`https://help.jiraalign.com/hc/en-us/articles/115000095234-10X-Portfolio-Room`.

As previously mentioned, the Investment by Theme report can be useful for budgeting programs and/or value streams. It shows how the portfolio allocates budget and effort to implement business strategy via themes. To access it, go to the navigation menu and then select **Portfolio | Track | Investment by Theme**. Be sure to set your context in the configuration bar. In the following screenshot, we've generated the report for the `Mobile` program and `PI-5`:

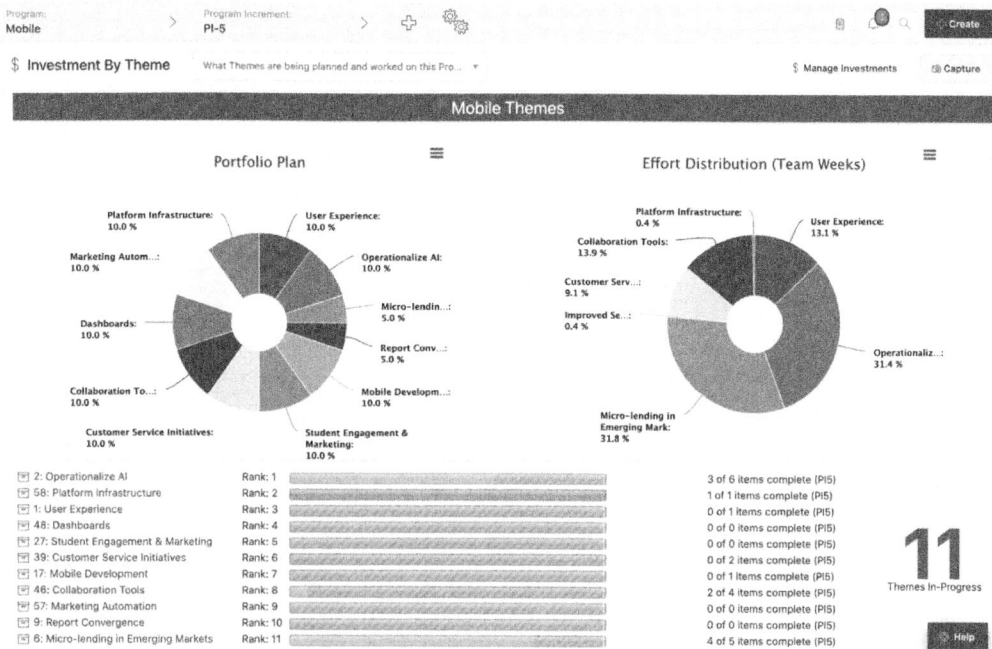

Figure 7.12 – Jira Align investment by theme report

The left pie chart shows how the portfolio apportioned the budget across themes. This is done by clicking on the **Manage Investments** button in the top-right corner of the workspace to open the **Theme Planning View** panel, where you can set the percentage of the total PI investment for each theme. The right chart shows the actual distribution of effort, enabling portfolio leadership to see how closely actual execution aligns with planned budget allocations.

The bottom section of the report lists the in-progress themes, with progress bars showing the percent complete. Hover over the bars for details. The count of competed epics and stand-alone features for each theme is listed to the right of the progress bars. Hover over the counts for details.

Another useful budget report is Investments vs. Actuals, which shows the PI allocation, estimated spend, and actual spend per theme in one report. To access it, go to the navigation menu and then select **Portfolio | Track | Investment vs. Actuals**. Be sure to set your context in the configuration bar. In the following screenshot, we've generated the report for the `Digital Services` portfolio and `PI-5`:

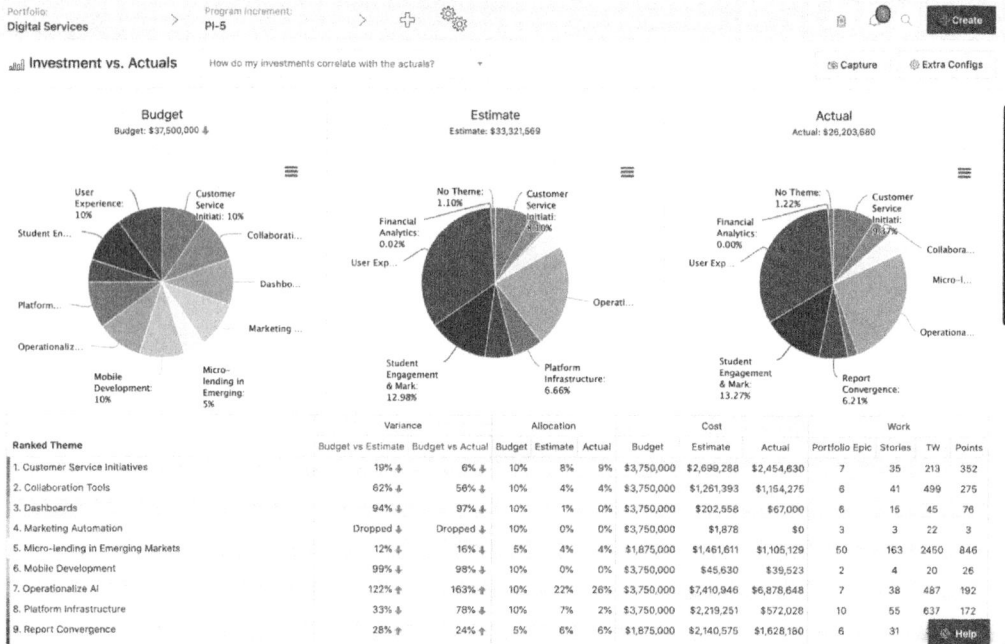

Ranked Theme	Variance		Allocation			Cost			Work			
	Budget vs Estimate	Budget vs Actual	Budget	Estimate	Actual	Budget	Estimate	Actual	Portfolio Epic	Stories	TW	Points
1. Customer Service Initiatives	19% ↓	6% ↓	10%	8%	9%	$3,750,000	$2,699,288	$2,454,630	7	35	213	352
2. Collaboration Tools	62% ↓	56% ↓	10%	4%	4%	$3,750,000	$1,261,393	$1,164,275	6	41	499	275
3. Dashboards	94% ↓	97% ↓	10%	1%	0%	$3,750,000	$202,558	$67,000	6	16	45	76
4. Marketing Automation	Dropped ↓	Dropped ↓	10%	0%	0%	$3,750,000	$1,878	$0	3	3	22	3
5. Micro-lending in Emerging Markets	12% ↓	16% ↓	5%	4%	4%	$1,875,000	$1,461,611	$1,105,129	50	163	2450	846
6. Mobile Development	99% ↓	98% ↓	10%	0%	0%	$3,750,000	$45,630	$39,523	2	4	20	26
7. Operationalize AI	122% ↑	163% ↑	10%	22%	26%	$3,750,000	$7,410,946	$6,878,648	7	38	487	192
8. Platform Infrastructure	33% ↓	78% ↓	10%	7%	2%	$3,750,000	$2,219,251	$572,028	10	55	637	172
9. Report Convergence	28% ↑	24% ↑	5%	6%	6%	$1,875,000	$2,140,575	$1,628,180	6	31		

Figure 7.13 – Jira Align investment vs. actuals report

Let's examine the three charts from left to right:

- **Budget**: The value above the chart represents either the program increment budget or the sum of portfolio epic budgets, depending on the setting made by clicking on the **Extra Configs** button at the top right of the workspace. The chart shows the same percentage allocation across themes we saw previously, which is set by going to the Investment by Theme report and clicking on the **Manage Investments** button. Hover over the segments of the pie chart to see the dollar values.

- **Estimate**: The value above the chart is the sum of estimated portfolio epic costs based on total story points in the PI and cost per point. Cost per point is derived from the average team cost per sprint divided by average velocity. The chart shows each theme's estimated portfolio epic costs for the PI as a percentage of the total estimated portfolio epic costs for the PI. Hover over the segments of the pie chart to see the dollar values.

- **Actual**: The value above the chart is the sum of actual story costs for accepted stories connected to portfolio epics in the PI based on total story points and cost per point. Cost per point is derived from the average team cost per sprint divided by average velocity. The chart shows each theme's actual story costs as a percentage of the total actual story costs for the PI. Hover over each segment of the pie chart to see the dollar values.

The bottom section of the report shows several other data points for each theme, including variance, allocation, cost, and work. Now that we've seen some useful reports for portfolio leadership to plan and monitor investments, let's see how the portfolio connects execution to enterprise strategy.

Connecting the portfolio to enterprise strategy

Enterprise strategy is formed on the basis of several inputs, including mission, vision, and values; business drivers; financial goals; and competitive analysis. The outputs of enterprise strategy are portfolio budgets and strategic themes.

In SAFe, themes are differentiating business objectives that drive the future state of the portfolio, connect the portfolio to enterprise strategy, and provide context for the portfolio vision and lean budgeting. According to SAFe, they are best described in the form of OKRs, with the objective being the theme, and the key results being the quantifiable measures of the theme's progress. While SAFe considers themes a type of objective, we follow the approach supported by Jira Align, where the theme represents a large work item and the OKR represents its corresponding business outcomes. This provides a consistent approach, documented in *Chapter 2, Implementing Jira Align, Figure 2.9*, where each level of scale has a set of people, work, time, and outcome dimensions.

The following screenshot provides an example of how themes in Jira Align correspond to OKRs:

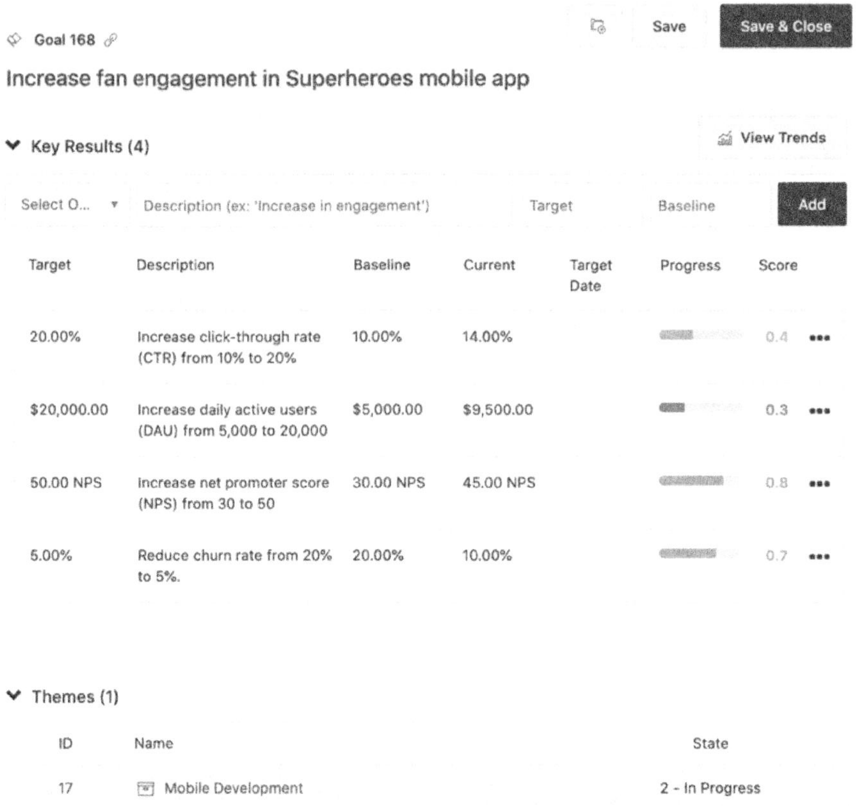

◇ **Goal 168** ⬚   ⬚ Save   Save & Close

Increase fan engagement in Superheroes mobile app

∨ **Key Results (4)**   ⬚ View Trends

| Select O... ▼ | Description (ex: 'Increase in engagement') | | | Target | Baseline | Add |

Target	Description	Baseline	Current	Target Date	Progress	Score	
20.00%	Increase click-through rate (CTR) from 10% to 20%	10.00%	14.00%			0.4	•••
$20,000.00	Increase daily active users (DAU) from 5,000 to 20,000	$5,000.00	$9,500.00			0.3	•••
50.00 NPS	Increase net promoter score (NPS) from 30 to 50	30.00 NPS	45.00 NPS			0.8	•••
5.00%	Reduce churn rate from 20% to 5%.	20.00%	10.00%			0.7	•••

∨ **Themes (1)**

ID	Name	State
17	⬚ Mobile Development	2 - In Progress

Figure 7.14 – Jira Align OKR linked to a theme

Here, we've set a yearly goal to "Increase fan engagement in the Superheroes mobile app" and associated key results and a theme with it.

A key function of LPM is to provide clarity on the direction and purpose of work in order to connect strategy to execution. Clarity enables decentralized decision making to improve the flow of value at each level of scale. OKRs, such as the yearly goal in the previous screenshot, help encapsulate the direction and purpose driving the work.

Themes and their corresponding OKRs influence portfolio strategy and provide context for decision making. They influence the portfolio vision; portfolio epic backlog and kanban; program, solution, and team-level backlogs; value stream budgets; and lean budget guardrails. Let's now examine portfolio vision.

Maintaining the portfolio vision

In SAFe, the portfolio canvas defines the portfolio's domain and development value streams and is a key input for creating and maintaining the portfolio vision. Jira Align makes creating a portfolio canvas easy. Begin by going to the navigation menu and selecting **Enterprise | Canvas**. Then name your canvas and choose **Portfolio Canvas** from the list before clicking on the **Create new Canvas** button. This will open a blank canvas with empty content blocks. In the following screenshot, we have created a portfolio canvas for the **Mutants** portfolio:

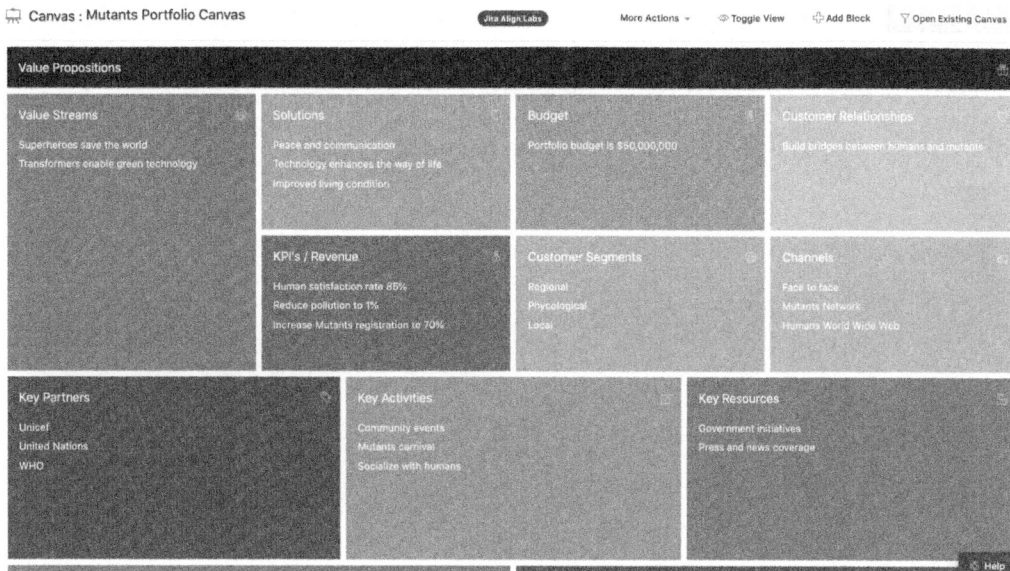

Figure 7.15 – Jira Align portfolio canvas

Here we see several content blocks for defining the portfolio's value proposition, value streams, budget, and much more. Hover over a block to perform the following actions to configure the look and feel of your canvas:

- Edit the title.
- Change the background color.
- Change the icon.
- Add content, including a link.

- Select a state to reflect content status: **Not Started**, **In Progress**, or **Done**. The states appear as color-coded icons (gray, red, and green, respectively) when you click on the **Toggle View** button near the top-right corner of the workspace to toggle from **full** to **note** view.

- Drag and drop to move the block or adjust its size.

- Delete the block.

To create a content block, click on the **Add Block** button near the top-right corner of the workspace. Then, click on the **More Actions** button at the top of the workspace, right of center, to access the following options: click on **Edit Canvas** to rename the canvas, **Delete Canvas** to remove it, or **Create new Canvas**. Note that if you delete a canvas, it cannot be recovered. You can open an existing canvas by clicking on the **Open Existing Canvas** button in the top-right corner of the workspace.

Now that we know how to create a portfolio canvas, let's see how the portfolio can leverage lean budgets to improve outcomes.

Establishing lean budgets and guardrails

A typical challenge of the traditional project funding approach is that it causes friction, overhead, and delays. LPM solves this by funding value streams, guided by budget guardrails, to increase the speed of value delivery.

One of the guardrails is to guide investments by horizon. SAFe recommends the following horizons:

- **Horizon 3 – Exploring**: Investment to evaluate potential new solutions.

- **Horizon 2 – Emerging**: Solutions that emerged from horizon 3.

- **Horizon 1**: Solutions that deliver more value than their cost. There are two subcategories of horizon 1:

  Investing: Solutions that require significant ongoing investment

  Extracting: Stable solutions that deliver high value with minimal new investment

- **Horizon 0 – Retiring**: Investment to decommission solutions.

We recommend that the Jira Align administrator adds the preceding horizons to the **Strategic Driver** dropdown on the portfolio epic details panel. To do so, the administrator would go to **Administration | Settings | Platform** and then click on the **Dropdowns** tab and select **Strategic Driver** to manage the field values.

Tips and tricks

The standard **Strategic Driver** drop-down values are **Innovate**, **Expand**, **Sustain**, **Contain**, **Exit**, and **Unknown**. We recommend renaming the existing values to identify the horizons as follows:

Horizon 3 - Innovate

Horizon 2 - Expand

Horizon 1 - Sustain

Horizon 1 - Contain

Horizon 0 - Exit

Setting up investment horizons in this way enables several helpful visualizations for the LPM function that we'll explore shortly. Before we do, note that Jira Align has a standard dropdown called **Strategic Horizon**. However, there are three disadvantages to using this when capturing investment horizons:

- It has only three options and these are not editable: Defend & Extend; Expand to New Markets; and Explore Future Options.

- You cannot group a portfolio epic roadmap according to these fields, as you can for **Strategic Driver**.

- You cannot generate a report according to these fields as you can for **Strategic Driver**.

Therefore, we recommend using **Strategic Driver** for horizons. To see the horizons in the portfolio epic backlog, go to **Columns Shown | Portfolio Epic** and select **Strategic Driver**, as shown in the following screenshot:

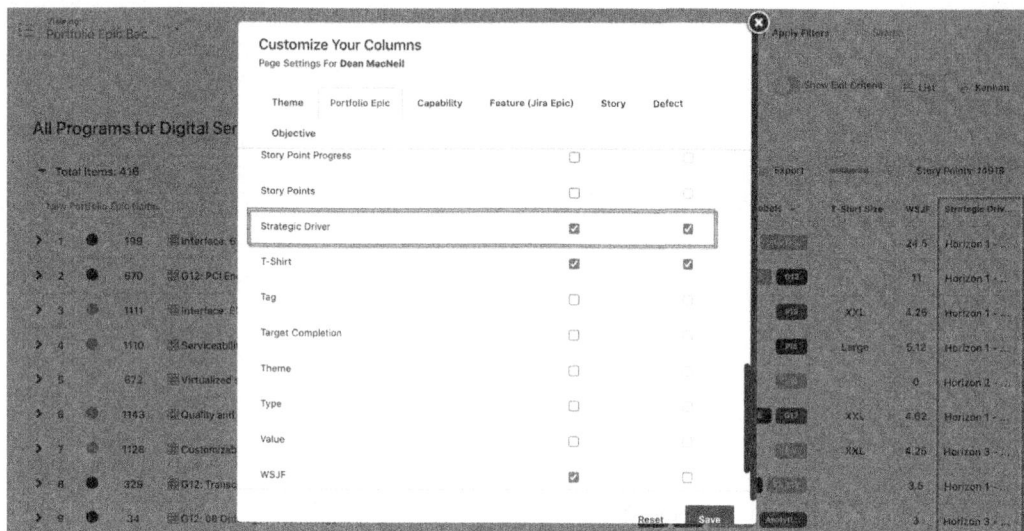

Figure 7.16 – Jira Align portfolio epic backlog with strategic driver

To create a portfolio epic roadmap by horizon, you need to perform the following steps:

1. Go to the navigation menu and select **Program | Manage | Roadmaps**. Be sure that PIs are selected in the configuration bar and that **Work** and **Portfolio Epics** are selected from the dropdowns.

2. Next, click on the **View Configuration** button at the top of the workspace, right of center.

3. Then, click on the **Other Options** tab and select **Strategic Driver** under **Group By Property**.

You will now have a roadmap of portfolio epics grouped by horizon, as shown in the following screenshot:

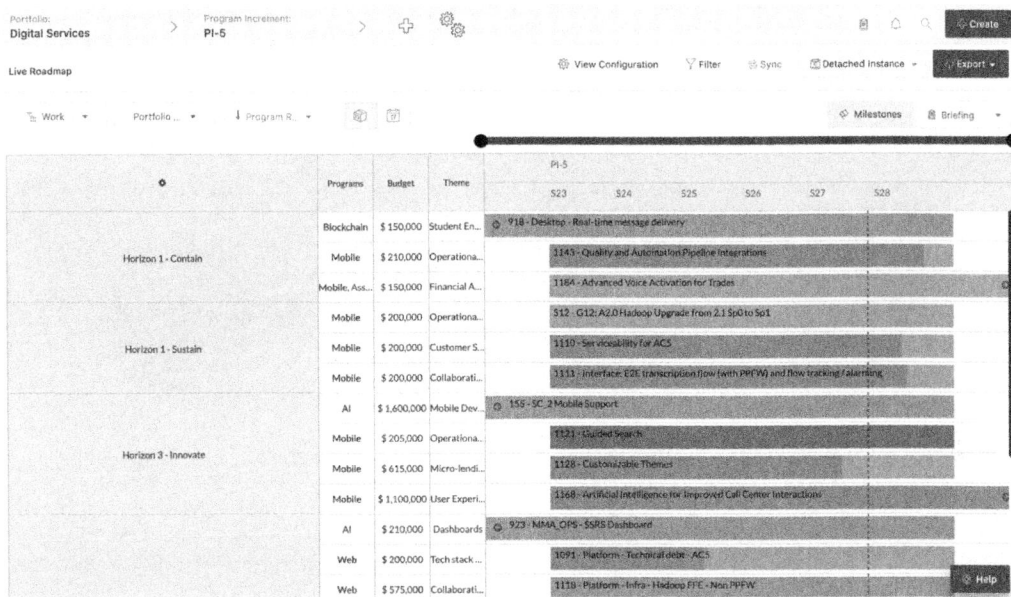

Figure 7.17 – Jira Align portfolio epic roadmap with strategic driver

Note that roadmap swim lanes are grouped by strategic drivers that reflect the horizons on the left. A prerequisite is that a strategic driver must be selected in the details panel for each portfolio epic.

Another budget guardrail is to determine and apply capacity allocation by activity type. Jira Align supports capturing the activity type at the feature work item level by using the category field. The standard categories are **Customer Funded**, **Grow / Protect Base**, **Innovation**, **New Market / Product**, **R&D**, **Tech Investment**, and **Technical Debt**. The Jira Align administrator can edit this list by going to **Administration | Settings | Platform** and then clicking on the **Dropdowns** tab and selecting **Feature Category**. Note, too, that categories must be enabled by going to **Administration | Settings | Details Panels Settings**, selecting the portfolio from the **Portfolio** dropdown, and **Feature** from the **Work Item** dropdown, and then sliding on the **Category** toggle.

To see the percentage allocation by horizon, go to the navigation menu, click on the **Reports** menu item near the bottom, and then search for `strategic driver`. Click on the search result to open the **Strategic Driver Report** as shown in the following screenshot:

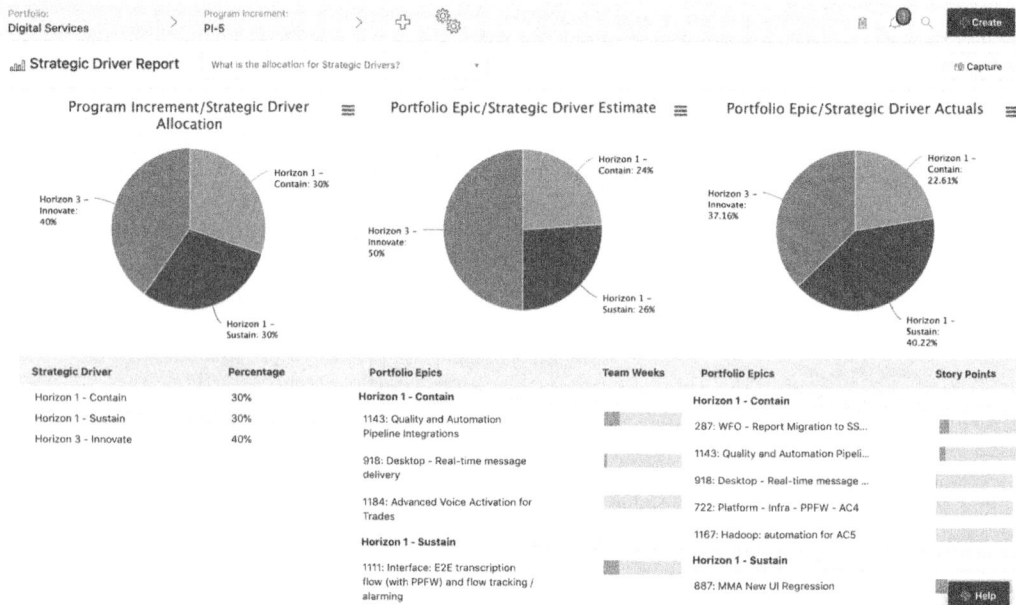

Figure 7.18 – Jira Align strategic driver report

Here you see the PI's planned, estimated, and actual allocations for each strategic driver. This enables portfolio leadership to determine whether the planned strategic allocation for the work is aligned with the work the teams are actually doing or planning on doing. For example, if leadership planned to spend 25% of the quarterly effort on expanding to new markets and the chart indicates that only 10% will be spent, then the portfolio could miss its revenue targets.

The left chart is based on the percentage allocations set in the PI details panel. To set these, go to the navigation menu and select **Program | Manage | Program Increments**. Next, click on a PI in the grid to open its details panel. Finally, click on **+ Full Details** and then on **Manage Strategic Driver allocations**.

The middle chart is based on portfolio epic estimates for the PI and the right chart is based on actual story points for accepted stories connected to portfolio epics in the PI. Further details below the charts include portfolio epics by horizon with progress bars. Hover over the progress bars for details. The report also displays an allocation trend across PIs when multiple PIs are selected in the configuration bar. This can be seen by scrolling down.

> **Tips and tricks**
>
> If your report search didn't return the Strategic Driver report, you can ask your Jira Align administrator to enable the report for your role.
>
> To do so, the administrator would go to **Administration | Access Controls | Roles**, select your role, click on **Additional Options** to expand the section, and then toggle on the **Strategic Driver Allocation** option under **Reports**.

Another budget guardrail of LPM is that approval is required for significant initiatives, in other words, portfolio epics. The portfolio's vision is realized through portfolio epics. Continuous business owner engagement is also encouraged. This can be formalized in regularly occurring meetings such as the portfolio sync recommended by SAFe.

The traditional categories of **capital expenses (CapEx)** and **operational expenses (OpEx)** are still relevant when using LPM. Jira Align supports tracking CapEx at the portfolio epic level. To designate a portfolio epic as CapEx, go to the portfolio epic's details panel and click on + **Full Details** to see the **Capitalized** dropdown. Select **Yes** for CapEx:

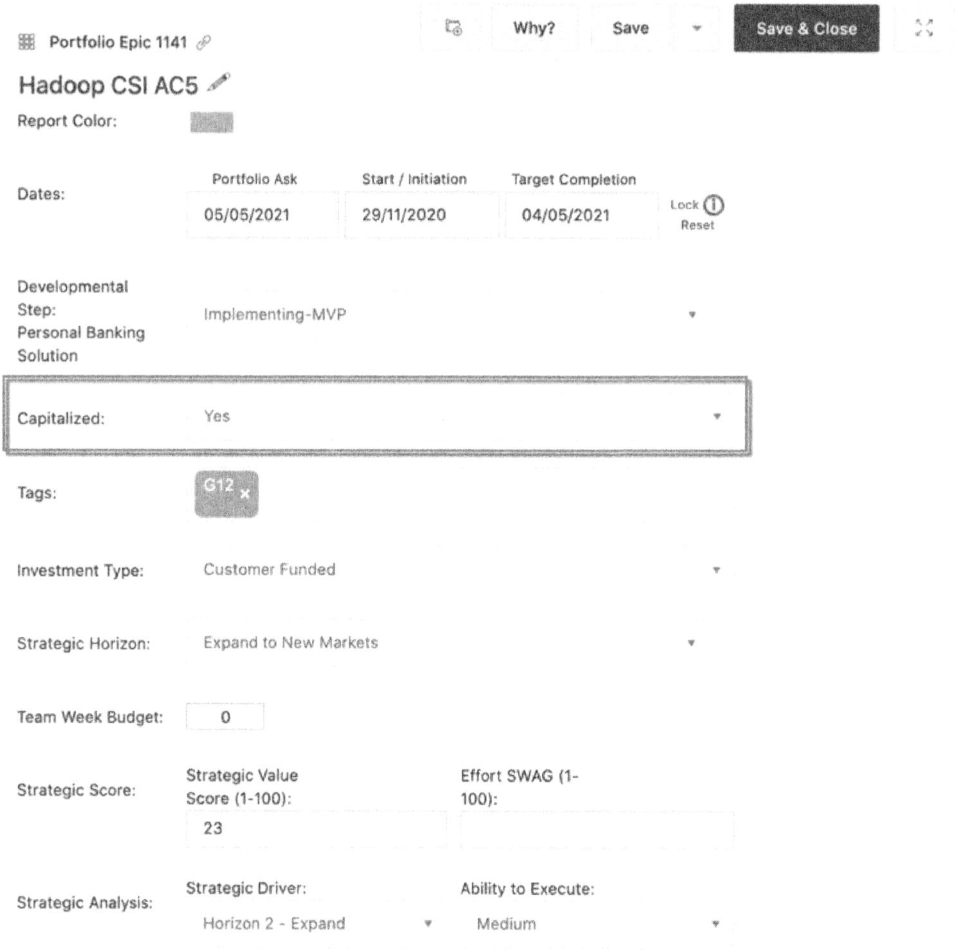

Figure 7.19 – Jira Align portfolio epic, capitalized

You can add this column to your portfolio epic backlog by clicking on the **Columns Shown** button at the top of the backlog workspace, and then clicking on the **Portfolio Epic** tab and selecting the **Capitalized** checkbox. In order to add the planned budget totals for CapEx and OpEx to the portfolio epic, click on the **Finance** tab in the details panel, as shown in the following screenshot:

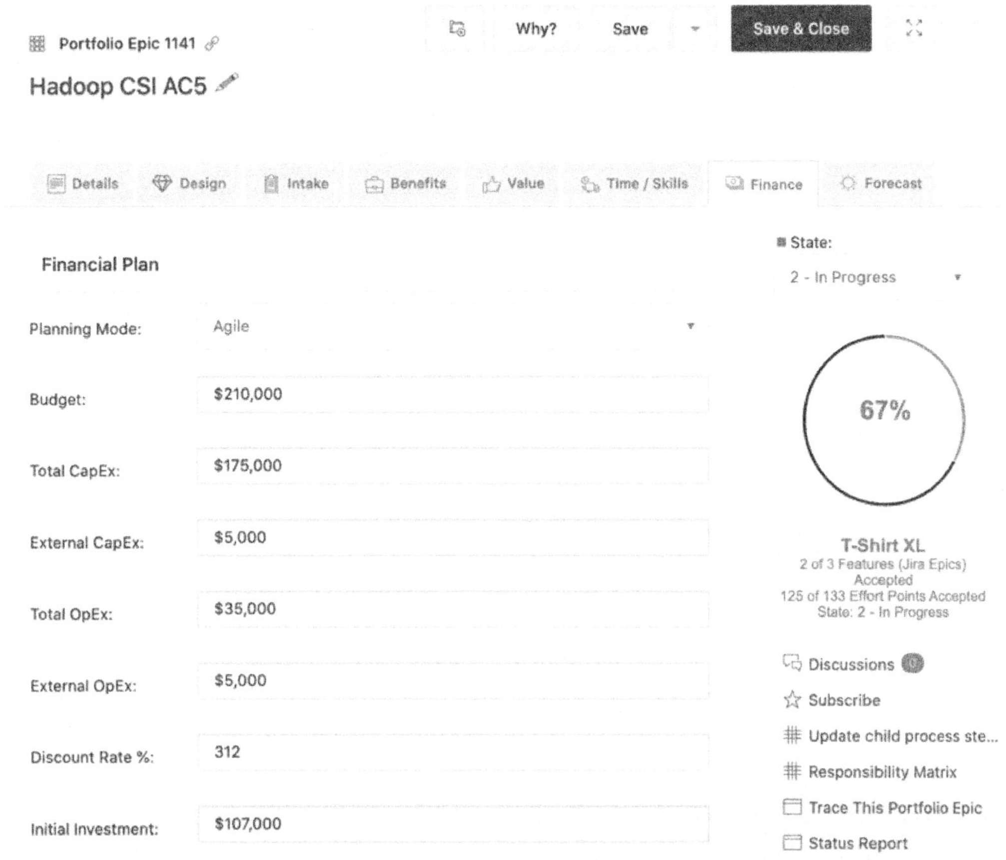

Figure 7.20 – Jira Align portfolio epic, finance

Here you can enter and track the CapEx and OpEx data. A useful visualization of this data is the status report, financials view. To access it, go to the navigation menu and select **Enterprise | Track | Status Reports**. Next, click on the **Portfolio** button and then on your portfolio. Finally, click on the **View Financials** button near the top-right corner of the workspace.

The status report, financials view provides portfolio epic financials, status, and health information broken down by program for the PI(s) selected in the configuration bar. Click on a program, portfolio epic, or its associated theme to drill down for more information. There are numerous columns of data, so you will need to scroll horizontally to see the CapEx and OpEx columns shown in the following screenshot:

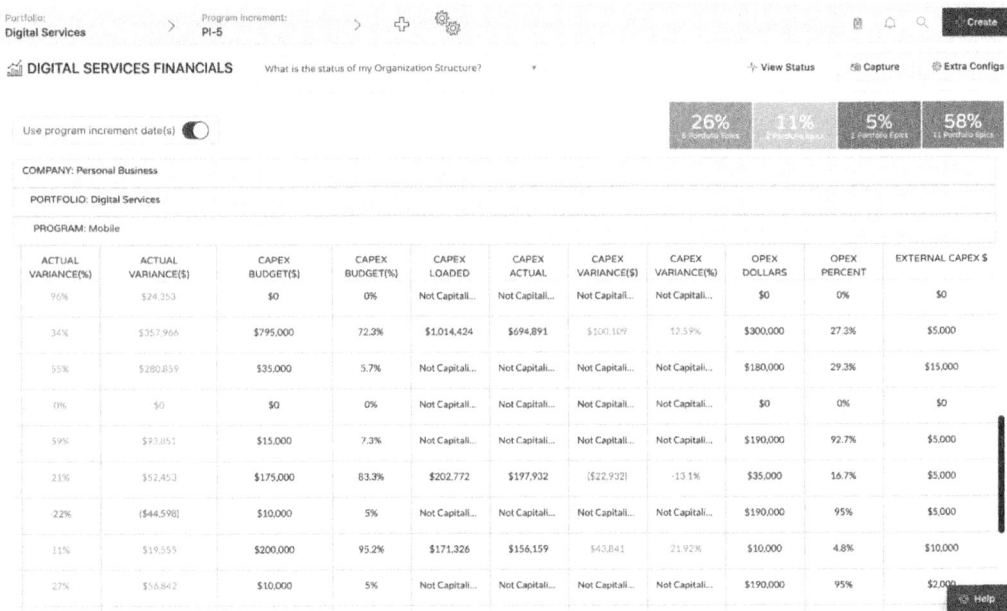

Figure 7.21 – Jira Align status report, financials view

Now that we've explored portfolio budget reports and guardrails, let's see how to establish portfolio flow.

Establishing portfolio flow

Another challenge of traditional portfolio management is that poor control of demand and **work in process** (**WIP**) reduces throughput. LPM's solution is to match demand to capacity to increase the flow of value.

The portfolio kanban enables the LPM function to match demand to capacity based on WIP limits, visualize bottlenecks in each process step, and identify opportunities for relentless improvement. The kanban also includes policies governing the entry and exit of portfolio epics in each process step.

To create a portfolio kanban, you'll first need to specify the underlying process steps. To begin, go to the navigation menu, select **Portfolio | Manage | Process Steps**, and then click on the **Add Process Steps** button to open the panel shown in the following screenshot:

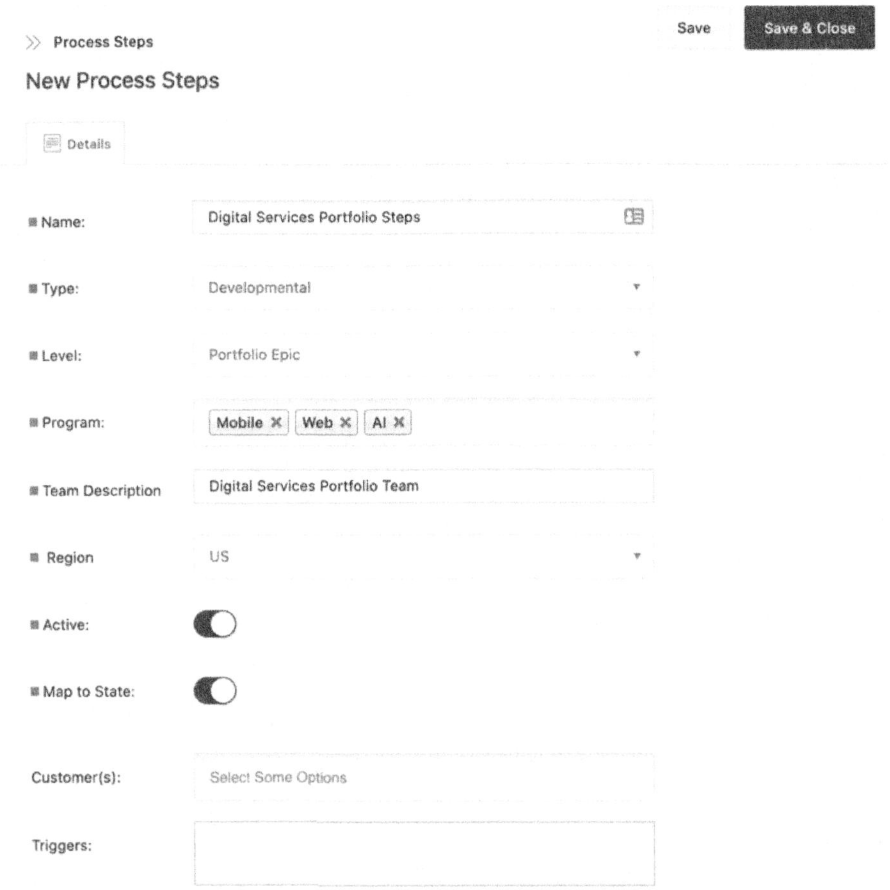

Figure 7.22 – Jira Align new process steps

Next, enter the following details:

- **Name**: Add a meaningful name to your portfolio kanban.

- **Type**: Select one of the two following types:

  Developmental: Steps required to develop new products, systems, or services capabilities. Choosing this option will allow you to map process steps to Jira Align's work item states. This is the standard option to use most of the time.

Operational: Steps required to provide goods or services to a customer, whether internal or external. This could be useful when modeling future business operations, but is rarely used.

> **Tips and tricks**
>
> If you don't see the **Operational** type in the dropdown, ask the Jira Align administrator to enable operational value streams.
>
> To do so, the administrator would go to **Administration | Settings | Platform**, click on the **Solution** tab, set the **Enable Operational Process Steps** dropdown to **Yes**, and then click on the **Save Settings** button.

- **Level**: Select the work item level – theme, portfolio epic, capability, feature, or story. Here, we will choose **Portfolio Epic**.
- **Team Description**: Add a description of the team responsible for the kanban.
- **Region**: Select a region applicable to the kanban.
- **Active**: Specify whether the kanban is active and available to use.
- **Map to State**: If you chose the **Developmental** type, then you can toggle this on to map process steps to work item states.

In addition, you can add the following optional information:

- **Customer(s)**: List the relevant customers.
- **Triggers**: Specify the events that trigger the flow of value; for example, a customer places an order or requests a new feature.
- **Inputs**: Specify any necessary inputs.
- **Outputs**: List any relevant outputs.
- **Includes**: Provide additional information in terms of the scope of the process steps.

Finally, click on the **Save** button. You will now see the **Process Steps** tab, where you can add steps for your kanban and link them to states, as shown in the following screenshot:

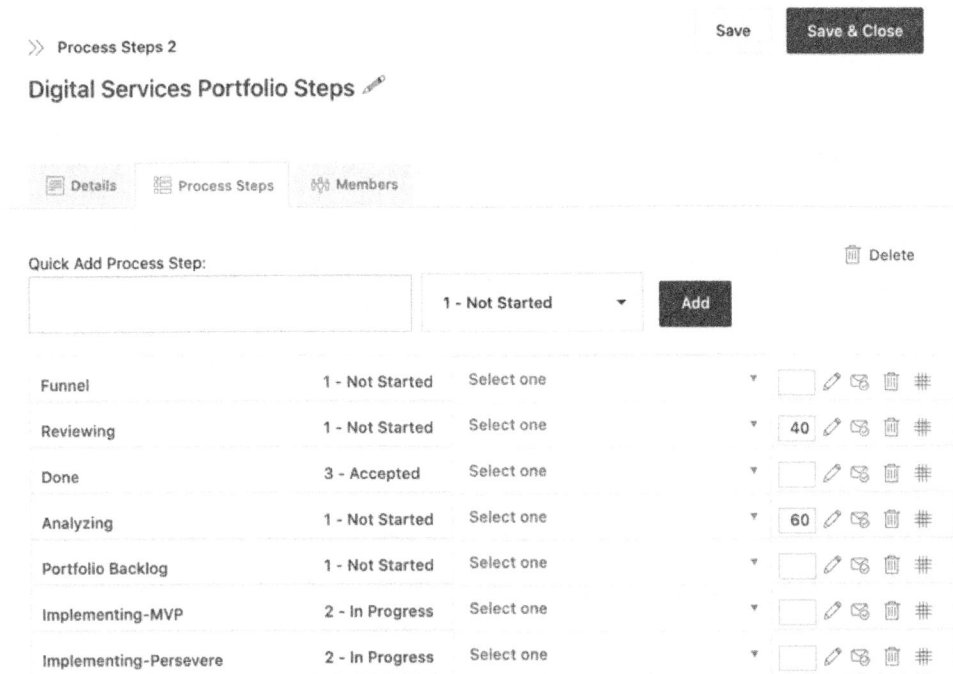

Figure 7.23 – Jira Align process steps

Here, we've added the portfolio kanban steps recommended by SAFe and mapped them to Jira Align work item states. For example, **Funnel** is mapped to **1 - Not Started**. Note that if a process step maps to a functional area of your organization, you can select it from the dropdown to the right of the work item state; however, this is rarely used.

> **Tips and tricks**
>
> To maintain the list of functional areas, go to **Administration | Setup | Functional Areas**.
>
> As a prerequisite, the Jira Align administrator must enable **Functional Areas** for your role under **Administration | Access Controls | Roles | Administration | Other Setup**.
>
> Note that **Functional Areas** is often renamed **Business Units** under **Administration | Settings | Platform Terminology**.

At the far right of the **Process Steps** tab, click on the matrix icon to maintain the **RACI (responsible, accountable, consulted, informed)** matrix. Remove a process step by clicking on the trash icon. Toggle on/off email alert notifications by clicking on the email icon. Click on the pencil icon next to each step to add or edit details, including exit criteria, as shown in the following screenshot:

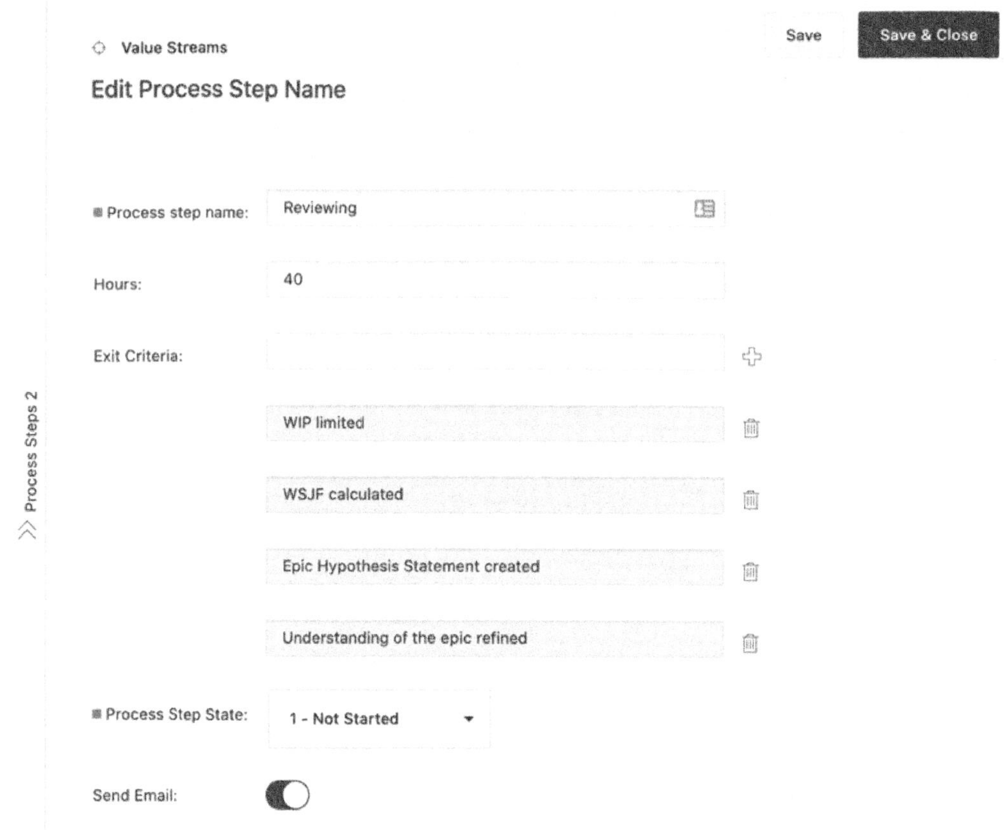

Figure 7.24 – Jira Align edit process steps

Here we are editing the **Reviewing** process step. The red squares indicate required fields. First, note that we entered 4 0 as the estimated process step time in **Hours**. These are used to measure efficiency, defined as the total estimated hours for steps divided by the total actual hours for steps, visible in the Work in Process report.

Tips and tricks

To see the process step metrics, including efficiency, go to the navigation menu and select **Portfolio | Track | Work in Process**. Make sure that your context is set in the configuration bar.

Next, click on the **Value Stream View** button and slide on the **Stats** toggle, both near the top-right corner of the workspace.

Finally, select your kanban name from the **Process Steps** dropdown and then expand it by clicking on the right-pointing angle symbol. You can select multiple kanbans for display and then expand or collapse them.

At the top of each swim lane, you will see **Efficiency**, discussed earlier, as well as **Throughput** (count of items that have moved into the final step in the last 30 days) and **Cycle Time** (average number of hours it took the items, within the last 30 days, to move to the final step).

Next, notice that we added a list of four **Exit Criteria** for the **Reviewing** process step, mapped it to the **1 - Not Started** state, and toggled on email notifications. When done editing on this tab, click on the **Save** button. Finally, click on the **Members** tab to add team members for **Digital Services Portfolio Team** and then click on the **Save & Close** button.

Now that we have created the process steps, we can view the portfolio kanban to visualize portfolio flow. This is often done during the portfolio sync, a cadence-based event for reviewing and managing the epics on the portfolio kanban board. The advancement of each portfolio epic through the process steps on the kanban is coordinated by the epic owner.

To view the portfolio kanban, begin at the portfolio epic backlog by going to the navigation menu and selecting **Portfolio | Backlog**. Next, click on the **Kanban** button near the top-right corner of the workspace and then select the **Process Step View** option to view the kanban board, as shown in the following screenshot:

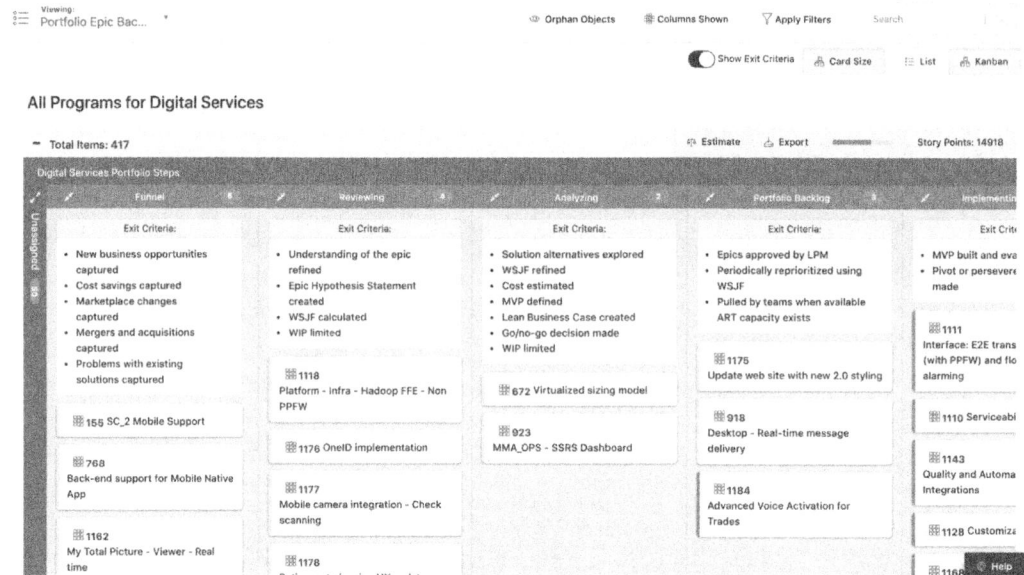

Figure 7.25 – Jira Align backlog process step kanban

Here we are viewing the kanban for the `Digital Services` portfolio. You may set your context in the configuration bar to filter by program and/or program increment. Note that we toggled on the **Show Exit Criteria** option near the top of the workspace to the right of center. This displays the exit criteria we added earlier for each process step. Click on the **Card Size** button and then select **Normal**, **Small**, or **Heat Map View**. Click on the arrows on each column to collapse or expand them to better visualize the end-to-end flow. In the preceding screenshot, we collapsed the **Unassigned** column.

Now that we can visualize the portfolio flow, let's view the Process Step Cycle Time report to evaluate how the portfolio epics are flowing through the process steps. To access the report, go to the navigation menu, click on the search icon (magnifying glass), search for `Process Step Cycle Time`, and then click on the result. Next, select the kanban name from the **Process Steps** dropdown and enter a date range in the corresponding fields. Note that the date range is automatically populated when you have a PI selected in the configuration bar. This will generate the report shown in the following screenshot:

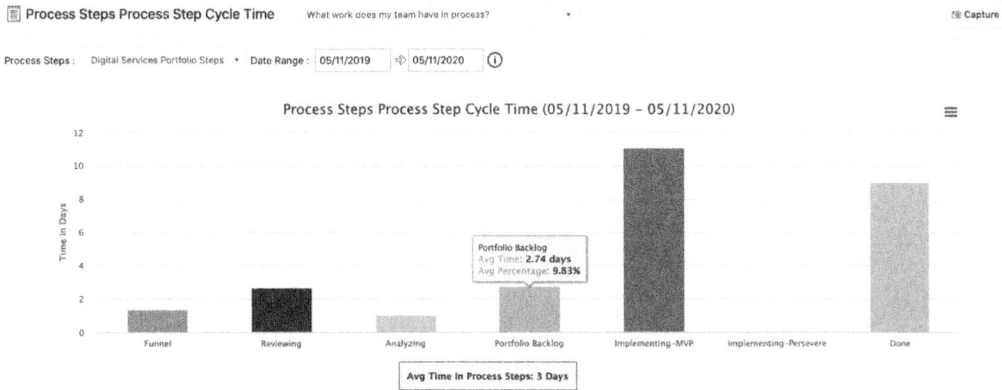

Figure 7.26 – Jira Align process step cycle time report

For this report, we selected the `Digital Services` portfolio in the configuration bar and set a date range of 1 year. As you scroll down, you will see three key statistics:

- **Process Step Cycle Time**: The bar chart shows the average time work items spend in each process step. Below the bar chart is a line chart that allows you to change the date range by clicking and dragging to highlight the time period you'd like to see. You can then click on the **Reset Zoom** button in the top-right corner to reset the timeline.

- **Process Step WIP**: Another bar chart that shows the average number of work items in each process step. Below is a line chart plotting the number of work items in each process step over time. Click and drag on the line chart to highlight the time period you'd like to see and then click on the **Reset Zoom** button in the top-right corner to reset the timeline.

- **Cycle Time Control Chart**: Displays the following information in the form of a line chart:

  Rolling Average: The average number of days all work items have been in process steps on the kanban, for that specific date.

  Overall Average: The sum of all rolling averages from each day divided by the number of days in the chart.

  Completed Work Items: The sum of days spent within process steps divided by the number of work items completed on that day. A work item is completed when it is moved into the final process step.

The report helps to identify bottlenecks and delays where work items are remaining in a process step for too long. It establishes an understanding of the end-to-end delivery process and how it can be improved in terms of velocity, quality, and time to market.

Applying lean governance

The final challenge associated with traditional portfolio management that we will mention in this section is that annual planning and rigid budget cycles impede the ability to respond to change. The practice of big, upfront planning and budgeting of portfolio epics is ineffective, often causing work items to become irrelevant by the time they're delivered.

LPM's solution is rolling wave planning and dynamic budgeting to enable rapid response to change. One aspect of this approach is to budget only the portion of a portfolio epic required to validate a hypothesis. For example, the hypothesis that epic delivery will result in enhanced security can be proven by fewer security breaches. We will discuss this aspect further in the next section.

Promoting innovation

Organizations of all sizes seek to innovate like a start-up in the quest for true business agility. The methods outlined in *The Lean Startup*, by *Eric Reis* (2011), have gained credibility and popularity over the years. For example, SAFe has incorporated them into its LPM approach. Simply put, the lean startup cycle of build-measure-learn fosters innovation.

When following SAFe, the lean startup cycle begins with a newly defined portfolio epic and hypothesis statement. A **minimum viable product** (**MVP**) is then defined for the epic. The MVP represents the smallest portion of the portfolio epic needed to understand whether or not the hypothesis statement is validated. The MVP flows through the portfolio kanban to the **Implementing** state. Based on whether or not the MVP has proven the hypothesis, the portfolio team then decides to either pivot to a new portfolio epic and hypothesis or persevere and continue developing the portfolio epic. When the portfolio team's oversight is no longer required, they move the portfolio epic to the **Done** state.

Tips and tricks

SAFe provides the epic hypothesis statement as a Word template. You can easily select all content from the Word template and then paste it into a web-based wiki such as Confluence. You can then add a link to the epic hypothesis statement in the portfolio epic details panel, under the links section.

Jira Align visualizes the flow of value on the portfolio epic kanban and provides advanced functionality for tracking the MVP from the hypothesis statement to the decision to pivot or persevere. The focus is on outcomes over outputs. To track and measure outcomes, open a portfolio epic's details panel, and then click on the **Value** tab, shown in the following screenshot:

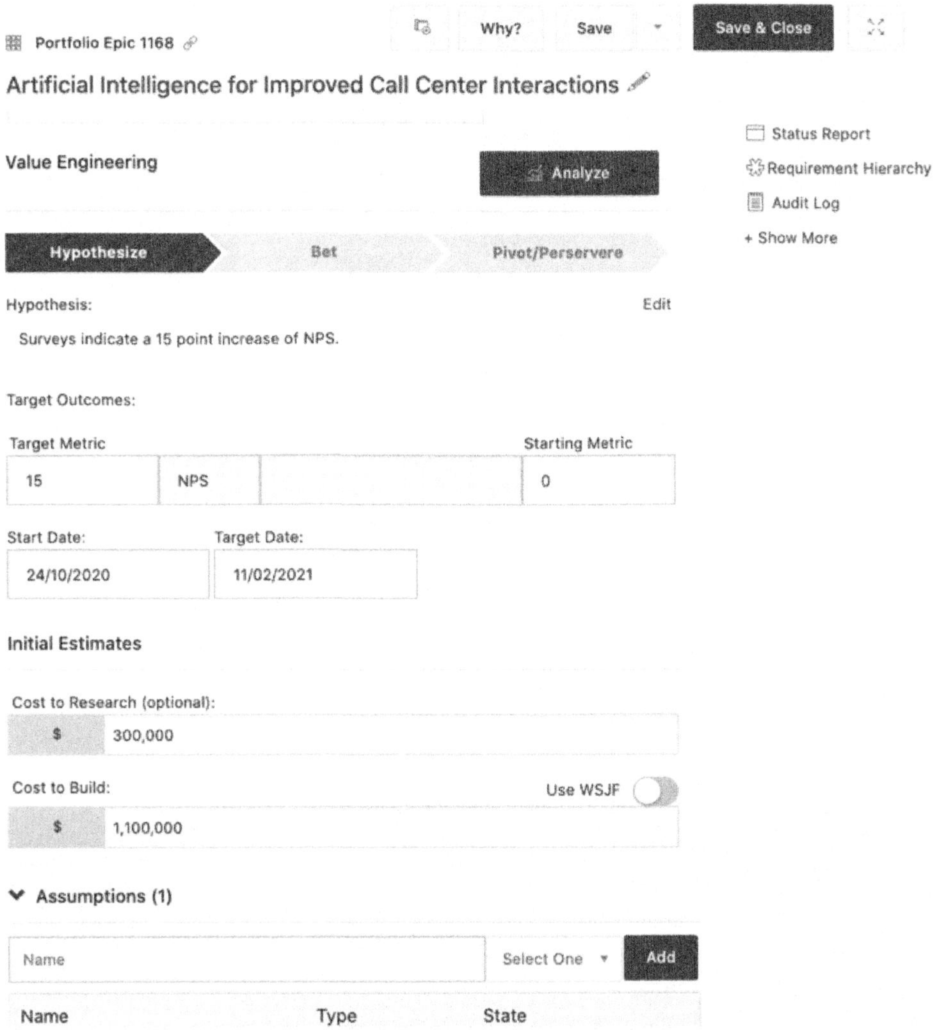

Figure 7.27 – Jira Align value engineering hypothesis

This tab provides strong support for value engineering. It allows you to define a hypothesis and, with minimal investment, ensure that the work is delivering the desired outcome. If not, it provides the opportunity to pivot away.

In this example, we believe we can validate our hypothesis with a research cost of $300,000 and a build cost of $1,100,000. We can begin to conduct the research and track our spending against the budget by adding expenses, as shown in the following screenshot:

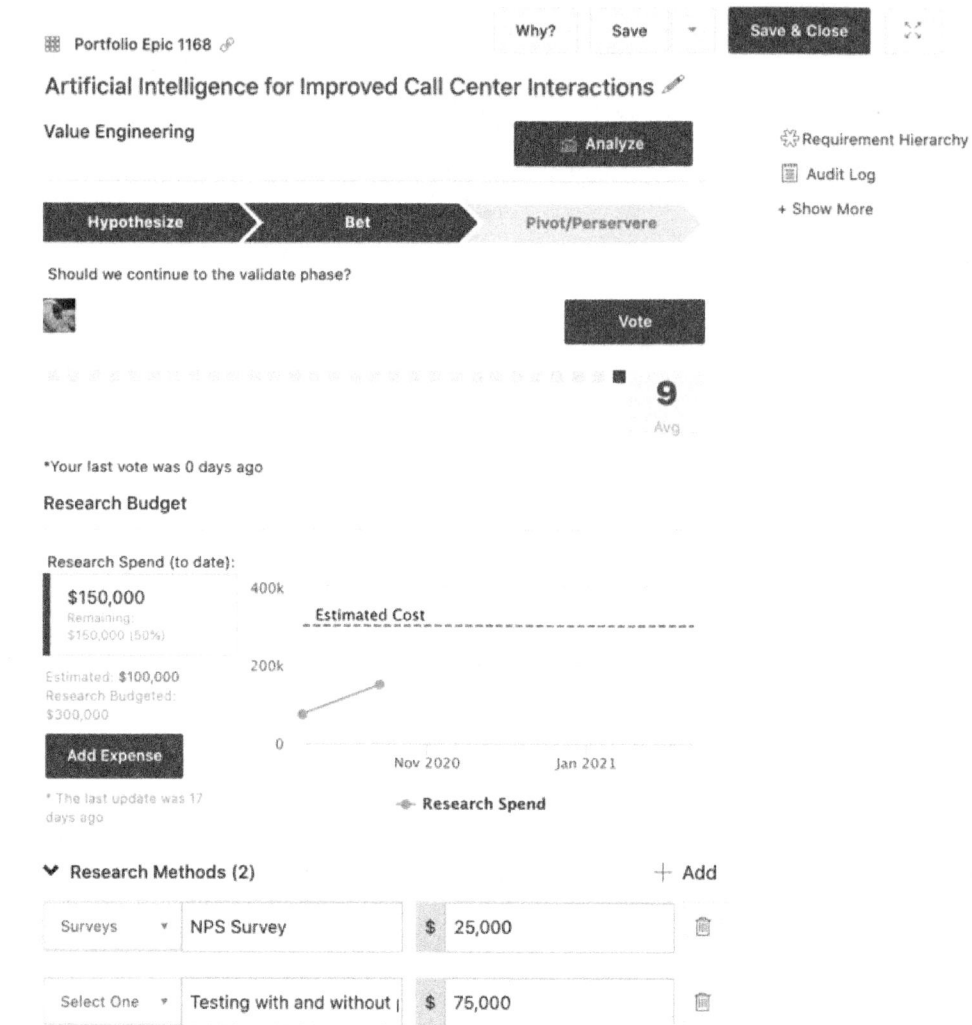

Figure 7.28 – Jira Align value engineering bet

This allows us to track our actual development costs and compare them to the value being realized. Portfolio leadership can cast their vote daily to decide whether we should continue on to the validate phase. Once we move to the next phase, we can decide whether we should pivot or continue investing and persevere:

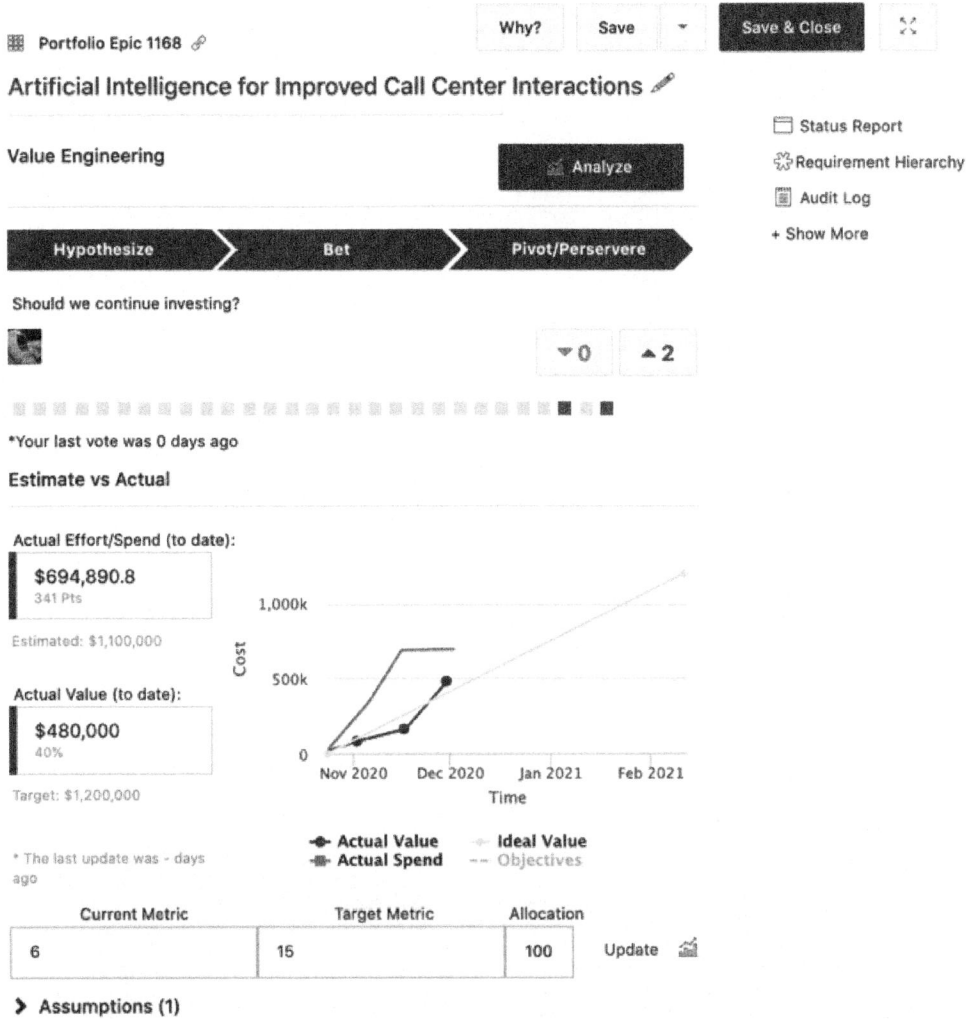

Figure 7.29 – Jira Align value engineering pivot/persevere

Jira Align automatically calculates the cost to deliver a story point, and rolls that cost up to the feature and then portfolio epic to tell us that we've spent **$694,890** thus far in delivering **341** story points and realized **$480,000** in value.

This measure of value here is not revenue, but rather a **net promoter score** (**NPS**) because, in the hypothesis phase, we associated a dollar value with each incremental point of increase in the NPS. We can analyze the performance of not only this particular portfolio epic, but of all the portfolio epics we're developing, and then have the opportunity to pivot or persevere as appropriate.

Now that we've learned how to track and measure MVPs from hypothesis to pivot or persevere, let's step back to see how new ideas can be collected directly from our customers and from people throughout our organization.

Collecting ideas

Jira Align's ideation module allows product management to collect ideas for future products and features from customers, both internal and external, and others. Let's begin by going to the navigation menu and selecting **Product | Ideas | Ideation**. Here you can submit an idea, such as an enhancement request for an existing product, or a question. You can also vote on ideas, as shown in the following screenshot:

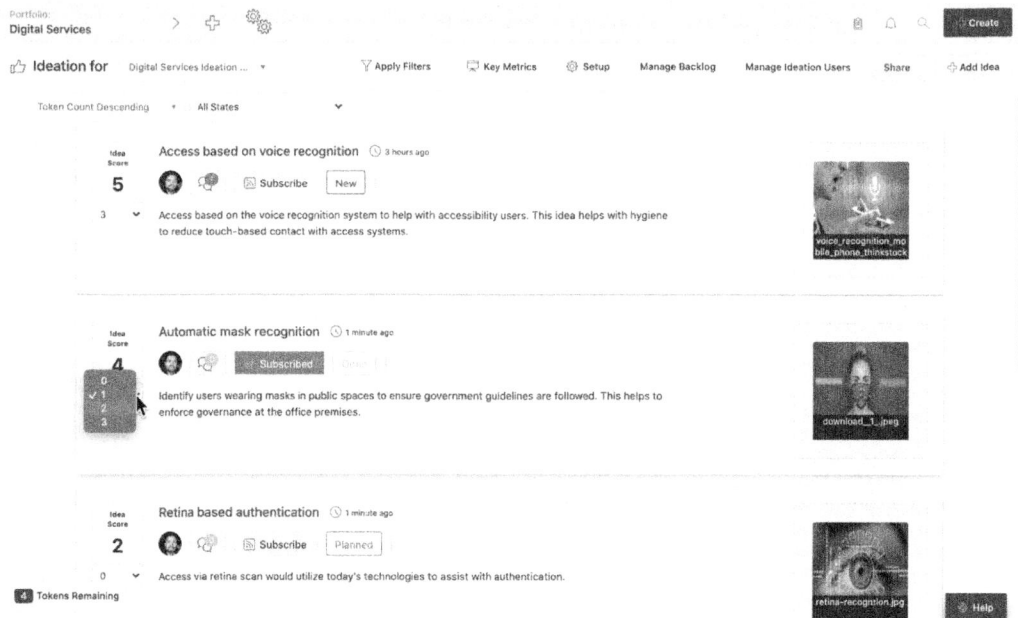

Figure 7.30 – Jira Align ideation

Click on the **Manage Ideation Users** button near the top-right corner of the workspace to grant or revoke access to the ideation module. Monitor the submission of ideas and voting results by clicking on the **Key Metrics** button at the top near the center. Share the contents of the workspace by clicking on the **Share** button near the top-right corner to generate an internal link.

A typical ideation process starts with a campaign to collect ideas related to a particular product or product line over a fixed period of time, such as a PI or business quarter. Begin by creating or modifying an existing idea group. To do so, click on the **Setup** button at the top of the workspace, right of center, to open the group details panel shown in the following screenshot:

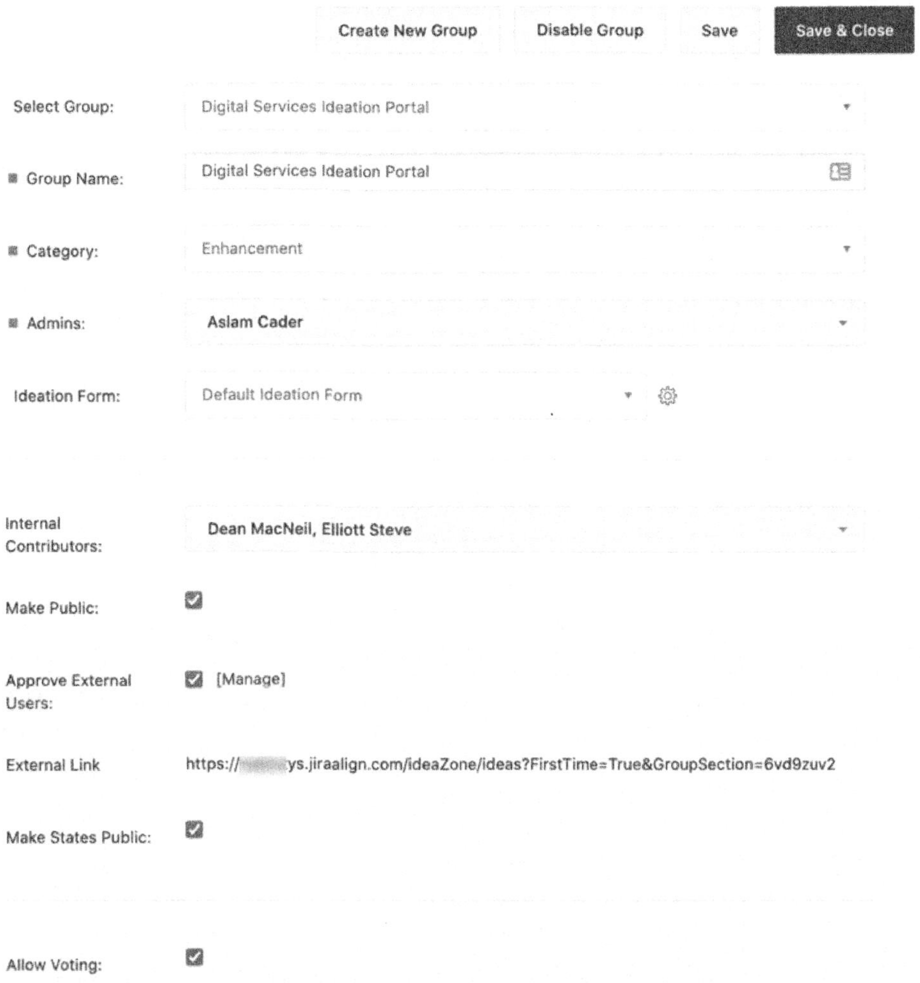

	Create New Group	Disable Group	Save	Save & Close

Select Group:	Digital Services Ideation Portal ▾
▪ Group Name:	Digital Services Ideation Portal ▣
▪ Category:	Enhancement ▾
▪ Admins:	**Aslam Cader** ▾
Ideation Form:	Default Ideation Form ▾ ⚙
Internal Contributors:	**Dean MacNeil, Elliott Steve** ▾
Make Public:	☑
Approve External Users:	☑ [Manage]
External Link	https://▮▮▮▮ys.jiraalign.com/ideaZone/ideas?FirstTime=True&GroupSection=6vd9zuv2
Make States Public:	☑
Allow Voting:	☑

Figure 7.31 – Jira Align ideation campaign

Note that red squares indicate required fields. To create a new campaign, click on the **Create New Group** button at the top center of the panel. Click on the **Disable Group** button to pause or stop the campaign and to reactivate it, and then click on the **Enable Group** button. The following are the attributes you can enter and track for a campaign group:

- **Select Group**: Switch between idea groups.

- **Group Name**: Provide a name for your idea group or campaign.

- **Category**: Select the category of what you'd like to collect in the campaign: **Enhancement**, **Question**, or **Ticket**.

- **Admins**: Choose who will be administering the campaign.

- **Ideation Form**: Choose an ideation form or click on the cog button to create a new form or add fields to an existing form to collect more details.

- **Internal Contributors**: Select the internal contributors or participants for the campaign.

- **Make Public**: Enable external access to the idea group.

- **Approve External Users**: Manage and approve external access to the idea group (the **Make Public** checkbox must be selected).

- **External Link**: When **Make Public** is selected, a link for you to provide to external users is displayed here.

- **Make States Public**: Make the idea status visible to external users.

- **Allow Voting**: Enable voting on ideas. By default, you can either vote up (+1) or down (-1).

- **Token Voting**: Enable token-based voting, as shown in *Figure 7.30*.

- **Max Votes Per Idea**: Set a limit on how many token votes you can cast for an idea (the **Token Voting** checkbox must be selected).

- **Total User Tokens**: Set how many tokens will be granted to each user (the **Token Voting** checkbox must be selected).

Click on the **Save & Close** button to submit changes and return to the workspace. Now, you can create an idea as an internal user by clicking on the **Add Idea** button in the top-right corner. This opens the new idea panel shown in the following screenshot:

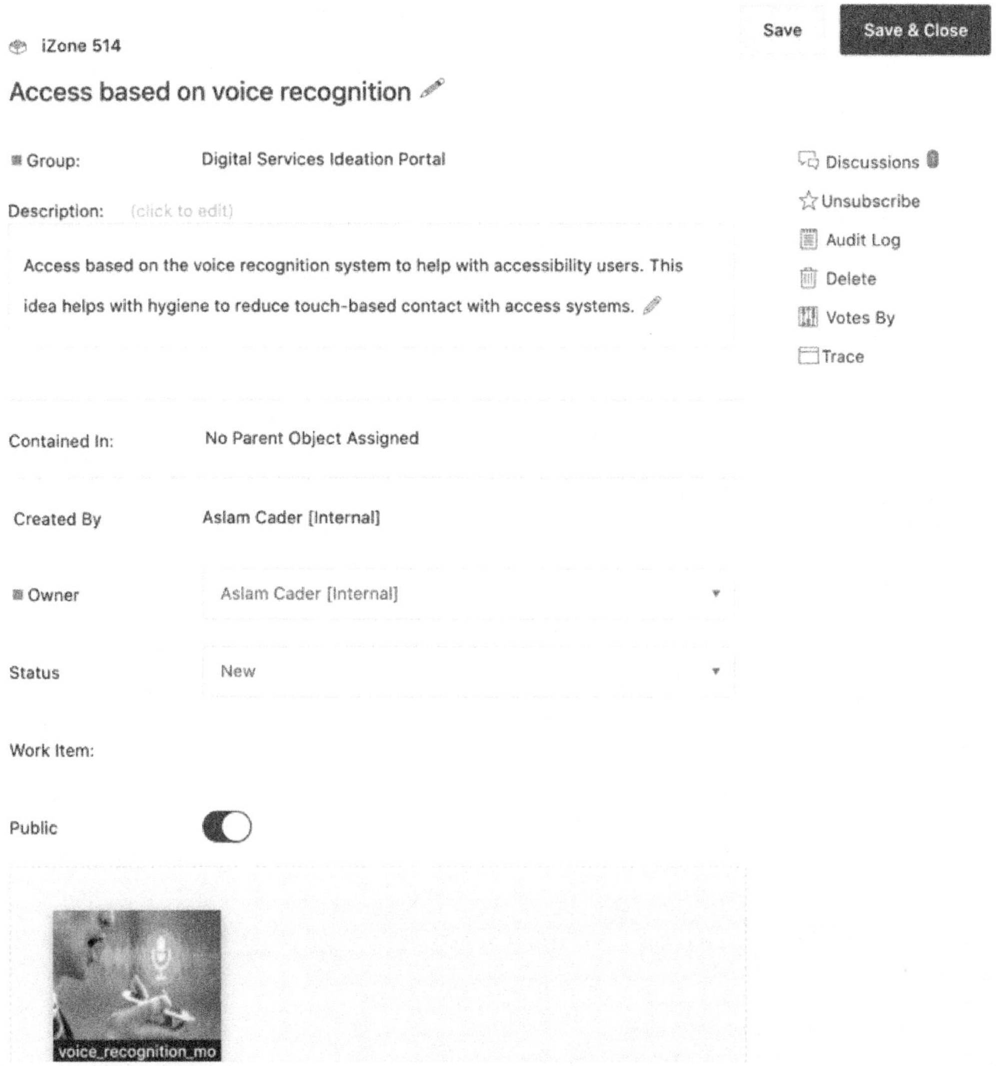

Figure 7.32 – Jira Align new idea

Here you see an idea submitted for the **Digital Services Ideation Portal** campaign. The following are the default attributes you can enter and track for an idea. These may vary, and others such as **Product** or **Customer** may appear depending on the ideation form that was selected for the campaign:

- **Group**: Select the idea group if you have access to more than one.

- **Title**: Add a summary of the idea.

- **Description**: Add more related details.

- **Contained In**: Displays a link to an associated work item after an idea gets promoted. We'll discuss promoting an idea shortly.

- **Created By**: Defaults to the user who creates the idea.

- **Owner**: Choose who owns the idea.

- **Status**: Choose **New** for a new idea that can later move through the following states in the idea backlog: **Open**, **Planned**, **Completed**, and **Shelved**.

- **Category**: Choose the type of idea: **Enhancement**, **Question**, or **Ticket**.

- **Public**: Make the idea available to external users.

- **Attachments**: Add attachments to your idea after clicking on the **Save** button to submit the idea.

Product management and campaign administrators manage ideas in the idea backlog. Click on the **Manage Backlog** button near the top-right corner of the ideation workspace to open the backlog, as shown in the following screenshot:

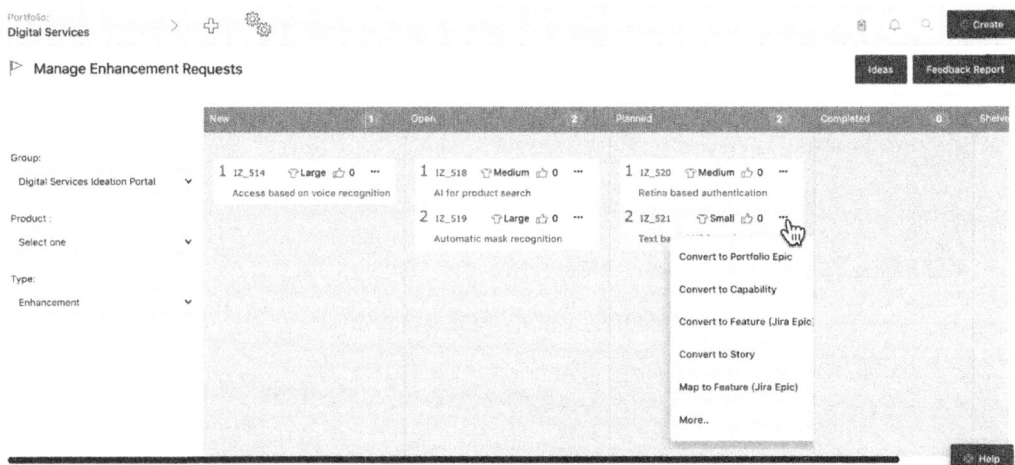

Figure 7.33 – Jira Align ideation backlog

Here you can click and drag ideas to rank them higher or lower and move them through the states on the kanban. Click on the ellipses to promote an idea by converting it to a story, feature, capability, or portfolio epic, as shown in the screenshot, or click on **More** to assign the idea to a different group or give it a t-shirt size. Filter the kanban by **Group**, **Product**, and **Type** using the dropdowns on the left-hand side.

In addition to collecting ideas, it is important to create spaces that can nurture an innovation culture. This is key to achieving a state business agility, meaning that the whole organization, not just engineering or development teams, is engaged in continuous and proactive delivery of innovative business solutions faster than the competition. Furthermore, an even greater level of discipline is required given the current trend of remote working, which can create barriers in team collaboration and impede innovation.

> **Tips and tricks**
>
> Jira Align provides robust functionalities to support innovation through tools such as **Mind Maps**, **Brainstorming**, and **Innovation**. These create spaces for better team collaboration, which leads to a culture of innovation. Access these modules under the navigation menu's **Product | Ideas** section.

Two companies we've discussed throughout this book can perhaps serve as inspiration in this regard. Atlassian nurtures an innovation culture by dedicating a 24-hour team hackathon called *ShipIt* every quarter. This event focuses on bringing teams together, improving collaboration, and innovating. You can read more at `https://www.atlassian.com/company/shipit`. Scaled Agile, Inc., the creators of SAFe, practice what they preach and foster an innovation culture by dedicating an iteration of each PI to **Innovation and Planning** (**IP**). You can read more at `https://www.scaledagileframework.com/innovation-and-planning-iteration/`.

Summary

In this chapter, we examined how to broadly connect strategy to execution in Jira Align. We then explored how LPM methods solve the problems of traditional portfolio management, and how Jira Align supports these methods. Lastly, we examined the important topic of innovation, so critical for enterprises in the modern digital landscape. With the help of these topics, you can now efficiently tackle the common challenges faced by organizations at the portfolio level.

In the next and final chapter, we turn to some special use cases and discover how Jira Align supports them. From hybrid waterfall/agile development to government reporting requirements, we've got you covered.

Questions

1. Which field in Jira Align is recommended for tracking investment horizons?
2. How does the Investment vs. Actuals report support portfolio leadership?
3. Which kanban view is used for a portfolio kanban?
4. How do you extend the ideation module to external users?
5. Why is it important to nurture an innovation culture?

Section 3: Special Use Cases and Add-Ons

In this section, you will learn how Jira Align supports special use cases such as legacy and government reporting requirements, hybrid development approaches, highly secured deployments, and advanced business intelligence capabilities.

This section comprises the following chapters:

- *Chapter 8, Bimodal Development, Advanced Data Security, and Analytics*

8
Bimodal Development, Advanced Data Security, and Analytics

In this final chapter, we explore some special use cases that may be of interest to organizations that require the tracking of waterfall and agile delivery within the same tool, the advanced security that on-premises hosting may provide, and advanced **business intelligence (BI)** capabilities.

In this chapter we will cover the following:

- Developing products bimodally
- Handling time tracking
- Advanced data security
- Government reporting
- Integrating with BI and other solutions

By the end of the chapter, you will know how to support bimodal development, report on agile projects to executives who want waterfall style reports, replace legacy time tracking systems with an add-on for Jira Align, host Jira Align on-premises, use an agile approach to earned value that can satisfy reporting requirements for government projects, and integrate with BI and other solutions.

Developing products bimodally

Garter coined the term *bimodal* when advising companies to embrace a more innovative and nimble approach to product delivery. Mode 1 is the traditional approach of waterfall development with long cycle times. The analogy for mode 1 is the marathon runner. Mode 2 represents the newer agile approach to product development, with short cycle times. The analogy for mode 2 is the sprinter.

Many companies today have not embraced agile throughout their entire organization. Some have agile teams under waterfall management. Others have pure agile in some areas and waterfall in others. Furthermore, agile isn't a "one size fits all" approach. The sweet spot of agile is the realm of the complicated and the complex, when the *what* and/ or the *how* is uncertain or not agreed upon. When what you are developing and how you are going to develop it are both well understood and agreed upon, then waterfall is a great approach. Because of this, Jira Align has been built to accommodate bimodal development.

There's a helpful adage that comes into play here: you can "*waterfall*" an agile tool, but you can't "*agile*" a waterfall tool. Thus tools focused on traditional Gantt project schedules and methods are ill-equipped to handle things such as burndown and velocity charts, let alone program boards and OKR trees. We'll now cover some Jira Align features that support bimodal development.

First, it's important to establish a bimodal operating agreement. This includes a common lexicon, particularly for people, work, time, and outcome definitions. For example, a portfolio practicing agile may be defined as a collection of development value streams while one practicing waterfall may define it as a business unit with its own P&L (profit and loss) statement, or a product line. Likewise, an agile program is a team of agile teams, while a waterfall program may represent the people working on a particular product within a product line.

Work and outcome dimensions

For the work dimension, we recommend using the portfolio epic to represent a funded project for business units operating in a waterfall model. While agile teams will associate a hypothesis statement with an epic and break it down into features and stories, a waterfall portfolio can associate a business requirements document with the epic. Many companies change "Portfolio Epic" to the more generic term, "Initiative" in **Administration | Settings | Platform Terminology**. In this way, an initiative can represent an epic for agile portfolios and a project for a waterfall portfolio.

Portfolio epics support several popular waterfall practices such as milestone-based planning and execution. Simply click on a portfolio epic in the backlog to open its details panel and then click on the **Time / Skills** tab to enter **Fixed Date Milestones**. On the same tab as shown in the next figure, you can specify the required skill sets to execute work over periods of time, another common waterfall practice:

Skill Sets Requested

Manage Skill Sets

	S23 22/08	S24 05/09	S25 19/09	S26 03/10	S27 17/10	S28 31/10	S29 14/11	S30 28/11	S31 12/12	S32 26/12	S33 09/01	S34 23/01
Business Intelligence	2 MW	2 MW			2 MW	3 MW						
Oracle	2 MW	2 MW		1 MW		1 MW						
SAP	3 MW	3 MW	3 MW	2 MW	2 MW	2 MW						

Fixed Date Milestones

Deliverable	Portfolio Ask	Start / Initiation	Target Completion	
				Add

Deliverable	Portfolio Ask	Start / Initiation	Target Completion	Complete Status
1 Stakeholder Meeting	04 Dec 2020	20 Oct 2020	11 Dec 2020	Mark Complete ✕ ✏

Figure 8.1 – Jira Align portfolio epic time/skills tab

Here we see the requested **member weeks (MW)** for each skill set per sprint. You can manage skill sets by clicking on the **Manage Skill Sets** button to add or remove skills.

Next we see the fixed date milestone fields as follows:

- **Portfolio Ask**: The date that the requestor wants the item to be delivered. This date is not related to the planned or target delivery date by the development team.

- **Start/Initiation**: The projected start date used for strategic planning. This is not the actual start date based on when the first story is done, but rather the date on which the development team intends to begin work. Note that this date is not tied to actual work or time objects.

- **Target Completion**: The projected completion date used for strategic planning. It is the date on which the development team intends to complete work. Note that this date is not tied to actual work or time objects.

Note that people add skills to their profiles as we saw in *Chapter 3, Navigating Jira Align, Figure 3.8*. To manage the skills inventory, go to the navigation menu, and select **Enterprise | Manage | Skills Inventory**. Next, click on the **Forecast** tab to project the required effort per team, program, and program increment. The unit of measure here is "team weeks," and we'll provide more info on these shortly.

The portfolio epic status report, financials view that we looked at in *Chapter 7, Enterprise and Portfolio Challenges, Figure 7.21*, is useful for both agile and waterfall audiences. Aside from financials, including CapEx and OpEx, it provides popular **RAG (red, amber, green)** reporting indicators for budget, people, quality, risk, and schedule.

For the outcomes dimension, OKRs are common practice across both agile and waterfall development teams. We recommend providing a roadmap to executives used to Gantt charts, and a popular view is to group portfolio epics by OKR. To do so, follow the instructions used for *Chapter 7, Enterprise and Portfolio Challenges, Figure 7.17*, but select **Objectives** under **Group By Property**. We also recommend adding **Programs** under **View Configuration | Custom Columns** to provide more context for the portfolio epics shown.

People and time dimensions

For the people dimension, we recommend that agile and waterfall teams roll up to separate portfolios and that portfolios are single mode, not bimodal. However, agile and waterfall teams can still collaborate. Themes are the work item that can span portfolios, so leverage them to consolidate epics from both agile and waterfall portfolios and then generate a theme status report to see the combined data across portfolios.

To view the theme status report, go to the navigation menu, select **Enterprise | Track | Status Reports**, and then click on the **Theme** button. Be sure your context is set in the configuration bar, then click on your theme to view the report where you'll find work item status by portfolio and program. Scan the report for off-track items with red status indicators, then click on an item to drill into its specific status to see risks, dependencies, and other key info.

For the time dimension, we've previously discussed the best practice that all programs in a portfolio follow a common cadence. For an agile portfolio, the program increment is comprised of sprints that sync with Jira Software and represent the shared agile team cadence. For a waterfall portfolio, you can create a program increment with sprints representing the toll gates or phases of a project. These would sync with sprints in Jira Software that have names and dates to match the phases in Jira Align.

Estimation is the last bimodal aspect we'll cover. Jira Align provides three methods for estimating work items: T-shirt size and points for agile estimation and team weeks for traditional estimation. A **team week (TW)** is similar to a **member week (MW)** except that it relates to the team level rather than the individual. Note that a team week is a measure of time independent of the size of a team. Therefore, if a portfolio epic is sized at 30 TW, it doesn't matter if it's a team of 5 or 11 members doing the work, the capacity is still the same. Each portfolio can have its own estimation method. The selection is made in **Administration | Settings | Platform | Portfolio | Estimation System**.

Now that we've been introduced to Jira Align's bimodal capabilities, let's take a deeper dive into time tracking.

Handling time tracking

While it's helpful for teams at an early stage of agile maturity to break their stories into tasks and provide estimated and actual hours at the task level, time tracking is generally not considered core to agile methods. Since organizations transitioning to agile or operating in a bimodal manner may require time tracking concurrent with agile estimation in story points, Atlassian provides a time tracking module for Jira Align. This goes beyond the roll-up of task hours flowing in from Jira Software to include time cards, booking time against various cost centers, and more.

The main benefits of handling time tracking in Jira Align are as follows:

- **Submission Governance**: Enforces timesheet submission windows and tracking, useful for regulated businesses and compliance.

- **CapEx and OpEx Accounting**: Enables you to categorize investments to optimize company financials.

- **Output Measurement**: Allows you to measure and report on actual work output. The agile focus on outcomes over outputs doesn't mean that output tracking needs to fall by the wayside.

> Tips and tricks
>
> To find out if your Jira Align instance is enabled to use Time Tracking, go to **Administration | Support | Version** and see if **Time Tracking** is set to **True**. If not, you can speak with your Atlassian solution partner about licensing your users to use time tracking.

Accessing time tracking

Access to the time tracking module is role-based and maintained by the Jira Align administrator under **Administration | Access Controls | Roles | Time Tracking Roles** as shown in the next figure:

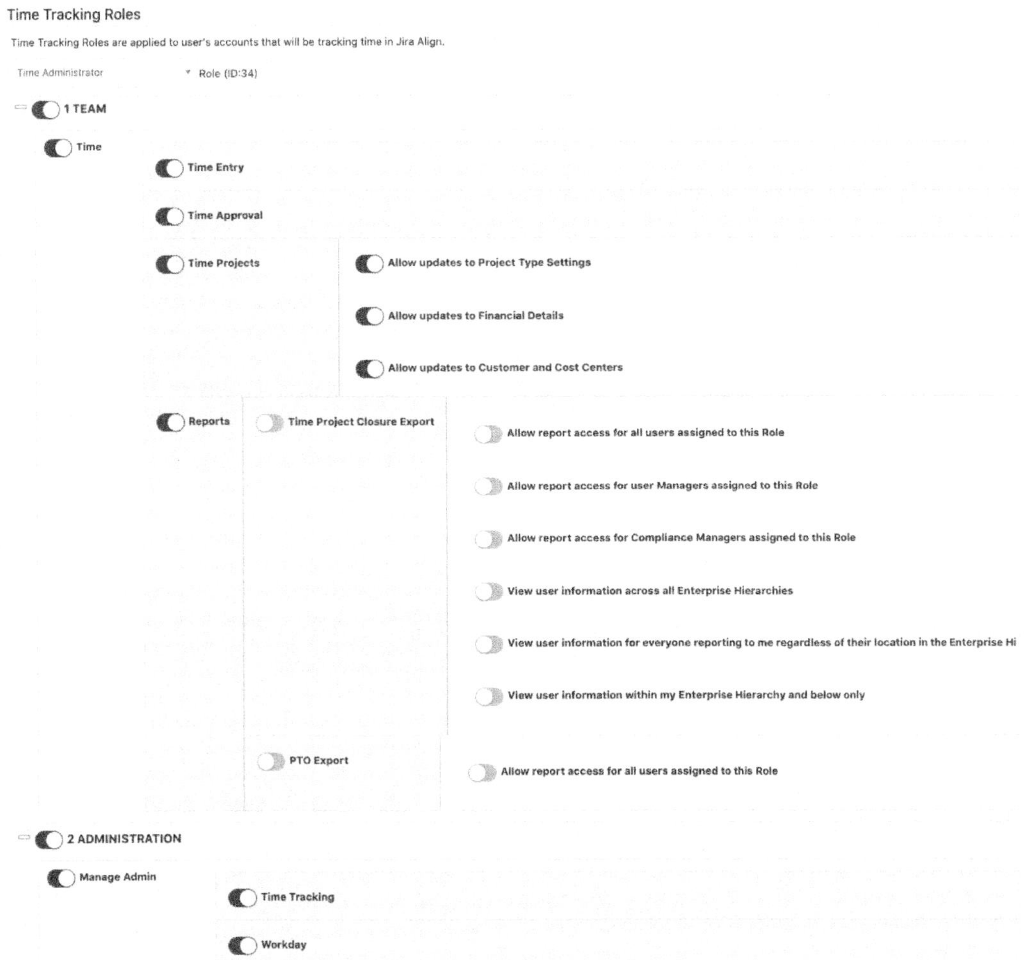

Time Tracking Roles

Time Tracking Roles are applied to user's accounts that will be tracking time in Jira Align.

Time Administrator   ▾ Role (ID:34)

- **1 TEAM**
  - Time
    - Time Entry
    - Time Approval
    - Time Projects
      - Allow updates to Project Type Settings
      - Allow updates to Financial Details
      - Allow updates to Customer and Cost Centers
    - Reports   Time Project Closure Export
      - Allow report access for all users assigned to this Role
      - Allow report access for user Managers assigned to this Role
      - Allow report access for Compliance Managers assigned to this Role
      - View user information across all Enterprise Hierarchies
      - View user information for everyone reporting to me regardless of their location in the Enterprise Hi
      - View user information within my Enterprise Hierarchy and below only
    - PTO Export
      - Allow report access for all users assigned to this Role
- **2 ADMINISTRATION**
  - Manage Admin
    - Time Tracking
    - Workday

Figure 8.2 – Jira Align time tracking roles

Here the administrator enables various permission toggles for each of the three default time tracking roles:

- **Time Administrator**: Able to configure and manage time tracking settings; the highest level of time tracking permissions.

- **Time Approver**: Able to approve timesheets; enabled under the Team time tracking roles permission.

- **Time Entry**: Able to enter time; enabled under the Team time tracking roles permission.

Note that users with the time tracking administrator role have permission to configure **Time Tracking** and **Workday** settings, which are accessible by navigating to the **Administration | Settings** section.

Tips and tricks

The Jira Align administrator can associate time tracking permissions with system roles such as Super Admin by navigating to **Administration | Access Controls | Roles | Jira Align Roles**. However, we recommend maintaining time tracking roles apart from system roles for better maintainability and control.

Most organizations find the default roles sufficient for time tracking. However, if you need additional roles such as a view-only role for reporting purposes, your Jira Align administrator can create custom roles with selective permissions by going to the **Add New Role** section found by scrolling down under the **Time Tracking Roles** section shown in *Figure 8.2*.

Now that time tracking roles are configured, let's see how the Jira Align administrator grants access to the time tracking module.

To provide access, the Jira Align administrator adds a time tracking role to each user account as shown in the next figure. Note that red squares indicate required fields and that you'll need to scroll down to see all options:

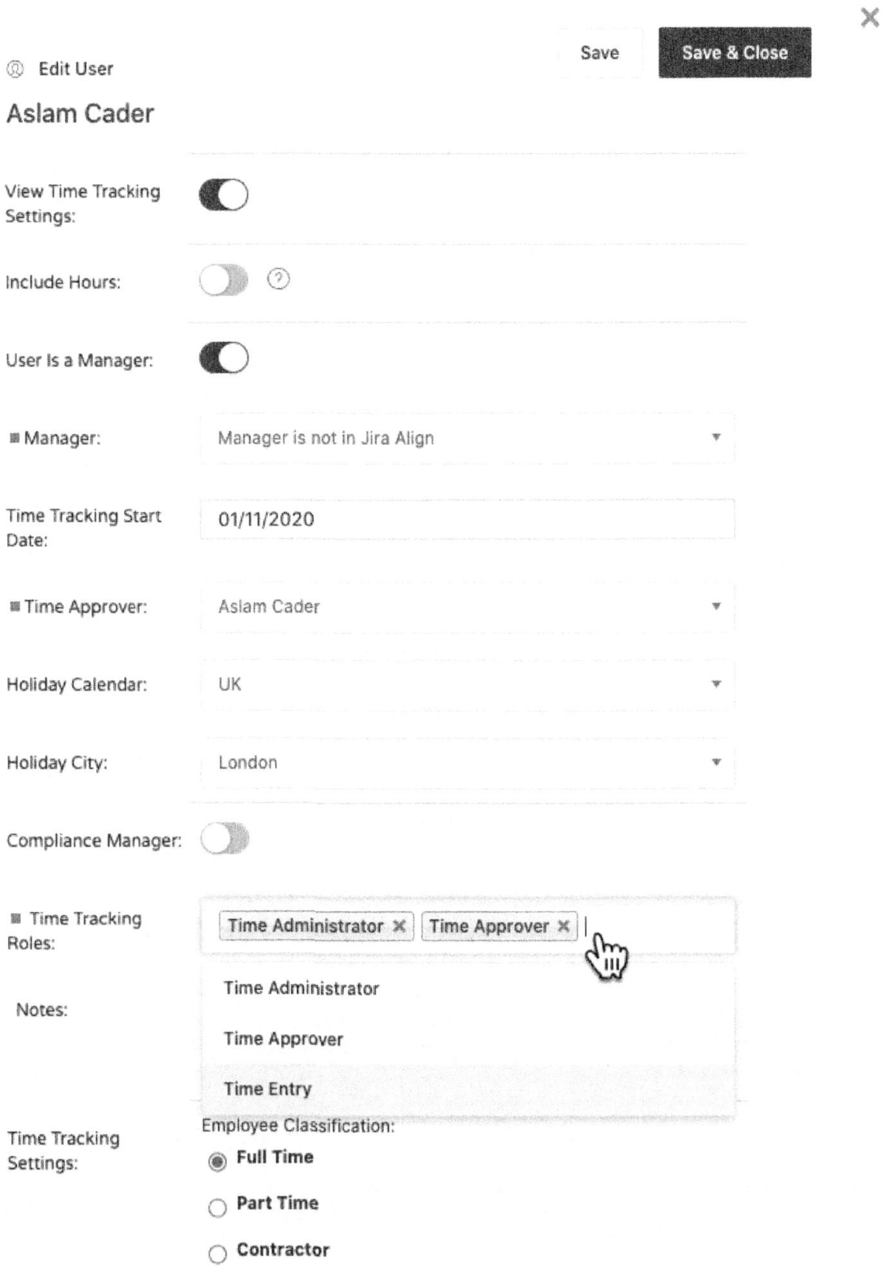

Figure 8.3 – Jira Align time tracking user account settings

Here the following time tracking user settings are maintained:

- **View time tracking settings**: Enable the time tracking module. The selected user region needs to be enabled under **Administration | Workday**.

- **Include Hours**: Specify whether to include or exclude the user's hours in your financial system. For example, you can choose to disregard time entries for non-billable users.

- **User Is a Manager**: You may set the user as a manager so they will appear in the **Manager** dropdown field for other users.

- **Manager**: Select the user's manager from the list or choose the option **Manager is not in Jira Align**.

- **Time Tracking Start Date**: Specify the start date for time tracking; required for users with time entry permission.

- **Time Approver**: Select a user with the time approver role to approve the user's time, for example, the scrum master of their team; required for users with time entry permission.

- **Holiday Calendar**: Select an applicable holiday region.

- **Holiday City**: Select an applicable holiday city.

- **Compliance Manager**: Slide this toggle on to indicate that the user is a compliance manager, for example, someone who approves time tracking during audits.

- **Time Tracking Roles**: Select the applicable time tracking roles for the user: **Time Administrator**, **Time Approver**, and **Time Entry**.

- **Time Tracking Settings**: Choose an employee classification for the user: **Full Time**, **Part Time**, or **Contractor**.

Now that users have been granted access to time tracking, they'll have a stopwatch icon near the bottom of the navigation menu as shown in the next figure:

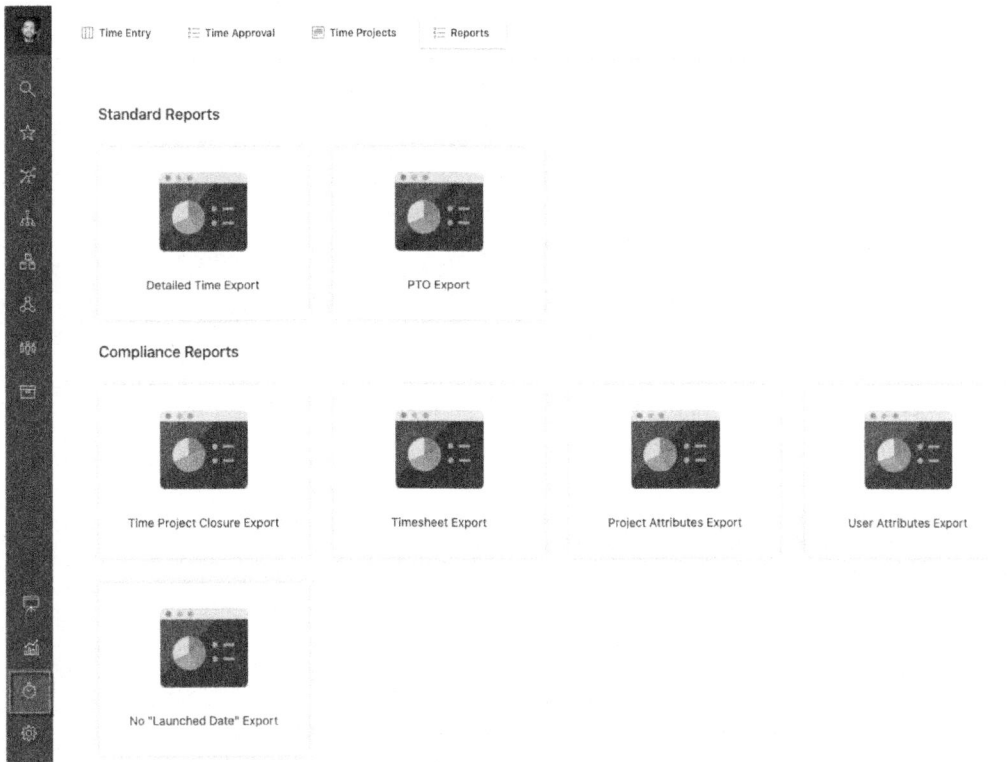

Figure 8.4 – Jira Align time tracking module

Based on how the time tracking roles were configured in *Figure 8.2*, users will have access to views accessible by clicking on the buttons along the top left of the workspace: **Time Entry**, **Time Approval**, **Time Projects**, and **Reports**.

In *Figure 8.4*, we've clicked on the **Reports** button to show the reports configured for the user's time tracking role. Let's take a moment to learn about the key time tracking reports and the filters they provide:

- **Time Submission Metrics**: Provides a dashboard of time tracking metrics so you can determine when to perform data extracts and manage outstanding items within your organization. You can filter your report based on the time submission metrics, which include time period, additional filters, and employee classification.

- **Detailed Time Export**: Shows the breakdown of all time entered in an exported `.xls` document. You can filter your report based on the time period, enterprise hierarchy, time approver, manager, contractor manager, user, user cost center, time project cost center, and time project name.

- **PTO Export**: Shows the **personal time off** (**PTO**) taken by team members within the organization. You can filter your report based on the time period, administration code, or enterprise hierarchy, and you can group by manager or contractor manager.

- **Time Project Closure Export**: Shows the time projects that are complete and can be closed each month. You can filter your report based on the year and month.

- **Timesheet Export**: Allows you to export timesheets for users within your organization. You can filter your report based on the time period, or filter by user or user-related filters.

- **Project Attributes Export**: Shows a list of time projects and their details. You can filter your report based on the time project type, time project owner, display name, time period dates, enterprise hierarchy, cost center, modified by, modified date range, capitalization, and work codes.

- **User Attributes Export**: Shows a filtered list of Jira Align users along with their attributes so that you can compare users against a system of record. You can filter your report based on the user start date range, and all user-related properties.

- **No "Launched Date" Export**: Shows any time projects that are past their Expected Completion date and do not have a **Launched** date. You can filter your report based on the owner, year, and month.

- **Timesheet Compliance Export**: Shows the compliance metrics for groups within your organization so that you can be sure that time is submitted and approved on time and your team members are in compliance. You can filter your report based on the time period, compliance, enterprise hierarchy, group by manager, time tracker, or time approver, and roll up results to the enterprise hierarchy.

Now that we've learned how to configure and assign time tracking roles and been introduced to reporting, let's see how to configure time tracking and workday settings.

Configuring time tracking

As previously mentioned, users with the time tracking administrator role have permission to configure time tracking and workday settings, which are accessible by navigating to the **Administration | Settings** section. In the next figure, we are viewing the **Time Tracking Settings**:

Time Tracking Settings

Fiscal Year Start

Select the start of the fiscal year for your organization.

January ▼   Save

Time Tracking Week

Select the start and end of the team work week.

Work week runs from   Monday   ▼   to Sunday   Save

General Settings for Email Notifications

Send email notifications for the following actions.

Approve
Reject
Recall
                                                                                                       Save

Time Submission and Approval Compliance

Set days and times when the time must be submitted and approved to be considered compliant within your organization. Timesheets submitted and approved after these dates would be considered out of compliance.

Name	Type	Day	Hour	Date Applied		
Weekly Submission	Submission	Friday	11:59 PM	01/11/2020		
Weekly Approval	Approval	Wednesday	12:00 AM	01/11/2020		

Create New

Time Tracking Terminology

Customize the terminology used throughout Jira Align's time tracking module.

Help

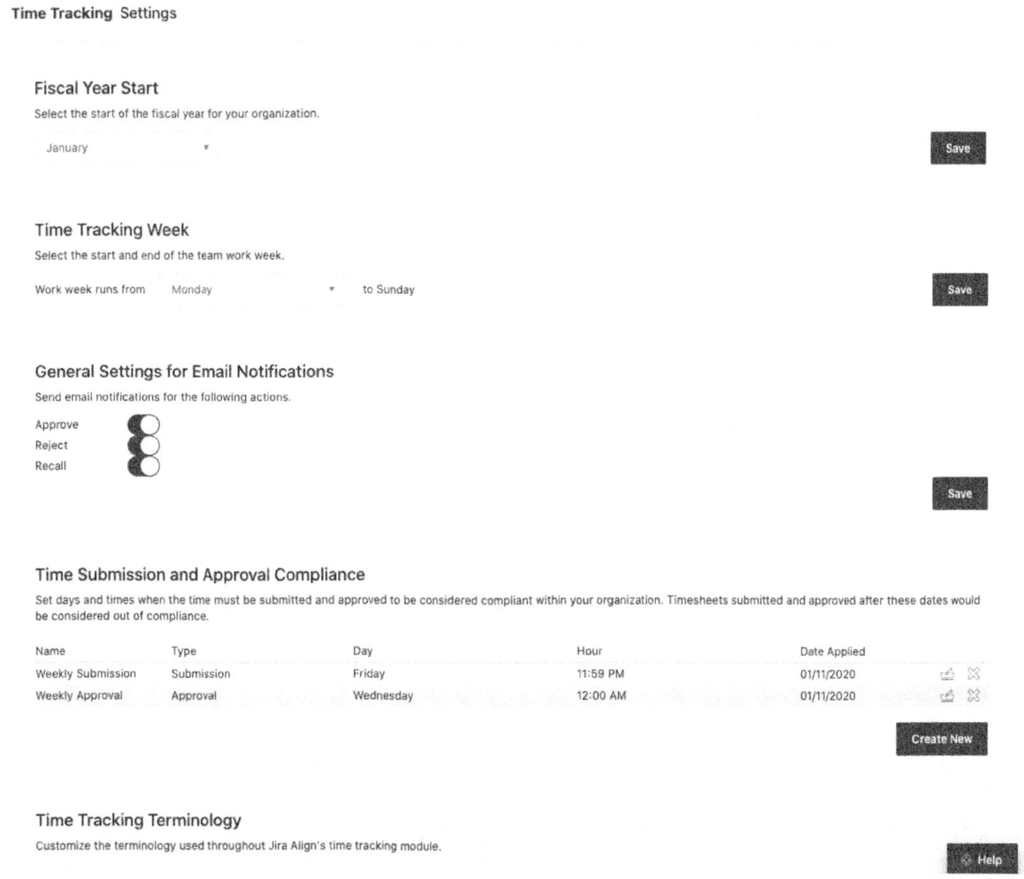

Figure 8.5 – Jira Align time tracking settings

Here, the time tracking administrator can view and configure the following settings. Note that you will need to scroll down to see all options:

- **Fiscal Year Start**: Set the start of your organization's 12-month accounting period. This may vary based on the country you operate in; for example, the UK fiscal year starts in April.

- **Time Tracking Week**: Specify when a week starts and ends. This impacts time tracking periods, timesheets, and data exports.

- **General Settings for Email Notifications**: Toggle on email notifications for users to receive when timesheets are approved, rejected, and recalled.

- **Time submission and approval compliance**: Set compliance rules for when timesheets should be submitted and approved. This allows you to report against any outstanding timesheets.

- **Time tracking terminology**: Configure your time tracking terminology to match your organization's processes.

- **General time tracking settings**: Create and associate custom time-tracking tasks. For example, create a task set for meetings and add time tracking tasks for planning, stand-ups, demo, and retrospective. Additionally, manage the number of flexible holidays for each region and enable the ability to record time in the future.

- **General time tracking settings | Time Approvers**: Set the scope for time approval; for example, the approver can approve any time tracker or only those within their enterprise hierarchy. Additionally, you can require approvers to be internal employees, excluding contractors.

- **General time tracking settings | Administration Codes**: Associate administrator time codes with cost centers and/or operating work codes.

- **General time tracking settings | Time Projects**: Associate time projects with release vehicles, portfolio epics, or stand-alone time projects. Enable cost center, identification code, and product fields. Enable editing of the launch date after it has passed. Automatically close launched time projects and set a warning when a time project is past its due date.

> **Tips and tricks**
>
> Associating time with portfolio epics can help facilitate CapEx and OpEx time reporting. To do so, obtain licenses for your Jira Software users to enter their time in Jira Align's time tracking module.
>
> We recommend exploring a combination of Jira Software and marketplace apps if you require time tracking and reporting at any level below the portfolio epic.
>
> To account for time not associated with a portfolio epic or release vehicle, for example, time spent on support activities, associate time with a stand-alone time project in Jira Align.

- **Time tracking periods**: Set the periods for which time will be tracked. Lock completed time periods so that data can be extracted and loaded into a financial system.

- **Administration codes**: Create internal work codes used for company holidays, personal time off, sick leave, jury duty, and so on. The codes can be associated with an employee classification and will appear on the user's timesheet.

- **Custom employee classifications**: Manage employee classifications like full time, part-time, and contractor, and add additional classifications. Most custom time tracking configurations are based on employee classifications.

- **Blended rates**: Set blended rates based on employee classifications to obtain accurate accounting from the system. Rates are per hour and can be set as a single rate, by region, or by role.

- **Manage identification codes and work codes**: Manage time tracking identification codes and work codes. To view the codes, you need to do a search first.

> **Tips and tricks**
>
> Permission to manage work codes is granted per system role. The Jira Align administrator grants this by going to **Administration | Access Controls | Roles | Jira Align Roles**, selecting the system role from the dropdown, expanding the **Administration** section, sliding the **Work Code Admin** toggle on, and then clicking on the **Save** button. Note that users will need to log out and back in for the change to take effect.
>
> Work codes can also be imported from an external business application into Jira Align using the REST API. Speak with your Atlassian solution partner about your integration requirements.

Now that we've examined the time tracking settings, let's take a look at workday settings where you set your employee work hours and company holidays per region. This is important because access to time tracking is enabled based on the region. You can further refine settings based on specific cities as shown in the next figure:

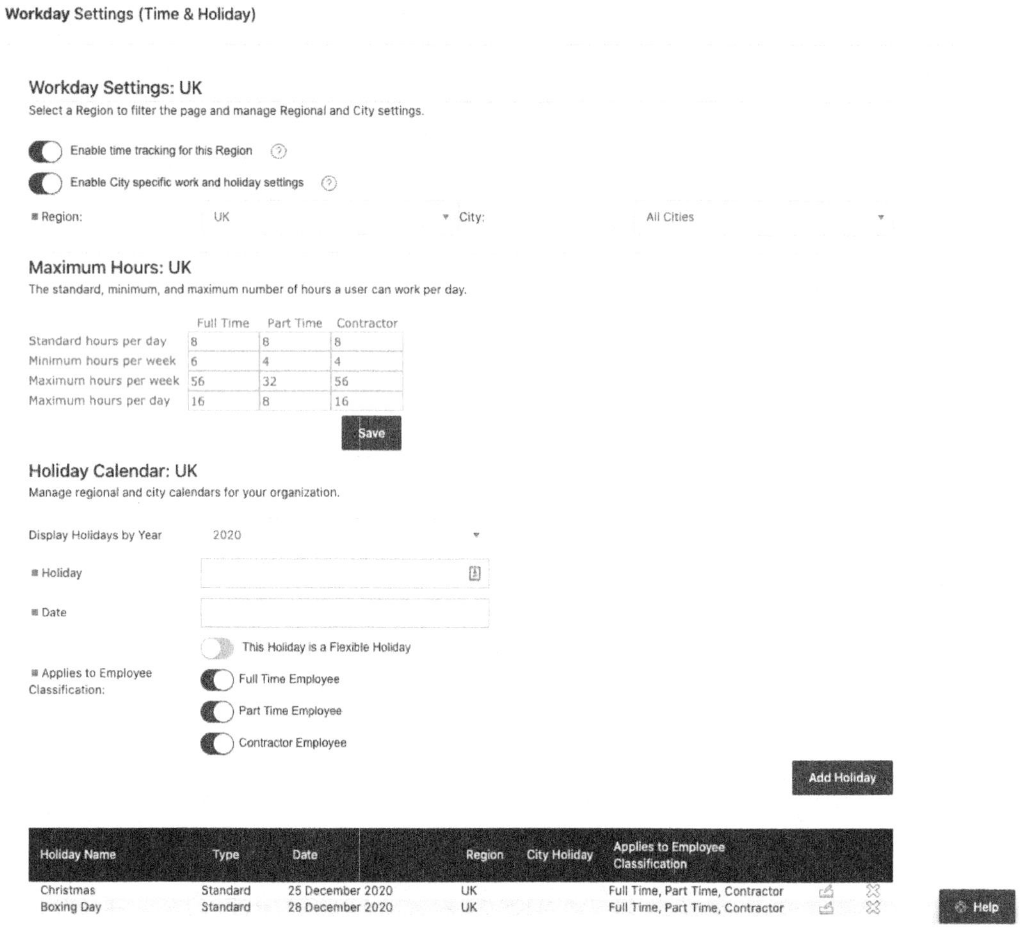

Workday Settings (Time & Holiday)

Workday Settings: UK
Select a Region to filter the page and manage Regional and City settings.

⬤ Enable time tracking for this Region   ⊙

⬤ Enable City specific work and holiday settings   ⊙

* Region: UK   ▾   City: All Cities   ▾

Maximum Hours: UK
The standard, minimum, and maximum number of hours a user can work per day.

	Full Time	Part Time	Contractor
Standard hours per day	8	8	8
Minimum hours per week	6	4	4
Maximum hours per week	56	32	56
Maximum hours per day	16	8	16

Save

Holiday Calendar: UK
Manage regional and city calendars for your organization.

Display Holidays by Year   2020   ▾

* Holiday

* Date

◯ This Holiday is a Flexible Holiday

* Applies to Employee   ⬤ Full Time Employee
Classification: ⬤ Part Time Employee
                            ⬤ Contractor Employee

Add Holiday

Holiday Name	Type	Date	Region	City Holiday	Applies to Employee Classification		
Christmas	Standard	25 December 2020	UK		Full Time, Part Time, Contractor	✎	✕
Boxing Day	Standard	28 December 2020	UK		Full Time, Part Time, Contractor	✎	✕

⊙ Help

Figure 8.6 – Jira Align workday settings

Now that we've seen how to configure time tracking and workday settings, let's take a look at how to manage timesheets.

Managing timesheets

Let's begin by creating a time project. To do so, go to the navigation menu and select **Time Tracking**. Next, click on the **Time Projects** button near the top left corner of the workspace and then click on the **Add Time Project** button at the top right corner to open the panel shown in the next figure:

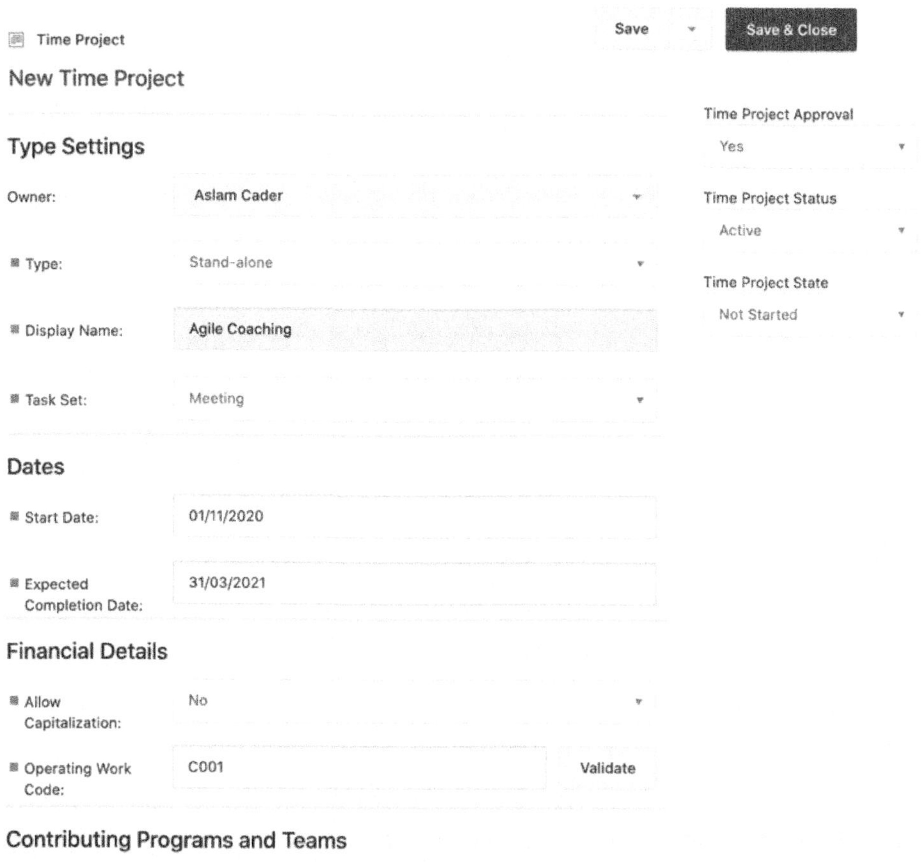

Figure 8.7 – Jira Align time project

Here we will create a stand-alone time tracking project and track the following attributes. Note that red squares indicate required fields:

- **Owner**: Select a user as the responsible owner for the time project.

- **Type**: Specify whether the time project is stand-alone or pertains to a portfolio epic or release vehicle. Here we will create a **Stand-alone** time project. Note that if you select **Portfolio Epic** or **Release Vehicle**, a search box appears for you to select the associated item.

- **Display Name**: Provide a meaningful name for your time project. This will be displayed in the timesheets for time entry.

- **Task Set**: Select the task set template with associated time task breakdown.

- **Time Project Approval**: Near the top right corner, select Yes if the time project requires approval.

- **Time Project Status**: Near the top right corner, set the project status as Inactive or Active. Setting to **Active** allows you to set a time project state.

- **Time Project State**: Near the top right corner, set the project state as Not Started, Started, Launched, Closed, or Cancelled. It is required to move the status to Started in order for the time project to appear on timesheets. Moving the status to Launched ensures that the Launched Date field is populated and locks the time entry on CapEx cost category tasks. Moving the status to Closed or Cancelled sets the time project status to Inactive and will populate the Closed/Cancelled date field and time entry on timesheets will be closed.

- **Start Date**: Add a start date for the time project and timesheet entry.

- **Expected Completion Date**: Add an end date for the time project and timesheet entry.

- **Allow Capitalization**: Specify if the CapEx work code is allowed.

- **Operating Work Code**: Provide OpEx work codes.

- **Capitalized Work Code**: If **Allow Capitalization** is set to Yes, then provide CapEx work codes.

- **Programs**: Select the programs applicable to the time project.

- **Teams**: Select the teams applicable to the time project.

- **Billable**: Specify if the time project is billable.

- **Customer**: Select a customer to associate with the time project.

Next, click on the **Save & Close** button to create the time project. The users of a team who belong to the time project can now add time against it. To do so, they'd go to the navigation menu, select **Time Tracking**, and then click on the **Time Entry** button to open the time entry workspace shown in the next screenshot:

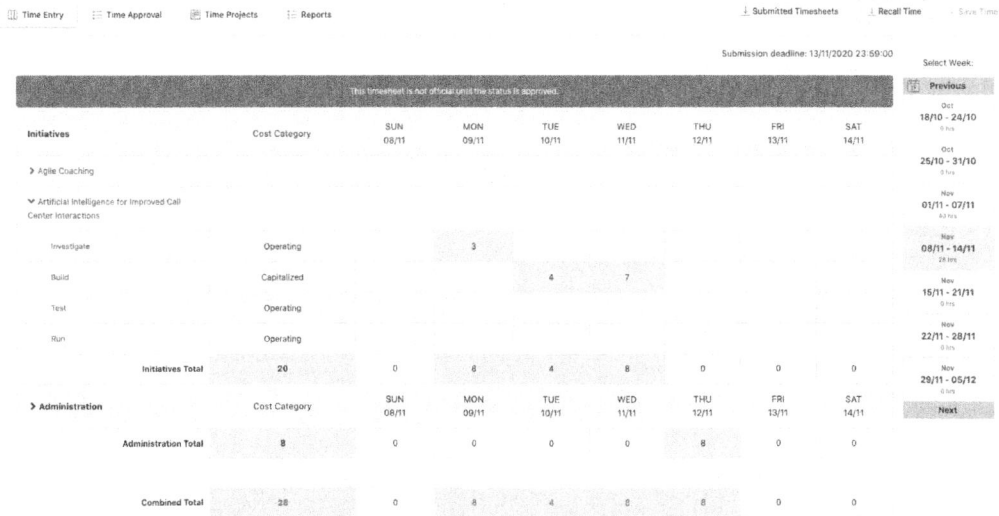

Figure 8.8 – Jira Align time entry

Here we see that time is logged against the time project associated with a portfolio epic, "Artificial Intelligence for Improved Call Center Interactions." Note the associated task set, with tasks categorized as **Operating** expense or **Capitalized**. The submission deadline based on the compliance rules in the time tracking settings displays above the timesheet on the right.

Navigate between the weekly timesheets using the **Select Week** panel along the right side of the workspace. On the top-right toolbar, click on the **Save Time** button to save time entries or on the **Save & Submit Time** button to submit a timesheet. Click on the **Recall Time** button to recall a submitted timesheet or on the **Submitted Timesheets** button to view all submitted timesheets.

Next, let's take a look at approving timesheets. As a time approver, you will receive your team's timesheet submissions for your approval as shown in the next figure:

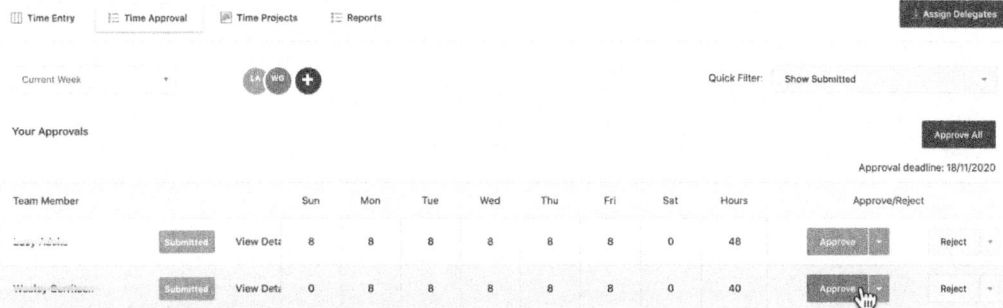

Figure 8.9 – Jira Align time approval

You will see all timesheet submissions filtered for the current week, and you can switch weeks using the dropdown near the top left corner of the workspace. Click on the **Approve** or **Reject** buttons to act on the timesheet approvals. You may choose to include a comment when approving or rejecting a timesheet to inform the user of the next action. Click on the **Approve All** button to approve all timesheets for a given week. Below that button, note the approval deadline based on the compliance rules set in the time tracking settings.

The quick filter dropdown near the top right corner of the workspace allows you to filter timesheets based on status: **Open, Submitted, Recalled, Rejected**, and **Approved**. If you are not available to approve timesheets, you can delegate the time approver task to a fellow time approver by clicking on the **Assign Delegates** button at the top right corner of the workspace.

Now that we have learned the details of time tracking and how it supports an organization's finance and accounting reporting, let's see how Jira Align supports advanced data security.

Advanced data security

Jira Align is a highly secure, cloud-based **SaaS (software as a service)** product. Atlassian takes a standards-based approach to security and holds industry-accepted certifications. Atlassian holds SOC 2 Type 2 and SOC 3 certifications that are validated by external third-party audits over an extended period. Details including the auditors' report can be found at `https://www.atlassian.com/trust/compliance`.

Atlassian's Trust Center is the source for everything compliance-related and can be found at `https://www.atlassian.com/trust`. For security-related questions, Atlassian has completed a generic **Consensus Assessments Initiative Questionnaire (CAIQ)** published by the Cloud Security Alliance. Full details of the CAIQ can be found at `https://www.atlassian.com/trust/security/vendor-security-risk-response`.

Atlassian uses **Amazon Web Services (AWS)** and **Microsoft Azure** to provide physical safeguards, environmental safeguards, infrastructure support and management, and storage services. Furthermore, as we discuss next, you can select one of two deployment options depending on your security needs.

SaaS deployment

The standard SaaS deployment option for Jira Align uses common data architecture patterns of multi-tenant database applications that run in a **virtual private cloud** (**VPC**) environment. The multi-tenant VPCs have an underlying SQL structure that separates each Jira Align customer's data on the database service into separated data stores.

By customer request, Atlassian can create "dedicated" VPCs, meaning that the VPC network is not shared with other customers, to essentially provide a dedicated database for additional security. This approach also allows customer-managed keys for encryption at rest, the ability to audit at will, penetration testing, and improved capacity overhead.

There is another option to consider for organizations requiring the utmost in security, which we discuss next.

On-premises deployment

Even with the industry-recognized SOC 2 Type 2 Audit, CAIQ, and trust overview, there are organizations that require the highest level of security. As recently as 2016, some large Fortune 500 companies were reluctant to use the standard SaaS deployment and opted instead to host Jira Align on-premises. The on-premises option carries a higher price tag and requires that the organization's own tools team apply the upgrades that Jira Align releases every two weeks. The added licensing and internal maintenance costs can add up. We've therefore seen the same Fortune 500 companies move to the SaaS product within three years.

Yet there are some organizations that may never be comfortable with the cloud. Government agencies such as the U.S. **Department of Defense** (**DoD**), a customer of Jira Align and of SAFe, host Jira Align on-premises so it's likely to remain an option into the foreseeable future. Agile practices and the tools to support them have been gaining in popularity among government organizations in recent years.

Organizations that provide contract services to the government are also candidates for a scaled agile approach. SAFe as a methodology and Jira Align as a tool both support earned value reporting as mandated by government contracts, which we examine next.

Government reporting

Earned value management (**EVM**) is a methodology that integrates scope, time, and costs to objectively measure performance and progress. Performance is measured by determining the budgeted cost of work performed, also known as **earned value** (**EV**), and comparing it to the **actual cost** (**AC**) of work performed. Progress is measured by comparing the EV with the **planned value** (**PV**).

Two other important EVM measures are the **cost performance index** (**CPI**) and **schedule performance index** (**SPI**). CPI is the ratio of earned value to actual costs (EV divided by AC). SPI is the ratio of earned value to planned value (EV divided by PV).

Government use of EVM originated with the DoD in the 1960s and continues to this day with many agencies required to use it by law. Some agencies provide guidance for contractors using EVM with agile delivery methods and numerous SAFe for government resources are available online. It's no surprise then that Jira Align offers agile EVM reporting.

To get started, be sure your Jira Align administrator has populated the EVM fields under **Settings** | **Platform** | **Program** and toggled on **Earned Value** for your role under **Access Controls** | **Roles** | **Portfolio** | **Track**. To access the report, go to the navigation menu and select **Portfolio** | **Track** | **Earned Value**. Be sure to set your context in the configuration bar. In the next screenshot, we selected the `Web` program and `PI-5`:

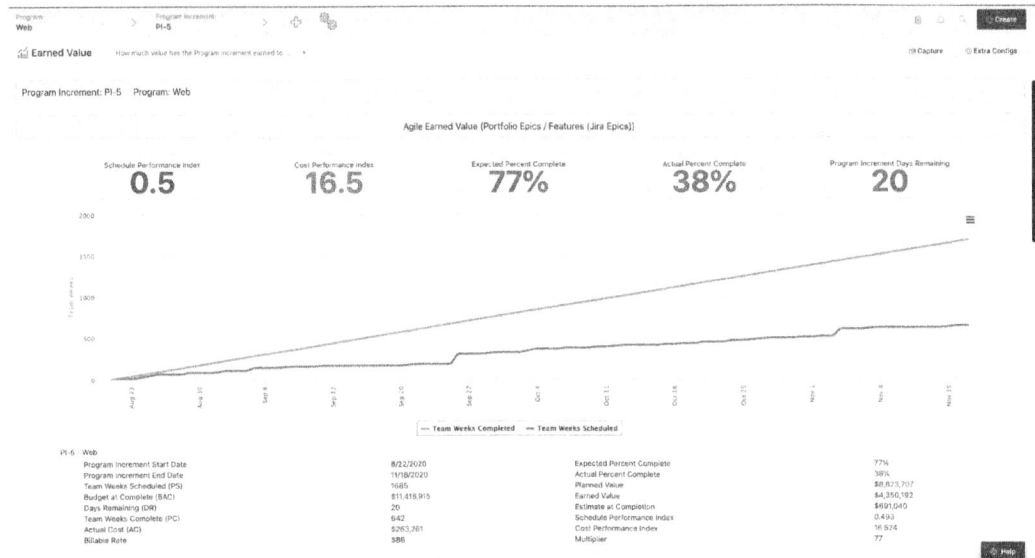

Figure 8.10 – Jira Align earned value report

The chart represents all portfolio epics and standalone features in the portfolio for PI-5, with team weeks on the vertical axis and weeks of the PI on the horizontal axis.

The chart shows team weeks completed against team weeks scheduled. Unlike a burndown chart, this report captures cost information, enabling you to validate whether teams can complete all of the work planned for the PI within both schedule and budget.

Team Weeks Completed is calculated as the sum of all team weeks on accepted portfolio epics and standalone features on each day of the PI. **Team Weeks Scheduled** is the sum of all team weeks on all portfolio epics and standalone features scheduled in the PI, expressed as an ideal upward trend from the PI start date to the PI finish date. Ideally, the team weeks completed line would closely match the team weeks scheduled line.

Note the SPI and CPI measures above the chart to the left. Values equal to or greater than one indicate a favorable condition and are shown in green. Values less than one indicate an unfavorable condition and are shown in red. There are many more EVM metrics available by scrolling down in the workspace.

Now that we've seen how Jira Align can meet the needs of government reporting, let's see how its data can be leveraged for advanced analytics.

Integrating with BI and other solutions

Jira Align is a solution that provides something for everyone at each level of scale. There are over 165 reports from the enterprise to team levels. And yet, there are inevitably unique analytical needs at every organization that can luckily be met with an add-on for Jira Align called Enterprise Insights.

If you are looking for specific insights that the standard report set does not offer, Enterprise Insights allows you to connect to data in Jira Align using your current BI tools (Power BI, Tableau, and so on) in a highly structured, tabular data model. This enables you to explore advanced analytics, KPIs, and metrics from either Jira Align alone, or in combination with data from across your organization. With Enterprise Insights, your team can focus on analytics and reporting rather than on complex data integration and transformation efforts. It leverages your existing data visualization capabilities and ensures that your transactional Jira Align system performance is not affected while positioning the big queries including machine learning on a dedicated data warehouse as shown in the next figure:

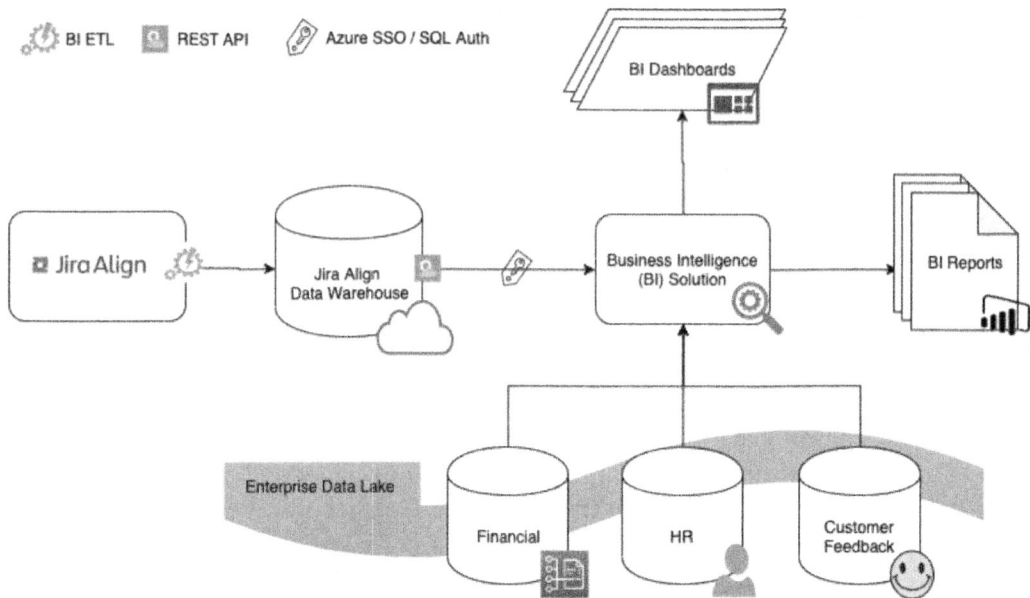

Figure 8.11 – Jira Align Enterprise Insights

The Enterprise Insights data warehouse and tabular semantic models are built on the Azure platform. The warehouse receives data from Jira Align via an **ETL** (**extract**, **transform**, and **load**) process. Connection to Enterprise Insights is made from your existing BI solution via Azure SSO, SQL Auth, and a REST API. The BI solution enables visualization of dashboards and reports from multiple systems connecting your organization's enterprise data lake in real time to make successful business decisions.

You can speak with your Atlassian solution partner to begin your journey with Enterprise Insights. Let's now take a look at other ways you can integrate Jira Align with critical business systems.

Integrating via APIs

Jira Align offers a **representational state transfer (REST) application programming interface (API)** that exposes key objects in the people, work, time, and outcomes dimensions. The REST API allows you to perform most actions available through the Jira Align user interface, as well as simplify user management, mass update work objects, and develop integrations between Jira Align and other critical business applications.

You can obtain access to the complete REST API documentation in your Jira Align instance using the URL `https://ORGANIZATION-NAME.jiraalign.com/rest/align/api/docs/index.html`, where `ORGANIZATION-NAME` is replaced by your organization's subdomain. The next figure shows the REST API documentation that provides access to the latest version of the Jira Align REST resources, along with HTTP responses and sample requests:

Figure 8.12 – Jira Align REST API

> **Tips and tricks**
> Jira Align's REST API is behind a feature flag and inaccessible by default.
> If you are interested in using the REST API, speak with your Atlassian
> solution partner or contact the Atlassian support team to enable it in your
> Jira Align instance.

The **uniform resource identifiers** (**URIs**) have the following structure `https://ORGANIZATION-NAME.jiraalign.com/rest/align/api/2/<resource-name>`. The REST API uses **JSON** (**object notation**) as its communication format, and the standard **HTTP** (**hypertext transfer protocol**) methods like GET, PUT, POST, and PATCH. Jira Aligns's REST APIs provide access to resources (data entities) via URI paths. To use a REST API, your other business applications will make an HTTP request and parse the response.

The Jira Align REST API 2.0 supports the following object types: theme, portfolio epic, capability, feature, story, task, defect, objectives, key results, portfolio, value streams, program, team, user, release/PI, sprint, product, customer, region, city, and ideation. Read more about the Jira Align REST API by going to the user menu, selecting **Help | Knowledge Base | Integrations | 10X: API 2.0**, and then clicking on **Getting started with the REST API 2.0**.

The REST authorization is based on the authenticated user and it authenticates using API tokens. The tokens are generated by going to the user menu, **Edit Profile** page, and then clicking on the **API Token** button as follows:

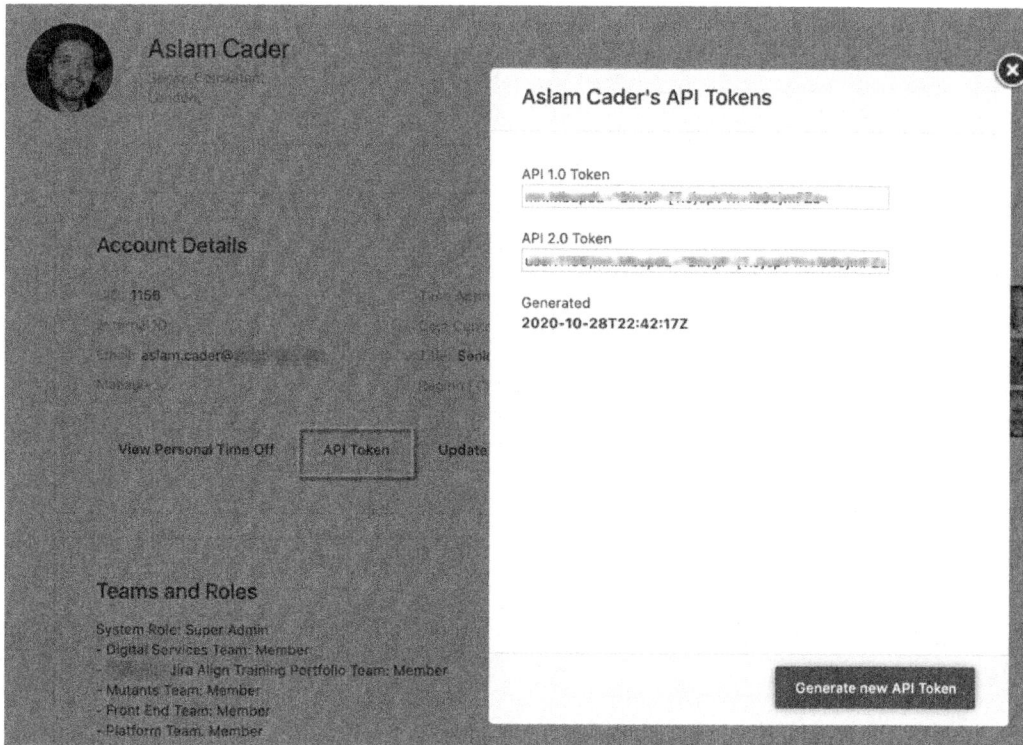

Figure 8.13 – Jira Align API token

When REST APIs are called, access privileges mirror the user's access to data and pages via the user interface. For example, if the user is assigned the **Team Member** role and has read-only access to portfolio epics in a single portfolio, the user will not be able to create or update portfolio epics via the API and will only be able to read portfolio epics from the single portfolio.

Jira Align APIs are rate-limited to ensure that they don't affect platform performance and that the instance remains stable. Currently, if calls from the same IP address exceed 600 requests per 60 seconds, calls are blocked for 60 seconds. When this threshold is met and calls are blocked, you'll receive the HTTP **429 Too Many Requests** error status response. It is recommended to use industry-standard techniques for limiting calls, caching results, and re-trying requests responsibly.

Atlassian is continually investing in the future bringing more REST API capabilities that may extend its REST to the object attributes such as fields and so on.

Summary

In this chapter, we learned the basics of bimodal product development, time tracking, data security, government reporting, and integrating with BI and other solutions. These topics provide a sense of Jira Align's advanced capabilities to round out the topics we've learned throughout this text. With the help of these topics, you'll be able to address some common edge cases around Jira Align deployments.

This agile platform is continuously improving, so we expect to update this text in the future to provide you with the latest understanding from both the practices and tools perspectives in support of your quest for business agility. Additionally, we recommend connecting with the Jira Align Community to stay current on articles, discussions, and questions from fellow community members: `https://community.atlassian.com/t5/Jira-Align/ct-p/jira-align`.

Congratulations, you now have the foundational understanding necessary to implement Jira Align from the team through the enterprise levels. We are pleased to have offered Jira Align insights to help you on your journey and wish you all the best in your agile undertakings.

Questions

1. What deployment options are available for Jira Align?

2. Which government-mandated report is available in Jira Align?

3. What are the three default time tracking roles?

4. When should you consider integrating through the Jira Align REST API?

Assessments

This section contains answers to the questions set in all the individual chapters.

Chapter 1 – Introducing Jira Align

Questions

1. What circumstances gave rise to the agile platform now known as Jira Align?
2. Which scaling framework has a longstanding relationship with Jira Align?
3. How many agile teams can belong to a program or "team of teams"?
4. What role does leadership play in a Jira Align implementation?
5. Why is it important to have a Jira Align Core Team?

Answers

1. The rise of agile frameworks in the 1990s and formalization of the Agile Manifesto in 2001 provided principles and practices that enabled iterative and incremental delivery by a single team or handful of teams. By the mid 2000s, the need to coordinate larger groups of agile teams to deliver more complex systems inspired the platform that became Jira Align.
2. Jira Align has had a close working relationship with the **Scaled Agile Framework (SAFe)** since SAFe was launched in 2011.
3. The general rule suggested by Jira Align and SAFe is that a program, or "team of teams", consists of 5 to 12 agile teams.
4. Leadership is critical to a Jira Align implementation. The role of leadership is not just to provide funding, but to actively participate in, and lead, the effort for change.
5. The Jira Align Core Team functions as the guiding coalition for the transformation effort. It is comprised of individuals "with skin in the game" who are willing to embrace change and lead by example.

Chapter 2 – Implementing Jira Align

Questions

1. Why is it important to align the organizational language and reflect it in Jira Align?

2. What are the most critical health checks when analyzing existing programs in Jira?

3. How do you organize projects/boards in Jira to map with teams in Jira Align?

4. What is the integration mapping between Jira and Jira Align?

5. What are the three practices adopted by organizations that have achieved success at portfolio level?

Answers

1. Aligning the organizational language is a success factor for digital transformation. It establishes a common understanding, fosters cohesiveness, consistency, and credibility, and increases productivity.

2. Four of the seven health checks are critical. They are: #4 – There should only be one project assigned to a Jira board; #5 – Mark custom fields as optional, not required; #6 – A single sprint should only be tied to one board; and #7 – Sprints on a Jira board should not have overlapping dates.

3. There are two options for mapping projects/boards in Jira to teams in Jira Align: (1) One Jira project per program (team of teams) with one board per team and one active sprint per board – this requires a custom team field in Jira to drive each board; and (2) One Jira project per team with one board per team and one active sprint per board – this requires a separate project for Jira epics and results in a greater quantity of Jira projects than the first option.

4. The integration mapping between Jira and Jira Align can be found by going to the user menu, selecting **Help | Quick Links | Guides**, and then clicking on the **10X: Jira Integration Guide**.

5. Organizations that achieve the greatest success at the portfolio level adopt the following three practices: (1) Establishing a portfolio vision and roadmap, (2) Funding value streams and teams, not projects, and (3) Connecting the enterprise.

Chapter 3 – Navigating Jira Align

Questions

1. What are the three key areas to master in Jira Align?

2. How does Jira Align facilitate onboarding and continuous learning?

3. What is the importance of the **Why?** button?

4. How do you link a work item to a higher-level work item?

5. What are the options for estimating features, capabilities, and portfolio epics?

Answers

1. The three key areas are the navigation menu, configuration bar, and workspace.

2. Jira Align facilitates onboarding and continuous learning through **Framework Maps**, **Training Simulations**, and **Checklists**.

3. The **Why?** button provides context for team members' efforts, showing how their work connects to a high-level strategy and is valuable to the mission of their company.

4. Unlinked items are called "orphans." To review and connect them up to higher-level items, begin in the backlog and click on the **Orphan Objects** button near the top-right corner of the workspace. In the panel that opens, you can multi-select work items to assign to a parent item, which you can search for by ID, name, or tags. This makes it easy to connect each level of backlog item to its parent item.

5. There are three options for sizing features, capabilities, and epics: T-shirt size, points, and team/member weeks.

Chapter 4 – Team Challenges

Questions

1. What do you call the Jira Software users synced in Jira Align?
2. What are the two types of estimation games in Jira Align?
3. What are the key measures produced in the **Sprint Metrics (M1)** report?
4. What are the agile ceremonies you could facilitate within Jira Align?
5. How do you award team members in Jira Align for their great work?

Answers

1. Team members using Jira Software are considered *integrated users* of Jira Align.
2. The two types of estimation games are **Level of Effort Poker** and **Level of Value Poker**.
3. The **Sprint Metrics (M1)** report highlights variances between what was committed for the sprint versus what was delivered, a useful tool for scrum masters in their role as agile coaches.
4. The agile ceremonies that can be facilitated in Jira Align are sprint planning, daily standup, sprint review, and retrospective.
5. You can reward team members through shout-outs. It creates a sense of gamification and encourages teams to strive to do better.

Chapter 5 – Program Planning Challenges

Questions

1. What are the three roadmap types recommended by SAFe?
2. Which report allows you to predict the ability to deliver business value?
3. Which risk model does SAFe and Jira Align use for managing risks?

Answers

1. SAFe defines three types of roadmaps: the near-term PI roadmap, the long-term solution roadmap, and the portfolio roadmap.

2. The **Program Predictability Report** examines the percent of completed objectives achieved during a selected time period, providing a better understanding of a program's ability to deliver business value.

3. The ROAM model is used to manage and take action in relation to identified risks. ROAM stands for Resolved, Owned, Accepted, and Mitigated.

Chapter 6 – Program Execution Challenges

Questions

1. Which program room widget displays the program's average velocity?

2. Which dependency maps allow you to visualize external dependencies?

3. How does the **Work Tree** module support the reduction of waste?

Answers

1. The **Program Increment Load** widget displays the program's average velocity over the previous 2 PIs.

2. You can visualize external dependencies using the grid (matrix) and wheel view dependency maps.

3. The **Work Tree** shows how work items connect to one another from the top down and bottom up, providing enterprise-wide visibility into all work happening across the organization. It helps visualize duplicate and orphan work items to reduce waste.

Chapter 7 – Enterprise and Portfolio Challenges

Questions

1. Which field in Jira Align is recommended for tracking investment horizons?
2. How does the Investment vs. Actuals report support portfolio leadership?
3. Which kanban view is used for a portfolio kanban?
4. How do you extend the ideation module to external users?
5. Why is it important to nurture an innovation culture?

Answers

1. The **Strategic Driver** drop-down field is recommended for tracking investment horizons because of its extended reporting flexibility.
2. The **Investment vs. Actuals** report enables portfolio leadership to see how closely actual execution aligns with planned budget allocations.
3. The portfolio epic backlog kanban, process step view, is used for a portfolio kanban.
4. Select the **Make Public** checkbox in the idea group details panel to enable external access.
5. An innovation culture is key to achieving a state of business agility, meaning that the whole organization, not just engineering or development teams, is engaged in the continuous and proactive delivery of innovative business solutions faster than the competition.

Chapter 8 – Bimodal Development, Advanced Data Security, and Analytics

Questions

1. What deployment options are available for Jira Align?
2. Which government-mandated report is available in Jira Align?
3. What are the three default time tracking roles?
4. When should you consider integrating through the Jira Align REST API?

Answers

1. Jira Align can be deployed as a SaaS or on-premises solution.

2. An **Earned Value** report, suitable for government-mandated reporting, is available in Jira Align.

3. The three default time tracking roles are **Time Administrator**, **Time Approver**, and **Time Entry**.

4. The REST API allows you to perform most actions available through the Jira Align user interface, as well as simplifying user management and mass update work objects, and developing integrations between Jira Align and other critical business applications.

Other Books You May Enjoy

If you enjoyed this book, you may be interested in these other books by Packt:

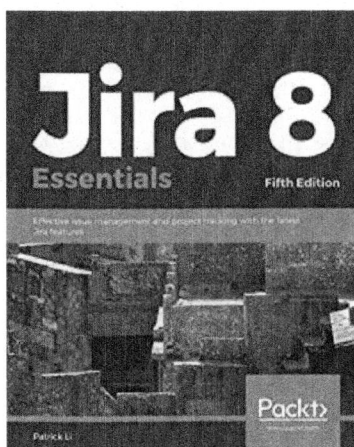

Jira 8 Essentials - Fifth Edition

Patrick Li

ISBN: 9781789802818

- Understand Jira's data hierarchy and how to design and work with projects in Jira
- Use Jira for agile software projects, business process management, customer service support, and more
- Understand issues and work with them
- Design both system and custom fields to behave differently under different contexts
- Create and design your own screens and apply them to different project and issue types
- Gain an understanding of the workflow and its various components
- Set up both incoming and outgoing mail servers to work with e-mails

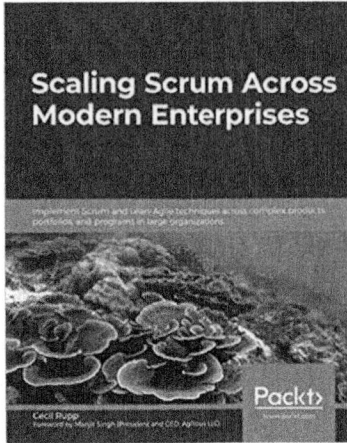

Scaling Scrum Across Modern Enterprises

Cecil Rupp

ISBN: 9781839216473

- Understand the limitations of traditional Scrum practices
- Explore the roles and responsibilities in a scaled Scrum and Lean-Agile development environment
- Tailor your Scrum approach to support portfolio and large product development needs
- Apply systems thinking to evaluate the impacts of changes in the interdependent parts of a larger development and delivery system
- Scale Scrum practices at both the program and portfolio levels of management
- Understand how DevOps, test automation, and CI/CD capabilities help in scaling Scrum practices

Leave a review - let other readers know what you think

Please share your thoughts on this book with others by leaving a review on the site that you bought it from. If you purchased the book from Amazon, please leave us an honest review on this book's Amazon page. This is vital so that other potential readers can see and use your unbiased opinion to make purchasing decisions, we can understand what our customers think about our products, and our authors can see your feedback on the title that they have worked with Packt to create. It will only take a few minutes of your time, but is valuable to other potential customers, our authors, and Packt. Thank you!

Index

Printed in Great Britain
by Amazon